2

TROILUS AND CRESSIDA TO THE TEMPEST

AN APPROACH TO SHAKESPEARE

2

TROILUS
AND
CRESSIDA
TO
THE TEMPEST

DEREK TRAVERSI

Third edition
revised and enlarged
in two volumes

HOLLIS & CARTER
LONDON SYDNEY TORONTO

PUBLISHER'S NOTE

The edition used as a basis for the act, scene, and line
references printed next to the quotations in the text is the
Oxford University Press *Complete Works of Shakespeare*,
edited by W. J. Craig.

This edition © Derek Traversi 1969
ISBN 0 370 00322 5
Printed and bound in Great Britain for
Hollis & Carter Ltd
9 Bow Street, London, WC2E 7AL
by William Clowes & Sons Ltd, Beccles
Set in Monotype Bembo
First published 1938
Second edition revised and enlarged 1957
Third edition revised and enlarged 1969
Reprinted 1978

AUTHOR'S NOTE TO THIRD EDITION

The present study is conceived as an expansion of my earlier book, originally published under the same title as long ago as 1938, and re-issued in a considerably longer form in 1957. It has long been apparent to me that this study suffered, even in its more extended form, by being concentrated almost exclusively on the later stages of Shakespeare's dramatic career. I hope that the new book, which deals with every undoubted play in the canon, may go some way towards correcting the balance.

The book is divided into two parts. The first aims at tracing Shakespeare's growing grasp of the full possibilities of his various forms, poetical and dramatic, and discusses in the process a number of undoubted masterpieces. The second part is almost entirely concerned with masterpieces and is on that account more compressed in its treatment of them: but here too it is my hope that something like a continued argument emerges, though not of the kind that forces the uniformity of a thesis upon material inexhaustibly rich and suggestive in its implications.

There has been, inevitably, some overlap with previous publications. In the first part, Chapter IV on the Sonnets reproduces, with some amendment, what I first wrote in 1938, and Chapter VII on the later series of English History Plays largely sums up the argument of my book, *Shakespeare: From Richard II to Henry V*, first published in Great Britain in 1958 by Messrs. Hollis & Carter, and in the United States by the Stanford University Press. Chapter III on the Early Comedies also owes a good deal to an essay on the same plays published in the *Writers and Their Work* series (Longman's and the British Council) in 1960. Eleven plays, however, are studied for the first time and I hope that the argument as a whole will throw some light on the development of the dramatist's art in its earlier stages.

In the second part the original essay has been largely re-written to take into account changes of view or emphasis in the intervening years.

I have added studies of six plays—*All's Well that Ends Well*, *Timon of Athens*, *Julius Caesar*, *Pericles*, *Cymbeline*, and *The Tempest*—and have drawn heavily, in the relevant chapters, on my two books, *Shakespeare, The Last Phase* (1954) and *Shakespeare, The Roman Plays* (1963), both issued in Great Britain and the United States by the publishers named above. Permission to make use of this material is in each case gratefully acknowledged.

The first part of the book, which includes the greater part of the entirely new material, was conceived and largely written during a semester spent in the Autumn and early Winter of 1965–6 as Visiting Professor at Swarthmore College, Pennsylvania. I am conscious of a great debt of gratitude to my colleagues and friends there; and also to my seminar students in discussion with whom not a few of the points here made were formulated or clarified. The views expressed are, of course, entirely my own, but without these advantages the book might well not have been written.

DEREK TRAVERSI
Rome, December 1967

CONTENTS

INTRODUCTION

IT IS PERHAPS worth recalling at the outset of this study that its origins lie in a very short and perhaps rather dogmatic essay originally published thirty years ago and entitled, like the present volume, *An Approach to Shakespeare*. The point of departure for this essay was an assertion that the great nineteenth-century tradition of Shakespearean study—running from Coleridge and Goethe to Bradley's *Shakespearean Tragedy*[1]—had reached 'something like the limits of its usefulness'. Little more, it was suggested, remained to be discovered in that particular direction; nor, at the time of writing, were the assumptions which this school of criticism had taken for granted entirely acceptable. More particularly, the Victorian insistence upon *character*, when carried to the point of excluding other aspects of an essentially *dramatic* action, had its foundation in the subjectivism of 'Romantic' thought. *Hamlet* the tragedy—to take the stock example—became, when considered in the light of this tradition, a fruitful mirror for the dissatisfactions of the romantic self, and even the greatest students of the plays—who gave us a great deal that was very valuable—found it difficult to avoid confusing Shakespeare's aims with their own, often quite different concerns. Above all—and to this we shall return—this type of criticism found its theatrical counterpart in a conception of the stage, and of the dramatic action as a whole, which tended to distort Shakespeare's intentions and even to make some of the greatest plays[2] almost impossible to represent.

This, however, as the introduction to the 1938 essay also suggested, was not the whole of the story. 'We all know that to discuss Hamlet's life *outside* the limits of the play, to attempt to deduce the manner of his upbringing in order to explain his subsequent behaviour, is an illegitimate extension of the critic's proper function. Nor can we share the confidence with which some writers fathered their own philosophies on to Shakespeare's work. But, although we are certain that the old outlook was incomplete and sometimes misleading—just as we know that the sumptuous and realistic productions, which were its theatrical equivalent, were not the last word in the production of the plays—we are far less sure what is to replace them.' The essay went on to say that

many valuable lines of approach had been opened out since the
beginning of the century; we might now add, thirty years later, that
many more have become available. Among these is a notable advance
in our knowledge of the Elizabethan background of thought in
cosmology, psychology, rhetoric, and in ideas on literature in general
and drama in particular, which has the negative virtue of discouraging
us from reading the plays too directly in the light of subsequent experience. Side by side with this, and largely complementary to it is the
remarkable growth in our understanding of Elizabethan stage conditions
and of their relevance for a proper understanding of the plays; already
in 1938, it was possible to mention the pioneer work of Granville
Barker,[3] and a great deal has been accomplished in this direction in
subsequent years. Finally, the introduction to the original essay mentioned the rise of a double-edged approach to the plays in the kind of
interpretation proposed by Professor Wilson Knight and still a relatively
new development in the thirties.

Each of these 'approaches', however, though important and fruitful,
brought with it its accompanying dangers. The increased modern
interest in Elizabethan thought and knowledge has led us back, truly
and significantly, to the contemporary setting of the plays and so has
helped, among other things, to avoid the nineteenth-century errors of
misplaced emphasis; but—it must be added—the criticism which has
followed from this approach has shown itself apt to ignore the element
of essential *discontinuity* which separates a genius from the commonplaces of his age. A writer of Shakespeare's stature is of his time in the
ideas he uses, and we shall always be unwise to forget this; but he uses
these ideas in ways of his own, which are not necessarily those of his
time alone. Shakespeare's plays on English history, for example, lean
heavily upon contemporary notions concerning such subjects as mon-
archy, its origins, its *rôle*, and its justification; but to interpret the series
of chronicles from *Richard II* to *Henry V* as no more than exercises in
Tudor patriotic propaganda is, in my submission, seriously to underestimate their originality. What truly emerges from these plays—as I
shall seek to show[4]—is a thoroughly personal vision, increasingly tragic
in its implications, of man as a political being; so that, properly read,
they speak to us not less than they did to the late sixteenth-century, and
speak moreover in ways that very few minds of that age—with the
possible exception of Machiavelli—would have fully understood. To
compare Shakespeare, as a mature dramatist, to almost any other
Elizabethan writer is to be made aware of the degree to which he

evades, escapes from the current Elizabethan limitations. Such a writer, in other words, and to adapt a critical commonplace, both is of his time and transcends it. The scholar is by the very nature of his task inclined to stress those aspects of a Shakespeare that relate him to his own times. In the process of so doing he helps to save us from committing fundamental errors of appreciation; but the critic—if I may be allowed, *for my present purpose alone*, to separate him from the scholar—is there to redress a necessary balance, the failure to appreciate which will prevent a response to his subject's true originality.

Something of the same kind, though to a lesser degree, can be said of an 'approach' too exclusively limited to a knowledge of the theatre and, more particularly, of contemporary stage conditions. As I suggested in 1938, Granville Barker's very considerable contribution to our understanding of Shakespeare as a working dramatist was to some extent limited by the tendency to rest on established judgements where both poetry and the definition of characters were concerned. He stressed, in the body of his work, an important truth, and one that his immediate predecessors had tended to neglect; but it was possibly too much to expect that he should also transform our understanding of other and not less important aspects of Shakespeare's work to correspond to that truth and to produce a new vision in its totality. His Hamlet and his Othello, were, in other words, still close to those proposed by Bradley, though our view of the stage on which these characters appeared was re-vivified, largely transformed, by the line of study which he did so much to originate.

The third of our new lines of 'approach', as seen thirty years ago, was that which led finally to the methods of 'interpretation' largely associated with the work of Wilson Knight. The effect of these methods was to move away from the more traditional readings in terms of character or 'philosophic' content to another, by which a given play was regarded, to use Wilson Knight's own phrase, as 'an expanded metaphor'. In the light of this contention the critic's task became very largely that of tracing in the plays significant threads and patterns of imagery within a 'spatial unity', recurrent themes through whose study and correlation the full 'meaning' of the work as a whole was to emerge. This line of approach can be associated, on a more academic level, with that of Professor Caroline Spurgeon, who—in a pioneer study published at this time[5]—card-indexed and catalogued Shakespeare's images, following up the repetition of particular images in a

given play, and who even claimed as a result to be able to tell us something about the writer's own tastes and prejudices. Because, for example,
the dramatist can be shown repeatedly to associate spaniels with cloying
flattery, and because this association tends to produce in his poetry a
sense of almost physical revulsion, we are asked to conclude that Shakespeare the man—that dim and unsatisfactory abstraction—felt a particular dislike for this species of dog, and perhaps for dogs in general.
Whether this deplorably un-English trait contributes anything to an
appreciation of his work remains uncertain.

To leave the matter thus is clearly to be less than fair to what
Professor Spurgeon, and her method as developed by others in various
directions, in fact achieved. The best parts of her study were valuable
and important: how important we are perhaps now prevented from
seeing by the fact that not a few of her discoveries have become common
currency in later criticism. It helps us to understand *Troilus and Cressida*,
for example, to know that there can be found in it a notable concentration upon imagery of taste; it is relevant to the study of *Macbeth* to
remember that images of ill-fitting clothes appear repeatedly in the
course of the play. These real discoveries called for a development
which Professor Spurgeon herself was not always ready to give them: a
development that, in one way or another, takes us beyond the card-
index, beyond the more or less mechanical collation and counting of
the images used, into a response to the poetry as a living and dynamic
whole, a whole moreover that looks for its completion beyond itself,
through incorporation into the ultimate unity of the dramatic action to
which it belongs. This is the incorporation at which Professor
Wilson Knight has consistently aimed in what is possibly the most
ambitious attempt to interpret Shakespeare that the last half century has
produced.

There can be no doubt that Wilson Knight to an eminent degree,
and Professor Spurgeon in her own possibly more pedestrian way, have
greatly extended our understanding of Shakespeare, and for this we
have reason to be accordingly grateful. We shall do well, however,
whilst recognizing this, to look a little closely at the 'methods', so to
call them, upon which these real discoveries are said to be based. In the
case of Professor Spurgeon we shall see at once that the 'method', in its
essence, consists of card-indexing and counting images with a view to
establishing their relative frequencies and drawing the corresponding
conclusions. The image 'X' appears so many times and the image 'Y'
so many: from the preponderance of either we can draw all kinds of

conclusions, which seem to be 'scientifically' based, perhaps about the dramatist's own tastes and certainly, it is suggested, about the intentions which underlie a given play. We shall find, I think, on reflection, however, that the poetic image, even if we accept it as a kind of ultimate constituent of poetry, is not readily susceptible to this kind of treatment. Some images belong primarily to literary convention, others impress us as deeply personal in their effect; some, again, belong exclusively to the dramatic personage in whose mouth they are placed and to the situation in which he finds himself, others seem to answer more directly to the expression of the author's own experience. Above all, the poetic image is, more particularly as used by Shakespeare, a living and not a dead thing; and it lives, not dissected and placed in a card-index, but in a context, in relation to the intensity with which it is conceived (which varies greatly from one case to another), to the rhythm of the verse that conveys it, and to the total conception of the play in which it is found. Images, in fact, cannot be abstracted from their context, or counted up by a mechanical process as if they were all identical or similar in value. They live, develop, and change by their very nature, and it is precisely the life, the development, and the change which escape classification and call for the critic, or more simply the theatre-goer, to make his similarly living response. If the result is, as it must surely be, something less than a scientific certainty, that may be considered by some a pity; but the rest of us may derive some encouragement from the reflection that there are certain areas of life (it may well be the most important) which are, of their very nature, irreducible to the card-index and its overgrown and monstrous successor, the computer.

The case of Wilson Knight, which I have associated with that of Professor Spurgeon only on account of the tendency of both to start from a consideration of the poetic image and its function in the complete dramatic effect, is a good deal more complex. Whether we accept his conclusions or not, there is nothing of the card-index or the computer about Professor Wilson Knight's work; and it is just and necessary to say that there has been probably no writer on Shakespeare, in the period which here concerns us, who has opened out more new fields of vision to an understanding of the dramatist in his full life and complexity. Practically everyone who has since written on Shakespeare has had occasion to express his disagreement with many of Wilson Knight's conclusions, in which highly personal applications of ideas derived in varying degree from Nietzsche and from Christian tradition play a large part; but practically all those who have done so have also repeated or developed findings that he was the first to express. And yet, we must add, when all the debts have been fairly acknowledged, the numerous insights recognized for what they are, we often find ourselves asking, as we read or re-read these studies, how exactly all this was achieved. The moments of vision are unquestionably there, many and true (and not always recognized as a source by those who have subsequently used them): but there too, surely, are an almost fantastically confused set of religious, 'philosophical', and patriotic preoccupations often based, scarcely less than in the case of the card-indexers, upon an extraordinarily naive conception of what image and metaphor really are. The interrelation of these two aspects—remarkable, genuine insights and the tendency to force the text to say what the critic wants it to say—is not difficult to illustrate. An entire book by Wilson Knight—*The Shakespearean Tempest*[6]—sets out to show, for example, the existence through all the dramatist's work of a music-tempest opposition, and traces the presence of this line of imagery in every play that he wrote. The intuition is, beyond doubt, valid and important. The opposition between these two sets of constantly repeated images is *there* and, moreover, *means* something for our understanding of Shakespeare. In the proving of it, however, we are asked to believe that images taken from the early *Henry VI* plays are as valuable, have much the same degree of significance, as others from the unquestioned masterpieces, from *King Lear* and *The Tempest*; and that a burlesque piece spoken by Bottom in his first rehearsal for the Pyramus and Thisbe interlude in *A Midsummer Night's Dream*[7] has to all intents and purposes as much meaning as others drawn, for example, from the undoubtedly Shakespearean part of *Pericles*. This is surely absurd. Similarly in *Antony and Cleopatra*, perhaps the supreme test for a balanced criticism of Shakespeare, the romantic estimate of Antony in terms of 'vitality', 'transcendance', and 'immortality' is stressed by Wilson Knight, if not exclusively, certainly unduly in relation to the merciless realism that accompanies the poetry at each stage in the development of the action. This is, no doubt, for the excellent reason that Wilson Knight himself feels the play in this way; and, so feeling, he has indeed greatly extended our understanding of Shakespeare, but has also on occasion fallen into traps, one-sided and finally confused judgements which are the opposite of our author's dispassionate clarity and balanced strength.

One other tendency in modern Shakespearean studies, related to

though not directly deriving from Wilson Knight's work, can appropriately be mentioned at this point. This is the tendency, observable
to-day in many academic quarters, to read into the plays explicit statements of Christian belief and morality. The greater writers of the
nineteenth-century tended, on the whole, to underestimate the Christian
content of Shakespeare's thought, and it is perhaps in reaction to this
that many writers in our own time have tended to present him as a
moralist of orthodox tendencies and even, on occasions, as something
of a theologian. This reaction, if such it is, towards a new orthodoxy
has no doubt been carried too far in Shakespearean criticism, and has
ended in producing a set of mechanically orthodox readings which are
at least as far from what the plays actually offer as the interpretations to
which they are opposed. Once again, Shakespearean criticism can only
benefit in this situation from the capacity to draw and to maintain
necessary distinctions. In view of the admitted lack of external evidence
it seems clear that little can usefully be said concerning Shakespeare's
personal beliefs, and certainly none of his plays were written to
illustrate religious dogmas or to point preconceived moral judgements;
on the other hand, it is surely no more than natural that a writer of his
time and place should be aware of Christian tradition as an influence
moulding his thought and that he should even seek, more especially in
his later plays, to present in terms of a highly personal reading of that
tradition some of his final conclusions about life. The relation of the
final romances, in particular, to Christian notions of repentance, atonement, and 'grace', is certainly in no sense a matter of simple transcrip-
tion or direct reflection; but for taking the romances seriously in my
final chapter, for reading them as something more than poetic fantasies
in dramatic form, I offer no apology. The seriousness and originality of
these plays seems to me to be clearly written on practically every
page.

  In the situation outlined in the preceding paragraphs it seems that the
student of Shakespeare will do well to consider his own position with
some care. Once again my short introduction of 1938 may serve, even
in its one-sided incompleteness, as a starting-point. Following a line that
was more novel then than it is now—though, of course, I made no
claim to be originating anything[8]—I then suggested a possible 'approach' through the development of language and verse as seen in the
entire course of the dramatist's work, beginning with the individual
word and taking it on, in the first instance, into its verse setting. Or, as
I put it at the time:

If a writer's intention is apparent in his choice of subject and general treatment, it has an even closer relation to the words and phrases in which he expresses himself. The word, as we shall see again and again in dealing with Shakespeare, is the product of the most intimate relations of thought and feeling, nervous sensitivity and conscious emotion. Indeed, word and thought, word and feeling, form part of an indivisible process of poetic creation; and, in the greatest poetry, the relation is felt as an identity, so that it becomes impossible to separate the personal development of an experience from its formal expression in words.[9]

And, since the dangers of a mechanical counting of words and images, referred to above, were already apparent, I added: 'It only remains to add that the individual word cannot be considered apart from the verse in which it performs its function. ... The development of Shakespeare's versification is revealed in a growing flexibility of response to the increasingly complex implications of the individual word. The various stages in the process by which he masters his experience, projects it fully into his plays, are most easily traced by starting from his continual effort to adapt language and verse structure to the growing pressure of his emotions'.[10]

In the years that have passed since this point of view was put forward both the virtues and the limitations of this kind of 'approach' have become clearer, to the writer at least, than they were at the time of writing. I should not now be inclined to express the argument in quite the same terms as those I first used thirty years ago. In particular I should be less happy now to talk, a little less than precisely, of Shakespeare's 'experience', at least in so far as this might be held to have 'biographical' implications, to be related to facts and circumstances in his life about which we can know nothing: nor am I altogether sure that there is a valid distinction between 'thought' and 'feeling' as elements making up a work of literature, between what I called, rather obscurely as I now find, 'nervous sensitivity' and 'conscious emotion'. I would now say, perhaps more simply, that if it is our aim to define the total impact upon us of a given play, we shall do well to start with the words, the language through which that impact makes itself most immediately felt in any given moment, proceed to the incorporation of the word into the verse structure to which it belongs, see again how this bears fruit in the conveying of such things as character, motive conscious and unconscious, and, finally, draw all these connected and successively expanding aspects of the work with which we are concerned into the complete concept of a *dramatic action*, which is the end and *raison d'être* of the whole.

In other words, we can now see—perhaps more clearly than I originally saw—that the kind of 'approach' suggested above is only useful in so far as it leads beyond itself, linking up with the various elements which go to make up the complete dramatic reality. No analysis of the first stage, *the word*, that does not illuminate some part of the last, the complete *dramatic action*, can be valid; but—and to this extent I would stand by my original proposal—we shall understand the *action* itself better if we proceed initially from the smaller unit to the larger, from that in which the individual intention first makes itself felt to the final unity of concept and projection which is the complete work of art. Or, as I put it in 1957, modifying and extending my intentions of 1938:

> The application of this general conception will clearly vary greatly from one play, or one period, to another. When applied to Shakespeare's early work, it is bound to be largely concerned with detecting the birth of tendencies that later found full integration in the unity of his mature masterpieces. Only gradually will it become apparent how these early intuitions, these first motions of personal feeling, are assumed into an adequate dramatic form. If we wish to find traces of true individuality in the plays of Shakespeare's youth, we must look not to the complete work, which is normally still derivative, artificial in conception, but primarily to individual turns of phrase, the occasional striking choice of a word or image to be discerned in otherwise commonplace passages of verse. From these it is natural to pass to a study of the way in which the words thus personally used influence the run of the verse itself, expanding into images which are eventually seen to bear significant repetition and to form, with the presentation of character and action correspondingly developed, a more subtle and suggestive unity. It is at this last point that the poetic merges into the dramatic reality. To proceed from the word to the image in its verse setting, and thence to trace the way in which a pattern of interdependent themes is gradually woven into the dramatic action, unifying and illuminating it, is the most fruitful approach—the most accurate and, if properly handled, the least subject to prejudice—to Shakespeare's art.[11]

To turn back to this passage, over the intervening years, is to obtain the sense of a valid, but also a notably one-sided procedure. In the study of Shakespeare's early work, to which reference is made, it would rather seem that two simultaneous lines need to be developed. The revealing personal phrase or image is important, both in itself and in relation to the character who utters it or to the situation in which it is spoken. But, side by side with it, an equally valid field of study would show Shakespeare developing and extending his conception of a dramatic action in its entirety; it would explore progressively the way in which his dramatic personages throw light upon one another by their comments and reactions, and are defined at least as much by what others say of them as through the impact of their own words. Beyond this again, analysis of the same plays would reveal a dramatist engaged in studying the scope of the dramatic conventions he has accepted, defining the implications of comedy, extending the possibilities of the historical chronicle, even moving from relatively crude beginnings to a more unified and subtle concept of tragedy. All these things, side by side with the attention simultaneously given to the growth of his expressive possibilities in language and verse, show a Shakespeare engaged in realizing the full possibilities, for his own purposes, of an integrated dramatic action.

The stress laid in the preceding argument on the dramatic action implies, as a necessary corollary, awareness that the plays were written for the stage, and for a given type of stage at that. A growing recognition of this reality, indeed, constitutes one of the most fundamental conquests of modern scholarship. Reading in the study can greatly extend our understanding of what Shakespeare wrote, even bringing out points which would normally escape us in the rapid development of a stage action; but in the long run it is to the stage—and to a particular moment in the development of the theatre—that we find ourselves returning, not in a spirit of mere historical reconstruction, but because the conditions of the Elizabethan playhouse need to be present in the mind of those who aim to present the plays in a way that shall be at once modern and—in the deepest sense, one separated from mere historical accident—truly Shakespearean.

Every undergraduate knows that the stage with which Shakespeare was initially familiar, and for which most of his plays were written,[12] descended in a very real sense from the platform used during the Middle Ages to represent the so-called 'miracle' plays. Without entering into details, which are either too familiar to repeat or too intricate to find a place in these introductory remarks, it was like this platform, and unlike most modern stages, in being surrounded on three sides by the public towards which it was deliberately projected. Furthermore, as it seems hardly necessary to remind the reader, it was divided into various parts, corresponding to different dramatic needs and roughly distinguishable, to modern scholarship, by the names of main, back, and apron stages. These arrangements looked very primitive from a nineteenth-century point of view, but—as has again often been shown—they offered certain important advantages; without some appreciation of these Shakespeare's conception of a dramatic action must remain largely obscure. It was, in the first place, a stage on which contact between the actors and the public was remarkably direct and intimate: the stock example is the speaking of Hamlet's soliloquies, difficult to deal with on a modern stage without interrupting the flow of the action, but normal and natural in their effect when considered in relation to the stage for which they were written.

If *intimacy* was the first important advantage this stage offered, *flexibility* was certainly the second. The tripartite division of the stage made it easy to maintain a rapid and uninterrupted flow of action. The stock examples, again, are Romeo addressing Juliet on the balcony, Othello strangling Desdemona on the back stage after the main stage has been cleared of the 'public' action and the separating curtains have been drawn apart. We might add, in *Henry IV, Part I*, the contrast between the court scenes and their burlesque reflection in Eastcheap, between the aristocratic leaders invoking honour on the field of battle and Falstaff passing his comment on that same 'honour' in a spirit at once openly cynical and indicative of life and realism. In each case, dramatic tension and the continuity of the action are maintained to important ends; and the lack of complex scenic effects, apparently an intolerable limitation when considered through nineteenth-century eyes, in fact often supported both. All this is elementary, but it seems important, in considering Shakespeare's work, to remember what a dramatic action is *not*. It is *not*, properly understood, a spectacle to be contemplated externally, still less a photographic imitation of what is sometimes misleadingly called 'real life'. It is rather, on the contrary, a spoken action, non-realist and conventional by its very nature, requiring the *participation* of the audience as a necessary element; indeed, the concept of scenery and decoration as a kind of subsidiary art added to give more visual attraction, is contrary to any serious view of the drama. An outstanding example of the kind of effect at one time lost to the theatre, but abundantly open to Shakespeare, was that of the storm in *King Lear*, where the aged king, in the process of creating the external tempest in the only way open to the poet, through his own words, fuses it with the dramatic projection of his own tragic state. Everywhere present, beneath the apparent poverty of the stage conditions available to

Shakespeare and his contemporaries, was a wealth of opportunity for the more profound poetic effects which the complication of later ages has often threatened to destroy.

To sum up, then: from a knowledge of the Elizabethan and Jacobean theatre it is possible to derive certain consequences which illuminate the Shakespearean conception of poetic drama. In the first place, like his mediaeval predecessors, Shakespeare based his work on what was still, in its underlying presuppositions, a popular and social conception of the stage and of dramatic art. It is true that by the sixteenth century the participation of the craft guilds, which had been the most obvious sign of this participation, had given way to a more individualistic spirit; but the tradition that considered dramatic representation as a collective act, from which none need be excluded, however illiterate or lacking in social pretensions he might be, was still sufficiently alive to find reflection in Shakespeare's work. We shall not fully understand *Hamlet* if we do not see in the hero's tragedy, besides the intricate analysis of spiritual motives which it certainly conveys, the melodramatic and bloodthirsty story of revenge which so attracted the Elizabethan public. We shall not grasp *all* of the force of *Macbeth* if we only consider the drama of contrary impulses which moves the hero to his choices against a universal background of redemption and damnation, and forget the simple story of crime and punishment, of the destruction that evil brings upon itself, which is an essential part of the complete effect. Shakespeare's greatest plays have, in reality, something of the universal appeal of myth, of the expression of a universal consciousness deeply implanted in the popular mind and accessible, though in varying degrees and ways, to all levels of society. They appeal in different fashions to different levels of understanding, related to one another by the very fact of their common participation, but not identical. There is something in these great plays for the illiterate as for the intellectual, and it is part of their greatness that the immense field of experience they offer to the latter is still intimately related to the primary emotions which constitute the chief popular appeal of the drama.

Secondly, and possibly even more important: the very structure of the theatre in which these works were shown was such as to concentrate attention, not on a spectacle or on the character interpretation of a single actor, however gifted, but on the *action*, in which the artists appeared on the raised and central platform of the stage as intermediaries between the conception of the author and the public, requiring of the latter not only that they watch and listen, but that they participate in the development taking place before them. This sense of *participation*, which had been alive in the Middle Ages as part of a frankly religious manifestation, survived in the sixteenth-century in a form akin to that encouraged by myth and legend. In the case of Shakespeare's great tragedies, we are required to participate in the fortunes of the central protagonist—a king, a hero, deliberately exalted above common humanity—either directly or through the comments and reactions of those who surround him: the result is an emotional effect akin to that to which Aristotle, in his basic treatise on dramatic poetry, gave the name of *katharsis* or purification.

Finally (and here we return to our starting point and justify our proposal to use sensitivity to living language as a point of departure), this essentially public action is *poetic* in nature, though not—I need hardly say—tied to any particular form of versification. In the best works of the Elizabethan theatre poetry, the vehicle of emotion, and the drama into which it flowers constitute a single and inseparable whole, fused in a unity that goes beyond its separate elements and to which we give the name of *poetic drama*. The personal emotions of the poet extend themselves to the public emotions of the theatre, establishing contact with society through the highly conventional and unrealistic medium of the stage. This example has a permanent validity, in so far as the possibilities of the theatre, properly considered, lie primarily neither in psychological accuracy of portrayal nor in realistic truth to the surface appearances of life. They lie, rather, elsewhere. Of all artistic forms, the drama is perhaps the most thoroughly conventional, the one that requires from the author the highest degree of identification with the special conditions which its very existence implies. This apparent limitation can, however, if properly understood and accepted, constitute a source of life; because it permits the poetic impulse, with which it is so intimately related, to flower with the greatest intensity, and because it provides the poet with a field of action that, unequalled in emotional depth, transcends the expression of purely personal sentiment. The dramatic poet is as fully poetic, as intense in his expression of emotion, as any other writer in verse; and, in addition, his chosen form obliges him to pass beyond the purely personal, to aim at the creation of a world that, in so far as it is outside himself, is beyond the accidents and prejudices of his own experience. To create is, artistically speaking, to bring into the light an obscure personal emotion, giving it the external appearance of form; the example of Shakespeare shows us how dramatic necessity can be united, continuously and harmoniously, to the ends of personal expression. The theatrical conventions of to-day have changed in many ways since the sixteenth century, and we should not wish to re-create them in a spirit of mere historical accuracy; but the permanent lessons of the Shakespearean theatre are still available, still actual, and still waiting to be re-applied.

TROILUS AND CRESSIDA
to
THE TEMPEST

I
THE PROBLEM PLAYS

THE period that followed immediately on the completion of the English historical trilogy consisting of the two parts of *Henry IV* and *Henry V*[1] is one of peculiar importance for an understanding of the development of Shakespeare's art. His dramatic production at this time is marked by an intensifying of the tragic feeling already discernible in parts of *Henry V* and of the plays which preceded it. This tragic feeling, however, did not immediately attain clear, direct expression. The plays which followed *Henry V* are, on the contrary, remarkably obscure in intention and sometimes even in expression: so much so that Shakespeare criticism has generally agreed to give them the significant name of 'problem' plays. Comedies, in the formal sense, but conceived in a spirit almost entirely opposed to that of Shakespeare's earlier comedies and indeed of comedy in general; tragedies in which the heroes are actuated by no clear motives, but rather grope in a kind of spiritual darkness, seeking to clarify their own impulses—such are the typical productions, at once intensely interesting and deeply disquieting, of this moment in the dramatist's development. Though not the period in which he produced his greatest masterpieces, almost all the themes of the great tragedies made their first appearance in the obscure and difficult plays of these years.

From the point of view of Shakespeare's developing dramatic art, these plays show a notable concentration on two related problems—the consistent presentation of character and the projection into a coherent dramatic pattern of complex states of experience. The two problems are naturally related, and advance in dealing with the one is therefore accompanied by growing success in mastering the other. As we read the problem plays in the order in which they were presumably written, we shall see how the issues with which they deal are first sorted out, divided into clear-cut conflicts capable of dramatic representation, and then, by a further refinement, revealed as conflicting aspects within a single mind. In *Troilus and Cressida*, the prevailing impression is one of a separation into two opposed and mutually exclusive camps, each corresponding to one isolated reading of experience; the tragedy of the central pair of lovers lies in the incapacity of their pale emotion to bridge this gap, and such unity as the play achieves is obtained less through dramatic means than through the interplay of related images in a common poetic mood. In *Hamlet* on the other hand, the spiritual conflict, though still imperfectly defined, radiates from a complex central character, who simultaneously interprets the world around him and, in interpreting it, reveals the extent of his own infirmity; the hero is not perfectly fitted to his dramatic setting, but his awareness of the discrepancy constitutes the root of a genuine personal tragedy. In *Measure for Measure*, finally, contradictions related to those of the previous plays are set against an objective conception of law to see whether, or to what extent, they can be resolved by accepting it; and though the final result is rather a deepening of self-knowledge in the protagonists than the achievement of spiritual coherence, the dramatic presentation of conflicting values is, at its culminating moments, clearer than ever before. All these plays are concerned, each after its fashion, with the effort to arrive at some kind of personal order in a world dominated by contradiction and obscurity. Though none of them can be said to attain more than a very partial measure of it, each represents in its own way an important step in Shakespeare's advance towards maturity of vision and in the mastery of his dramatic craft.

1 Troilus and Cressida

The close relationship between the values of love and war—one of the most marked features of *Troilus and Cressida*—corresponds to a conception of dramatic unity which, although its antecedents can be traced respectively to the sonnets and the historical plays, was, at the time of writing, new in his work. The novelty consists in uniting in a manner mutually illuminating, a personal theme and its public, 'social' extension. Instead of a political conflict objectively observed and commented on by a character (such as Falstaff) who stands, in a sense, outside it, we are presented with a personal issue—the story of two lovers of opposed parties—set in the context of the Trojan War. The situation of the lovers is variously connected with the cleavage between the warring parties to which they respectively belong; and the connection thus dramatically established is further strengthened by the pervasive presence of imagery which suggests disruptive tendencies barely contained within a common way of feeling. The result, in terms of poetic drama, is less a finished and coherent creation than a statement of emotional ambiguity, the reflection of an experience deprived of order and seeking clarification through its own expression.

This ambiguity, in so far as it affects the personal action is connected with themes that found expression, perhaps in some cases almost simultaneously, in the sonnets.[2] Taking as his point of departure the conventional subject of so many Renaissance sonneteers—the union with his mistress desired by the poet—many of Shakespeare's most individual sonnets convert this theme, which is applied to a variety of human relationships, into an apprehension of the parallel fulfilment and destruction of human values by time. Time, which brings passion to its consummation, implies equally its decline; for the union of love, the very desire for which is inconceivable apart from its temporal setting, demands as a necessary condition an unattainable eternity. The desire for unity is inevitably preceded by a state of separation, and to this tragic separateness it equally inevitably, in the flesh, returns:

> Let me confess that we two must be twain,
> Although our undivided loves are one. (Sonnet XXXVI)

The action of time, which is at the same time creative and destructive, which both makes love possible and destroys it, is the unavoidable flaw at the heart of passion. The dramatic presentation of this contradiction in the setting of a 'political' situation which in some sense reflects it, is the theme of *Troilus and Cressida*.

The flaw thus introduced by time into human experience is represented dramatically in the separation which overtakes the two lovers, a separation foreseen from the beginning and implicit in the logic of events. Of the spirit of this separation, Troilus' leave-taking is possibly the clearest expression:

> *Cressida:* And is it true that I must go from Troy?...
> Is it possible?
> *Troilus:* And suddenly; where injury of chance
> Puts back leave-taking, justles roughly by

> All time of pause, rudely beguiles our lips
> Of all rejoindure, forcibly prevents
> Our lock'd embrasures, strangles our dear vows
> Even in the birth of our own labouring breath;
> We two, that with so many thousand sighs
> Did buy each other, must poorly sell ourselves
> With the rude brevity and discharge of one.
> Injurious time now with a robber's haste
> Crams his rich thievery up, he knows not how;
> As many farewells as be stars in heaven,
> With distinct breath and consign'd kisses to them,
> He fumbles up into a loose adieu,
> And scants us with a single famish'd kiss,
> Distasted with the salt of broken tears.   (IV. iv. 30)

The verbal intricacy of this speech is highly characteristic of the play and helps to throw light upon the peculiar nature of its inspiration. The experience reflected in it is, verbally at least, tremendously rich, endlessly elaborate, but the ordering of it is not equal to the complexity. The adverse action of time upon the parting lovers is represented by an astonishing number of verbs—'puts back', 'justles roughly by', 'rudely beguiles', 'forcibly prevents', 'strangles'—but the emotion does not *develop*, does not acquire added coherence in the course of its expression. It remains a long and acutely sensed effort to express a state of conflicting feeling. It belongs, in short, to a period in Shakespeare's development in which the keenness of his apprehension of certain elements of experience was not accompanied by a corresponding sense of order and significance; for the attainment of that order and significance in his love poetry we shall have to wait until *Antony and Cleopatra*.

Nonetheless, though unsatisfactory, the experience behind these lines is highly individual. In each of the verbs of parting there is an element, sharply and vividly realized, of harsh and hostile physical contact. This laboured feeling is balanced by the poignant thinness of the positive love imagery which so inadequately accompanies it. Troilus, whose awareness of separation is so acute, so tangibly conceived, can only express his passion in images as intense as they are airy and essentially bodiless. Love is indeed 'rich' in his estimation, fit to be mentioned with the 'stars in heaven'; but it can only be expressed in 'sighs' and 'labouring *breath*', in the hurried breathlessness of 'distinct *breath* and consign'd kisses', and in the intensely palated but transitory delicacy of 'Distasted with the salt of broken tears'. Opposed to this 'airy', pathetic passion, the full brunt of the senses is felt in every phrase that stresses parting. 'Rudely', 'roughly', 'forcibly', time and hostile circumstance undermine the tragic brevity of love, so that the 'lock'd embrasures' which should normally convey the intensity of physical union are felt to be only an effort to snatch a moment's identity in the face of events which are forcibly drawing the lovers apart. The parting, imposed by external circumstances, indeed, is subsidiary to a certain weakness inherent in passion itself. The ideal, which is perfect union, is desired intensely, but is light as 'breath' or 'air'; and the bodies through whose coming together alone this intensity can be enjoyed are always, while they are united, 'labouring' against a tendency to separate. Their 'labour', irrevocably frustrated, issues in nothing tangible or permanent. Throughout *Troilus* the elements in love that make for separation are too strong for those that desire union, and 'injurious time' is the process by which separation is born out of desired consummation.

Troilus and Cressida, then, in so far as it deals with the central pair of lovers, projects a metaphysical situation into the evocation of a personal relationship. The play is, in this as in other respects, the product of a profound uncertainty about the value of experience. The consequence of this uncertainty, as it affects more particularly the love poetry of Troilus, is the corruption of romantic sentiment. Once again, we are taken back to the sonnets. The sensation conveyed by some of the most individual of these poems turns upon a combination of conventional Petrarchan devices with an intense and normally disturbing sensual quality: the familiar image of the lily, to take an obvious example, with its associations of beauty and purity, is transformed by a magnificent juxtaposition of convention and immediacy into the potent corruption of 'Lilies that *fester* smell far worse than weeds.'[3] A somewhat similar effect, dramatically presented, is apparent in Troilus' first account of Cressida:

> I tell thee I am mad
> In Cressid's love; thou answer'st 'she is fair';
> Pour'st in the open ulcer of my heart
> Her eyes, her hair, her cheek, her gait, her voice,
> Handlest in thy discourse, O that her hand,
> In whose comparison all whites are ink

Writing their own reproach, to whose soft seizure
The cygnet's down is harsh, and spirit of sense
Hard as the palm of ploughman. (I. i. 53)

The underlying convention here is clearly Petrarchan, romantically
abstracted from common reality. It makes itself felt in the assertion
that Troilus is 'mad' for love, in the strained use of 'pour'st' and
'handlest' to describe Pandarus' speech, in the comparison of Cressida's
hand to the 'cygnet's down', and in the introduction of 'ink' to bring
out by contrast its superlative whiteness. But the conventional imagery
is transformed, as it were, from within in a manner so closely bound up
with the convention that it acts as a corrupting agent, intimately
related to the surface sentiment. By giving deep sensuous value to the
Petrarchan images, it conveys simultaneously an impression of intense
feeling and an underlying lack of content. 'Handlest in thy discourse'
is a far-fetched literary image; but it brings with it a notable keenness
of touch which is developed in the contrast between harshness and the
'soft seizure' of the cygnet's down, between the hardness of the
ploughman's hand and the almost unnatural immediacy of 'spirit of
sense'. Yet the conventional note remains, and with it the feeling that
Troilus' passion, for all its surface intensity, has an inadequate foundation, is vitiated by the strained self-pity which allows him to refer to
'the open ulcer of my heart', and by the weakness to which he confesses in the course of the same scene: 'I am weaker than a woman's
tear'.

It is important to realize why this weakness, which Cressida after
her own fashion shares with her lover, does not produce a tragedy of
character, but of situation. The tragedy indeed consists less in the personal suffering of the lovers than in the overriding influence exercised
by time upon all human relationships and feelings. In *Antony and
Cleopatra*, at least while the lovers are united by their feeling for one
another, personal emotion has become strong enough to override
mutability; in *Troilus*, the supremacy of time is never really questioned,
and so a consistent status as persons inevitably eludes the lovers. Their
weakness reflects the uncertainty of mood in which the play was
conceived and to which they owe the peculiar poignancy, more than
sentimental and less than tragic, with which they meet their personal
fortunes. Antony and Cleopatra, as lovers, are fully drawn human
beings because their love, while it lasts and within its own clearly
defined limitations, is valid and confers upon their emotions a full

personal value. Conversely, the complete realization in evil of Regan and Goneril in *King Lear*, with the sensual ferocity that characterizes their behaviour, proves that when he wrote that play, Shakespeare felt himself able to distinguish between the various elements in his moral experience without falling into ambiguity and confusion. Antony and Cleopatra, Regan and Goneril have full reality as characters precisely because they proceed from a clear understanding in their creator of the value of human emotion as distinct from the evil possibilities implied in it. *Troilus and Cressida*, however, with its intuition of passion as vain and transitory, is compatible with no such individuality of presentation; for time, as it is understood in this play, destroys personal values and makes them invalid.

This limiting observation can be applied with equal force to the behaviour of both lovers, and through the entire action. Cressida's falseness does not spring from a deep-seated perversity or even from a strong positive attraction for Diomedes, but from the mere process of events, from a flaw inherent in the human situation. Her tragedy, such as it is, derives from awareness of her helplessness. We feel it in her pathetic appeal when Troilus prepares to leave her after the night they have spent together:

> Prithee, tarry;
> You men will never tarry,   (IV. ii. 15)

and in the moment of self-knowledge in which she tells him:

> I have a kind of self resides with you,
> But an unkind self that itself will leave
> To be another's fool.   (III. ii. 155)

There is something in the expression of this uncertainty, half punning and conventional, that makes it difficult to conceive of Cressida as a fully realized being. At most, she lives for us only in the mood of the moment, with barely a sign of that responsibility and consistency which is involved in the very conception of character. Any attempt to subject her inconsistency to a moral judgment, of the kind that the mediaeval elaborators of this legend had in mind when they denounced her 'faithlessness', is out of place because the spirit in which Shakespeare created her made it impossible for her to be shown as really responsible for her actions; and without responsibility there can be no moral evaluation. When she comments in the early part of the play on her refusal to reveal her feelings for Troilus:

> Yet hold I off. Women are angels, wooing;
> Things won are done; joy's soul lies in the doing,   (I. ii. 310)

her aphoristic lines are not a revelation of wantonness, but simply an impression of the sense, which constitutes the only true tragedy of this play, of the impossibility, the meaninglessness of constancy in a world where time dominates human relationships and where attraction and separation seem necessary and connected aspects of a single situation.

This impossibility also dominates the poetry of Troilus himself and is there further developed from its original basis in romantic sentiment. Troilus' passion, even before it is faced with the necessity for separation, is strong only in anticipation. The intensity of its sensations is conveyed in a refinement of physical feeling, in an attempt to embody in terms of the senses an insubstantial and incorporeal emotion:

> I am giddy; expectation whirls me round.
> The imaginary relish is so sweet
> That it enchants my sense; what will it be,
> When that the watery palate tastes indeed
> Love's thrice-repured nectar? death, I fear me,
> Swounding destruction, or some joy too fine,
> Too subtle-potent, tuned too sharp in sweetness,
> For the capacity of my ruder powers:
> I fear it much, and I do fear besides
> That I shall lose distinction in my joys ...   (III. ii. 17)

The sensations of this passage are intense enough, but only through the palate and the senses; like the corresponding emotions of Cressida, they scarcely involve any full personality in the speaker. Troilus' emotions are concentrated on 'expectation', on the '*imaginary* relish', and he feels that the 'watery palate' will be too weak to sustain the actual consummation. The whole speech turns upon this contrast between the refined intensity of feeling which he seeks, self-consciously and with a touch of indulgence, in 'Love's *thrice-repured* nectar', and the giddiness, the 'swounding destruction', which would follow its impossible consummation. The experience of love, it is suggested, is so fine, so 'subtle-potent', that it surpasses the 'ruder powers' of the body and remains an incorporeal aspiration which the senses strive vainly to attain.

Yet, by a strange contradiction, it is precisely because fulfilment in love is sought by Troilus exclusively on the sensual level that it proves unattainable. We can see now why the poetry of this play makes such extensive use of the imagery of taste, why Cressida, for example, says, before she leaves Troy for the Greek camp:

> The grief is fine, full, perfect, that I taste.   (IV. iv. 3)

Taste is a sense at once luxurious, delicate, and transitory; also it can be connected, in gross opposition to Troilus' bodiless idealism, with digestion and the functioning of the body. For the weakness of Troilus' passion, as we have already suggested, implies that it is patent of corruption; and that corruption—it can now be added—is the logical consequence of an effort to extract from the refinement of the sensual a substitute for spiritual experience. Immediately before the speech just quoted there is a striking turn of phrase in his appeal to Pandarus:

> O, be thou my Charon,
> And give me swift transportation to those fields
> Where I may *wallow* in the lily-beds
> Proposed for the deserver.   (III. ii. 10)

The ideal aspirations of Troilus remain abstract, intangible; such intensity as they achieve derives from their subjection to time, from his awareness of their own transitory nature. But this impermanence makes them bodiless, so that the sensual instincts, unable to associate themselves fully with the insubstantial ideal of union in a mutual passion, express themselves both weakly and basely, 'wallowing' like a pig in clover, in what would be, if it were more forceful, a corrupt satisfaction.

This special use of the contrasted implications of sensual experience is extended in the course of the play from the personal to the public action, and contributes thus to the unity of its conception. The refined imagery of taste given to the Trojans, and especially to Troilus, reflects a bodiless ideal which becomes, in the mouths of the scurrilous Thersites and the Greek cynics, a series of clogged, heavy references to the digestive processes. Thersites has 'mastic jaws', and Achilles calls him 'my cheese, my digestion', whilst Agamemnon tells Patroclus that Achilles' virtues

> like fair fruit in an unwholesome dish
> Are like to rot untasted.   (II. iii. 130)

In fact, the very sense that expresses the related intensity and lightness of Trojan passion becomes, in the Greeks, a symbol of inaction and distemper out of which issue the boils, the 'botchy core' (II. i. 7), of Thersites' disgust.

In this way we pass from the individual to the public action, from the love of Troilus and Cressida to the war between the Greeks and Troy. This connection between the private and the public theme is indeed the most original feature of the play. The two parties, like the two lovers, are divergent within a common type of feeling. The Trojans share the fragile intensity of Troilus. They are deeply concerned with the value of 'honour' and with a view of love that aspires to be idealistic, while Hector shows the virtues of war which are so noticeably absent from the bulky Ajax and the graceless Achilles. Typical of them is the speech in which Troilus explains the case for continuing the war:

> But, worthy Hector,
> She is a theme of honour and renown;
> A spur to valiant and magnanimous deeds,
> Whose present courage may beat down our foes,
> And fame in time to come canonize us. (II. ii. 198)

Yet the lightness and grace of this idealism covers a certain artificiality. The verse itself is unsubstantial and the expression vague and high-flown. It reads, at this stage in Shakespeare's development, like a survival from earlier plays set against the contortions and involutions of so much of *Troilus*. The impression is neither accidental nor isolated. Hector's reasoning in the same scene shows clearly that the arguments advanced by Troilus are as flimsy in content as their expression is tenuous. For all this 'honour', for which Troilus is ready to fight and, if need be, to die, is directed to the defence of Helen, whose worth has been destroyed by the manner in which she has been stolen from Menelaus. Even Paris can only argue that the original dishonour of her rape should now be redeemed by the heroism shown in her defence. The tone of the Trojan references to Helen contrasts strangely with the idealism of their declared intentions. Paris pleads that he

> would have the *soil* of her *fair* rape
> Wiped off in honourable keeping her, (II. ii. 148)

and Troilus, conveying a slight but unmistakable twist to conventional imagery, declares that Paris

> brought a Grecian queen, whose youth and freshness
> Wrinkles Apollo's and *makes stale* the morning. (II. ii. 78)

The juxtaposition of 'fair' and 'soil', 'freshness' and 'stale', touches the basic weakness of Trojan idealism, and points to the way in which that idealism is organically connected in its expression with the sluggish inertia that prevails in the Greek camp.

The true nature of this Trojan weakness is perhaps most explicitly stated by Troilus when he sets forth, in an attempt at reasoned expression, his argument for the continuation of the war:

> I take to-day a wife, and my election
> Is led on in the conduct of my will;
> My will enkindled by mine eyes and ears,
> Two traded pilots 'twixt the dangerous shores
> Of will and judgement: how may I avoid,
> Although my will distaste what it elected,
> The wife I chose? There can be no evasion
> To blench from this, and to stand firm by honour. (II. ii. 61)

Troilus' terminology is indefinite and the expression of his argument, like so much of what passes for discussion in this play, far more complicated than its content. There seems at one point to be an opposition of 'will', which we may associate here with sensual impulse, and 'judgment', by which this impulse should normally be restrained and directed; the opposition, in short, of sensuality and moral control, which becomes a little later a central theme of *Measure for Measure*.[4] In that play, however, the moral conflict is explicitly stated, and—what is more important—takes shape in a dramatic clash of clearly defined personalities; in *Troilus and Cressida* there is only an uncertainty, a sense of uneasiness, which the notable incoherence of the expression reflects. The conclusion reached by 'judgment' is that affirmed by Hector—that purposeful action must follow from a dispassionate weighing of alternatives in the light of the principles of reason—but the whole trend of Troilus' reply is to annihilate, or at least wilfully to confuse, the distinction between 'will' and 'judgement' themselves, to show that 'judgement' is powerless and irrelevant once the sensual will has impelled man towards action. In other words, the basis of Troilus' 'honour' is simply sensual impulse, and its weakness lies largely in his unwillingness to recognize this fact, and in the abstraction and lack of content which follow in the train of this evasion.

In a way very typical of this play, the discussion turns into a debate, conducted on lines that recall the traditional procedure of the schools, on the relative merits of reason and honour as guides in life. Its central *crux* is a conflict between opposed interpretations of *value*. Troilus, the romantic, if we may so agree to call him, needs to feel himself supported by a belief that man can create his own values, that he can confer worth upon the object of his strivings by the unsupported strength of his own subjective engagement. 'What's aught but as 'tis valued?' he asks; but Hector, older and more experienced, better able to contemplate his own motives and to distinguish in them between what is genuinely valid and what proceeds from the need to justify illusion, replies by arguing the need for an external confirmation of value, the support of subjective estimation by a genuinely objective consensus. In his own words, spoken in answer to his brother:

> value dwells not in particular will;
> It holds his estimate and dignity
> As well wherein 'tis precious of itself
> As in the prizer. (II. ii. 53)

Acting upon this conviction, Hector is sufficiently outspoken on the subject of Troilus' infatuation:

> Is your blood
> So madly hot that no discourse of reason,
> Nor fear of bad success in a bad cause
> Can qualify the same? (II. ii. 115)

The argument—though Troilus rejects it and Hector himself fails to follow it to its conclusion—once more binds the personal love theme to that of the justification of public action. Troilus—and in this he is typical of the Trojans—refuses to admit the weakness of his conception of honour, which is, however, implied in the very situation which brought the war into being: for the reality of Helen, as Hector points out, does not correspond to Troilus' embroidered and Marlovian conception of her:

> Brother, she is not worth what she does cost
> The holding. (II. ii. 51)

But this same lack of solid foundation is apparent, as we have seen, in the undertones of Troilus' own poetry, where the unacknowledged sensual basis of his idealism refuses to be entirely suppressed. Underlying the 'poetical' quality of Troilus' emotional flights, there is a distinct strain of coarseness and inertia. It appears in the references, so typical of this play, to the 'soiled silks' and the 'remainder viands' which are thrown away 'because we now are full'. Most typical of all,

in the determination to hide its own weakness which it implies, is
the Trojan reaction to reason:

> Nay, if we talk of reason,
> Let's shut our gates, and sleep: manhood and honour
> Should have hare hearts, would they but *fat* their thoughts
> With this *crammed* reason: reason and respect
> Make *livers pale* and lustihood deject. (II. ii. 46)

This insistence upon mental inertia and the obstruction of physical
processes, as applied to reason, stands in significant contrast to the
lightness and artificiality of Troilus' idealistic outbursts, but they are
organically related to them. The Trojan devotion to honour, Shakespeare would seem to infer, is devotion to an abstraction that has no
sufficient basis in reason, that is, in fact, no more than an empty justification of impulse; but—it is equally important to realize—to abandon
honour for its lack of rational foundation is to expose oneself to the
danger of lethargy, to a rooted disinclination to act at all.[5] Once more
we are faced with the split between motive and impulse, moral *value*
and sensual substitutes, which dominates this play without a real
glimpse of resolution.

The analysis of this important scene suggests how the contrast
between the Greek and Trojan parties, which most critics of the play
have noted, is modified by significant points of contact. The Trojans,
for all their concern to defend 'honour', as they conceive it, against
the Greeks, are strangely related to their enemies. This relationship,
of course, is openly 'symbolized' in the combat between Hector and
Ajax (IV. v), when Hector refuses to carry on the duel with his
'cousin-german' and Ajax agrees to call a truce. But the contacts
established through a common type of imagery are still more important
for an understanding of the play. In the Greek camp, we find fully
explicit the staleness which Trojan 'honour' has tried to ignore. Where
the Trojans reject reason in favour of ill-considered action, the Greeks
accept it and are reduced to inaction. Agamemnon's very first speech,
as the head and cornerstone of Greek unity, shows how inconclusive
are the intellectual processes so painfully followed by the leaders who
accompany him and how closely related they are to the views expressed
by Troilus on 'crammed reason':

> Princes,
> What grief hath set the jaundice on your cheeks?
> The ample proposition that hope makes

In all designs begun on earth below
Fails in the promised largeness; checks and disasters
Grow in the veins of actions highest reared,
As knots, by the conflux of meeting sap,
Infect the sound pine and divert his grain
Tortive and errant from his course of growth.
Nor, princes, is it matter new to us
That we come short of our suppose so far
That after seven years' siege yet Troy walls stand;
Sith every action that hath gone before,
Whereof we have record, trial did draw
Bias and thwart, not answering the aim
And that unbodied figure of the thought
That gave it surmised shape.   (I. iii. 1)

Agamemnon's thought proceeds not from point to point according to
a definite rational sequence, but by a series of indeterminate digressions
which reveal his incapacity to come to a conclusion. His laboured
illustrations and the theoretical observations which accompany them
destroy the coherence of an argument which they do nothing to further;
as so often in this play, there is no recognizable development of thought
to justify the complexity. The repeated doublings of words—'tortive
and errant', 'bias and thwart'—all lay emphasis upon obstruction,
upon the speaker's struggle against obscure impediments which hinder
the Greeks from successful action; and the use of unusual and unassimilated Latinized words, such as 'conflux' and 'tortive', produces
a similar sense of resistance and difficulty. More significantly still, these
obstructions are associated with disturbances and interruptions in
organic growth. The prospect of hope 'fails in the promised largeness',
does not grow to its anticipated stature. 'Checks and disasters' are
intertwined with natural growth, and the very rising of the sap in the
'sound pine', which is so eminently a natural process, produces
infection and distortion in the growth of the tree. Most important of
all, because corresponding to the spirit expressed by Troilus, thought
is 'unbodied' and its processes, separated from the actual course of
events, are equally cut off from the sensual immediacy which finds
irresponsible expression in the comments of Thersites. The keen
nervous quality so noticeably lacking in the theoretical observations
of the Greek leaders breaks out significantly in Thersites' sweeping
affirmation of anarchy and disorder; in a similar manner, Troilus'

disembodied idealism covers a sensual impulse which he refuses to recognize.

It is only natural that this discrepancy in the Greeks between thought and action should be expressed in terms of physical disorder; and here the link with the Trojans becomes even more explicit. Thersites' boils and plague-spots are related to Agamemnon's laborious thoughts on authority just as Troilus' contempt for 'crammed' reason and his insistent sense of soilure and physical obstruction are connected with his abstract idealism. The vital point in Shakespeare's presentation of the Greeks is this association of continual ratiocination with a complete overthrow of 'degree' in their ranks; they are entirely unable to turn counsel into united action. The position in the Greek camp is briefly summed up by Thersites, whose clear-sightedness can produce nothing but stagnation: 'Agamemnon is a fool to offer to command Achilles; Achilles is a fool to be commanded of Agamemnon; Thersites is a fool to serve such a fool; and Patroclus is a fool positive' (II. iii. 67). While Agamemnon, Nestor, and Ulysses scheme and discuss, Ajax and Achilles 'fust' out of action; the hand that executes is out of touch with the 'still and mental parts' that contrive the conduct of the war. Perhaps the point is most clearly made by Ulysses in his account of the pride which keeps Achilles in his tent:

> imagined worth
> Holds in his blood such swoln and hot discourse
> That *'twixt his mental and his active parts*
> Kingdom'd Achilles in commotion rages
> And *batters down himself.*   (II. iii. 184)

The conflict in Achilles between personal pride and duty to the Greek cause is stated here in terms of 'blood', of sensual passion; the implications of 'swoln and hot', suggesting feverish disorder due to extreme intemperance, are unmistakable. The adjective 'kingdom'd', like so many of the words which characterize the poetry of this play, is not fully explicit, but it clearly refers the personal issue back to the general theme of 'degree'. The individual warrior, like the Greek polity at war, should be a unity founded upon 'degree'; and 'degree' in the individual is an ideal correspondence between thought and action, impulse and control, 'blood' and 'judgement'.[6] It is Achilles' tragedy, like that of all the Greeks, whose hope of final victory depends upon his return, to find himself involved in strife between his 'mental' and his 'active' parts to an extreme which leads him, in self-consuming conflict, to destroy his own manhood, to 'batter down himself'.

On both sides in this presentation of the Trojan War, indeed, it would seem that the balance between emotion and reason is profoundly disturbed. The 'cunning' of the Greek leaders is manifestly out of touch with practical considerations and expends itself in an activity completely disproportionate to the desired end: 'it will not in circumvention deliver a fly from a spider without drawing their massy irons and cutting the web' (II. iii. 16). Himself like a boil on a disordered body, Thersites dismisses the warrior Ajax—the incarnation, after Achilles, of Greek prowess in the field—as a mindless brute—'thou hast no more brain than I have in mine elbows'; 'thou art here but to thrash Trojans' (II. i. 48)—and sees in the war itself nothing but lechery and unreason. On the Trojan side the infidelity of Cressida finally undermines Troilus' faith in 'honour' as a basis for action and leaves him dimly aware of the incompatible and contrary elements which underlie what he had assumed to be the indivisible simplicity of passion. Confronted by Ulysses with the direct proof of betrayal, he says:

> Within my soul there doth conduce a fight
> Of this strange nature, that a thing inseparate
> Divides more wider than the sky and earth;
> And yet the spacious breadth of this division
> Admits no orifex for a point as subtle
> As Ariachne's broken woof to enter.
> Instance, O instance! strong as Pluto's gates;
> Cressid is mine, tied with the bonds of heaven:
> Instance, O instance! strong as heaven itself,
> The bonds of heaven are slipp'd, dissolved and loosed:
> And with another knot, five-finger-tied,
> The fractions of her faith, orts of her love,
> The fragments, scraps, the bits and greasy relics
> Of her o'er-eaten faith, are bound to Diomed.   (V. ii. 144)

All the characteristics of the love poetry of Troilus can be recognized here—its tenuous and unnaturally refined expression, its subtlety in dealing with distinctions within an apparent unity, its sensuous thinness balanced by the imagery of disgust and repletion which connects it with the verse given to the Greeks and indicates the unifying factor in this play. For the ambiguous attitude towards experience which so deeply exercised Shakespeare in many of his sonnets is the determining factor in his presentation of both parties. Proceeding from his sense of the disharmony introduced by their subjection to the temporal process into the love of Troilus and Cressida, it extends to embrace the two parties in their fantastic and unreasonable conflict. The Trojans follow a false idealism, which deceives itself with talk of 'honour', but is really based on 'blood' and ends in a pathetic and helpless realization of its own insufficiency; the Greeks elaborate endlessly a 'judgement' that is out of touch with the instinctive sources of action, until Agamemnon's chaotic reasoning finds its proper counterpart in the distorted bitterness of Thersites' diseased sensibility.

Read in this way, *Troilus and Cressida* emerges as an attempt to give expression to a fundamental flaw felt to exist at the heart of human experience, and not readily to be described. The final difficulty is the lack of that *degree*, proper and natural order in distinction, which Ulysses abstractly perceives in the longest and most famous of his speeches:

> Take but degree away, untune that string,
> And, hark, what discord follows! each thing meets
> In mere oppugnancy: the bounded waters
> Should lift their bosoms higher than the shores,
> And make a sop of all this solid globe:
> Strength should be lord of imbecility,
> And the rude son should strike his father dead. (I. iii. 109)

From this general proposition he goes on to paint, in words of universal resonance, his culminating picture of a world in anarchy:

> Force should be right; or rather, right and wrong,
> Between whose endless jar justice resides,
> Should lose their names, and so should justice too.
> Then everything includes itself in power,
> Power into will, will into appetite;
> And appetite, an universal wolf,
> So doubly seconded with will and power,
> Must make perforce an universal prey,
> And last eat up himself. Great Agamemnon,
> This chaos, when degree is suffocate,
> Follows the choking. (I. iii. 116)

In this speech, which represents so much more than a mere reflection of political orthodoxy, we find supremely expressed, in terms of the disorder introduced by passion or 'appetite' into the human organism, the nightmare of mere 'chaos' which, present on both sides in the conflict between Greeks and Trojans, is the real theme of this fascinating and disturbing play. The Trojans seek to ignore the limitations of passion in a bodiless idealism; the Greeks, quite incapable of idealism, are weighed down by all that the Trojans try to forget. Both sides are bound together by the occasion of their quarrel; as Thersites says: 'All the argument is a cuckold and a whore' (II. iii. 79). Troilus, in one magnificent phrase, sums up the crux from which the varied contradictions of the play draw their interest:

> This is the monstruosity in love, lady, that the will is infinite and the execution confined, that the desire is boundless and the act a slave to limit.   (III. ii. 85)

The infinity sought by the will is the idealistic love of Troilus, which neglects the wearing action of time and the related inability of passion to live up to ideals of love and honour which can only be redeemed from abstraction by integration into an adequate conception of value; and the very boundlessness of the desire, when it encounters the limits imposed by time and the body to which, in the absence of such an integration, it feels enslaved, turns to the clogged inertia of Achilles and the endless self-scrutiny of the Greek camp.

2 Hamlet

In their various ways the critics of *Hamlet* agree that the subject of the play is a frustration. The hero's speculations on action proceed from his creator's consciousness of a flaw felt to exist at the heart of human experience, the nature of which we can only hope to understand in so far as it has been projected into a dramatic sequence adequately corresponding to it. This, stated in general terms, is the key to the problems which the tragedy so notoriously raises. A frustration of the kind reflected in *Troilus and Cressida* or in *Hamlet* can never convey an initial effect of clarity, because it implies that the experience with which it is concerned has not been previously mastered, that the action which reflects it on the stage—though not necessarily confused or contradictory in its dramatic effect—is itself conceived as in some sense an act of definition. *Hamlet* is a problem play precisely because

Shakespeare, when he wrote it, was engaged, for reasons which it cannot be the task of criticism to establish, in reducing to order a whole world of disturbing ideas and emotions by giving them significance in a balanced and dramatically effective creation.

Some part of the difficulty of interpreting the play is no doubt due to the fact that a commonplace Elizabethan story of revenge, already popularized in all probability by Thomas Kyd some ten years before Shakespeare may have written his play, does not lend itself naturally to the type of experience which Shakespeare wished to make it express. Revenge implies swift action based on clear-cut and primitive convictions leading, as its principal theatrical attraction, to the remorseless shedding of blood. It thrives, dramatically speaking, on an undeveloped passion for melodrama; the one thing not readily squared with it is the subtle exploration of states of conscience and feeling issuing in profound inaction. In making this point it is not suggested that the difficulties of *Hamlet* are purely or principally of an external order, to be ascribed in any important sense to an imperfectly judicious choice of plot. As a dramatic structure the play is admirably conceived, supremely effective in the theatre, clear and concrete in its development and final resolution. The difficulties proceed rather from the nature of the experience which the play so uniquely reflects. *Hamlet* dramatizes a story, chosen in part out of external considerations, in which intense personal engagement makes its presence felt; but the emotion which this engagement generates is of its nature such that it can only attain a due measure of objectivity in the process of working itself out. *Hamlet* is—to put the matter briefly—a masterpiece of exploration, and the initial effect of obscurity which it is apt to make upon us is a necessary part of the price we pay for participating in the process of relentless probing by which this exploration is conducted.

Hamlet, however, though it recalls many motives of *Troilus and Cressida*, is a great deal more than a repetition of that play. The thwarting of action by self scrutiny which is connected with the development of disease in the human organism is indeed common to Hamlet and the Greek leaders. Fortinbras' attack on Poland becomes

> the imposthume of much wealth and peace,
> That inward breaks, and shows no cause without
> Why the man dies. (IV. iv. 27)

The feeling of this, and of a good deal else in the play, could be paralleled from Ulysses' speeches. But the advance in *Hamlet* is apparent in its more dramatic quality and in its more profound penetration of the instinctive foundations of character. Hamlet's soliloquies are far less 'rationalized', less theoretical and exterior in their effect, than Ulysses' reflections upon time, order, and human motivation. The laborious machinery of ratiocination is replaced by subtle and truly dramatic shifts of feeling. In the 'To be or not to be' speech—to limit ourselves to the most familiar example of all—Hamlet's contrasted moods are *felt* in the movement of the verse, in language that reflects through the varied and precise operation of the senses the constantly fluctuating relation of thought to emotion. More ample resources of language are being brought into play; we feel the sharp immediacy of the vernacular ('To *grunt* and *sweat* under a weary life') contrasted with the remote Latinity of 'quietus' and 'consummation'. The conflicts in Hamlet's mind are no longer arguments but *states* of experience in which sense and thought are fused in the study not of an idea, but of a character.

The mention of character suggests a further new development in *Hamlet*. The divisions upon which the story of *Troilus* turns belong, as we have seen, to the metaphysical rather than to the human order. The central clash of feeling is between living emotion and impersonal, destructive time, and the love of Troilus for Cressida, hopelessly involved in a situation not of its own making, is felt as a light, almost a disembodied aspiration. In *Hamlet*, on the other hand, contradictions too complex and, so to speak, too *human*, to be thus neatly separated are brought together into one person whose relation to the action, though not completely clarified (for he is himself engaged in an inconclusive effort to achieve self-definition), is varied and continuous. Instead of a division of opposites, conceived in relative abstraction, we are presented with a central figure whose motives penetrate the action at every point, seeking clarification through contact with it and illuminating it, in turn, by the centrality of its presence. In pursuing the duty laid upon him by his father's ghost, Hamlet brings to light a state of disease which affects the entire field presented to his consciousness; and, in the various stages through which this infection, this 'imposthume', is exposed, he explores progressively the depths of his own infirmity.

In accordance with this conception, the first part of the play gradually concentrates its latent discords upon the revelation of the Ghost. This is not, as we may assume it to have been in the original melodrama, a simple call to action, an unambiguous appeal to filial piety; nor, on the other hand, can Hamlet's attitude towards it be accounted for, as some writers have argued,[7] principally by his uncertainty as to the nature, good or evil, 'heavenly' or 'hellish' in its origins, of its inspiration. The matter is more complex than either of these attitudes would suggest, more closely related to the intimate contradictions of the play. *Both* aspects are in some degree relevant to a proper understanding of the Ghost, and the link that unites them is to be sought ultimately in Hamlet's own mind. The Ghost, in fact, acts upon Hamlet as a disturbing influence, imposing upon him a clear-cut filial obligation, to which all that is positive in his being responds, at the same time that it confirms the presence around him of sinister realities which he feels, even as he repudiates them, to be obscurely related to stresses in his own nature. In this way, far from leading to resolution through the action proposed by the original story, its message plunges the hero and his surroundings into obscurity and doubt.

Obscurity and doubt, indeed, accompany the first appearances of the Ghost. Horatio says that at the cock-crow 'it started like a *guilty* thing' (I. i. 148), and that its coming 'bodes some strange eruption' (I. i. 69) to the state. This 'eruption' is present as an ill-defined foreboding in the minds of those who await its coming on the battlements of Elsinore. Francisco, the common soldier, is 'sick at heart' (I. i. 9), and his 'sickness', after finding an external projection in the feverish preparations for war reported by Marcellus, is more intimately related to the latent tensions of the play in Horatio's account of the threat from Norway which has inspired them:

> young Fortinbras,
> Of unimproved metal *hot* and *full*,
> Hath in the skirts of Norway, here and there,
> *Shark't up* a list of *lawless* resolutes,
> For *food* and *diet*, to some enterprise
> That hath a stomach in't.   (I. i. 95)

This type of imagery, describing social maladies in terms of the unbalance which 'blood'-inspired 'appetite' provokes in normal physical processes links *Hamlet* in spirit to the other problem plays. Its dramatic counterpart is the revolt, repeatedly revealed in the course of the action, of youth against age, impulse against experience, restless self-will against the complacency of established authority. Fortinbras is expressly described as a young man defying his 'impotent and bed-rid' uncle

in pursuit of his own predatory ends. His behaviour, which provokes
from Denmark the correspondingly tense and strained reaction implied
in Marcellus' talk of 'sweaty haste' and 'nightly' toil (I. i. 72), will be
paralleled by that of Laertes and, in a certain sense (in so far as Claudius
claims 'parental' tutelage over his nephew), of Hamlet himself; they
point to a widespread dislocation of natural functioning, centred
ultimately upon the inversion of normal relationships which accompanies the usurped royalty of the Danish king.

At this point it is well to bear firmly in mind, as we follow the
deliberately slow and intricate development of the action, with its
sense of plot and counter-plot, its references to the 'old mole' (I. v. 62)
working below the surface of the earth and to the 'enginer' 'hoist
with his own petard' (III. iv. 206), that *Hamlet* is something more than
the inwardly directed tragedy of an exceptionally complex and self-
aware individual. Not all criticism of the play has recognized sufficiently
the importance of its *political* aspect, the fact that its hero is, whatever
else he may also be, a public figure, a prince and an heir-apparent,
whose relation to Claudius is coloured from the outset by the ambiguous
relationship in which they stand with respect to one another. When
Hamlet, on his initial appearance, stands pointedly aside in the presence
of his uncle's assembled court, listening to the flow of bland, respectable
commonplace which comes so readily and, it seems, so impressively
from the throne, and inserts from time to time the obscure comments
which reflect what is to us his still unexplained bitterness—'I am too
much i' the sun'; 'A little more than kin and less than kind' (I. ii. 65)—
it is not the barbaric drama of some remote Danish principality that
stirs our interest but something nearer both to Shakespeare and
ourselves: the intrigue and the treachery that accompanied the
manœuvring for power in a Renaissance court. Beneath Claudius'
impressive ability to assume, on the surface and in the public eye, the
appropriately judicious and authoritative mask, which has even led
some students of the play to minimize the full extent of his malignity,[8]
lie the obsessive realities of insecurity, ruthlessness, and hunger for
power which it is Hamlet's tragedy that he can only meet on their own
level, by answering spying with counter-espionage, cruelty with the
deliberate suppression of pity, and usurpation with murder. By so
doing, by experiencing to the full the claustrophobic quality of this
corrupt and unnatural court, he finally exposes the 'imposthume'
implicit in Claudius' rule and rids Denmark of the poison at its heart;

HAMLET   47

but this is not accomplished before he has himself been destroyed by his recognition of the link which binds him, in his own despite, to the reality he is called upon to destroy.

The revelation of this state is, in accordance with the essentially exploratory spirit of this play, gradual and indirect. The reversal of the natural foundations of authority in Claudius' rule is first reflected in a strictly subsidiary fashion, through the relation of Polonius to his children. In Polonius, with his mixture of 'policy' and self-satisfied 'experience', impotence, and complacency, the claim of paternity to proper respect appears as a mockery. His senile distrust of youth, which fails to assert itself against Laertes when the latter presses his determination to return to Paris, imposes upon Ophelia his own interpretation of love, at once cynical and life-denying:

> I do know,
> When the blood burns, how prodigal the soul
> Lends the tongue vows ...
> Do not believe his vows, for they are brokers,
> Not of that dye which their investments show,
> But mere implorators of unholy suits,
> Breathing like sanctified and pious bawds,
> The better to beguile.   (I. iii. 115)

The sense of resentful distrust, of natural emotion belittled and entangled in ambiguous complexities of expression, will be linked in due course to Hamlet's own repudiation of love to contribute to the final definition of his tragedy. Polonius the moralist, as he denounces passion, involves his own counsel in equivocation. Envy inspires, at least in part, his repudiation of 'blood', of an experience which age no longer permits him to feel; and the reference to 'brokers' and 'investments' ('broker' with a subsidiary sense of 'pander' and 'investments' in the double sense of financial interests and transforming garments), the intricate relationship between the surface of 'pious' propriety and the compound of cynicism and resentment that underlies it, corresponds to the spirit of courtly dissembling which the speaker, in his position of trusted, experienced authority, so weightily upholds. Polonius' treatment of his children, and their contrasted reactions to him, rebellious and unnaturally submissive respectively, indicate in the personal order the profound dislocation of normal relationships which prevails beneath the bland surface of Claudius' rule and extends like a stain over the entire field of his authority.

Only gradually, as his own misgivings find expression, is this dis-location related to the sense of intimate betrayal which Hamlet, still obscurely, associates with his father's loss and the 'appetite' so un-naturally revealed in his mother. The disgust revealed in his first soliloquy (I. ii) still precedes rather than derives from his external situation. It is a revulsion against the 'too too solid flesh'—'solid' and, if a relevant subsidiary meaning be accepted, 'sullied', stained by its unescapable materiality[9]—that oppresses him, producing the desire, essentially unstable, immature, self-centred, that it should 'melt', 'resolve into a dew'; and this in turn is extended to find expression in his vision of the world as an 'unweeded garden', possessed by 'things *rank* and *gross* in nature', 'weary, stale, flat, and unprofitable'. The tone at this point reveals rather an internal disaffection, not devoid of emotional self-indulgence, than a mature judgment, and the 'incest' attributed to Gertrude, referred to in such a context, is at least as much a projection as a source of inner conflict. Not for the first time in Shakespeare's writing of this period, the type of physical reference which pervades the speech indicates the presence of unassimilated feeling. Already the world has been spoken of in terms which convey, in many of the sonnets and in *Troilus and Cressida*, a repudiation of 'appetite'; the effect produced by 'rank and gross', the sense of dregs and disenchantment implied in 'stale', point to the disillusionment which overtakes time-conditioned love. The attempt to provide this type of emotion with an objective equivalent, to project it into a dramatic conception, is fundamental to the play.

A certain projection, indeed, is achieved during the same speech in Hamlet's comparison of the two kings, his father and his uncle, to Hyperion and a satyr respectively;[10] but the terms of the comparison, far from reflecting the moral clarity at which he aims, confirms the persistence of the infirmity which inspired it. A figure noble, remotely classical, and *dead* has been replaced by another, a gross, repellent threat to purity, but alive; and in this substitution is reflected not so much the particular tragedy of a son, or even the degradation of a mother's affections, as the inevitable corruption of human feeling. *Both* kings, the living as well as the dead, bear relation to Hamlet's own state; bound to him by ties of blood, *both* affect aspects of his being from which he cannot, in the last analysis, free himself. The sources of his disgust, though never fully explicit, can be derived, still in the course of this speech, from his account of the relations between Gertrude and her dead, her idealized husband. His father's love for his mother had, as their son now recalls it, a precarious artificial quality, as though its object needed to be protected from physical contact, even to the extent of not permitting the wind to 'visit' her face 'too roughly'; but her response to it is associated, still in his memory, with a passionate intensity of craving that again reminds us of certain passages from *Troilus*:

> she would hang on him,
> As if *increase of appetite* had grown
> By what it *fed* on.   (I. ii. 143)

Such a passage will show why some critics[11] have found the emotion expressed in *Hamlet* excessive, imperfectly related to its causes as dramatically presented. It is—be it noted—Gertrude's relation to her first, not her 'incestuous', husband that is being recalled; and the impression conveyed is not that of a particular, unlawful relationship, nor even simply of the sensual weakness which has borne fruit in his mother's infatuation for Claudius, but of a corruption present at the heart of passion and affecting all human relationships. That corruption, both in love and in the experience which finds in love one particularly intense expression, seeks in this tragedy an adequate dramatic projection.

Because Hamlet's infirmity, by its very nature, resists full definition, the final revelation of the Ghost (I. iv, v), while it relates his disgust at last to an external motive, deepens the sense of conflict which envelops his being. It shows Claudius to be not only the supplanter of his father's love but his murderer; it adds a public cause of resentment—that of having been deprived of the royal succession—to Hamlet's intimate grief. Yet, rather than illuminating, the Ghost's story extends the area of obscurity which surrounds Hamlet's malady. As a result of it, his mind and the condition of the world are united as aspects of a single infirmity. That 'something is rotten in the state of Denmark' (I. iv. 90) he has known from the start, though his sense of Gertrude's 'incest' has never seemed a sufficient cause of his reaction; but now, when it appears that such a cause has been revealed, the infamy he is called upon to destroy is linked to the unease that already weighs upon his heart:

> The time is out of joint; O, cursed spite,
> That ever I was born to set it right.   (I. v. 188)

External disease and inner disaffection, far from finding resolution in the prospect of the action imposed upon them, exasperate one another in mutual aggravation. The rest of the play will mainly confirm that in the world which the author's experience at this stage postulates as uniquely and obsessively real they are incapable of resolution.

After the revelation of the Ghost, the main action is concentrated on the efforts of the protagonists to clarify their position with regard to one another. Here, perhaps, more obviously than at any other stage in its development, a claustrophobic sense of Renaissance court intrigue permeates the action. Both Claudius and Hamlet, while suspecting that their own situation is not in certain important respects what it appears to be, have suspicions to confirm. Claudius increasingly relates to Hamlet's person the insecurity which he senses beneath the surface tranquillity of his rule, and Hamlet has learned from the Ghost that his own disaffection is connected with his uncle's criminality and, more obscurely, with the unnatural relationship that binds the latter to his mother. Each, therefore, sets himself to observe the behaviour of the other, with a view, ultimately, to clarifying his own situation; but each, by a twist deeply characteristic of this play, does so by dissembling, by reflecting in a deliberate tortuousness of approach the obscurity of his moral state. Claudius, seeking to involve Hamlet in a double intrigue, makes use of elements which derive from the ambiguous character of his royal authority. Besides setting Rosencrantz and Guildenstern to spy upon him, thus bringing him into contact with the corrupt servility that has replaced true loyalty at Elsinore, he involves his relations to Ophelia in the servile manœuvrings of the 'politic' Polonius. To these devices, each calculated both to confirm his sense of the 'rottenness' that surrounds his uncle's authority and to magnify his intimate disgust, Hamlet responds with a counter-intrigue, which equally corresponds to his own abnormal condition, for the madness he feigns is at once a disguise deliberately assumed and the manifestation of a true moral infirmity. The threads of the action, thus involved in plot and counter-plot, are finally drawn together in the play scene (III. ii), which serves as a point of focus, concentrating upon itself the preceding intrigue and making possible the progressive revelation of disease which follows. Itself a fiction, but a fiction reproducing life, it exposes the false foundations of Claudius' rule and, at the same time, makes it possible for Hamlet, who alone is in a position to grasp the full significance of his uncle's involuntary self-betrayal, to begin his exposure of the relationship which binds the remaining protagonists (grouped as they are round the dramatic representation of their king's actual crime) to the central corruption.

At this stage, then, the area of Hamlet's infirmity is extended by contact with the external world. The verbal duel with Rosencrantz and Guildenstern concentrates his mind, already possessed by an inner incompatibility, upon the courtly fiction which surrounds him. They are, by their own admission, parasites, reflections of the falsity which emanates from Claudius and disguises itself under the outward appearances of duty; 'indifferent children of the earth', dwellers 'in the secret parts of Fortune' their phrases seem expressly fashioned to touch the hidden roots of his loathing, to confirm his estimate of a society to which, even as he repudiates it, he feels himself obscurely connected. As always, his distaste expresses itself in the extension to his surroundings of his own unease. His thought, embracing the universe in the process of turning in upon itself, offers him the prospect of feeling himself, in abstraction from the outer world which he cannot accept in its common reality, 'king' of a space at once 'infinite' and finally empty; but, in so doing, it leaves him the victim of the 'bad dreams' to which he is led by the contrast between the vague 'infinity' of his aspirations and the reality of the 'prison'—Denmark, the world, his own mind— in which an inner incompatibility compels him to live. The exposure of this situation culminates in the great prose speech (II. ii) in which the spiritual dignity of man ('*noble* in reason', '*infinite* in faculty', angelical, divine) is set against the vanity implied in 'quintessence of dust'; while its setting, the 'goodly frame' of the firmament, becomes, as he contemplates it in the light of his rooted distaste, 'a most *sterile* promontory'. Here, as elsewhere, Hamlet's thought at once embraces and rejects a thin, abstract 'infinity'. In the name of this 'infinity', for which it craves without being able to embody it, it spurns the concrete, the limited, which it persistently associates with corruption but to which its expression is obstinately tied.

The second intrigue to which Hamlet is exposed touches even more closely the roots of his malady. In his love for Ophelia, his desire for purity—purity, nobility, and infinity represent the persistent but abstract aspirations of his thought throughout the play—might have found expression in an emotion which, while partaking of the flesh, could have been raised to the spiritual; this love, however, becomes the occasion for the cynical devices by which Polonius offers to discover the truth for his master. Polonius, indeed, has from the first involved Ophelia's purity in his own impotent resentment against the flesh. Her love, tender, abstract, and inexperienced, like most of the shades of positive emotion which so ineffectually cross the stage in this tragedy, has been subjected to a process of denigration against which it can offer no positive assertion of its own validity. It is this denigration which finally penetrates Hamlet's own mind, finds its ally there in the obscure resentments which are so prominent in his nature, and pro-vokes—more especially when he realizes that Ophelia's love is being turned into a trap against himself—the bitter, self-centred cruelty of his repudiation. For Hamlet's anger is only in part caused by his dis-covery of the intrigue to which he has been so shamefully exposed. Its sources are ultimately more personal, more closely related to his own moral dilemma. Love, trapped in the 'prison' of the flesh and unable to conceive other than an abstract, bodiless 'infinity', is exposed to decay; and so, reacting against it with an asceticism based finally on resentment, Hamlet incorporates his intimate disgust into the mad-ness which is at once a disguise, a refuge, and a manifestation of despair. Divorced by an obstacle which remains beyond definition from its natural roots in the flesh, and moved by a passionate loathing of physical processes, his reason turns upon his former love in a mood akin to hatred: 'I say we will have no more marriages ... To a nunnery, go!' (III. i. 156). To grasp the full range of feeling here, we should be aware that 'nunnery', in Elizabethan low speech, could bear the sense of 'brothel'; so that among other things the bitter references to 'painting' in which Hamlet, with a self-righteousness that is also part of the character, expresses his disgust fall naturally into place. The ideal of chastity, remote but intensely desired, and the reality—as the speaker conceives it—of universal and inevitable promiscuity are united in one complex reaction. 'Go thy ways to a nunnery!' he repeats, because otherwise physical union with Ophelia may produce more creatures 'indifferent honest', condemned to experience the decay of 'nobility' which has become for Hamlet a universal attribute of life. Thus inspired to revulsion, he first shatters Ophelia's spirit and is finally responsible for her death.

To this exposure of Hamlet's infirmity through its relation to the world around him corresponds, in these same scenes, the gradual under-mining of Claudius' apparent confidence and royal control. Although

the self-betrayal induced by the play scene is the first clear revelation
of his divided state, the discrepancy between inner reality and surface
appearance has already been indicated in his comment, delivered as an
aside, on Polonius' plans to entrap Hamlet through Ophelia:

> *Polonius:*   We are oft to blame in this—
> 'Tis too much proved—that with devotion's visage
> And pious action we do sugar o'er
> The devil himself.
>
> *Claudius:*   O, 'tis too true;
> How smart a lash that speech doth give my conscience!
> The harlot's cheek, beautied with plastering art,
> Is not more ugly to the thing that helps it
> Than is my deed to my most painted word. (III. i. 46)

The action of *Hamlet* is, in its inner logic, the progressive revelation
of a state of disease. The king's reference to 'painting' belongs to the
same range of feeling as that of Hamlet's own denunciation of woman.
It reduces the show of regality in Claudius to a mask, sugared over with
a false surface, plastered to conform to a fictitious pose; and by so
doing, it both prepares the way for Hamlet's exposure of the corrupt
reality beneath it and indicates the presence of contradictions not
unrelated to those in the hero's own mind. The effect is the highly
disturbing exposure of what, before being an external reality, is an
intimate state of disharmony.

It is at this turning-point in his relationship to the world around him
that Hamlet, left to digest these shattering revelations of intrigue and
treachery, utters the most famous and most intimate of his soliloquies.
It would be wrong to see in his reflections the unfolding of a consistent,
'philosophic' line of thought; what is in fact conveyed is the fluctuation
of feeling in response to the contradictory and frustrating impulses of
emotion. Ostensibly, indeed, the soliloquy presents an incitement to
action. 'To be or not to be': in other words, to act or not to act, for
action is the necessary confirmation of being, even—so Hamlet initially
appears to propose to himself—when it has become the act of self-
destruction. If all action in life has been made to appear senseless,
there may even be an attraction, a kind of *nobility* ('whether 'tis
nobler . . .'), in the act of killing oneself to escape this necessary sense-
lessness:

> To die: to sleep;
> No more; and by a sleep to say we end

> The heart-ache, and the thousand natural shocks
> That flesh is heir to, 'tis a consummation
> Devoutly to be wish'd. (III. i. 60)

Here, if anywhere, we have the play's nearest approach to a 'romantic' Hamlet, a Hamlet who considers, nostalgically and with a certain complaisance, the prospect of annihilation as release, restful abdication from the need to make senseless decisions and to undertake useless and equivocal duties.

The best comment on the 'nobility' of this resolve is that it does not maintain itself. In what follows, Hamlet's reflections, though he still attempts to present them to himself as rationally persuasive, turn into the expression of a flawed and disaffected consciousness:

> To die, to sleep,
> To sleep, perchance to dream; ay, there's the rub. (III. i. 64)

Brusquely interrupted by this sharp recall to reality, as it cuts across the accumulated nostalgia of the preceding lines, Hamlet's meditations turn once again to dwell upon the all too human and tangible causes of his disaffection. The long and laboriously built-up list of indignities to which he now gives free rein—

> the whips and scorns of time,
> The oppressor's wrong, the proud man's contumely,
> The pangs of despised love, the law's delay,
> The insolence of office, and the spurns
> That patient merit of the unworthy takes— (III. i. 70)

are still intended, by the gathering force of their massed emphasis, to carry him to his self-annihilating decision; but they lead only to a sharp confrontation with the nakedly sensed reality of the instrument of suicide—the 'bare bodkin'—and stand revealed by the end of the speech as expressions not of determination, but of his innate desire to regard *all* action as inescapably flawed.

Under the impulse of these sombre reflections Hamlet's thought turns back upon itself in the direction of the obscure stagnation which is finally congenial to his nature. After recognizing the existence of a 'dread' of 'something' beyond definition, some dark and indefinitely menacing reality concealed in the aftermath of annihilation, the pressure of emotion gathers momentum, emotional commitment, in the carry-over of the period which evokes

The undiscovered country from whose bourn
No traveller returns,   (III. i. 79)

only to be pulled up yet again in the brief and vivid phrase '*puzzles
the will*', where the emphasis is set plainly and tensely upon personal
disorientation. In this way, a response to the rhythmic development
of the soliloquy allows us to feel the successive stages by which real
uncertainty overcomes the initial show of resolve, by which 'conscience'—or self-awareness—supports intimate disorientation, and by
which a 'cast of thought' recognized to be 'pale' and ineffectual ends
by tainting—the implication of infirmity in 'sicklied o'er' is full of
meaning in its relation to the imagery of disease which so abounds
throughout the play—what Hamlet, as a rational human being capable
of 'nobility', needs to consider 'the native hue of resolution'. In the
absence of inner consistency 'enterprises' potentially of supreme
value as acts of decisive self-affirmation ('of great pith and moment')
fade from their illusory attraction,

turn awry
And lose the name of action.   (III. i. 87)

In this speech, significantly placed at the very heart of Hamlet's
tragedy, the possibilities of verse as an immediate reflection of inner
tensions are exploited as never before in Shakespeare's work. The
conflicts in his mind, far from being merely arguments or even statements of a clear-cut moral dilemma, are revealed as states of conscience
in the very act of seeking self-definition, subjected to the ebb and flow
of a constantly shifting and developing emotion.

The various strands of intrigue which have been used to explore
Hamlet's malady and its relation to 'the state of Denmark' are finally
brought together in the play scene (III. ii). This, by re-enacting the
past, recalls the occasion of the corruption which now covers the
entire action with its ramifications. Above all, it shatters the appearance of royal self-control which Claudius has so far presented to the
world—like a painted mask covering the reality beneath—and brings
to the surface the split which his guilty act first introduced into his
conscience. Immediately after the end of the play episode, we see him
striving impossibly to pray, caught in an awareness of his state, but
unable—like Macbeth after him—to retreat from the position in which
he has placed himself:

> O limed soul, that struggling to be free,
> Art more engaged!   (III. iii. 68)

The contamination produced by association with Claudius' rule affects to some degree all those who surround him, so that none—from the moment of his self-betrayal—can live at ease with himself or his surroundings. All of them, indeed, are involved through Hamlet's bitter asides in the falsity, the inner hollowness, of the central situation. The appearance of ordered peace hitherto offered by his uncle's rule having been finally destroyed, his nephew is ready to probe ever deeper into the corruption which surrounds him and which, as we have seen, ultimately covers the central action as a reflection of his own state.

If the scenes which lead up to the play episode are concentrated upon it, as upon a central point of focus, those which follow expand from it as consequences of the situation which it has revealed. The next decisive moment is represented by Hamlet's interview with his mother (III. iv). This penetrates more deeply than ever before into the roots of the disease which, emanating from Hamlet himself, expands from his wounded nature to cover the entire action. The sense of his mother's guilt in relation to his uncle has been from the first a pervasive though imperfectly defined presence in Hamlet's mind. Only now, however, after the situation revealed by the Ghost has been confirmed, is he ready for a direct attack upon it. The attack opens, after the elimination of Polonius—dismissed as 'a wretched, rash, intruding fool', an irrelevant intruder who has so far merely obscured the central clash of 'mighty opposites'[12]—with a contrast that can be linked significantly to Hamlet's first soliloquy. 'Look here', he tells Gertrude, 'upon this picture, and on this':

> The counterfeit presentment of two brothers.
> See what a grace was seated on this brow;
> Hyperion's curls, the front of Jove himself,
> An eye like Mars, to threaten and command;
> A station like the herald Mercury
> New-lighted on a heaven-kissing hill;
> A combination and a form indeed,
> Where every god did seem to set his seal
> To give the world assurance of a man:
> This was your husband. Look you now, what follows;
> Here is your husband; like a mildew'd ear

Blasting his wholesome brother. Have you eyes?
Could you on this fair mountain leave to feed,
And batten on this moor? (III. iv. 53)

The point of this contrast can only be understood after due appreciation
of its linguistic qualities; for, as so often occurs in this play, what is
stated is not in perfect accord with the manner of its expression.
Ostensibly the passage contrasts two realities, one uniformly perfect,
the other equally uniformly corrupt; but a careful reading will show
that, while the corruption is indeed beyond question, its presence is
not entirely without relation to the perfection set against it. That the
representation of the two brothers should be described as a 'counterfeit' already indicates that Hamlet, even as he elaborates his comparison,
is following his familiar course of loading it with an ambiguous
content that reflects his own instability. The son presents his father's
memory in terms of literary comparisons of classical origin—Hyperion,
Jove, Mars, Mercury[13]—and the result is a perfection abstractly,
decoratively conceived. Memory, indeed, is thin, transient, so that if
his father lives still in Hamlet's mind, it is in the main nostalgically,
because his 'wholesomeness'—the word has also been used before[14]—
represents at best a distant aspiration to set against the presence, active
and sensibly conceived, of corruption. It is only when we pass from the
dead father to the living uncle that the force of direct expression is felt
in the image of the 'mildew'd ear', in the positive power of 'blasting',
and in the implications, so often paralleled in *Troilus and Cressida*, of
'feed' and 'batten'. The speaker's mind is clearly involved in dis-
tinguishing between abstract perfection and concrete deficiency,
between a spiritual concept precariously projected into literary imagery
and a sense of corruption, ultimately physical in its expression, as
pervasive as it is disturbing.

This sense of frustration, of an inability to impose his idealism upon
reality, is no doubt connected with the cruel, destructive tone of
Hamlet's moralizing. This cruelty, the product of a kind of inverted
self-indulgence, indicates once more the presence of a rooted spiritual
infirmity; and in giving rein to it, his emotions induce in those around
him the disintegration of their seeming integrity by exposure to the
stresses present in their own natures. As he arraigns Gertrude, Hamlet
at once leaves her hopelessly divided—that is implied in her exclamation, 'O Hamlet, thou hast cleft my heart in twain!'—and, under the

guise of performing a salutary act of moral surgery, finds a certain
savage satisfaction in exposing further the roots of the division in his
own soul. The presence of the 'flesh' as an object of loathing which
weighs upon his consciousness inspires, at least as much as it proceeds
from, his revulsion against his mother's 'incest':

> Rebellious hell,
> If thou canst mutine in a matron's bones,
> To flaming youth let virtue be as wax
> And melt in her own fire; proclaim no shame
> When the compulsive ardour gives the charge,
> Since frost itself as actively doth burn,
> And reason panders will. (III. iv. 82)

The sources of Hamlet's disgust, here as always, are intimate rather than
external, moved by the tension within himself which divides flesh from
spirit, leaving the latter, as in *Troilus*, thin, abstract, and disembodied,
but expressing the former with a force and consistency of repudiation
unequalled in the more abstractly conceived play. When he proceeds
to accuse Gertrude of living in 'the rank sweat of an enseamed bed',
of being

> Stew'd in corruption, honeying and making love
> Over the nasty sty, (III. iv. 93)

we must feel at once that there is something excessive about the emotion conveyed, that its roots lie not in the external facts of Hamlet's
situation, but in an intense distortion, imperfectly understood by the
speaker himself (and perhaps by his creator) within his own experience.

Once again we have touched upon that discrepancy, so to call it,
between the inner emotion and its dramatic manifestation which is
so persistently to be felt in *Hamlet*. The 'nasty sty' is not primarily the
reality that underlies the marriage of Claudius and Gertrude, but the
conviction, produced by the stress of imperfectly balanced feelings,
that the unsavoury quality of this particular relationship covers a
universal human weakness. Dramatically speaking, no doubt, the emotion is not fully dominated, projected into the external action; and yet,
as we compare this utterance with its parallels in *Troilus and Cressida*,
we must feel the advance in *weight*, in concrete reference, to be as
notable as it is disturbing. In *Troilus*, the flesh is felt only in separation,
in the frustration of a disembodied desire. In *Hamlet* this subsidiary
presence of the flesh is in process of becoming an essential element in

experience; its immediate relevance is felt in new linguistic power, in a subjection to ends which, if still in some respects incoherent, are truly dramatic, free of that sonnet artifice which the other play never entirely loses. Reason, which one side of Hamlet's nature wishes to see allied to the natural human functions in action, takes the form of a loathing of all bodily contacts; it leaves the field open, by its withdrawal into a disembodied 'spirituality', for a repudiation, itself pervertedly sensuous, of the life of the senses. The feeling thus expressed brings to a head reactions spread through the play in the form of a bitter preoccupation with physical decay: 'The sun *breeds maggots* in a dead dog, being *a god kissing carrion*' (II. ii. 183).[15] The mention of 'god' is to be associated with the same 'god-like' reason which, as the force of 'breed' indicates, serves in Hamlet's mind only to pander to the lust-inflamed will.

Thus far, the course of this tragedy can be conceived as corresponding less to a consecutive series of events moving logically towards an appointed end (in the manner of Shakespeare's mature plays) than as a succession of attempts at self-clarification on the part of the hero, each of which culminates in an analytic soliloquy and reaches out, as it were, to seek illumination through relation to the surrounding world. Self-clarification, however, is conceived as a necessary prelude to action: in this case the filial duty exacted from Hamlet by his father's Ghost. Hamlet's concern with action, upon which his dilemma is finally concentrated, is most fully developed, immediately after his confrontation with his mother, in the course of his meditations upon the martial enterprise of Fortinbras (IV. iv). It is essential to realize that Hamlet, following one of the principal convictions of traditional thought, regards action as natural to the rational and undivided personality. The ability to act is the mark of 'god-like' reason in man, the chief sign of his superiority over the 'beast', whose only concern is 'to sleep and feed'. There is, in other words, no question of the rightness or otherwise of revenge. Hamlet's task chiefly interests Shakespeare as an act which requires the unity of purpose and sentiment in a harmonious personality. But, as the entire action shows, it is precisely the lack of this union which constitutes Hamlet's problem. In his own inaction he is moved to envy Fortinbras ('a most delicate and tender prince': we can feel the lightness, the spontaneity of the verse in contrast to the speaker's own clogged doubts), but with an envy which turns to criticism almost imperceptibly in the course of the expression. If the soldiers before him are moved by what Hamlet recognizes to be 'divine ambition' ('*divine* ambition': 'god-like reason'; the parallel is not without significance), it is nonetheless to be noted that they are 'puffed' by its presence in them—the word carries a suggestion of vanity and inflation—so that we are prepared, in Hamlet's following meditations, to coincide with him in seeing them as absurdly 'making mouths at the invisible event', grotesquely agitating themselves, with a vain conviction, for a mere 'egg-shell'.

Thus far the criticism, expressed in verse which reflects the shifting consciousness of the speaker has followed the lines of Falstaff's attitude towards 'honour'.[16] The next sentence, however, while it continues the train of thought turns upon an ambiguity which involves a further complication of feeling:

> Rightly to be great
> Is not to stir without great argument,
> But greatly to find quarrel in a straw
> When honour's at the stake. (IV. iv. 53)

The two statements thus combined have the appearance of a noble and consistent attitude based on 'honour', but they are actually in virtual contradiction. Reason, it is suggested, does not allow a man to act except upon a sufficient cause, upon the foundation of 'great argument'; but 'honour', based on natural feeling, insists that it is right and noble to act 'greatly', with magnanimity, even when 'reason' has concluded that the ground for action is an inadequate 'straw'. Falstaff's realistic scepticism has, in short, been taken up into a mood at once deeper and less conclusive, based no longer on the detached observation of reality but upon an intimate sense of conflict. 'Honour', satirically conceived in the earlier comic spirit, has now become a necessary good, an incentive to action of a kind with which Falstaff had never been concerned; but, in the mood in which Hamlet considers it, it is also less than acceptable to reason. The two contrary attitudes, thus assumed into a single character, constitute the basis of the tragic discord.

The expression of this dilemma gives a fuller meaning to the general definition attempted in the opening lines:

> What is a man,
> If his chief good and market of his time
> Be but to sleep and feed? a beast, no more.

Sure, he that made us with such large discourse,
Looking before and after, gave us not
That capability and god-like reason
To fust in us unused. (IV. iv. 33)

The argument seems simple enough, but once more the expression of
it suggests rather a conflict of feeling than the triumphant demonstration of a truth rationally established. The sense of man's nobility, his
'large discourse' and 'god-like' reason, is balanced by the sluggishness
of 'sleep' and 'feed' (we are reminded of the food imagery so prominent in *Troilus and Cressida*) and still more by the contrary implications
of 'beast' and the musty vanity of 'fust'. The intensity with which
these words underline the note of stagnation forbids us to pass them
by; they are the key to the emotional undercurrents which dominate
the speech. It is Hamlet's desire to see action and its rational sanction
fused in 'god-like' action. The exercise of reason, however, produces
an exactly contrary effect to that which is declared to be its proper
end. Instead of justifying, it convinces the speaker of the uselessness of
the action proposed to him; he has to choose between action, which is
natural and in itself desirable, but—to the eye of reason—'*gross* as
earth',[17] and rational thought, which is 'divine', but leads, in the
speaker's disaffected state, merely to immobility.

By this stage in the play the divisions in Hamlet's own nature are
amply reflected in the surrounding action. The last scenes, indeed, are
less the logical working out of a dramatic process than the revelation
of a complete disintegration. With the apparent self-control of
Claudius visibly broken, Polonius eliminated, and Gertrude divided
against herself, infection is spreading through the Danish court like a
stain; its next advance involves Ophelia. Gertrude and Ophelia, indeed,
occupy in *Hamlet* an intermediate position which turns finally into
their peculiar tragedy. Bound simultaneously to the corrupt royalty
of Claudius, Gertrude by marriage and Ophelia as the daughter of his
instrument Polonius, and to Hamlet as mother and lover respectively,
the growth of palpable division within the state is reflected in their
intimate disunion. Gertrude, like Claudius himself, though in a subsidiary sense, is subjected to an inner conflict beyond all possible
resolution; Ophelia is driven to a madness which is the true counterpart
of that feigned by Hamlet, and which has for its elements sorrow at
her father's death and a sense of personal betrayal. Her innocence, the
product of a calculated sheltering from the world, is finally brought

into touch with death and with its visible manifestation—corruption
in the 'cold ground' (Hamlet's irony, too, has dwelt insistently on 'the
convocation of politic worms' at work on the body of Polonius)—
at the same time that her shattered integrity reveals itself in the form
of equivocal songs. The final account, by Gertrude, of her suicide
mingles innocent beauty with artifice, the sad virginity implied in
'cold maids' with the '*grosser* name' given to the flowers of nature
by '*liberal* shepherds'. The whole description, moreover, is involved
as befits the victim, in a sense of elegiac helplessness:

> long it could not be
> Till that her garments, heavy with their drink,
> Pull'd the poor wretch from her melodious lay
> To muddy death. (IV. vii. 181)

That even innocence should find its pathos expressed through artifice
is indeed typical of the spirit, ambiguous and, to use one of its own
characteristic expressions, 'muddied', impure, which has now taken
possession of the play.

During these later scenes, the corruption in which the whole of
Denmark is involved is exposed in all its ramifications. Claudius,
acutely aware of himself as surrounded by the suspicions of the people

> *muddied*,
> Thick, and *unwholesome*, in their thoughts and whispers
> For good Polonius' death, (IV. v. 81)

also sees in the 'secret' return of Laertes another stirring of violent,
youthful 'blood' in the infected body of his state. The idea of infection
is now obsessively present in his utterances. Of his supposed 'indulgence' to Hamlet, he says:

> so much was our love,
> We would not understand what was most fit,
> But, like the owner of *a foul disease*,
> *To keep it from divulging, let it feed*
> *Even on the pith of life.* (IV. i. 19)

This intimation of infirmity can be supported by his further comment
on his own state:

> diseases desperate grown,
> By desperate appliances are relieved,
> Or not at all, (IV. iii. 9)

and, most significantly of all, by his own definition of his relation to Hamlet:

> like the hectic in my blood he rages,
> And thou must cure me.   (IV. iii. 69)

The bond which unites these 'mighty opposites' so closely in their common tragedy, and which is now approaching its final resolution in death, is nowhere more exactly stated. Claudius' final intrigues, indeed,—the dispatch of Hamlet to England, the use of Polonius' death and Ophelia's tragic end to involve Laertes in a web of intrigue— are no more than attempts to conceal what the remorseless development of events is already revealing, to cover the 'imposthume' of his own state, from which that of Denmark derives, by extending the area of the disease. His devices, however, like the state of mind which produced them, hopelessly divided against itself, are finally deprived of all true conviction.

Something not very different can be said, at this stage, of Hamlet himself. When he returns for the final reckoning, he does so in a state that is, in one sense, a reflection of clarity achieved—for the subsidiary issues of the action, personified in Rosencrantz and Guildenstern, in Polonius, even in Ophelia, all instruments of the central corruption which emanates from his uncle's power, have been cleared away— but with a lack of belief in the efficacy of his personal intervention which proceeds finally from his sense that the disease he aims at curing is intimately related to his own state. The king will die, because death is the end to which his nature tends, and Gertrude too will be carried away by the intrigue in which her own weakness has involved her; but restoration cannot be personified in Hamlet, who is himself mortally affected. His return is from the first involved in death—he reappears in a cemetery and struggles vainly with Laertes in Ophelia's grave (V. i)—and the final resolution which fate puts into his hands is surrounded by obscurity and misunderstanding. Claudius, intending to poison him, in fact poisons Gertrude; Laertes, hoping to avenge his father's death, is caught in the trap he has agreed to lay for his enemy; and Hamlet himself only carries out the Ghost's command after he has realized that he is finally, inescapably involved in the pattern of death which has woven itself round his person. The whole of the last scene represents rather the final working out of a mortal process of disease than the triumphant execution of a natural duty. It is as though the poison originally poured by Claudius into his brother's ear, like

> a most instant tetter, barkt about,
> Most lazar-like, with vile and loathsome crust,   (I. v. 71)

has extended its action from the 'smooth body' of Hamlet's father to cover the entire court of Denmark grouped for death round the infected person of its usurping king.

In this way the last scene reflects the spirit which, in greater or lesser degree, has prevailed throughout the play. Hamlet's efforts to follow the course of duty have been throughout obstructed by an inner conflict, a settled disgust, the true extent of which is only gradually revealed in the course of the action. This conflict, or disgust, is spread through the entire tragedy, into which it instils a pervasive, violent poison, associated in some degree with the disorder of the 'blood' in and through which it works. The poison is present in all the protagonists and in the state which is their common environment; but it works always *from within* outwards, revealing its full power to destroy in the course of its development. It is supremely present beneath the suave surface of Claudius, whose usurped authority is undermined in the course of the play by guilt and fear; but it is also present in Gertrude, whose weakness has led to the marriage which her son, finding in it an exterior projection of his inner disgust, regards as 'incestuous'. It can be found in the senile self-regard of Polonius, more especially in his attitude towards youth and passion, and eventually breaks through to the surface in the madness of the shattered Ophelia; Laertes, the representative of hot, idle youth, shares it, and so does even the active, confident Fortinbras in his irresponsible military adventures. Above all, it is present in Hamlet himself, whose actions throughout are peculiarly calculated to bring about its exposure in those around him. By the end of the play Hamlet has revealed all the evils which surround him and has shown them to be variously, if obscurely, related to the stresses, which constitute the real centre of the tragedy, in his own soul. By bringing them to the light, and by finally carrying out as a passive instrument the mission imposed upon him, he leads those who surround him, with himself, to the death that is their common end. The spirit of this tragedy is still involved in contradiction, still imperfect in its clarity of conception; but never so far in Shakespeare's work has an emotional situation been so variously reflected in an elaborate

dramatic action. The fact is of decisive importance for an understanding
of the dramatist's complete development.[18]

3 Measure for Measure

Few of Shakespeare's plays have given rise to more contrasted interpretations than *Measure for Measure*. Most of the difficulties derive
ultimately from the discrepancy which is generally felt to exist between
the play's formal assumptions and a prevailing spirit which is, for the
greater part of its development, notably incompatible with them.
Formally speaking, *Measure for Measure* is a comedy, and as such
dedicated to a reconciling and harmonizing conclusion, which is
indeed worked out with considerable ingenuity in the long and intricate
final scene. The most individual episodes, on the other hand, are
notably uncomic, dedicated not to reconciliation but to the exploration
of insoluble conflicts and sombre moral realities. The preoccupation
with the flesh, already present as one element among many in *Hamlet*,
acquires greater weight and consistency in *Measure for Measure*, and
to it corresponds a 'law' which is 'reason' made more personal, more
immediately realized in answer to a more concrete sense of moral
realities.

The need for constant moral standards, and for their enforcement
by the civil power, is the starting point of the action. It is to strengthen
this enforcement that the Duke, at the beginning of the play, calls
upon Angelo to replace him; and even Claudio, who is most interested
in the loosening of bonds that condemn him to immediate death,
agrees that the sentence passed upon him is just. His plight, he tells
Lucio, proceeds

> From too much liberty, my Lucio, liberty;
> As surfeit is the father of much fast,
> So every scope by the immoderate use
> Turns to restraint. Our natures do pursue,
> Like rats that ravin down their proper bane,
> A thirsty evil; and when we drink we die. (I. ii. 134)

Claudio's words, however, do more than confirm the necessary
severity of the law. Their apparent directness is capable of sustaining

the weight of the moral contradiction upon which the whole play turns. The linguistic power of *Measure for Measure*, far from expanding easily into lyricism or rhetoric, is subordinated to a supple bareness and concentrated most often upon an intense underlining of the value of single words. This does not mean that the effect is necessarily simple. No word in Claudio's speech is logically superfluous, but more than one is, in its context, surprising. The verb 'ravin', for instance, suggests bestial, immoderate feeding, and so 'appetite', but the next line proceeds, through a 'thirsty evil', to transfer the metaphor to drinking; the shift of the image and the sharp focusing of impressions by which it is accompanied are characteristic of Shakespeare's mature art. The effect is to transfer attention almost imperceptibly from the idea of Claudio's condemnation to another which, without directly questioning the first, yet profoundly modifies it. The repellent impression summoned up by 'ravin' and maintained by the reference, at once contemptuous and loathing, to 'rats' is unobtrusively transformed into an evocation of natural thirst; the evil remains, and is uncondoned, but its relation to the normal human situation has gone through a decisive change. The whole passage, indeed, is designed to stress the deep-seated contradiction involved in the very nature of passion. Human nature, Claudio says, is driven to pursue the object of its desire like a rat whose natural, or 'proper', thirst impels it to swallow the 'bane' which must inevitably, once swallowed, kill it. Passion, indeed, coveted and pursued in full 'liberty' beyond the limits of the moral law, leads fatally to destruction; but—and here Shakespeare restores the balance necessary to his conception—it is a bane *proper* to humanity, which craves free satisfaction as the thirsty animal craves for water and which man cannot therefore, even if he should so desire, hope to suppress.

The reservations implied in Claudio's confession of guilt gain fresh power, a little further on, from one of the few speeches in *Measure for Measure* in which strong and simple emotion triumphs over the discipline habitually imposed upon it. When Lucio brings news of Claudio's arrest to Isabella, he describes her brother's sin in lines where intensity of feeling breaks with tremendous effect through the deliberate, restrained tonelessness of so much of this play:

> Your brother and his lover have embraced:
> As those that feed grow full: as blossoming time,
> That from the seedness the bare fallow brings

To teeming foison; even so her plenteous womb
Expresseth his full tilth and husbandry. (I. iv. 40)

The writing of such a speech implies new possibilities in Shakespeare's
art. Not only are various of its images vastly developed in *King Lear*
and later plays, but the very movement of the verse is more rich and
complex in the command of words behind 'seed*ness*' and '*plenteous*
womb', in the concentration that can use both 'feed' and 'husbandry'
to express the fertility of passion. The effect is to give to the natural
instinct behind Claudio's sin a full and triumphant expression. The
bane is, after all, inescapably 'proper' to humanity. His love for Juliet,
expressly related to the fullness of the harvest and to the physical
satisfaction that follows eating, is as inevitable as the return of the
fertile 'blossoming time' to the dead, bare fallow; and, like that
return, it is life-giving, 'plenteous', 'teeming'. In the light of the
undeniable vitality so expressed, the problem of 'liberty' in its relation
to the moral order acquires a new urgency. It represents an intuition
which must not indeed overstep the restraining limits of the law but
which must somehow, in the interests of harmony, be freely incor-
porated in them.

The balance thus held in the individual utterance is consistently
maintained in Shakespeare's presentation of life in Vienna. The life of
the city is based upon the natural order uncurbed by any reference to
the moral law; the Duke himself, we are told, has withdrawn into the
cultivation of his personal interests, allowing common life to develop
in accordance with its own instincts. The result has been an unchecked
spread of what the moral law condemns as vice and this spread is
associated, in the realistic scenes presenting the street life of the city,
with corruption and death. Vienna is undermined by decay, and the
imagery of venereal disease dominates Shakespeare's presentation of
its life. The jesting conversation of the courtiers and men of the world
in this play turns insistently, even monotonously, upon the threat of
sexual disease; but beneath the levity which springs from long familiar-
ity there appears a deeper note of fear. The courtiers of Vienna and the
parasites who prey upon them are aware of the frightening moral
emptiness which their maladies imply. When one of his friends
observes to Lucio, 'Thou art always figuring diseases in me; but thou
art full of error—I am sound', he replies, with at least a hint of the
profound religious seriousness which animates this play: 'Nay, not as

one would say, healthy; but so sound as things that are hollow: thy bones are hollow; impiety has made a feast of thee' (I. ii. 56). Beneath this hollowness, which is more than physical, lies that fear of death which is in *Measure for Measure* the beginning of wisdom.

Here too, however, there is another side to the picture. The 'bane' that has poisoned Viennese society is still, to return to Claudio's key phrase, 'proper' to it. It is still a consequence, however tainted by human perversity, of natural human failings. This is a fact with which the law itself must eventually come to terms. The examination of the bawd, Pompey, by Escalus, the representative of the Duke's justice, sets before us in concrete form some of the intricacies which human nature imposes upon the necessary administration of justice. Pompey, when challenged, makes no attempt to deny his trade. He simply denies the utility of trying to suppress it. 'Truly, sir,' he says, 'I am a poor fellow that would live.' The discussion that follows proceeds in the most direct and telling simplicity:

> *Escalus:* How would you live, Pompey? by being a bawd? What do you
>   think of the trade, Pompey? is it a lawful trade?
> *Pompey:* If the law would allow it, sir.
> *Escalus:* But the law will not allow it, Pompey; nor it shall not be allowed in
>   Vienna.
> *Pompey:* Does your lordship mean to geld and splay all the youth of the city?
>   (II. i. 240)

The point is crudely, even cruelly made, but its implications are tremendously serious. To re-establish the law in Vienna is, as we have seen, vitally necessary. Failure to deal with the diseases of which Pompey is a symptom involves the collapse of society under the double burden of physical disease and moral dissolution. Yet upon what human instinct, if Pompey is right, can the law be based? For Pompey, and for the great unconscious mass of humanity, the law is no more than a matter of verbal caprice. The trade of bawd is 'unlawful' in Pompey's eyes, not because it degrades man's true dignity, but simply because the law in its mysteriousness 'will not allow it'. To find for the law a necessary sanction in experience without depriving it of the firmness and impartiality upon which its maintenance depends is the task which ultimately faces the Duke in *Measure for Measure*.

Before he has gained the experience necessary to carry it out, however, the Duke has to learn from two simplified solutions of the moral problem. His own error has been an excessive faith in 'liberty', in permitting human instincts to grow uncurbed until they threatened to undermine the fabric of society. His abdication, besides clearing the way for Angelo's rigid enforcement of the letter of the law, brings him into contact, through Isabella, with a virtue whose perfection implies a complete withdrawal from human affairs. Both Angelo and Isabella have their own way of imposing 'law' upon the flesh: ways which are found to be inadequate and, indeed, by a strange irony, mutually destructive, but through the contemplation of which the Duke gains at least some of the understanding upon which true justice rests.

The attempt to enforce the law by delegating authority to Angelo fails. It fails ultimately because of the deputy's lack of self-knowledge. Angelo believes that he has, by the force of his own virtue, dominated passion, whereas in reality he has simply passed it by. Lucio, whose remarks are so often revealing, describes him as a man whose blood is 'very snow-broth', who 'rebates and blunts' his 'natural edge'— the adjective is important—by opposing to it an abstract discipline conceived in 'the mind', in 'study and fast', and ultimately powerless before what Escalus calls 'the resolute acting of [the] blood' (II. i. 12); his inexperience is enough to disqualify him as a lawgiver. That is what is implied in the offhand and unsubstantiated claim with which he backs his rejection of Escalus' plea for Claudio:

> You may not so extenuate his offence,
> For I have had such faults. (II. i. 27)

Angelo condemns Claudio in reality because he finds his crime inconceivable, and for the same reason he eventually falls. Self-deception, however, is only the first stage in his progress. The ignorance upon which his virtue is so precariously based can turn, with catastrophic suddenness, into the complications of vice.

Measure for Measure is not the only play in which Shakespeare suggests the possibility of a development of this kind. In the preoccupation which other plays reveal with the conflict between passion and controlling reason, his heroes are often moved to admire the man who seems to have dominated his lower instincts. 'Give me'—says Hamlet to Horatio—'that man that is not passion's slave' (III. ii. 76); and his desire is simply an extension into the personal sphere of Ulysses' abstract insistence upon 'degree'. Yet here too there is another side of the picture. Reason that is not fully harmonized with a rich and free emotional life may easily become an imposition concealing every kind of dangerous thwarted instinct; and *Measure for Measure* is only one of several plays written at this time in which Shakespeare concerns himself with situations where that balance is difficult to maintain. The man born free of passion is evidently to be admired and envied; but his freedom may imply a coldness, an indifference to feeling that only partially covers latent impulses of cruelty and domination. The position is perhaps most clearly stated in a famous sonnet:

> They that have power to hurt and will do none,
> That do not do the thing they most do show,
> Who moving others, are themselves as stone,
> Unmoved, cold, and to temptation slow;
> They rightly do inherit heaven's graces ...   (Sonnet XCIV)

The application to Angelo is obvious. In him too there is a stony virtue which depends upon the innate sluggishness of the blood, upon the fact that he has been from birth 'cold' and 'to temptation slow'. More important still, he has 'power to hurt' and exercises it implacably against Claudio; and, most significantly of all, the blamelessness upon which his claim to judge rests is a deception, a concealment of deeper and more unrealized instincts. Angelo, like the man in the sonnet, does not do the thing he most does show. The deception is not less dangerous for being, at the outset, unconscious. Indeed, it is more dangerous, for the ignorance that covers it makes it peculiarly liable to perversion. Angelo's control is of the kind that can turn, almost without warning, into a desire for domination which aims in complete ruthlessness at the goal appointed by his lower instincts.

This is precisely what happens when he meets Isabella. When he finally becomes aware of his feelings towards her he expresses himself in terms which are pregnant with sexuality and self-will:

> I have begun:
> And now I give my sensual race the rein;
> Fit thy consent to my sharp appetite;
> Lay by all nicety and prolixious blushes,
> That banish what they sue for; redeem thy brother
> By yielding up thy body to my will.   (II. iv. 160)

The most remarkable thing about this speech of Angelo's is the completeness with which it accepts, and makes its own, the impulse to recognized evil. For it is not sufficient to say that Angelo is weak-willed or that his normal self-control has been undermined by irrational forces. It is rather that the passion to which he has denied all natural expression has now taken complete control of his will, which reveals itself as forcibly in the direction of carnal desire as it had previously been affirmed in moral rigour and 'firm abstinence'. Thus impelled, it proceeds, by a remorseless internal logic which will become more and more characteristic of Shakespeare's tragic figures, along the road that leads to destruction.

Isabella's virtue, though standing at the other extreme from Angelo's, is related to it by a common foundation in inexperience. When the play opens, she is about to take her vows of profession as a nun. The fact is in itself significant. Virtue in *Measure for Measure* is habitually on its guard, defending itself by withdrawal against the temptations that so insistently beset it. Isabella's opening exchange with the nun who accompanies her stresses the note of retreat and mortification. Considering the rules to which she is shortly to submit herself, she desires an even stricter seclusion from the world:

> *Isabella:* And have you nuns no farther privileges?
> *Francisca:* Are not these large enough?
> *Isabella:* Yes, truly. I speak not as desiring more;
> But rather wishing a more strict restraint
> Upon the sisterhood, the votarists of Saint Clare. (I. iv. 1)

It is significant too, in view of all that is to follow, that Francisca goes on to emphasize one particular feature of the enclosure:

> When you have vow'd, you must not speak with men,
> But in the presence of the prioress;
> Then, if you speak, you must not show your face. (I. iv. 10)

To grasp the spirit in which this retirement is conceived, we must see it in relation to the necessity for enforcing the law at any cost. Virtue and chastity need to be restored in a world where every unrestrained instinct threatens to violate them; and just as the lawgiver must defend them by imposing 'The needful bits and curbs to headstrong weeds',[19] so must the individual preserve them in himself even at the cost of renouncing a society which seems to incline almost universally to corruption. Isabella, by entering the convent, is simply carrying to its logical extreme the fulfilment of a moral duty.

Mere restraint, however, is not in her case enough. Before she can

take her vows, human claims of a kind which no exclusion can solve
call her away from the cloister. Lucio brings the news that her brother,
at the point of death, places his last hope in her intervention. The terms
in which this hope is expressed by Claudio himself are an indication
of the hazards, so far unsuspected by Isabella, which beset virtue in
this play:

> bid herself assay him:
> I have great hope in that; for in her youth
> There is a prone and speechless dialect,
> Such as move men; besides, she hath prosperous art
> When she will play with reason and discourse,
> And well she can persuade.   (I. ii. 192)

The qualities upon which Claudio relies are not, typically enough,
those of simple virtue. In his view, at least, his sister can 'play with
reason' and mould the wills of men subtly—even if innocently, in
complete unconsciousness of artifice—to her purpose. Most significantly of all, her main power lies in the 'prone and speechless' attractions
—there is even a faint suggestion of invitation and artful passivity in
the adjectives—of her youthful person. It is not of course that she is
dishonest or that she sets out to appeal deliberately to Angelo's baser
instincts. It is simply that she is a woman and that therefore her power
over men, which she has yet to begin to understand, is bound to become
a temptation. If Isabella's virtue does not fully satisfy, that is not
primarily through any obvious moral deficiency in her own nature
(though attempts have been made to find one) but simply because the
state of simple virtue does not exist in *Measure for Measure*. Chastity
there is surrounded by reservations not of its own making, flaws
related to the flesh and inherent in the human situation. If Isabella has
any fault, it is that she is unaware of these flaws and reservations. Her
retirement is too simple, her virtue too little grounded in experience
to correspond to the spirit in which this play is conceived. In the very
readiness with which she accepts the mission that Lucio urges upon
her—

> Commend me to my brother: soon at night
> I'll send him certain word of my success—   (I. iv. 88)[20]

there is, besides proper feeling for her brother, a touch of inexperience
that will eventually lead her into a situation with which she is in some
respects unqualified to deal. It is certain that the path to Claudio's
salvation will be longer and harder than she yet realizes.

The two scenes which portray the encounter between Angelo and Isabella (II. ii, iv) owe much of their effect to the fact that each is peculiarly fitted to bring out the weakness of the other. The first is devoted substantially to the downfall of Angelo. His utterances, short and ambiguous in her presence, become after her departure charged with the imagery of desire:

> she speaks, and 'tis
> Such sense, that my sense breeds with it. (II. ii. 141)
>
> . . . . .
>
> The tempter or the tempted, who sins most?
> Not she, nor doth she tempt, but it is I
> That, lying by the violet in the sun,
> Do as the carrion does, not as the flower,
> Corrupt with virtuous season. Can it be
> That modesty may more betray our sense
> Than woman's lightness? Having waste ground enough,
> Shall we desire to raze the sanctuary,
> And pitch our evils there? (II. ii. 163)

The peculiar verbal texture of these speeches is already familiar in works of this period. The play, in the first tentative aside, on the double meaning of 'sense'—'sense' as 'meaning' or 'understanding' and 'sense' as 'sensuality'—conveys perfectly the half-conscious process by which Angelo's self-control has been undermined; the type of ambiguity so prominent in the more analytic sonnets is being effectively projected into a personal and dramatic situation. The opening lines of the later speech, in turn, clearly recall the 'god kissing carrion' of *Hamlet* and, perhaps even more clearly, the 'lilies that fester' of the sonnet. Compression in the syntax is once more a sign of emotional pressure, though still scarcely understood by the speaker. Angelo does not pause to develop the comparison between 'I' and the 'carrion'; he gives them simultaneous existence in a single image which brings out, in the first dim moment of realization, the significance of his new state. His will, clarifying its sinister purpose in the very process of expression, reveals itself as a destructive instinct perversely incited by the mere presence of virtue to the satisfaction of its corrupt desires. The 'carrion' element of passion, always present beneath his modesty, is breaking out in a form even more dangerous than the evils he had so confidently undertaken to suppress.

The connection between Angelo's 'foulness' and its opposite in

Isabella is the key to all that follows. Having abandoned himself to his instincts, he proceeds at their next meeting to work upon her with consummate dialectic skill. Desire, far from undermining his intelligence, sharpens it, gives it fresh power to penetrate and destroy. When he repeats his sentence, she takes her stand on the contrast between the absolute claim of the law and the pitiful incapacity of its human instruments. ''Tis set down so in heaven, but not in earth' (II. iv. 51). The argument is dangerous because, though just, it can be turned logically against herself. If Claudio's sin is not, at least on earth, beyond forgiveness, if frailty can indeed be an adequate reason for relaxing the severity of the law, then

> Might there not be a charity in sin
> To save this brother's life? (II. iv. 64)

Isabella, still ignorant of the sinister purpose behind all this, falls into the trap. She declares her readiness to take upon herself responsibility for the decision to which she is pressing Angelo:

> Please you to do't,
> I'll take it as a peril to my soul,
> It is no sin at all, but charity. (II. iv. 65)

The exclamation, generous as it is, proves fatal. Isabella's plea, taken up with evil intention, recoils against her own position. If pity is a sufficient reason for relaxing the statutes, she herself can plausibly be summoned to relax them too. The conscience of the lawgiver, if—as Isabella has still every reason to suppose—his intentions are pure, is not necessarily less inviolate than that of the virgin; indeed, if the present state of Vienna is any indication, his responsibility may be greater and the call for firmness more urgent. As Angelo, taking up her very words, at once retorts:

> Pleased *you* to do't at peril of *your* soul,
> Were equal poise of sin and charity. (II. iv. 68)

Angelo does not go so far as to deny that the act which he is about to urge upon Isabella is a sin. He merely shows that the charity upon which she so passionately calls can be invoked against her; events will show how far she can maintain the rigidity of her virtue without sacrificing some of her own humanity.

Isabella, of course, when she has understood the drift of Angelo's proposal, refuses to consider it. She refuses in terms that, besides

reflecting the impulsiveness of her character, point to the presence of
tense and unrecognized elements, finally not devoid of erotic implications, beneath the emphasis of her repudiation:

> were I under the terms of death,
> The impression of keen whips I'd wear as rubies,
> And strip myself to death, as to a bed
> That longing have been sick for, ere I'd yield
> My body up to shame. (II. iv. 101)

It is not necessary to go so far as to find this actually repellent; but it
does show a remarkable insight into the psychological pressures that
sometimes find issue in the craving for martyrdom and which fore-
shadow, in the case of Isabella herself, a comprehensible but nonetheless
self-centred breakdown into hysteria. When she has finished, Angelo
can quietly, logically return to his point:

> You seem'd of late to make the law a tyrant;
> And rather prov'd the sliding of your brother
> A merriment than a vice. (II. iv. 115)

At this point Isabella begins to realize the weakness of her position.
She admits as much in her reply—'To have what we would have, we
speak not what we mean.' This is not the kind of answer likely to
dissuade Angelo. 'We are all frail,' he insists, and once more Isabella
falls into the trap laid for her. 'Else let my brother die,' she exclaims,
and Angelo uses her appeal to press home the implications of his
original argument. 'Nay, women are frail too,' he insinuates, and goes
on to make his logical deduction:

> Since, I suppose, we are made to be no stronger
> Than faults may shake our frames—let me be bold—
> I do arrest your words. Be that you are,
> That is a woman; if you be more, you're none. (II. iv. 133)

The argument, though perverse, brings out complexities which Isabella
is unfitted to recognize. She originally brought forward the admission
of man's natural weakness as a reason for relaxing the rigour of the law;
Angelo, not less logically, though moved by the selfishness of his own
desire, bases upon the very same recognition his demand that she should
surrender herself to his will.

What are we to conclude from this? Not, certainly, that Angelo is
right and Isabella wrong. Her main point—the essential distinction
between 'ignominy in ransom' and the graciousness of 'free pardon'—

stands, and Angelo's lust is clearly the enemy of virtue. Yet we do wrong, beyond this, to simplify Shakespeare's conception by looking for 'solutions' to clear-cut moral problems. The dilemma set before Isabella—to surrender her virginity to buy her brother's life—the play is not primarily concerned to solve; it merely gives her two opposed attachments, both right and both involved in contradiction by an evil quite beyond her control. But once this has been granted, it is hard not to feel in her virtue at least a touch of wilful egoism:

> More than our brother is our chastity . . .   (II. iv. 186)

> Take my defiance!
> Die, perish! Might but my bending down
> Reprieve thee from thy fate, it should proceed.
> I'll pray a thousand prayers for thy death,
> No word to save thee.   (III. i. 141)

It is not the sentiment that surprises, but the manner of its expression. That Isabella should, in such a case, refuse indignantly is natural; that she should turn upon her brother, accuse him of cowardice and even— as she condemns him to death—cast upon him the shadow of bastardy is less so.[21] The egoism which promoted Angelo to will the evil conceived in his 'appetite' is not totally absent from Isabella's defence of her chastity. 'Virtue', as each of them conceives it, is still a partial and abstract thing, still an imposition of the reason planted a little aridly upon a whole world of sentiments and reactions which remain outside it and take refuge in the humanity, corrupt and hollow though it be, of Pompey and Lucio. Both lack the self-knowledge that true moral maturity requires. Both are themselves in need of judgment and both, before they can be adequately judged, must be considered in the light of an experience more mature and impartial than their own.

That experience, to the degree in which this play offers it, is provided by the Duke. The figure of the Duke, as Shakespeare conceives him, hesitates between two aspects. He is both inside the action, as the indispensable instrument of a remarkably involved and tortuous plot, and outside it, judging with compassionate detachment the events to which his own abdication have given rise. As a character within the action, the Duke's self-confessed weakness, born though it is of tolerance and the readiness to understand, has contributed to the intolerable state of Viennese society. As a detached 'symbol' of truth in judgment, on the other hand, his understanding is presented in a way that tends to affirm it as absolute and perfect. Angelo himself, when finally exposed, ascribes to Vincentio certain attributes of divinity:

> O my dread lord,
> I should be guiltier than my guiltiness,
> To think I can be undiscernible,
> When I perceive your grace, *like power divine*,
> Hath look'd upon my passes. (V. i. 367)

The transition between these two positions takes place during the course of the action. A retired and even ambiguous figure in the early scenes, the Duke comes forward increasingly as the plot advances. In the later episodes he holds the threads in his hands, directs them, and provides by his observations upon them the most impartial comment. No other Shakespearean character, at this stage in the poet's career, had been conceived with an intention so clearly, if intermittently, 'symbolic'; it is even possible to think of the Duke, in this light, as a first approximation to Prospero.[22]

The emphasis upon superior detachment must not lead us to think of the Duke's function in terms of providing solutions, more or less clearly defined, to the problems raised in the course of the play. Shakespeare was elaborating a state of experience, not answering an abstract question; and this state was essentially a strife, a disharmony still far from resolution. 'Solutions' in Shakespeare are not intellectual statements; they are only apprehensible in a gradual harmonizing of themes, to which the functions of plot and character become increasingly knitted. The contradictory elements of experience are reconciled, if at all, in the process of living them out. The reconciliation towards which they are moved is not imposed in abstraction, but slowly and patiently attained through a steady incorporation of the most diverse elements. In *Measure for Measure*, at any rate, in spite of its 'comic' presuppositions, it is still premature to speak of this kind of resolution. The Duke does not, in any primary sense, offer solutions; rather he is steeped in the mystery and obscurity so typical of the play. To Lucio he is 'the old fantastical duke *of dark corners*' (IV. iii. 167), and Escalus tells us that he has always been 'one that, *above all other strifes*, contended especially *to know himself*' (III. ii. 252). This description is significant. Both Angelo and Isabella have failed in self-knowledge, in awareness of the complex knot of good and evil which centres on human passion.

A lawgiver must be aware of this complexity, must seek to harmonize the natural sources of experience with the moral 'law'. The Duke's own self-knowledge, however, still hangs in the balance. It is still a 'strife', a 'contention', a matter of working out obscure and even contradictory impulses that refuse, so far, to submit to a common unity. The fact that he exists at all, that Shakespeare was able to conceive a judgment based upon true impartiality, points to the direction in which his interests were moving; but between the conception and such fulfilment of it as was attained in the plays of his later maturity lies the prolonged experience of the tragedies.

The Duke's distinctive contribution to *Measure for Measure* really begins when, having assumed the Friar's role, he confesses Claudio (III. i). He introduces in his great opening speech a fresh fact in relation to which the problems raised by the desires of the flesh need to be reconsidered. This fact is the universal relevance of death:

> Be absolute for death; either death or life
> Shall thereby be the sweeter. (III. i. 5)

To Claudio's confession of hope—'I've hope to live, and am prepared to die'—the Duke replies with a reasoned pessimism whose acceptance of death places it beyond the uncertainty which inevitably accompanies and often flaws all human desire. Death is the common destiny of man and simply to rebel against it is the act of a child; but to consider in the light of it the passions and appetites which have brought Claudio—and Vienna—to such tragic consequences is the beginning of wisdom.

The beginning but not the end. Men do well to accept the idea of death as an element inextricably interwoven, through the action of time, into every moment of our living experience. Without that acceptance there is no true maturity, but without a corresponding sense of life there is no vitality at all. The reaction against death, like that against the letter of the law, affects *Measure for Measure* at every level. The problem of Pompey, as it faces Angelo and Escalus, is balanced for the Duke by that of Barnardine. Like Pompey, like so many other characters in the background of this play, Barnardine has no conception of the moral law. He is, in the words of the Provost, 'a man that apprehends death no more dreadfully but as a drunken sleep; careless, reckless, and fearless of what's past, present, or to come: *insensible of mortality, and desperately mortal*' (IV. ii. 148). The Duke,

whose sense of the moral law is so closely bound up with his awareness of mortality, cannot consent to his execution in such a state. He
finds Barnardine

> A creature unprepared, unmeet for death;
> And to transport him in the mind he is
> Were damnable. (IV. iii. 74)

Damnable: the sense of moral issues implicit in our acts and prolonging
themselves to eternity is throughout distinctive of the Duke's outlook.
The acceptance of the moral law is bound up with a deeper, profounder
respect for human life. This does not, of course, invalidate the law
itself, or diminish the need for its enforcement; but it does underline
the almost infinite patience and understanding which that enforcement
involves. Barnardine, though only a minor presence in *Measure for
Measure,* has a distinctive part to play in it; and Shakespeare, in allowing
him to play it, enriches notably the moral pattern of his conception.

The reservations represented by Barnardine are taken up on a higher
level—as they were with Pompey in the matter of judgement—by
Claudio and Isabella. As the dialogue between these two proceeds
after the Duke's departure, the emphasis slowly but decisively shifts
from death to its opposite—that is, to Claudio's keen desire for life.
Even in the Duke's speech, where the feeling for death is most intense,
we feel the horror of the

> soft and tender fork
> Of a poor worm. (III. i. 16)

This horror can be paralleled in *Hamlet*. So much can hardly be said
of the way in which Isabella's attempt to minimize the pangs of death
turns into an acute realization of the actual nervous 'pang' of dying:

> Darest thou die?
> The sense of death is most in apprehension;
> And the poor beetle that we tread upon,
> In corporal sufferance finds a pang as great
> As when a giant dies. (III. i. 75)

Clearly this is no sort of argument for death. The emphasis is no longer
where the Duke had left it, upon the peace of death, but rather upon
the pain involved in the passage to extinction. The body reacts with
vivid sensual immediacy against the consolation offered to it. The
reaction, proceeding as it does from the nervous sensibility, is completely spontaneous; and gradually it communicates itself to Claudio.

At first he is resolved to die that his sister's honour may be saved; but the resolution that expresses itself in the phrase 'I will encounter darkness as a bride' (III. i. 82) is really a rhetorical effort to force himself to accept a fate which he regards as inevitable. It does not live long. As Claudio slowly comes to realize that he *might* live, his resolution palpably wavers. The first resolve had been clear-cut, decisive: 'Thou shalt not do it'; but when his sister, with that strain of moral ruthlessness which is part of her nature, and—as we now know—of her weakness, forces him to face his position with the unambiguous order: 'Be ready, Claudio, for your death to-morrow,' he hesitates. 'Yes,' he answers, but with deliberation and as though his thoughts were fixed elsewhere; and indeed they pass, in the phrase that immediately follows, to considerations that affect him more nearly:

> Sure, it is no sin;
> Or of the deadly seven it is the least.   (III. i. 108)

The phrase amounts to a plea to Isabella to change her mind. To meet death boldly when no hope of life remains is a thing a man owes to his self-respect, but to choose it when it might be avoided, even with shame, is far harder. It calls for a degree of detachment and determination which few young men—or indeed, few of any age—can claim to possess. Claudio tries to show he has acquired them, but fails.

In the remark just quoted, if anywhere, lies the moral issue beneath the whole incident. The conception of *Measure for Measure* rests upon a balance between two aspects of human passion: the natural and proper instinct upon which it rests and the dissolution and disease to which its unchecked indulgence leads. Claudio's phrase holds the balance perfectly. The idea that it would be 'no sin' for Isabella to lie with Angelo is no part of Shakespeare's conception. It *is* a sin, and *deadly*, barely redeemable. Claudio has committed this same 'deadly sin'— and the phrase has behind it the force of a Christian tradition to which Shakespeare in this play firmly adheres—but he has also committed the most natural, the most spontaneous of the seven; for his sin, though he recognizes it to be grievous in social terms, has involved that offering of self which is, in Shakespearean terms, the law of love, and so of life. Isabella, when she turns on him in her anger, fails to take this into account. It is not her decision which is wrong, but her expression of it which is—from the level of compassionate understanding at which the Duke aims—inadequate; and Claudio's profoundly human

observation compels us to recognize this. Having made it, he falters
and then visibly breaks down. His instincts, refusing to accept the
extinction decreed for them, react against the abstract resolution
previously imposed upon them:

> Ay, but to die, and go we know not where . . .
> The weariest and most loathed worldly life
> That age, ache, penury, and imprisonment
> Can lay on nature, is a paradise
> To what we fear of death.   (III. i. 116)

This is the fear of *Hamlet* once again, the dread of uncertainty following
extinction; but it is that fear expressed with a physical immediacy
rarely known in the earlier play. The emphasis in Claudio's tremendous
outburst of horror is all upon the sensitive apprehension of life, upon
the immediate opposition between the 'sensible warm motion' of the
living body and the 'cold', rotted 'obstruction' which reduces it to a
'kneaded clod'; even the life of the 'delighted spirit' in the cosmic
obscurity of the afterstate is sensually conceived. The impending
presence of death has brought out in Claudio a fear whose very weakness is natural, human: a fear which Isabella's virtue has not sufficiently
allowed for, but which the Duke in his compassionate understanding
will accept.

It is from this point, indeed, that his activities of reconciliation begin
to take shape. Having overheard the dialogue of Isabella and Claudio
he begins to take steps to ward off the consequences of Angelo's
wickedness. These steps are plunged for a time into obscurity during
which the issues are delicately balanced, poised between life and death.
He works, it is worth noting, at night. This part of the play, in which
the mysterious intrigues of the Duke and Angelo strive for supremacy,
is full of references to 'the heavy middle of the night' (IV. i. 37), to
'dead midnight' (IV. ii. 67), and—perhaps most significantly of all in
its sense of deception and disappointment—to 'lights that do *mislead*
the morn' (IV. i. 4). The intricate mechanism of the plot at this point,
which is often brought forward as evidence of Shakespeare's lack of
interest in his theme, but which is better seen as corresponding,
however obscurely, to the harmonizing conventions of comedy, may
be more significant than it looks. The Duke, for all his detachment, is
not fully in charge of events. He is learning, not less than the others,
from experience, and only differs from them in the wider range of his
sympathy. The control of evil is *not* in his hands; its machinations often

find him unprepared, leave him groping hastily in the darkness for an improvised remedy. That is why the resolution of this play, directed toward a clarification which has no place in the outlook of the characters themselves, cannot completely satisfy. The external and the inner situation simply do not correspond. When Angelo, by a crowning perfidy, sends word that Claudio's execution is to be put forward so as to take place before the meeting in which Isabella is to buy his life, the Duke is almost forestalled. Only by a rather unconvincing trick of substitution does he avert tragedy. This is clearly no way for an allegedly semi-'divine' figure to behave, and Vincentio, no less than Prospero after him, is strangely capable of very human contradictions and irritability; but perhaps we should be wrong to stress excessively the 'divine' attributes in either figure. Both, after all, are involved in events which they themselves have helped to bring about, and are in the process of understanding their own situation in relation to these events. In the confusion which life offers to the seeker after moral clarity the opportunity to do good presents itself in strangely haphazard ways; and the Duke, with no more than an unusually awakened moral sense to see him through the surrounding darkness, grasps them and turns them to his own ends. In so doing, he increases the area of his understanding and shows his humanity.

Measure for Measure, then, offers no real 'solution' to the problems it raises. The problems, indeed, interested Shakespeare at this moment more closely than the possible solutions. The contradictions so essential to the play were to be worked out later, with far greater resources and in other styles. Here the resolution is no more than hinted at. The clearing-up in the last scene is little more than a piece of able manipulation. In spite of its undoubted technical skill, the full body of experience never really informs it, as it has informed the episodes of anguish and division, to give it a corresponding life. But suggestions of greater clarity can be found. They express themselves, in that very fourth act which seems so given over to tortuous obscurities, in a rising series of dawn images, which become more powerful as the Duke begins to feel his mastery of the situation. These culminate in his great prose speech to the Provost:

> Look, the unfolding star calls up the shepherd. Put not yourself into amazement how these things should be: *all difficulties are but easy when they are known* ... Yet you are amazed; but this shall absolutely resolve you. Come away; *it is almost clear dawn.* (IV. ii. 219)

But the 'symbolism', if such we may call it, remains elementary. All the forces of life and fertility suggested in Lucio's great speech on Claudio's love[23] are not yet behind it to give it life and adequate content. This strengthening has yet to grow out of the whole body of the tragedies. The theme of *Measure for Measure* is still the inter-dependence of good and evil within human experience as centred in the act of passion. The mature tragedies which follow are to separate the elements within this complexity; this separation will result in a more complete projection of the individual experience into a more plastic and sensitive dramatic form.

4 All's Well that Ends Well

All's Well That Ends Well, which shows in the matter of plot con-trivance superficial points of contact with *Measure for Measure*, is by any account a curiously indecisive piece. Two distinct themes are clearly intended to illuminate one another, but can scarcely be said to come together with complete harmony. The first aims at exploring, through the relationship of Helena and Bertram, the connection between personal *virtue* and inherited *honour*; the second relates this theme to the story of a sick and ageing king, his 'miraculous' cure through Helena's faith in her dead father's remedy, and the winning by her, through her own personal merits and faith, proved in adversity, of a Bertram who strikes us throughout as remarkably unworthy of her. It is, indeed, in the actions of Helena and in her relation to the courtly world around her that the play most consistently comes to life.

The virtues of Helena display themselves in a world notably domin-ated by an awareness of the adverse action of time. The King, as it opens, is said to have 'abandoned his physicians'; having 'persecuted time with hope', he has found at the last 'no other advantage . . . but only the losing of hope by time' (I. i. 16). His physician, whose skill and integrity were such that he was *almost* able to 'make nature immortal', is dead, and has confirmed by his death his share in what are evidently the limitations of all human effort: 'he was skilful enough to have lived still, if knowledge could be set up against mortality' (I. i. 35). The elaborate balance of the prose in these early scenes answers once more to Shakespeare's efforts to turn the conven-tions of comedy to distinctive use as the reflection of real life.

This situation produces in the King a deep nostalgia for the past. Like other Shakespearean comic characters, notably in *As You Like It*,[24] he habitually sees virtue in relation to the dead, and more especially in Bertram's father, in whom 'wit', divorced from its degeneration into modern levity, was still compatible with true 'honour', who was conscious of his appropriate place in society and was yet scrupulously deferential towards those of lower station; whom memory, in short, presents as an example, the incarnation of courtly virtue, to a decadent present:

> Such a man
> Might be a copy to these younger times;
> Which, follow'd well, would demonstrate them now
> But goers backward.   (I. ii. 45)

We shall not, if we wish to be true to the play's intention, equate this nostalgic attitude with the author's complete thought; but it remains true that these memories produce in the King a typical old man's pessimism, which he expresses feelingly in the remembered words of his departed friend:

> 'Let me not live,' quoth he,
> 'After my flame lacks oil, to be the snuff
> Of younger spirits, whose apprehensive senses
> All but new things disdain; whose judgements are
> Mere fathers of their garments; whose constancies
> Expire before their fashions.'   (I. ii. 58)

Although this is not what the play finally aims at saying, though its final affirmation will not be placed in the mouth of tired old age, there is strength enough in the expression—and more particularly in the equation of the rash judgment of youth with the outer 'garments' of reality—to lead us to give it due weight in the complete picture.

Inspired by these thoughts to a sense of his own irrelevance, the King goes on to express his desire to follow his generation into oblivion. The conflict in his exhausted frame between 'nature', the instinct for life and its acceptance, and 'sickness' is one that he is now conscious of lacking the strength or the living motivation to resolve. He, and his state with him, are aware of being dominated by the force of decline and death, and await—but not yet with the hope of receiving it— the continual, the daily re-created 'miracle' of life renewed.

Against this background, the comedy shows us two young people asserting their own natures in strongly contrasted ways. In the court a certain feverish craving for activity in the young answers to the impotent scepticism of old age: the 'gentry', we are told, are

sick
For breathing and exploit,   (I. ii. 16)

in much the way that Fortinbras, in the opening scene of *Hamlet*, was said to be defying his 'impotent and bed-rid uncle' in the pursuit of his predatory ends.[25] Bertram, the son, as we have seen, of a worthy but *dead* father, reflects a similar situation. He is the external copy of the parent whom the King in his nostalgic memory exalts:

thou bear'st thy father's face;
Frank nature, rather curious than in haste,
Hath well composed thee;   (I. ii. 19)

there remains the question whether the inner, personal reality of so noble a father—his 'moral parts'—have also descended to his son. For, as his mother clearly sees, Bertram, though resplendent in the superficial courtly virtues, enjoys these by inheritance rather than by merit of personal affirmation; he is, moreover, recognized by her to be, as a courtier, 'unseason'd', imperfectly prepared to cope with a dangerous and declining world, so that her advice to him as he leaves to seek his fortunes is defensively conceived. 'Love all', she urges him, but '*trust a few*'; and again:

be able for thine *enemy*
Rather in power than use;
... be check'd for *silence*,
But never taxed for speech.   (I. i. 75)[26]

Once these precautions have been taken for the defence of virtue in a treacherous environment, the rest must lie in the will of 'heaven', and his mother, beyond praying for him, can do little to save her son from the perils that must infallibly await him.

Already, however, Bertram is contrasted—still in the Countess' mind—with Helena, who backs the 'hopes' that her 'education' promises with a virtue that is not merely inherited but consciously and personally affirmed: 'she derives her honesty and achieves her goodness' (I. i. 52). Unlike so many of the older generation, Helena is not overawed by the recognition of mortality; she grieves, naturally, as in filial duty bound, for her dead father, but refrains from that 'excess' of grief which she truly defines as 'the enemy of the living'. As the

play opens, her life is concentrated upon the reality of the love which
she feels for Bertram and upon which she—after the fashion of other
Shakespearean heroines[27]—is ready to stake her being:

> there is no living, none,
> If Bertram be away. (I. i. 96)

It is typical, however, of the quality of Helena's devotion that it should
be compatible with a firmly realistic estimate of practical possibilities.
She is aware that the object of her love is, in terms of the worldly
values of the court, impossibly beyond her reach; ''twere all one,'
she confesses, with a characteristic combination of realism and commitment,

> That I should love a bright particular star
> And think to wed it, he is so above me. (I. i. 97)

Similarly the picture she draws of the object of her desire is one in
which idealization and realism are significantly blended:

> 'Twas pretty, though a plague,
> To see him every hour; to sit and draw
> His arched brows, his hawking eye, his curls,
> In our heart's table; heart too capable
> Of every line and trick of his sweet favour:
> But now he's gone, and my idolatrous fancy
> Must sanctify his reliques. (I. i. 104)

'Idolatrous'; 'sanctify'; the implications of these words, so often used
of love with a finally limiting implication in Shakespearean comedy,[28]
show Helena engaged in placing the image of courtly perfection which
she has herself a little artificially evoked. Bertram's 'arched brows',
his 'hawking eye', his 'curls': these things, though answering to true
emotion as written in her 'heart's table', are yet the reflections of a
reality in some sense strained and artificial. The heart, indeed, is only
'*too* capable' of responding to these superficial graces, of registering
'every line and trick' of these surface splendours; but the full reality
of her love, which is to be affirmed, through the comic convention, in
the experience of loss and repudiation, will be shown in the course of
the play to rest upon a deeper and more genuine human content.

It is through Helena's exchange, in this same opening scene, with
the incongruous Parolles that love begins to emerge, beyond these
initial limits of convention, in something of its true strength and weakness. Parolles, indeed, is a kind of touchstone, not altogether unrelated

in function to the character so named in *As You Like It*.[29] The product
of the disillusioned scepticism of the society upon which he lives as a
parasite, he touches the action at many points, alternately deflating
pretension by the assertion of his own distillation of cynicism and
prompting those around him to reaction. Parolles, indeed, is a kind of
desiccated Falstaff, deprived of the greater character's distinctive comic
energy but perhaps rendered by this deprivation even more indestructible, more obstinately and clingingly attached to the surface of existence; and as such Helena, with her ability to penetrate to fundamental
reality, responds to him. Helena is fully aware of Parolles' human limitations. She knows that he is 'a notorious liar', 'a great way fool', and
'solely a coward'. As such, she is ready to repudiate him and all that he
stands for; but beyond these indignities she can also appreciate in him
a certain consistency of outlook which is to be recognized, in contrast
to so many courtly attributes that pretentiously claim more, as belonging to the indestructible fabric of life. As she strikingly puts it:

> these fix'd evils sit so fit in him,
> That they take place, when virtue's steely bones
> Look bleak i' the cold wind.   (I. i. 114)

For it is also true to this play's intention that 'cold wisdom' should be
seen, in its self-satisfied superiority, as waiting ignobly on the 'superfluous folly' which everywhere surrounds it.

It is accordingly in contact with the reality represented by Parolles
that love begins to appear in something of its true nature; for, if it is
to be more than the matter of abstract idealization and verbal conceit
to which the courtly outlook habitually limits it, it will have to be
seen to come to terms with a more disillusioned and realistic estimate.
When Parolles urges, against facile idealization, that 'there was never
yet virgin got till virginity was first lost,' when he dismisses virginity
itself as 'against the use of nature,' he is at once echoing Falstaff and,
in his own cynically limited way, asserting certain claims of life:
though, yet again, his references to sale and 'commodity' as the ultimate
criterion—'off with't, while 'tis *vendible*'—point to his own anti-
romantic bias and worldly limitation. Again, when he comments
'your old virginity is like one of our French withered pears, it looks ill,
it eats drily,... it was formerly better' (I. i. 176), it is his own pessimism
that echoes Falstaff's phrases and attitudes[30] without sharing in Falstaff's
distinctive zest. It will be no part of Helena's reaction to endorse

positions so belittling of love, and therefore so far removed from her own frank positives; but it is in reaction to Parolles and all that he stands for that the central truths which it is her part to affirm will begin to take shape in the course of the play.

By her readiness to meet Parolles on his own ground Helena shows, indeed, that there is more behind her own attitudes than mere romantic yearning for an unattainable love. Her virtue is proved from the first to be compatible with a due measure of realism and plain speaking. She stresses, in terms familiar from the sonnets, her awareness of the infinite contradictions which love implies—'His jarring concord, and his discord dulcet', 'His faith, his sweet disaster' (I. i. 188)—but her estimate of Bertram and his ambitions is, at the end of it all, realistic and true. 'The court's a learning place, and he is one,' she reflects, leaving the phrase deliberately and ominously unfinished: 'one', in short, to whom she feels herself attracted even as she recognizes that mere attraction is no guarantee of permanence or objective worth, that the 'pity' is that 'wishing well' has 'not a body in 't'. She is equally clear concerning her own prospects in love, as one of 'the poorer born'

> Whose baser stars do shut us up in wishes;   (I. i. 199)

but against this, it is her own freedom and responsibility that she emphasizes, underlining in the deliberately stressed and sententious rhyme, with which the positive statements of this play are habitually put forward, her confidence in the capacity of human beings to shape their fate to their desires:

> Our remedies oft in ourselves do lie,
> Which we ascribe to heaven: the fated sky
> Gives us free scope; only doth backward pull
> Our slow designs when we ourselves are dull.   (I. i. 235)

In this conviction she brushes aside the 'impossible' and places her trust in the conscious possession of a 'merit' that has nothing to do with inherited position:

> Who ever strove
> To show her merit, that did miss her love?   (I. i. 245)

This is realism, though of a kind very different from that shown by Parolles: a kind which will prove effective precisely because it is not short-sightedly limited to the material appearance of things. The 'king's disease' will provide the opportunity, which her proper faith in herself and her love enables her to grasp, to work what will appear to the realists and the 'experienced' to be nothing less than a 'miracle'. It is perhaps the central paradox of this comedy that Helena's belief in 'miracle', or its possibility, is based in the last analysis upon a firmly realistic trust in her own resourcefulness, upon what her own faith, and her readiness to accept the risk implied in it, may be expected to achieve.

In this spirit Helena confesses to the Countess, Bertram's mother, the love which she bears her son. To the Countess' declaration of faith in her virtue and modesty, and in the naturalness of love itself—'Our blood to this, this to our blood is born' (I. iii. 139)—she responds by declaring, in terms of romantic convention, her readiness to live as Bertram's 'servant' and to die, if need be, as his 'vassal'. Beyond this, however, she stresses equally her determination to *merit* the love she is seeking:

> I follow him not
> By any token of presumptuous suit;
> *Nor would I have him till I do deserve him.* (I. iii. 205)

Given the values which prevail around her, Helena is bound to confess that she does not 'know how that desert should be'; but, though she is aware that, by the standards of the world, she 'strives against hope' and 'loves in vain,' it is of the nature of her love to persevere in the disinterested gift of self and to expect to generate further love in the process of giving:

> in this captious and intenible sieve,
> I still pour in the waters of my love,
> And look not to lose still. (I. iii. 210)

Her confidence in her love is related to her faith in her father's remedy, through which she expects to achieve the 'miracle' of the King's cure. To restore the King to health, and thereby to obtain her 'impossible' love, she is ready to stake everything, even her 'well-lost life'; by this declaration she unites the two central themes of the play in a common gesture of generosity and confidence in the positive laws of life, a readiness to give all in order to obtain the all-embracing fulfilment she so confidently and spontaneously seeks.

In Helena's programme of action we have been brought to see the reality of 'honour'. Bertram, meanwhile, is preparing to 'woo' the same deity under a more superficial aspect. His is the young man's enthusiasm for appearance, for the heady challenge of the 'brave wars' to which he is ready, neglecting the more prudent counsel of his elders, to 'steal away' (II. i. 29). Once more his attitudes receive their implicit evaluation in Parolles' echo of the soldier's bombastic talk of 'Mars' novices' and of Captain Spurio, 'with his cicatrice, an emblem of war,' and in his own bravado claim to have inflicted that wound: above all, in his avowedly cynical advice to Bertram to cultivate those who 'wear themselves in the cap of the time' and 'move under the influence of the most received star' (II. i. 56). Such, concludes Parolles, with a clear reflection of courtly values and the military pretensions which go with them, are to be followed, 'though the devil lead the measure' (II. i. 57).

In the central confrontation, to which all this leads, youth and age, faith and scepticism, meet face to face. The King, confirmed in his knowledge of the world, refuses to be 'credulous' where the possibility of his own cure is concerned; Helena in her reply stresses the *value* of her father's 'receipt', which she declares to be stored up,

> as a triple eye,
> Safer than mine own two, more dear. (II. i. 111)

This, indeed, is the turning-point of the entire action. Helena, having declared her readiness to face the supreme risk to obtain the prize of love, is brought to the decisive test. Her exchange with the King is once again given solemnity through the high sententiousness of rhyme. The emphasis rests, quite deliberately, on a supernatural intervention. In her plea, Helena stresses the discontinuity of what she offers with all merely human intervention, asserts the force of 'inspired merit' against 'worldly breath', and goes on to state:

> most it is *presumption* in us when
> The help of heaven we count the act of men, (II. i. 154)

before concluding: 'Of heaven, *not me*, make an experiment.' Following logically from this, she goes on to take up the King's challenge by laying her own existence in the balance. If she fails in her healing mission, her own life shall be forfeit: 'With vilest torture let my life be ended' (II. i. 177). Confronted by this gesture of faith, the King in turn accepts the offered 'hazard' against all the claims of 'common sense', the consensus of worldly wisdom and recognized experience. As he lays stress on the mortal consequences of failure Helena confirms, for the last time and unequivocally, her readiness to take up the challenge before her:

> King: Sweet practiser, thy physic I will try,
>   That ministers thine own death if I die.
> Helena: If I break time, or flinch in property
>   Of what I spoke, unpitied let me die.   (II. i. 188)

This gesture of faith, however, has its reverse side. In the event of success, Helena is ready to put forward her claim to the reward for which she has chosen to risk her life. She affirms her right, once the cure has been effected, to marry the lover of her choice; and this the King, following what we know to be the normal law of comedy, is ready to grant her.

A variety of standpoints, all in varying degrees worldly and sophisticated, surround this central confrontation. Lafeu, in particular, is inclined, as an old courtier, to hold that 'miracles are past' and belief in their possibility invalidated by the findings of 'philosophical persons' who have made 'modern and familiar, things supernatural and causeless' (II. iii. 2): though he tends ultimately to reject these sceptical attitudes in the light of his own conviction, scarcely less detached in its final implications, of the relativity of all human knowledge:

> Hence it is that we make trifles of terrors, ensconsing ourselves into *seeming knowledge*, when we should submit ourselves to *an unknown fear*.   (II. iii. 4)

Against this background, nonetheless, it emerges as a fact, true if incomprehensible in the eyes of the world, that the 'miracle', 'the rarest argument of wonder that hath shot out in our latter times' (II. iii. 7), has taken place. The King has indeed been restored to health, against his own expectations and those of the world; and it is left, most unexpectedly but with a kind of wry propriety, to Parolles to salute the cure as an effect of 'great *transcendance*' and to prompt Lafeu to declare in turn the 'showing of a heavenly effect in an earthly actor' (II. iii. 28). For the space of this incident, with its persistent overtones of spiritual meaning, we feel ourselves in a world not unlike that of certain prose scenes in *The Winter's Tale*.[31]

Having won her crucial victory of faith, Helena is asked to choose her reward from among those of 'noble father' set before her. In her own words, at once confident and profoundly humble, '*Heaven hath through me* restored the king to health' (II. iii. 70); and now, in the light of this achievement, she does not so much offer to 'take' Bertram as to 'give' herself to him, much as Portia in *The Merchant of Venice*[32] gave herself to Bassanio in response to his choice of the casket:

> I give
> Me and my service, ever whilst I live,
> Into your guiding power. (II. iii. 109)

Here, however, Bertram reveals himself inadequate. Unlike Bassanio, he has chosen no casket, made no demonstration of his readiness to accept the risk which love of its very nature implies. He refuses the 'gift', preferring false 'honour' to true 'value', for reasons typically self-centred and frivolous:

> She had her breeding at my father's charge.
> A poor physician's daughter my wife! (II. iii. 121)

In vain the King calls upon him to reflect that 'Good alone is good without a name,' whilst 'great additions', where they swell in the absence of virtue, can only produce 'a dropsied honour' (II. iii. 135). The matter has in fact passed beyond his control; for, when the young man boorishly insists in his attitude—'I cannot love her, nor will strive to do't' (II. iii. 152)—Helena answers his ungenerous repulse by declaring her refusal to take an unwilling lover and by assuming, in the moment of adversity, the guise of a penitent pilgrim.

From this moment until the end of the play, interest passes from Helena to Bertram, who, following his superficial values in the quest of 'fortune' through 'hazard', leaves for the wars with Parolles as his appropriate attendant. Parolles, as usual, stands in a double relationship to his master, whom he at once echoes and, by implication, exposes. His rhetoric is the hollow counterpart to Bertram's 'honour', though his observations are also those of one who knows, after his fashion, 'what is man' and who, in so far as his knowledge contains elements of truth, surpasses in some measure the confessed ignobility of his role. In accepting Parolles as experienced guide and mentor in the ways of the world, Bertram reveals the insufficiency of his own insight into life. Lafeu judges him more accurately when he penetrates to his essential hollowness: 'the soul of this man is in his clothes' (II. v. 49). Parolles lives parasitically upon a society which affirms indeed the values of war and 'honour', but which finds its appropriate symbol in the *drum*, hollow and high-sounding, for which he is verbally—but only verbally—ready to risk himself. His reality, as the Countess truly sees it, is that of 'a very tainted fellow' (III. ii. 89), corrupting and himself the product of corruption; although it is true that in his very ignobility he reflects life under certain of its aspects, more real after their own fashion than the empty verbiage of self-flattering honour by which so much of the world around him is inspired.

The 'drum' episode ends with the exposure of Parolles as an insubstantial 'bubble': an exposure which in turn implies that of the values followed by Bertram, who placed his trust in Parolles' supposed 'knowledge' and 'valiance' precisely because these, in their lack of solid content, mirrored his own defects. By comparison with Bertram, indeed, Parolles shows himself, in the moment of his downfall, at once more patently corrupt and, after his fashion, more honest. His reply to the Second Lord's contemptuous question, 'Is it possible he should know what he is, and be that he is?' is a plain affirmation of his obstinate will to survive. 'Let me live' (IV. i. 88): the very simplicity of this aspiration marks its separation from Bertram's more pretentious ignobilities, gives the speaker, within the limits which his nature imposes, a certain counter-balancing actuality and truth.[33]

Bertram, meanwhile, follows his own shabby path to personal degradation. His attempt to seduce Diana is marked by a typical combination of facile sentiment and shallow sensuality. 'Love is holy,' he pleads, only too easily, as he asks his intended victim to surrender to what he calls, revealingly enough, his '*sick* desires' (IV. ii. 35). We have here the familiar ingredients of Shakespearean 'doting',[34] the selfish and one-sided parody of true love: 'doting', moreover, turned to something more corrupt than itself, passing beyond mere folly to what remarkably resembles viciousness. Diana, the object of this mean assault, shows herself by contrast ready, with her feminine realism and refusal to be taken in by empty and high-sounding phrases, to expose Bertram's craving as an ignoble caricature of love. His behaviour she sees, as a woman, to answer to permanent aspects of weakness and egoism in the male sex:

> Ay, so you serve us
> Till we serve you; but when you have our roses,
> You barely leave our thorns to prick ourselves,
> And mock us with our bareness. (IV. ii. 17)

As Bertram confirms his willingness to surrender the ring handed down to him by his forebears—with all its associations of faith and 'honour' —in order to obtain the satisfaction which his 'will', his sensual desire, so ignobly craves, her attitude touches the heart of the matter. To Bertram's emphasis on the 'honour' that derives solely from inheritance, and which he is now in effect revealing in its true shallowness, she opposes a more personal and human conception—

> Mine honour's such a ring:
> My chastity's the jewel of our house,
> Bequeathed down from many ancestors;
> Which were the greatest obloquy in the world
> In me to lose—   (IV. ii. 45)

until he is driven to lay down the very nobility and honour to which he pretends—

> Here, take my ring
> My house, mine honour, yea, my life be thine—   (IV. ii. 51)

in a self-centred and selfish impulse which seeks in reality nothing beyond the satisfaction of its own craving.

It should be noted that the course of this singularly unattractive episode is marked by a further string of accompanying comment, put into the mouths of anonymous attendants and expressed in the play's typically disenchanted and sombre prose. The two Lords who observe Bertram's adventures are fully convinced both of the need to resist the baser promptings of the flesh and of the universal force of these promptings in relation to the human situation. 'Now, God delay our rebellion! as we are ourselves, what things are we!' as one of them puts it, only to arrive at a characteristically pessimistic conclusion: 'Merely our own traitors' (IV. iii. 24). These generalizations are shown in what follows to be compatible with a full measure of realism. The end of Bertram's line of conduct is clearly seen to be an ignoble self-destruction—'he that in this action contrives against his own nobility, in his proper stream o'erflows himself' (IV. iii. 28)—and against this perversity is set, as a redeeming feature, the reality of Helena's 'holy undertaking' and her supposed entry, after a sanctified death, into 'heaven'. The general reflection on human life by which these comments are rounded off—

> The web of our life is of a mingled yarn, good and ill together: our virtues would be proud, if our faults whipped them not; and our crimes would despair, if they were not cherished by our virtues—   (IV. iii. 83)

is typical, in its grave and balanced detachment, of the mood which prevails in the most individual passages of this least spontaneous of comedies.

Whilst Bertram is thus engaged in the pursuit of his ignoble ends—again in the words of the attendant Lord, 'this night he fleshes his will in the spoil of her honour' (IV. iii. 19)—the time of resolution is at hand. Its first stage is represented by the final exposure of Parolles, who maintains in the face of it his claim to represent a permanent and indestructible aspect of life. 'Simply the thing I am,' he affirms, 'shall make me live' (IV. iii. 373); in this obstinate relation to reality, exercised in the face of rejection and contempt, we are once again close to the prevailing spirit of this enigmatic and dryly conceived action. Helena, too, as she returns from her 'pilgrimage' to contemplate the disenchanting reality of her lover, echoes Diana in striking the note of man's frailty and irresponsibility. 'O strange men!' she exclaims,

> That can such sweet use make of what they hate,
> When saucy trusting of the cozen'd thoughts
> Defiles the pitchy night: so lust doth play
> With what it loathes for that which is away.   (IV. iv. 21)

In reality, however, though she is still dead in the eyes of the world, the moment of final clarification is already foreshadowed—'the time will bring on summer'; 'All's well that ends well' (IV. iv. 31)—and Helena herself, celebrated by the Clown as 'the herb of grace' (IV. v. 18), will be instrumental in bringing it into being.

The closing scene, intricate and drawn out in a manner familiar from earlier comedies, provides perhaps the closest parallel with *Measure for Measure*; it also displays fugitive points of contact with the 'symbolic' romances of Shakespeare's last years. As it opens, the King and the Countess are at one in condemning Bertram for his indulgence of self-will to the point of rebellion and at the expense of his true 'honour'; though the Countess is ready to allow his conduct the excuse of '*Natural* rebellion, done i' the blaze of youth' (V. iii. 6). By following his impulses to this unworthy end, Bertram is seen to have renounced the high good offered to him beyond his deserts:

> He lost a wife
> Whose beauty did astonish the survey
> Of *richest eyes*, whose words all ears took captive,
> Whose *dear perfection* hearts that scorn'd to serve
> Humbly call'd mistress.   (V. iii. 15)

In this way, it is made clear that Bertram, by rejecting Helena, has done *to himself* 'the greatest wrong of all'; but the King, in whom the sense of age and nostalgia for the vanished past remain strong, remarks that

> Praising what is lost
> Makes the remembrance dear,   (V. iii. 19)

and declares his readiness to forgive a fault which is in any event beyond human remedy:

> The nature of his great offence is dead,
> And deeper than oblivion do we bury
> The incensing relics of it.   (V. iii. 23)

At this point, we may feel the presence of the 'symbolic' overtones which will announce the prospect of reconciliation in the final romances, and which is clearly intended to set the tone, poised between resignation and understanding, for what is to come.

When Bertram finally makes his appearance the King confirms his readiness to forget the past. 'All is whole,' he declares; for

> we are old, and on our quickest decrees
> The inaudible and noiseless foot of time
> Steals ere we can effect them.   (V. iii. 40)

Bertram, on his side, seems to have learned wisdom, at least in relation to Helena,

> she whom all men praised and whom myself,
> Since I have lost, have loved.   (V. iii. 53)

The sense of a pervading regret for 'love that comes *too late*', the pessimism of an old age that sees life and perfection fading irreparably into the past ('That's good, that's gone'), continues to colour the King's reflections and answers to the spirit of an action concentrated now upon the contemplation of human values seemingly lost and awaiting, in a spirit that once again anticipates certain effects of the last comedies, the 'miracle' of resurrection.

The path to the final resolution, however, is still beset by obstacles. As the King recognizes as Helena's the ring now offered by Bertram to Lafeu, and as Bertram holds to his denial that it was ever hers, the direction of the action seems to change yet again. Bertram is still less than honest in his story of how he came by the ring. As though in response to his evasions the mood of the scene notably darkens; the

King confesses himself moved by 'conjectural fears' of foul play at
Helena's expense and orders the young man's arrest, whilst Diana
comes forward to confront him with his past behaviour towards
herself and to claim redress for the wrong supposedly done to her.
Bertram, ungenerous and frivolous almost to the last, thrusts her aside
as 'a fond and desperate creature' and makes a last appeal to his decidedly
soiled 'honour':

> let your highness
> Lay a more noble thought upon mine honour
> Than for to think that I would sink it here. (V. iii. 181)

The King, reverting to a principal theme of the play, retorts that this
honour can only be bound to the reality of his 'deeds', which stand
at present visibly compromised. As Diana challenges him on oath to
recognize the reality of his treatment of her, Bertram plunges deeper
into ignominy, dismissing her as 'a common gamester to the camp';
but the truth is by now ready to emerge, and he receives the eloquence
of his intended victim's retort:

> O, behold this ring,
> Whose *high respect* and *rich validity*
> Did lack a parallel; yet for all that
> He gave it to a commoner of the camp,
> If I be one. (V. iii. 193)

Out of his own vain words, Bertram stands most effectively condemned.
His former associate Parolles, the shadow of his earlier pretensions,
now emerges most appropriately to confirm the truth of Diana's
assertion in the face of her would-be seducer. The 'burr'[35] indeed
sticks, though Bertram is capable of a last desperate effort to shake
him off as 'one with all the spots o' the world tax'd and debosh'd'
and to present himself as a victim deceived, 'subdued to her rate' by
Diana's 'infinite cunning', before bringing his self-defence to a
typically ignoble close:

> I had that which any inferior might
> At market-price have bought. (V. iii. 220)

A modern view of Bertram might tend to find some excuse for him
as the victim of a deceitful stratagem, tricked into a marriage which he
has been from the first unwilling to contemplate. Such an interpretation,
however, though it may help to account for the notable lack of con-

viction with which Bertram's final acceptance of Helena is portrayed, would be contrary to the artificial laws of comedy, which regard substitution of the kind practised by Helena and Diana as justified by the nature of the good which is to be gained by their use. In terms of the action to which he belongs, and outside which we are not called upon to consider him, Bertram stands condemned by his own attitudes and behaviour, and his only prospect of redemption will lie at the last in the positive good of marriage which, once he has finally set aside his perverse and negative attitudes, he will be brought by Helena's faith and resourcefulness to accept.

Bertram's efforts at self-exculpation are indeed by now as vain as they are unattractive. As Diana continues to press him for the return of the ring the falsity of his account of how he came by it is exposed and he can only 'confess' the truth. Once more, and for the last time, Parolles has a relevant comment to offer. Bertram, he says, has indeed loved Diana 'as a gentleman loves a woman': in other words, and more explicitly: 'He loved her, and loved her not' (V. iii. 250). The King, in his reply, stresses with equal truth the equivocal standing of Parolles himself—'As thou art a knave, and no knave' (V. iii. 251)—even as Lafeu recalls the episode of the drum to his confusion.

Finally, as the comedy draws to its appointed close, the true history of the ring given unwittingly by Bertram to Helena is revealed in riddling form, and Helena herself, now pregnant with the fruit of her stratagem in the form of Bertram's child, is 'resurrected'. 'One that's dead is quick' (V. iii. 308): once again, in spite of Bertram's obstinate shabbiness and the notably perfunctory manner in which he asks for pardon and declares his readiness to be reconciled to Helena, we are in a world which foreshadows that of the final romances. 'The bitter past, more welcome is the sweet' (V. iii. 339): an apt phrase, indeed, to sum up the complex of mingled emotions which this play, so oddly balanced between faith and scepticism, innocence and cynicism, leaves us.

II
THE MATURE TRAGEDIES

IN THE series of great tragedies which followed *Measure for Measure*, Shakespeare's art attained a more varied and controlled expression. We are no longer dealing with 'problem' plays, in which the presence of unresolved dilemmas, uncertainties incapable of clear artistic statement, makes itself felt. The conceptions elaborated in the new plays are, indeed, more complex than ever before, the interrelation of themes even further extended; but there is no longer any sense of that gap, which we must feel even in *Hamlet*, between purpose and achievement, between emotion and the dramatic conception through which it expresses itself. Above all, the tragic conflicts which predominate in these plays correspond to states of feeling more firmly defined, more clearly conceived in terms of a possible resolution. If the range of experience is far more ample than any we have so far considered, certain possibilities of harmony have grown, tentatively at first and then more clearly, to keep pace with them. By the end of the series a definite clarity has imposed itself, always within the prevailing tragic conception, upon the dramatic presentation of these plays. Having passed through *Othello*, *Macbeth*, and *King Lear*, in which the heart of the tragic experience is revealed in its full intensity, we are ready for *Coriolanus* and *Antony and Cleopatra*, which are as clear, lucid, and controlled in their conception as *Hamlet*, at the other end of the series, was dark, contradictory, and intractable. But it is essential to realize, if we are to understand the nature of the Shakespearean experience, that the later works in the series could never have been conceived without the earlier.

As usual, the advance in artistic maturity first makes itself felt in greater linguistic range and power and then expands to cover the other elements of dramatic expression. As the contradictions of the problem plays are progressively mastered, the poetry which formerly expressed them becomes not only vastly extended in range but correspondingly harmonized, subject to a greater degree of emotional unity; and this unity is in turn reflected in a clearer conception of character and in a more truly dramatic presentation of conflict. There is not, at this stage, any suggestion of a change in the prevailing tragic mood. The subject of all these great plays can be described, in general terms, as the working out to its inevitable conclusion of the disruptive effect of the entry of passion into normal human experience. By this entry the balance, essential to right living, between the passionate and rational elements in the personality is overthrown, and what should have been orderly, vital, and purposeful is plunged into disorder, death, and anarchy. The novelty of Shakespeare's work at this period lies not in the mood expressed, but in the scope and growing clarity of the expression. As the tragedies follow one another, the conflict between passion and reason ceases to be shown in the form of an internal cleavage, such as that observed in *Hamlet*. It becomes something more truly dramatic, a clash between contrasted and opposed personalities and orders, which reflects in turn an effort to separate the factors within experience which, by accepting the place ascribed to them in a balanced set of values, move towards unity and development, from those which, by pressing their claim to absolute independence, make all harmonious integration impossible. In other words, the opposition between reason and passion, first isolated—through Othello and Iago—in a dramatic conflict of personalities and then projected, in *Macbeth* and *Lear*, beyond the individual hero to the state and universe which surround him, is merged increasingly into another, of greater significance and profundity, between highly personal conceptions of 'good' and 'evil'.

1 Othello

Othello is, by common consent, one of Shakespeare's most completely 'objective' plays. The internal conflict of *Hamlet*, the identification of the hero's tragedy with the effort to achieve self-definition, is now polarized into a more obviously dramatic opposition between the Moor and his envious lieutenant Iago. The substitution as vehicles of the tragic emotion of one complex and incoherent character by two sharply defined personalities in conflict implies a different kind of play, and brings with it a new and in some ways a clearer conception of the tragic protagonist. Othello is the first of a series of Shakespearean heroes whose sufferings are explicitly related to failings in themselves, but who manage in spite of this to attain tragic dignity. Like Antony and Coriolanus after him, he dramatizes as 'nobility' what emerges, in certain important respects, as his own incapacity to cope with life; and, as in their case, the very weakness by which Iago engineers his downfall is turned into true tragedy.

The dramatic construction of the play turns, accordingly, upon the close, intricate dovetailing of the two contrasted characters of the Moor and his Ancient. At the centre of the action, a tragic compound of nobility and weakness, stands Othello. That the Othello of the early scenes is truly and worthily a hero, who dominates his surroundings by the consistent simplicity of his attitudes and behaviour, is not seriously open to question. Leader in war of the armies of the republic to which, as an alien stranger, he has sworn allegiance, saviour of Venice from her traditional Turkish enemy, his merits are universally recognized, his authority in the moment of peril beyond discussion. Shakespeare, however, has been equally careful from the first to suggest the presence of certain weaknesses, potential if not yet actual, beneath the impression of strength and consistency which his hero initially presents to the world. One can detect in Othello from the first a revealing tendency to self-dramatization. His first utterance is a round assertion—full, splendid, rhetorical—of his royal lineage and of his services to Venice:

> My services, which I have done the signiory,
> Shall out-tongue his complaints. 'Tis yet to know,—
> Which, when I know that boasting is an honour,
> I shall promulgate,—I fetch my life and being
> From men of royal siege; and my demerits
> May speak, unbonneted, to as proud a fortune
> As this that I have reacht: for know, Iago,
> But that I love the gentle Desdemona,
> I would not my unhoused free condition
> Put into circumscription and confine
> For the sea's worth.   (I. ii. 18)

One need not deny the compulsive power of this rhetoric, whilst recognizing a certain theatrical quality in the gesture with which he underlines the nobility of his origins and which makes him say, not without a certain unconscious irony, 'When I know that boasting is an honour.' These rapt declarations do not constitute boasting, if only because boasting implies a self-consciousness in conceit which is far from the essential simplicity of the character; but they show a certain complacency, equally barbaric, which has already allowed Iago to dismiss his speeches maliciously as 'bombast circumstance' (I. i. 13), and which will shortly induce him to caricature his description of his love-making as so much 'bragging' and 'fantastical lies' (II. i. 226). The complement of this self-centredness—the defect, Iago again tells us, of 'a free and open nature'—is the simplicity that leads Othello to think 'men honest that but seem to be so' (I. iii. 406), to misread the motives of those around him in the light of his own naïve self-esteem.

These limitations are scarcely important for as long as Othello is confined to the field of action. In war, indeed, where confidence and self-affirmation are the order of the day, they may be positively advantageous; but in personal relations, more particularly in an alien society and in the unfamiliar complexities of love, the situation is very different. Othello, in spite of himself, submits with a touch of un-willingness to love, finding it somehow incongruous with the 'un-housed free condition' in which the active simplicity of his nature has so far found expression; and even the encounter with Desdemona, whose love can so easily become for him a cause of 'circumscription and con-fine', merely underlines the possibility of tragedy. For Othello, as the entire action will show, is rarely able to get sufficiently far from himself to offer Desdemona the disinterested dedication in which true love consists. His happiness in the opening scenes is genuine and moving; but it is also, like everything else in his character, self-centred, naïve, even egoistic in its expression, and his account before the Venetian senate of his manner of wooing makes this clear. He begins, not without a certain theatricality, by asserting his ignorance of life as lived beyond the narrow circle of soldiery:

> little of this great world can I speak,
> More than pertains to feats of broil and battle,   (I. iii. 86)

before going on to evoke, with his usual splendid vigour, the way in which he recreated for Desdemona the 'moving incidents' which befell him 'by flood and field', his imprisonment and slavery, his journeys through 'antres vast and deserts idle', to finish, with typical *bravura*, by recalling his sojourn among the grotesque beings who dwell in the remote and barely explored regions of the earth:

> the cannibals that each other eat,
> The Anthropophagi, and men whose heads
> Do grow beneath their shoulders.   (I. iii. 143)

The fact that all this is typical, not only of Othello's intensely imaginative nature, but also of an age in which adventures and discoveries had
married fantasy to daily life, should not prevent us from seeing in his
words the expression of a decidedly one-sided conception of love. It was,
in fact, by his passionate, simple-minded delight in his own magnificent
career that Othello won Desdemona, taking her from her aristocratic
surroundings and introducing her to a world at once elemental,
strange, and full of possible misunderstandings; and—we could fairly
add—it was in part because the conquest ministered to his self-esteem
that he valued her:

> She loved me for the dangers I had pass'd
> And I lov'd her *that she did pity them*.   (I. iii. 167)

There is nothing accidental about this declaration, before a foreign and
potentially hostile audience. If Desdemona's love for Othello was
founded on her spontaneous admiration for the person whose adventur-
ous story had captivated her youthful imagination, his for her was, by
his own account, less a return of personal feeling than an extension of
his self-esteem. 'I loved her that she did pity them': Othello's estimate
of his situation is nothing if not simple; but events will show that this
simplicity is terribly, tragically vulnerable.

For we can never forget that Othello is, after all, a foreigner in
Venice. For the cultured and sceptical Venetians around Desdemona,
her relations with the 'lascivious Moor' are mysterious, unnatural, and
deeply disturbing. In the eyes of her own father, who holds to the last
that his child has deceived him, Desdemona's action proceeds from a
perversion of the judgment and passion is a poison which acts through
the erring senses to enslave the will:

> A maiden never bold;
> Of spirit so still and quiet that her motion
> Blush'd at herself; and she—in spite of nature,
> Of years, of country, credit, everything—
> To fall in love with what she fear'd to look on! . . .
> I therefore vouch again,
> That with some mixtures powerful o'er the blood,
> Or with some dram conjured to this effect,
> He wrought upon her.   (I. iii. 94)

In his perplexity Brabantio lays exaggerated emphasis upon his
daughter's submissiveness until simplicity itself becomes, in this world

of sophistication and scepticism, faintly equivocal. The adjectives 'still' and 'quiet' and the suggestion, barely indicated, of shame in 'blush'd at herself' stand in a peculiar relationship to the mixtures 'powerful o'er the blood' which are said to have overcome her judgment. To say this is not, of course, to accept Iago's account of Desdemona as 'a super-subtle Venetian' who has moulded the 'erring barbarian' (I. iii. 362) to her purposes; though it is true that Brabantio's parting words—spoken, we may feel, in the resentful impotence of old age—do something to endorse this view:

> Look to her, Moor, if thou hast eyes to see:
> She has deceived her father, and may thee.   (I. iii. 294)

Iago—as we shall see—invariably pushes his own interpretations of human motive to the extreme which his peculiar logic demands and in so doing falsifies it. He represents only one possible attitude—the least flattering—to love, but Brabantio's reaction is there to underline its relevance to what we may call the Venetian atmosphere of the play and even to our estimate of Desdemona's part in it. Like Isabella and even Ophelia before her, Desdemona has the power to exercise upon men an influence of whose nature and strength she remains until the last moment very largely unaware; and this power, given a perversely logical interpretation in Iago's 'philosophy', becomes an occasion of dissolution and destruction.

In the light of all this, there is something ominous in the terms in which Othello begs the Duke and his counsellors to allow his wife to accompany him to Cyprus:

> Vouch with me, heaven, I therefore beg it not
> To please the palate of my appetite;
> Nor to comply with heat—the young affects
> In me defunct—and proper satisfaction;
> But to be free and bounteous to her mind.   (I. iii. 263)

The sentiment is unexceptionable, but the resolution is a little too easily made. Not for the first time, Othello dismisses confidently the very failings with which in the event he is to stand condemned. The references to 'heat' and to 'the palate of my appetite', which contrast so oddly with the vague, confident opulence of his plea, take us forward to his own behaviour as the tragedy unfolds itself. In view of the fact that the despised elements of sensuality are shortly to force their way into Othello's mind till his utterances are saturated with them we are justi-

fied in allowing them even at this early stage more importance than he
is ready to concede to them. Equally, in the second part of the same
speech we may read an unconscious irony into the contemptuous dismissal of the possibility that the mere 'disports' of love may undermine
his devotion to the serious business of war:

> when light-winged toys
> Of feathered Cupid seal with wanton dullness
> My speculative and offic'd instruments,
> That my disports corrupt and taint my business,
> Let housewives make a skillet of my helm,
> And all indign and base adversities
> Make head against my estimation.   (I. iii. 270)

Once more the facility of the contrast indicates danger for the speaker.
Othello, who here ostensibly dismisses love in the name of his 'specula-
tive and offic'd instruments', spurns it in effect as a 'circumscription' of
his simple, barbaric selfhood, of a conception of his own dignity which
is essentially instinctive, unreasonable; by so doing he reveals his peculiar vulnerability to the irrational forces of animal feeling. Indeed the
whole of his subsequent history is a tragic comment upon this facile
opposition between the 'serious and great business' of generalship, in
which he finds a satisfaction not less passionate for being ostensibly
divorced from love, and the fatal promptings of an 'appetite' whose
real power and importance he never admits or understands and which
therefore ruins him.

If Othello's 'nobility' provides one of the main conceptions upon
which the closely-knit structure of the play rests, the 'critical' scepticism of Iago is certainly the other. Through his plotting, the mysterious
poison which had worked, according to her father, on Desdemona's
'still and quiet' nature becomes an active and sinister reality. For Iago *is*
that poison, no longer hinted at or obscurely present in minds never
fully conscious of it, but turned to destructive activity. His acts present
themselves as the consequences of a 'philosophy'—if we may call it so—
which regards Othello's downfall as being as inevitable, as rooted in the
nature of things, as his love. Since time dominates human experience,
and since spiritual *value*—which Hamlet had so passionately and so
vainly sought—dwells only 'in particular will',[1] love becomes for Iago
merely an appetite, 'a lust of the blood and a permission of the will'
(I. iii. 339). One object, therefore, may satisfy desire as readily as
another. The 'permission of the will' is indeed required, suffices to

distinguish man from the beast; but, since, according to Iago, the object of this will can be nothing other than physical satisfaction, the attainment of this becomes the only imperative which the will can recognize.

This line of thought leads Iago, logically enough, to a pessimistic interpretation of love; for satisfaction, in experiences purely physical, leads necessarily to satiation, and this in turn to a craving for change. According to his 'philosophy', there is nothing in the world of 'nature' to prevent desire from passing easily—and meaninglessly—from one object to another. In the particular case of Desdemona he contends that it *must* so pass:

> Mark me with what violence she first loved the Moor, but for bragging and telling her fantastical lies; and will she love him still for prating? Let not thy discreet heart think it. Her eye must be fed; and what delight shall she have to look on the devil? When the blood is made dull with the act of sport, there should be, again to inflame it and to give satiety a fresh appetite, loveliness in favour, sympathy in years, manners and beauties; all of which the Moor is defective in; now, for want of these required conveniences, her delicate tenderness will find itself abused, begin to heave the gorge, disrelish and abhor the Moor; very nature will instruct her in it and compel her to some second choice. (II. i. 225)

Satiety; *second choice*: on these words, Iago will build something like a destructive 'philosophy' of love. The transient nature of all physical passion will do more than incline Desdemona to be unfaithful; it will *compel* her, with a determinism of its own, and once the original impulse towards Othello has been exhausted, to choose again. Love, being merely a prompting of the senses to which the will gives assent, needs to be continually 'inflamed' if the 'blood' is not to be 'made dull with the act of sport'. For love, as in *Troilus*, is simply an 'appetite', intense but impermanent, like all sensual experience, and in particular like the impressions of taste. That which was—to use another of Iago's characteristic phrases—as 'luscious as locusts' will soon become 'as bitter as coloquintida' (I. iii. 354); full, in the moment of fulfilment, of 'relish', of 'delicate tenderness', it must continually be 'fed', lest it turn to 'abhorrence', 'disrelish', and 'heave the gorge' in nausea at the object of its former choice. The original impulse, once satisfied, fatally demands renewal; without this, it turns to indifference and even to loathing.

We shall not understand fully the implications of Iago's reading of love unless we appreciate not only the extent to which they echo

prejudices actually present in what we may call the 'Venetian' atmosphere of the play, but also the nature of the bond that, beneath every
surface appearance unites him to the object of his envy and hatred. At
first sight, the Ancient is everything that his general is not, cynical,
'intellectual', and detached where Othello is passionate and trusting to
the point of folly. These qualities, however, are in certain important
respects less opposed than complementary. If Othello's passion tends to
express itself, as we have seen, with a certain remoteness from the
realities of sexual attraction, Iago's cynicism and belittlement of natural
emotion, though uttered from his mask of worldly commonsense and
'honest' plainspeaking, are saturated with the feeling of 'blood'.
'Blood', or sexual emotion, is the driving-force of his intelligence,
although it is a force always controlled and criticized by that intelligence. He tells Desdemona on her arrival at Cyprus that he is 'nothing
if not critical' (II. i. 119) and he shows Roderigo a passionate (that is the
only word for it) contempt for the operations of 'appetite'; but it is
'appetite', though belittled and despised by one whom a deep personal
impotence seems to debar from the experience of it, that is at the root of
the man, criticism and all. This is apparent in the temper of his remarks
to Roderigo advancing the claims of reason and control:

> If the balance of our lives had not one scale of reason to poise another of
> sensuality, the blood and baseness of our natures would conduct us to most
> preposterous conclusions; but we have reason to cool our raging motions, our
> carnal stings, our unbitted lusts. (I. iii. 331)

How intensely we feel 'blood' at work here in the very criticism of
passion! 'Reason' balances—'poises', as Iago so precisely puts it—the
scale of sensuality, foreseeing in the unchecked operation of our fleshly
instincts the 'most preposterous conclusions'; but the vigour of the
references to 'raging motions', 'carnal stings', and 'unbitted lusts'
demonstrates beyond all possible error the source of Iago's peculiar
vitality in action. His intellect dwells from the first pungently, insistently, upon the elements of bestiality which underlie human passion
and which he is driven by a compelling need to expose; but the
presence in his own thwarted and resentful mind of the despised emotions is implied in the very intensity with which they are contemplated.
It is impossible not to feel the obsessive sexuality which inspires his
feverish activity in the dark at the opening of the play. Revealing itself
in the persistent animality with which he incites Roderigo to disturb

the 'fertile climate' in which Othello dwells and so to 'poison his delight' ('poison', indeed, is one of the images most characteristically present in his mind, a key to his mode of operation throughout the play), it dominates both the man and the scene:

> Even now, now, very now, an old black ram
> Is tupping your white ewe. Arise, arise;
> Awake the snorting citizens with the bell,
> Or else the devil will make a grandsire of you.   (I. i. 88)

The grotesque tone of the last lines in itself reflects the intimate source of the intensity behind Iago's every action. The 'passionate' Othello never, until his enemy has injected his peculiar poison into his mind, expresses himself in love with such physical intensity as the 'sceptical', ostensibly controlled Iago; in this apparent paradox lies a principal key to the interpretation of the whole play.

   In the light of this situation, much of the dramatic action of *Othello* acquires a deeper meaning. Above all, Iago's 'philosophy' gives a clear logical expression to the doubts and reservations which from the first accompany the hero's love in the minds of those who surround him. Brabantio had believed that his daughter's choice was against the rules of nature; Iago, on the contrary, believes not only that the choice was natural, but that 'nature', which had brought her to it, would drive her inevitably to change. The facts appear to bear him out, in so far as he succeeds in undermining Othello's love for Desdemona; but before the beginning of the destructive process which he foresees and makes it his business to bring about, we are given one brief glimpse of Othello's happiness. Separated by stormy sea during their voyage to Cyprus, he meets Desdemona once more and enjoys a brief moment of fulfilment which, it seems, nothing in life can equal. His one desire is to hold this moment, to make it eternal:

> If it were now to die,
> 'Twere now to be most happy; for I fear,
> My soul hath her content so absolute
> That not another comfort like to this
> Succeeds in unknown fate.   (II. i. 192)

Yet, even here, at the moment of his 'absolute' content, Othello *fears*. This precarious moment, he senses, will never find its fellow, for the temporal process is one of dissolution and decay. Only death can come between this communion and its eclipse; but death, of course, implies the annihilation of the personality and the end of love. Like a harmony which has reached the culmination of its development, this love must either cease or turn to the discord which Iago, in a prophetic aside, foresees:

> O, you are well tuned now:
> But I'll set down the pegs that make this music.   (II. i. 202)

In the extended use, against a background of tempest at sea, of the musical metaphor of harmony as a symbol of spiritual concord, the play anticipates some of the techniques which will be developed, to very different ends, in *Pericles* and *The Winter's Tale*;[2] but the device remains inevitably unsustained in a play in which the elements of destruction and discord clearly prevail. Already Iago has been present to observe this reunion and to colour Desdemona's forthright declarations of devotion with the insertion of his own worldly and persistently disparaging comment; and, as soon as she and Othello have left the scene, his destructive cynicism returns—in the tone of his prose dialogue with Roderigo—to become the driving force of the action. From this moment until the final disaster it never really loses the initiative.

The transition from concord and the anticipation of married fulfilment is indicated with considerable care. In the scene which follows the reunion of the lovers (II. iii), the motives of felicity and disillusionment are simultaneously developed. It is night, the night in which Othello has announced 'the celebration of his nuptial', but also the night in which Iago's activity will turn rejoicing into savagery and drunkenness. His instrument to this end is Cassio, in whom all his unflattering conclusions with regard to love appear to him to find their confirmation. We shall only understand Iago's part in this tragedy if we realize that he plays throughout upon the real weaknesses of his victims. These weaknesses he elevates, following his 'philosophy', into consistent principles, reading into what is largely infirmity, susceptibility, or indecision a positive tendency to evil; but his observations, though they do not account fully for the behaviour of his victims, and indeed consistently pervert their underlying motives, invariably pick on something really vulnerable in them. That something is normally connected with desire or 'appetite'. Cassio is by inclination a courtier, proud of his ability to respond easily to beauty and to insinuate the pleasing compliment; he is also, as his regretted susceptibility to drink suggests, something of a sensualist. His imagination, stirred by Iago, lingers upon Desdemona with intense but passing approbation. She is 'exquisite', 'a fresh and delicate creature', with an 'inviting' though—he hastens to add—'a right modest eye'. There is nothing particularly vicious about all this, but it is enough to enable Iago—considering Cassio in the light of his own jealousy and of his disparaging convictions about life—to see him as one who puts on 'the mere form of civil and humane seeming for the better compassing of his salt and most hidden loose affection' (II. i. 244). The description is highly typical. Iago cannot conceive of human weakness as other than fully conscious. Believing in the controlling powers of 'corrigible authority' (I. iii. 330), because he senses in them his own instrument for the exercise of power over others, he is led to rationalize Cassio's failing, turning susceptibility into positive cunning; but the short encounter with Bianca (III. iv) is there, with its glimpse of callous and superficial worldliness, to show that his judgment is not altogether unrelated to reality. Having observed in Cassio just sufficient 'loose affection' to make his accusations plausible, he uses him to bring out Othello's unconsidered sensuality, to ruin his judgment and destroy his peace.

By inflaming the fuddled Cassio to riot Iago releases the forces of passion on the island. As the drunken revelry, prevailing, takes the mind prisoner, jealousy creeps into Othello's mind through Iago's action upon the instability which makes his will, unknown to himself, the slave of passion. Once his happiness has been disturbed, the tone of his anger contrasts significantly with his earlier assertions of self-control:

> Now, by heaven,
> My blood begins my safer guides to rule,
> And passion, having my best judgement collied,
> Assays to lead the way. (II. iii. 206)

For the first time, Othello admits that his anger may be powerful enough to poison his judgment, his 'safer guides' as he ominously calls them, and to carry him into ill-considered courses. Iago has already begun to work upon his weakness. He has known from the first that this is a victim who will allow himself to be led 'tenderly' by the nose, 'as asses are' (I. iii. 408). His confidence rests on his reading—one-sided and cynical indeed, but not on that account less effective for the end he proposes to himself—of the Moor's simplicity. Othello, as we have seen, tends to neglect the part played by physical desire in a love in the conduct of which he needs to feel himself 'free and bounteous', at once truly generous and flattered in his vulnerable self-esteem; Iago, for

whom *all* love is simply the gratification of this desire, gives a very
different interpretation of his victim's character:

> His soul is so *enfetter'd* to her love,
> That she may make, unmake, do what she list,
> Even as her appetite shall play the god
> With his weak function.   (II. iii. 354)

It was precisely this idea of being 'enfettered' by his love that Othello
had so confidently rejected in bringing Desdemona to Cyprus; it had
offended his belief in himself both as a warrior and, more intimately, as
a man. But Iago's action, based as always on the rationalization of
affection as 'appetite', aims at the dissolution of this heroic simplicity,
seeks to subdue Othello by rousing the bestial instincts which slumber
beneath the surface of his personality.

In this he succeeds with surprising ease: surprising, that is, unless we
remember how the way has been prepared by the stress laid upon the
Moor's disastrous ingenuousness. The long and intimate scene (III. iii)
placed at the very heart of the play, in which Othello is progressively
'infected' with Iago's malignant attitudes, is also a revelation of the
extent to which these two central characters are connected within their
opposition, related to one another as light to darkness, as contrasted but
finally complementary aspects of a single reality. Iago knows at the
outset that his victim, once confused, is lost, and so his primary aim is to
involve him in uncertainty. For Othello, once placed in doubt, is quite
incapable of suspending judgment. Suspense affects his self-confidence,
contrasts with the capacity for quick and firm decision upon which he
prides himself. He demands an immediate resolution, which can in
practice be nothing but an acceptance of Iago's insinuations:

> to be once in doubt
> Is once to be resolved; exchange me for a goat,
> When I shall turn the business of my soul
> To such exsufflicate and blown surmises,
> Matching thy inference.   (III. iii. 179)

Few things in Othello are more revealing than this habitual tendency to
protest rhetorically against the presence of the very weaknesses that are
undoing him. He refers contemptuously to the 'goat', the most
notorious symbol of sensuality, just as Iago is engaged in poisoning his
mind through his 'blood'-inspired imagination; and the reference,
strengthened by the sense, in 'exsufflicate', of the beast breathing

heavily in the external signs of passion, is at once grotesque and significant.

Flattering the 'free and open' nature in which his victim so naïvely prides himself, Iago proceeds to clip the wings of his freedom and to convert his frankness into suspicion. He recalls the persistent misgivings that have from the first surrounded this marriage—'She did deceive her father, marrying you' (III. iii. 206)—and stresses the inequality of 'clime, complexion, and degree' in a way at once calculated to hurt Othello's pride and to emphasize his ignorance, as a foreigner and a man of alien race, of Desdemona's true motives. Above all, he insinuates that her apparent purity of purpose may conceal a sensual corruption of the will:

> Foh, one may smell in such a will most rank,
> Foul disproportion, thoughts unnatural.   (III. iii. 232)

The last assertion is really the important one. The others do little more than prepare the ground for it. Iago's purpose is, in his own words, to 'act upon the blood' (III. iii. 329) to make the sensual basis of Othello's passion come to the surface, not to give body and content to the reality of love, but in the form of passionate and destructive jealousy. The victim's mind must be infected. Iago's conception of love as so much corrupt 'appetite' is to take possession of him, exploiting unsuspected facets of his nature, demoralizing him and destroying his integrity. He must be brought to see Desdemona as Iago, in his 'philosophy', insists that she really is. She is natural, 'the wine she drinks is made of grapes'; therefore her 'blest condition' must be fatally, inevitably subject to inconstancy.

It is worth noting that Iago has begun to act upon Othello by throwing doubt upon the purity of his own thoughts. The Moor believes that men 'should be what they seem' (III. iii. 126); his whole life has been founded on the assumption that our motives are few and our spiritual needs simple, our actions completely and unequivocally under our control. Iago implies that the assumption is dubious, that not only the motives of others, but even our own are open to obscure and scarcely apprehended reservations:

> Utter my thoughts? Why, say they are vile and false;
> As where's that palace whereinto foul thoughts
> Sometimes intrude not?   (III. iii. 136)

This is a typically sophisticated 'Venetian' conclusion, and one which perfectly fits Iago's purposes. It is because his 'philosophy' enables him

to establish contact with the lower, unconsidered elements of his
victim's emotional being that he is able to destroy Othello's simplicity
and to reduce him to a mass of contradictions and uncontrolled impulses. Having once deprived him of the certainty which his nature
craves, he plays upon his sensual fancy, re-creating Cassio's 'dream'
with obsessive insistence—the product, perhaps, of a certain thwarted
'appetite' in himself—upon the grossness of physical contacts, makes
him *visualize* the sin by which Desdemona is offending his self-esteem.
Othello has already offered a glimpse of how completely his being is
anchored upon his faith in his love; as Desdemona leaves him he has
said, in a first obscure glimpse of the horrors which await him:

> Perdition catch my soul,
> But I do love thee! and when I love thee not,
> *Chaos is come again.*   (III. iii. 90)

Now, dimly aware of the prospect of this 'chaos' opening before him,
he makes his impossible, absurd demand for instant proof. The completeness of his fall is reflected in the grotesque irony which his demand
implies. 'Villain, be sure thou prove my love a whore' (III. iii. 360);
from which point Iago leads him on with a sneer that works like poison
on his fantasy:

> how satisfied, my lord?
> Would you, the supervisor, grossly gape on?
> Behold her topp'd?   (III. iii. 395)

Here, besides rousing still further the sensual elements in his imagination,
Iago touches Othello at a most vulnerable point; he offends him intimately in his personal respect. The reaction is a characteristic mixture
of pathetic bewilderment and defiant self-esteem. Conscious of the
racial difference which separates him from the Venetians around him
and vaguely aware of a mortifying social inferiority—

> Haply, for I am black,
> And have not those soft parts of conversation,
> That chamberers have—   (III. iii. 263)

he thrusts aside the doubt that assails him with the man of action's
superior reference to 'chamberers', only to fall at once into further
uncertainty of a more concrete and, perhaps, for him of an even more
mortifying kind:

> or, for I am declined
> Into the vale of years.   (III. iii. 265)

The instinctive reaction—'yet that's not much'—is not sufficient to
undo the final impression of failure, openly recognized in the conclusion—

> I am abused, and my relief
> Must be to loathe her—   (III. iii. 267)

in which misery and offended self-respect compete for precedence.
Iago's very boldness has won his point. He must have been very sure of
the Moor's blindness to work upon him with so gross a caricature, but
his confidence has been justified by the event. For the caricature, for all
its grossness, has roused not Othello's indignation, but his outraged self-
esteem and has brought to the surface the destructive forces of his
neglected animal instincts.

A few ambiguous phrases from Iago have been enough—with Cassio's
invented intrigue and a handkerchief fallen and found by chance—to
reduce Othello to an absolute slavery to passion. The slender basis of
the intrigue, far from being a sign of weakness in the play,[3] is a deliberate and necessary part of its intention. Iago himself, in a solitary
moment, describes perfectly his own method and achievement:

> The Moor already changes with my poison:
> Dangerous conceits are in their nature poisons:
> Which at the first are scarce found to distaste,
> But with a little act upon the blood,
> Burn like the mines of sulphur.   (III. iii. 326)

The relation of poison to taste, and of both to the action of the 'blood',
is by now familiar. It has marked the process which has reduced Othello's
barbaric egoism to incoherence, his heroic rhetoric to a grotesque echo
of his enemy's cynicism. Above all, he has been induced to see himself
as betrayed, and it is typically the knowledge, rather than the betrayal,
which affects him:

> I had been happy, if the general camp,
> Pioners and all, had tasted her sweet body,
> *So I had nothing known.*   (III. iii. 346)

The form of this confession is highly revealing. The problem of
Othello is revealed here as a problem of consciousness, of the relationship of instinctive life to critical detachment. The intense and pathetic
sense of isolation, of the irrevocable loss of what might have been, as it
makes itself felt in the evocation of Desdemona's 'sweet', 'tasted' body,
is balanced in Othello by an infantile readiness to be deceived, to accept

OTHELLO 115

as true less than what his reason—however unreasonably, even per-vertedly—has told him to be the truth.

By the end of this scene, Othello's new 'knowledge' has had two consequences. It has destroyed his heroic simplicity of judgment, upon which his real nobility has been based, and it has roused his own sensual impulses to destructive fury. From now on, sensual passion and prowess in action are, in Othello, mutually exclusive; the entry of the one implies the dissolution of the coherence and self-confidence necessary to the other. It is significant that, when he becomes aware that his peace is undermined beyond hope, he refers to his loss, not first of Desde-mona, but of his integrity as a warrior:

> Farewell, the tranquil mind, farewell, content!
> Farewell, the plumed troop, and the big wars
> That make ambition virtue. (III. iii. 349)

For the last time, Othello looks back in this speech to his former greatness. From now on, he is a man submitted to two main influences, both equally destructive: on the one hand the loss, so intimately felt, of his military glory, on the other, that sense of Desdemona's supposed promiscuity which grows upon his imagination until Iago can make the ironic comment: 'I see, sir, you are eaten up with passion!' (III. iii. 392).

The scene in which these developments take place forms a kind of pivot upon which the whole subsequent action turns. The end of it is marked by an exchange which, in another context, would strike us as a piece of grotesque parody, but which here, confirming Othello's conse-cration to self-deception, conveys an appalling irony which is all its own. Prompted by Iago's deliberate sneer—'your mind perhaps may change'—the barbaric warrior vows himself, finally, once and for all, in the name of the very consistency he has always prized, to destruction:

> Like to the Pontic sea,
> Whose icy current and compulsive course
> Ne'er feels retiring ebb, but keeps due on
> To the Propontic and the Hellespont;
> Even so my bloody thoughts, with violent pace,
> Shall ne'er look back, ne'er ebb to humble love,
> Till that a capable and wide revenge
> Swallow them up. Now, by yond marble heaven,
> In the due reverence of a sacred vow
> I here engage my words. (III. iii. 454)

The vow, made in the name of a 'compulsive', an irreversible passion, to which the speaker is now enslaved, is offered to a 'marble' heaven, reflects the motion of an 'icy' current, answers to a will petrified or frozen, caught in the savage and unreasoning thrust of its own egoistic and 'blood'-inspired purposes. Thwarted in a love which he has never really understood in its true nature of mutual dedication, Othello's egoism announces itself as consistent in revenge, decisive, irresistible; all the intensity of personal feeling which was never fully gratified in his relations with Desdemona are to be exercised in exacting retribution for the ruin of his integrity.

To the rhetoric of this inhuman resolve, Iago's voice, shriller and more highly pitched, answers as he too kneels in a grim parody of the un- natural dedication which he has himself brought into being:

> Witness, you ever-burning lights above,
> You elements that clip us round about,
> Witness that here Iago doth give up
> The execution of his wit, hands, heart,
> To wrong'd Othello's service! Let him command,
> And to obey shall be in me remorse,
> What bloody business ever. (III. iii. 464)

To the ample, barbaric gesture, at once irresistibly powerful and 'stony', deprived of life and flexibility, of the hero who has just renounced his heroism with his humanity, answers the clipped, almost falsetto tones of the betrayer who, by engineering the 'currents' of Othello's passion into the channels he has prepared for them, is engaged in completing the destruction of love, the ruin of 'nobility', in accord- ance with his consistent and all-absorbing aim.

The increasing insolence of Iago's attitude as he comes to realize that his success is assured is brought out with increasing force in the scenes that follow. Perhaps the irony reaches its climax when the plotter makes his victim stand aside and assist in silence at what he imagines to be Cassio's account of Desdemona's infidelity (IV. i). Every word is a mortal wound for Othello's pride. Iago sneers, and disclaims the sneer with a phrase that is itself an affirmation of contempt:

> Othello: Dost thou mock me?
> Iago: I mock you! no, by heaven,
>   Would you would bear your fortune *like a man!* (IV. i. 61)

He roundly taxes the heroic Othello with lack of manliness:

Whilst you were here o'erwhelmed with your grief—
A passion most unsuiting such a man—
Cassio came hither . . .
                    Marry, patience;
Or I shall say you are all in all in spleen,
And *nothing of a man*. (IV. i. 77)

Nothing could do more than this savage element of caricature in Iago's
treatment of Othello to convey the degradation of the victim; no better
foil to the Moor's earlier rhetoric—rhetoric which stands in the closest
relationship to the subsequent tragedy—could be conceived.

As the plot advances, and as Iago's control over his intrigue grows,
the sensual element becomes increasingly intense and disturbing in the
victim's utterances. We see and feel its effects when he falls into a fit,
drags himself along the ground, and mutters frenziedly, in the presence
of his exultant enemy, about 'noses, ears, and lips' (IV. i. 43). We feel
them in those bestial phrases in which his outraged egoism, deprived
of expression in the natural simplicities of action, gropes blindly towards its revenge: 'I'll tear her all to pieces!' 'I see that nose of yours,
but not that dog I shall throw it to' (IV. i. 144); and still more in the
combination of affronted self-respect and rising savagery which prompts
the exclamation, 'I'll chop her into messes; cuckold me' (IV. i. 210).
But they appear most clearly of all, and in closer relation to the love
they are corroding, in that terrible scene (IV. ii) in which the crazed
Othello turns, with a mixture of intensely frustrated physical attraction
and open repulsion, upon Desdemona. The feeling is, at certain
moments, curiously reminiscent of the sonnets. Desdemona is addressed
as a '*rose*-lipp'd cherubin'—such imagery, a compound of poetic convention and deep emotion, is very characteristic—and his loathing for
her finds expression in typical sense imagery:

Desdemona: I hope my noble lord esteems me honest.
Othello: O, ay; as summer flies are in the shambles,
              That quicken even with blowing. O thou weed,
              Who art so lovely fair and smell'st so sweet
              That the sense aches at thee, would thou had'st ne'er been born
              (IV. ii. 64)

The mention of 'weed', the reminiscence of convention behind 'lovely
fair' and the keen evocation—almost unnaturally sensitive—of the

faculty of smell are all suggestive of the sonnets.[4] Like 'lilies that fester',[5] their effect depends upon a sharp opposition of acute sense impressions. The intensity of desire implied in 'sense *aches* at thee' and the feeling for life behind 'quicken' are set against the loathing which produced 'shambles' and the 'blowing' of the flies. 'Blowing' is especially subtle in that it speaks of the generation of flies out of corruption whilst using a word that suggests the opening of the rose-bud into mature beauty. The reminiscence of the sonnets is not accidental, for the story of *Othello* is precisely a dramatic representation of the inevitable degeneration of desire, in a world where 'value' appears to have no foundation, into selfish and destructive appetite.

The whole of this part of the play shows Othello, as his personal integrity collapses, taking up Iago's attitudes and becoming impregnated with Iago's obsessions. By the end of the tragedy, this once splendid figure of a man has been reduced to a barely human state, in which broken remnants of astonished resentment grope in vain for an appearance of certainty upon which to found the action which he so intensely and so impossibly craves. As his ruin proceeds, the egoism which has always been a part of his nature comes to the fore, no longer in relation to military glory, but rather in his attitude towards his own folly. The great final speeches in which he attains a true measure of tragic stature are also merciless exposures of weakness. In the first, addressed to Desdemona, there emerges, besides a profound note of pathos, the speaker's unpreparedness to meet the situation in which he finds himself. 'Had it pleased heaven', he says,

> To try me with affliction; had they rain'd
> All kinds of sores and shames on my bare head;
> Steept me in poverty to the very lips;
> Given to captivity me and my utmost hopes;
> I should have found in some place of my soul
> A drop of patience.   (IV. ii. 46)

If life, Othello seems to say, had presented to him a problem which could have been met by asserting a nobility at once true and flattering to his self-esteem, all might have been well. As he lists the forms of trial which he believes himself able to resist, we feel the speaker recovering a kind of confidence, assuring himself that in resistance too there is a sort of heroism, that the exercise of patience to the limit of endurance is not, after all, incompatible with his conception of his own moral dignity. Only at the end are we shown the true source of Othello's suffering:

> But, alas, to make me
> A fixed figure for the time of scorn
> To point his slow, unmoving finger at!   (IV. ii. 52)

To become an object of ridicule without being able to react, to assert his own 'nobility'—this is the shame from which Othello feels that there is no escape, and which accompanies him to his tragic end.

That end, when it comes, adds little to what we already know of his character. Having set himself up, impossibly, as accuser, judge, confessor, and executioner in his own 'cause',[6] Othello advances to the final catastrophe with something of the quality of a sleep-walker about him. To the last, in his meditation over the sleeping Desdemona before he stifles her, we find intensity matched by coldness, sensuous feeling by a strange remoteness from living passion. Beginning with an invocation to 'you *chaste* stars', he goes on to speak of a skin 'whiter than *snow*' and 'smooth as *monumental alabaster*'; while there is something intense but distant in the apostrophe to 'thy light' which follows, and in the almost studied reference to 'Promethean heat' (V. ii. 12). Putting together these impressions, we come to feel that Othello's passion at this critical moment is, as we have felt it to be before, as cold on the surface as it is intense just below; it combines a certain monumental frigidity with a keen impression of the activity of the senses.

That the senses are present is clearly guaranteed—at this stage—by Othello's own behaviour; and, indeed, the same speech proves that this is so. As he gazes upon his sleeping victim his underlying sensuality is felt in the comparison of Desdemona—once more—to the 'rose' and in the keenness with which the sense of smell asserts itself in 'balmy breath' and in 'I'll smell it on the tree.'[7] Even here, however, the note of incompleteness persists. The impression is once again of overwhelming passion unable to express itself otherwise than in cold and distant imagery: the imagery, never quite freed from the conventional, of the sonnets. Even when he is stressing the full happiness he had hoped to find in his love Othello sees perfection, not in terms of warm life, but in the chill flawlessness of a precious stone:

> Nay, had she been true,
> If heaven would make me such another world

> Of one entire and perfect *chrysolite*,
> I'ld not have sold her for it.   (V. ii. 141)

As we have seen, the strength of his passionately emotional being finds
adequate expression, not in love, but in the poetry of action, untram-
melled by reference to objects and needs beyond itself. In his love
poetry the same intensity has habitually failed to express itself completely towards another person; but precisely because he has, in spite of
this, become involved in another person's needs and committed to her
his own, the moment of his awakening to reality is also the moment of
his ruin.

   In the last scene, in which dignity and weakness are blended in the
process of awakening to the extent of his disaster, in which he kills
Desdemona and falls, dead by his own hand, across her body, the
nearest approach to an impartial comment is made in terms of common
realism by Emilia when she calls him 'dull Moor'; an accusation to
which he can only answer, once the enormity of his error has come
home to him, with the simplicity of truth: 'O fool, fool, fool!'
(V. ii. 322) Yet, in spite of this, Othello retains to the end the simplicity
which formed part of his egoism throughout, and with it a good measure
of tragic dignity. His weakness and his tragedy are, indeed, closely
united to the last. As T. S. Eliot noted,[8] his last speech is both a splendid
expression of self-centred poetry and a final attempt at self-justification
in an irrelevant pose:

> I have done the state some service, and they know't . . .
>   . . . then must you speak
> Of one that loved not wisely but too well;
> Of one not easily jealous, but, being wrought,
> Perplexed in the extreme.   (V. ii. 338)

We shall recognize that this speech, as we follow it, carries us with the
speaker to the culminating moment in which he kills himself, to fall,
as in a final gesture of expiation, over the body of his murdered wife.
And yet there is more than this. If we are not mistaken in finding here
the last words of a hero of true tragic stature, we should nonetheless not
allow this to blind us to other realities, those to which Othello has so
painfully awakened in the course of this same scene. For who, in point
of fact, has been 'more easily jealous' than Othello? For all the declama-
tory splendour of his final words, much of what is said has nothing to do
with the burden of responsibility that rests so heavily upon him. For the

real point, or a great part of it, lies in the presence of Desdemona's body, killed by the speaker himself in his blindness, wantonly and unnecessarily sacrificed; and his last words are not only 'poetry', but a final confession of failure. 'Perplexed', by his own admission, betrayed by emotions he has never really understood, Othello's last words are a pathetic return to his original simplicity. Unable to cope effectively with the complicated business of living, he recalls his generous past and commits the 'simple' act of suicide. But already the critical acid applied by Iago has destroyed the structure of his greatness.

We may say with some justification that the spectacle of Othello's fall is excessively painful. The prevailing spirit of the tragedy tends undoubtedly to destruction, so much so that it possibly lacks balance and fails to satisfy completely as a reflection of human experience. Other elements, however, also emerge from a balanced view of the play. Iago, so triumphantly in charge of his intrigue, loses control of it at the last and is faced unexpectedly, in the person of the wife whom he has consistently used and despised, with the reaction of elementary human decency.[9] ''Tis proper I obey him, but not now'; 'Perchance, Iago, I will ne'er go home' (V. ii. 194). The truth 'will out', in spite of all the efforts of malignant and self-confident cunning to conceal it. It will destroy Othello, who has contributed to his destruction by his own folly, but it will also reduce Iago from his wonted command of events to a final enigmatic silence:

> Demand me nothing; what you know, you know:
> From this time forth I never will speak word.   (V. ii. 302)

In spite of all his shortcomings, we feel at the last that Othello has been connected with love and natural emotion; nor is there anything grudging about the nobility conferred upon him at his best moments. Iago, on the other hand, is felt, for all his claim to superior 'intelligence', to be at once limited, mean, and evil. His attitude, repellent as it is, represents truth in so far as it answers to flaws truly present in the character of his victim; but there is no suggestion in the play that his acceptance of these flaws as final is anything other than a perverse interpretation of human reality, against which it is necessary to fight by gaining that degree of self-knowledge which Othello so conspicuously lacked. Within the unity which it imposes upon contradictions still present in its author's experience, *Othello* allows us to glimpse the decisive orientation of Shakespearean *good* and *evil* in *Macbeth*.

2 Macbeth

Macbeth, which represents in more ways than one a crucial stage in the
development of Shakespeare's art, exhibits the conflict between reason
and passion—the constant theme of the great tragedies—under aspects
notably different in kind and implications from any he had hitherto
attempted.[10] The play deals this time with the overthrow of harmony,
not merely in an individual tragic hero (such as Othello) but in an
ordered society: and the conflict is worked out in terms that are more
clearly and unequivocally moral than in any of the preceding plays.
The plot, reflecting this modification of purpose, turns upon a clear
contrast between two completely opposed orders. Duncan and
Malcolm, who both suffer at the hands of a usurper, are not bound, as
Othello had been, by egoism or weakness to the evil which aims at their
overthrow; rather do they stand over against Macbeth less as characters
in the generally accepted sense than as 'symbols' of order, loyalty, and
goodness. *Macbeth* is, in the first place and above all, a play about the
murder of a king; and there is a very real sense in which the centre, the
focal point of the conception is to be found neither in the criminal
usurper nor in the wife who initially urges him to crime, but in the
figure, too easily neglected in its central, normative function, of
Duncan.

To say this is clearly to depart in some degree from the conceptions
of dramatic character which have inspired so much past study of the
play. The significance of Duncan, however we may choose to conceive
it, clearly cannot depend upon a character study carried out on conventional lines; some critics, starting from the method of analysis often
associated with the name of Bradley, have even found him weak and
ineffectual, which was certainly no primary part of Shakespeare's
intention. Duncan's function in the play emerges rather, as we shall
shortly see, from the images of light and fertility which surround his
person and confer substance and consistency upon the 'symbolic' value
of his rule. The universal implications of this value, again, are only fully
appreciated after due weight has been given to the short initial appearance of the Witches, which establishes the climate, moral as much as
merely physical, within which the action is to be conducted.[11] The
Witches, as a prelude to the human tragedy, introduce us to a situation
in which 'Fair is foul, and foul is fair' (I. i. 11); through the calculated

ambiguity of their utterance and through the elemental commotion
which surrounds them, they prepare the way for the entry of evil and
disintegration into a state which has been, under Duncan, positive,
natural, and orderly. When the evil obscurely present in Macbeth's
mind is stirred to conceive and execute the murder of Duncan, he
introduces both into the Scottish realm and into his own nature a disrupting evil which must work itself out through the process it has
initiated. The play, thus conceived as a harmonious dramatic construction, deals with the overthrow of the balance of royalty by Macbeth's
crime, with the full development of the malignity which that overthrow implies, and, finally, with the restoration of natural order under
the gracious successor of the murdered king.

Macbeth's murder of Duncan is, accordingly, in the first place a crime
against the natural foundations of social and moral harmony; it is at the
same time an attack by the destructive elements contemplated in
Shakespeare's experience upon those which make for unity and un-
trammeled maturity. As we have already suggested, the positive values
of the tragedy are concentrated on the 'symbolic' function of Duncan's
royalty and upon the poetry in which it finds expression. As king,
Duncan is the head of a 'single state of man' (we shall see later the full
implications of this phrase of Macbeth's), whose members are bound into unity by the accepted ties of loyalty. By virtue of this position he is
the source of all the benefits which flow from his person to those who
surround him; receiving the free homage of his subjects, he dispenses to
them all the riches and graces which are the mark of true kingship, so
that the quality of his poetry is above all life-giving, fertile. The early,
light-drenched scenes of the tragedy are dominated by this rich, vital
relationship between service spontaneously given and abundant royal
bounty. Macbeth himself, still speaking as the loyal general who has
saved his country from the consequences of internal rebellion and
foreign invasion, describes the subject's duty in repeated protestations
of devotion that only in the light of his own later behaviour become
ironic[12]; in his expression of them his poetry attains, though fugitively
and imperfectly, a breadth, a completeness of emotional content, that
it will never recover. Duncan, in turn, replies to these professions of
loyalty with an overflowing bounty expressed in terms of harvest
fullness:

> I have begun to plant thee, and will labour
> To make thee full of growing,

to which the devoted Banquo replies by taking up the same image—

> There if I grow,
> The harvest is your own—

and receives from his king a final expression of abounding joy:

> My plenteous joys,
> Wanton in fullness, seek to hide themselves
> In drops of sorrow.   (I. iv. 28)

Duncan and his subjects, in short, vie with one another in the celebration of a relationship that is not one of mastery or subjection, but essentially free, expansive, life-giving. It is in accordance with the spirit of his kingship that Duncan's brief appearances before his murder are invariably invested with images of light and fertility to which are joined, at his moments of deepest feeling, the religious associations of worship in a magnificent, comprehensive impression of overflowing *grace*.

This impression, which is at this stage new in Shakespeare (we shall see something similar, expressed in a different context, in the conception of Cordelia in *King Lear*), from now on acquires growing significance in his work. It is perhaps most finely conveyed in this play at the moment in which Duncan and Banquo, when the former makes his last living appearance, pause before they enter Macbeth's castle at Inverness. The exchange between them is more than decorative in its effect:

> Duncan: This castle hath a pleasant seat; the air
> Nimbly and sweetly recommends itself
> Unto our gentle senses.
> Banquo: This guest of summer,
> The temple-haunting martlet, does approve
> By his loved mansionry that the heaven's breath
> Smells wooingly here: no jutty, frieze,
> Buttress, nor coign of vantage, but this bird
> Hath made his pendant bed and procreant cradle:
> Where they most breed and haunt, I have observed
> The air is delicate.   (I. vi. 1)

The combination of natural sweetness and supernatural 'grace' is here achieved in an amplitude of reference that gathers its component images into a single triumphant effect. The 'martlet'[13] that builds on the castle walls its '*pendant* bed and *procreant* cradle' (note the sense of

weight, of life concentrating itself naturally in the process of birth, reflected in the sound and meaning of the adjectives) is 'temple-haunting',
a dweller in the shadow of sanctity; and the 'loved mansionry' of its
home, 'loved' both as an auspicious presence and as itself the home
of love, is attracted to spots where the breath of heaven 'smells
wooingly' with a sense of fulfilment that is the prelude to generation.
The combination of spring with the delicate air which so 'nimbly and
sweetly' lends itself to senses described as 'gentle', purged of all grossness and yet intensely, naturally alive, is an achievement so richly and
finely compacted as to be new in Shakespeare. It marks a fresh stage in
the dramatic ordering of his experience, and in the resulting liberation
of its full possibilities for life and harmony. The 'canker' of frustration
which was still eating into Othello's love is now fully mastered,
artistically worked out in the evil of Macbeth; and all the vitality and
goodness so freed finds expression in a new intuition of life as fertile and
sanctified.

In accordance with this conception there is between Duncan and the
loyal Macbeth of these early scenes a relationship rich in honour and
fertile in royal bounty. As Duncan's instrument in war, Macbeth wins
two arduous battles and becomes Thane of Cawdor. No sooner has he
heard the prophecy of the Witches, however, than a new quality enters
his meditations, expressing itself in verse of a very different kind. The
verse of *Macbeth*, apart from that associated with the loyal personages
of the play, is often, at a first reading, so abrupt and disjointed that
some critics have felt themselves driven to look for gaps in the text.
Yet the difficult passages do not look in the least like the result of
omissions; they are demonstrably necessary to the feeling of the tragedy.
In practically every one of Macbeth's speeches there is a keen sense of
discontinuity, a continual jolting of the sensibility into disorder and
anarchy. Macbeth, from the time when the thought of murder first
forces its way into his consciousness, moves almost continuously in a
remarkable state of nervous tension, a state in which a very palpable
obscurity is suddenly and unexpectedly shot through by strange revelations and terrifying illuminations of feeling. This state is fully significant only as an inversion of the rich, ordered poetry of Duncan; it is the
natural consequence of his murder, a reflection of the entry of evil both
into the individual and the state. The quality of this disturbance, which
changes with the various stages of Macbeth's own situation, should be
closely considered.

Immediately after his first meeting with the Witches, when the thought of his crime first claims his attention, Macbeth, standing for a moment aside from his companions, speaks with typical disjointed intensity:

> This supernatural soliciting
> Cannot be ill, cannot be good: if ill,
> Why hath it given me earnest of success,
> Commencing in a truth? I am thane of Cawdor;
> If good, why do I yield to that suggestion
> Whose horrid image doth unfix my hair
> And make my seated heart knock at my ribs,
> Against the use of nature? Present fears
> Are less than horrible imaginings:
> My thought, whose murder yet is but fantastical,
> Shakes so my single state of man that function
> Is smothered in surmise, and nothing is
> But what is not.   (I. iii. 130)

Nothing quite like this following of thought in the very process of conscious formulation can be found in Shakespeare's early work; it is another development new to *Macbeth*. There is nothing accidental about the telescoping of the syntax in the last few lines; the strange juxtaposition of 'thought' and 'murder' conveys perfectly the actual birth of the unnatural project in the tangled chaos of ideas. Taken with the rest of the speech it conveys even more. It anticipates the whole disturbance of natural 'function', of the 'single state of man', which the very thought of such a crime implies; it expresses with unsurpassed nervous directness the shaking to its foundations of what has been a harmonious personality. The speech, indeed, is much more than a mere statement of the ambiguity and tension present in Macbeth's mind. It is a *physical* apprehension of ambiguity, a disordered experience expressing itself in terms of a dislocated functioning. There is a tremendous sense of heightened animal feeling about the unfixed hair and the hammering of the heart. And yet (and it is here that the moral judgment which the whole play will be concerned to enforce is implicitly revealed), keen as it is in its operation, this almost bestial sensitivity is quite meaningless. It introduces unreality even into the thought of murder, in a way which the following scenes will make apparent. When Lady Macbeth, immediately after the killing of Duncan, tries to rouse her husband to a fuller awareness of himself, she says:

the sleeping and the dead
Are but as pictures; 'tis the eye of childhood
That fears a *painted* devil.   (II. ii. 54)

The terms in which this attempt to encourage the bemused Macbeth is couched themselves incorporate it into the spirit of unreality, of hideous mockery, which dominates this part of the action. Divorced from its proper place in the 'use of nature', the most intense feeling has only a quality of hallucination—that is the full force of 'horrible imaginings' and 'fantastical'. Feeling is 'smothered in surmise', and the same keen senses which so effectively seconded the gracious gentleness of Duncan are directed only to a muffled fumbling among uncertainties.

The full meaning of Macbeth's first aside should now be clear. The fertile poetry of Duncan, based upon so delicate and so complete an organization of the 'gentle' senses, depends upon a right ordering of the 'single state of man'. Harmony in the individual is balanced by harmony in the Scottish *state* under its lawful king. Macbeth's poetry, however, reflects the growth into consciousness within his mind of a wilful determination to break down this 'single state'; and, by means of it, Shakespeare identifies the evil of his play with the disrupting of a most harmonious experience. The result in psychological terms is presented with rare immediacy in Macbeth's early meditations upon his future course of action. It produces in him a discontinuity between the senses and the mind, between the mind and the conscience (note how the speech already quoted opens with a vain fumbling at the meaning of 'good' and 'ill'), and, between these gaps, nothing but an intense awareness of their existence. Considered in this way, *Macbeth* can be related to the whole line of development traced in the earlier plays. Its subject is still the 'degree' theme of *Troilus and Cressida*, but now immeasurably enriched by a firmer grasp of personality and by a new, more mature organization of feeling. By the side of this contrast between Duncan and Macbeth, the conception behind Ulysses' discourse on 'degree'[14] must strike us as sluggish and, dramatically speaking, unrealized. Here, unlike the earlier play, there is no gap between the statement of the argument and its apprehension in terms of immediate experience. Ulysses, on the whole, *tells us* about the breakdown of 'degree' in abstract terms, whereas here we *feel* the personality in dissolution, striving vainly to attain, on the basis of its own illusory desires, an impression of coherence. To the gain in poetic immediacy corresponds an advance in dramatic presentation. The 'single state of man', a state which depends for both the individual and the social organism on the due observance of ordered loyalty, is here replaced by a cleavage in the innermost fabric of the mind, an uncertain groping in the bottomless pit of psychological and spiritual darkness, in the first obscure glimpses of a state where fundamental values are inverted, and where 'nothing is But what is not'.

Darkness, indeed, is from now on Macbeth's native element. From the decisive moment in which his crime is conceived he is excluded from the light which radiates from the royal figure of Duncan, so that it is no surprise when, in the very next scene, we meet with his exclamation:

> Stars, hide your fires;
> Let not light see my black and deep desires:
> The eye wink at the hand; yet let that be,
> Which the eye fears, when it is done, to see.   (I. iv. 50)

In point of fact, Macbeth himself, already involved in obscurity, is not at this moment clear as to the true nature of these desires. The decisive part in clarifying his still confused thoughts is played by Lady Macbeth, whose first significant utterance, on receiving her husband's letters with an account of his meeting with the Witches, turns upon two closely associated ideas. The first is the recognition of his lack of clarity, expressed in her own concise definition of him as one who

> wouldst not play false,
> And yet wouldst wrongly win.   (I. v. 22)

The second is her determination to oppose to this contradiction in his nature the conviction (which she, in her own way, shares with all the great Shakespearean 'villains': Iago, Edmund, Antonio) that success in action implies, as a necessary condition, the abolition of any gap in the mind of the agent between the act itself and the will whose decision alone makes action possible. It is the elimination of this gap, the equivalent on an avowedly moral level of Hamlet's rooted disinclination to carry out the duty imposed upon him, that she is determined to produce in her vacillating husband; for, as she says:

> that which rather thou dost fear to do
> Than wishest should be undone.   (I. v. 25)

By introducing this element of logic, spurious though it be, into Macbeth's uncertainty, she makes the crime possible. The relationship between the two characters, in the course of which one of them takes the initiative in bringing to the surface elements obscurely present in the mind of the other, is a characteristic feature of Shakespeare's dramatic constructions. We have already seen it in operation in the disintegration, by Iago, of Othello's heroic nobility: applied here in a different context, and to a very different purpose, it confers upon the plot a dynamic element, a sense of development essential to the complete effect.

The connection between *Macbeth* and Shakespeare's previous work becomes still clearer once it is seen that the murder of Duncan is the result of a movement of the 'blood', of the deeper sources of passion exercising their potent influence upon the will. The nature ot the relationship that unites husband and wife is worth careful consideration. It is implied in the words in which Lady Macbeth, having read her husband's letter, greets him upon his arrival:

> Thy letters have transported me beyond
> This ignorant present, and I feel now
> The future in the instant,   (I. v. 57)

and in the ecstatic quality of his response: 'My dearest love!' It is precisely this intensity of passion which, diverted from its natural channels, is turned into a craving for power and issues in murder. To follow the common line of interpretation and call this craving 'ambition' is not enough, for ambition is an abstraction and this is something that comes, as we have seen, from the 'blood', from the hidden instinctive foundations of the personality. Lady Macbeth's attitude, indeed, logical though it be once its premises are granted, involves a passionate distortion of normal humanity which balances that which she herself helps to produce in her husband. Born of a reversal of nature, its expression is consistently unnatural. Her first prayer, as her purpose takes shape, is '*Unsex* me here!' Her second—prefaced by the significant apostrophe, 'Come, thick night!'—is an appeal to the darkness that makes possible the exclusion of reason and pity. From this to the expressions of forced, unnatural determination which follow—the declared willingness to kill her own child rather than fail in the course of action which her 'blood'-impelled craving for power has dictated, the final conquest of her feeling that the sleeping Duncan resembled her own father—the passage is as easy as it is monstrous, inhuman. The whole crime is, in the words of Ross, from the moment of its conception to that of its final execution, 'against nature still' (II. iv. 27). The overthrow of the royal symbol of order and fruitful unity is the result of a preceding disturbance of the balance between impulse and conscience, instinctive 'blood' and reasonable will; and this, in turn, naturally produces a dissociation of bodily function, an anarchy in which animal feeling works in an isolation divorced from all control, and so void of continuity and significance.

After this, the actual murder of Duncan comes as the grotesque climax of a process that has involved from the first an inversion of every natural bond and feeling. Macbeth moves towards it in a state of hallucination, still invoking the darkness in which evil thoughts have at least the illusion of free play. 'Each corporal agent' in him is 'bent up' (I. vii. 80), as by a conscious, strained effort, to the deed that awaits him. Even at this stage, however, more is involved than a statement, conveyed with the greatest linguistic immediacy, of psychological disorder. The supernatural sanctions against which Macbeth has rebelled in conceiving the murder of his king make themselves felt, in a broken form indeed, because they are reflected in a mind already irretrievably shattered, but with the power to impose their validity in his own despite. The speech in which Macbeth pauses in a final attempt to take stock of his situation is at once a ruthless revelation of character and a contribution to the dominant spiritual theme:

> If it were done when 'tis done then 'twere well
> It were done quickly; if the assassination
> Could trammel up the consequence, and catch
> With his surcease success; that but this blow
> Might be the be-all and the end-all here,
> But here, upon this bank and shoal of time,
> We'ld jump the life to come.   (I. vii. 1)

Macbeth is trying to persuade himself that the only valid reason for hanging back from the murder he is about to commit is one of expediency, the fear of rousing to retribution the public opinion which an attack on Duncan must inevitably outrage. From the first, however, the expression of his position is anything but dispassionate or clear. The succession of uneasy suppositions with which his reflections open, and the very avoidance, through the repeated use of 'it', of all direct reference to the absorbing object of his meditations, show that even his efforts at logical expression are caught up in the incoherence, the broken continuity, which has dominated his thought ever since he first considered the revelation of the Witches. The breathless confounding, so superbly echoed in the sound of his words, of 'assassination' with 'consequence', 'surcease' with 'success', reflects a mind involved in the incoherent flow of its own ideas, while the force of 'trammel' and 'catch', each stressing with its direct impact a break in the rhythm of the phrase, conveys perfectly the peculiar disorganized intensity which Macbeth will bear with him to the final extinction of feeling.

Disorganization and incoherence, however, are not the only aspects of Macbeth's condition revealed by the speech. Beneath them, rising to take possession of his mind in a swelling flood of emotion, is a tide of feeling which, while reflected through the speaker's own state, derives ultimately from the outraged spiritual values of the play. The true sources of the murderer's fear are not what he declares them to be. Self-ignorance and self-deception are essential parts of his nature, and as his words bring them to light, they are seen to be connected, in his own despite, with the supernatural terrors which he has just declared his readiness to 'jump':

> Besides, this Duncan
> Hath borne his faculties so meek, hath been
> So clear in his great office, that his virtues
> Will plead like angels, trumpet-tongued, against
> The deep damnation of his taking-off;
> And pity, like a naked new-born babe,
> Striding the blast, or heaven's cherubin, horsed
> Upon the sightless couriers of the air,
> Shall blow the horrid deed in every eye,
> That tears shall drown the wind.   (I. vii. 16)

To discuss the logic of this passage in terms of mixed metaphor would clearly be to miss the whole point of the speech, dramatic not less than poetic (and how, indeed, shall we separate one aspect of the total effect from another?). Macbeth's emotion grows in the course of its expression, and in a way which involves the presence of the whole in each of its stages. It passes from a consideration of the inexpediency of murdering Duncan to embrace a sense of supernatural terror which is at once, in itself, a sign of hysterical weakness, and, in the general design of the play, a reflection of the positive sanctions that dominate the entire action. His first impulse is to contrast the brutality of his projected deed with the 'meekness' of his victim, the guilt he feels in himself with the 'clarity' of the king he is about to kill. 'Meekness' and 'clarity', however, when associated with the royal office, are not merely innocent and pacific qualities. They have, by virtue of the spiritual foundation on which the royal office rests, a force that will impose itself by pleading 'trumpet-tongued', with apocalyptic power, against the horror of his death; and the sense of this horror is itself fused, in Macbeth's mind, with a growing fear of the 'damnation' that the intrinsic evil of his act will bring upon him. The supernatural sanctions associated with the holiness of the royal office, based themselves on a coherent, unified conception, are reflected in the weak, divided mind of the murderer in the form of a hysterical and disintegrating sense of terror.

In this way Macbeth's thoughts, still developing his reaction to Duncan's innocence and the public effect, as he foresees it, of his death, rise to the great complex image in which the speech culminates. The universal pity which he feels to be an obstacle to the carrying out of his project is now seen to combine the attributes of innocence ('a naked new-born babe') already associated with his victim, with that of a supernatural power rising, as it were, out of the depths of his own consciousness to overthrow him. The speech thus affirms the relevance of the very values it is engaged in setting aside, recognizes in its own darkness the existence of light, albeit seen through distortion and obscurity. The 'new-born babe' becomes, in his distraught imagination, an avenging power 'striding the blast', carrying on the sense of irresistible denunciation already conveyed in 'trumpet-tongued' and finally projected as 'heaven's cherubin'

> horsed
> Upon the sightless couriers of the air,

to make his hidden crime universally, inescapably known. Fear, not less than loyalty, testifies in its own despite to the validity of the order it is engaged in outraging. Finally, the emotion which has thus risen to its distraught climax subsides as Macbeth returns to a consideration of his own situation, isolated before the fear which now possesses him and acutely conscious of his lack of genuine motivation:

> I have no spur
> To prick the sides of my intent, but only
> Vaulting ambition, which o'erleaps itself
> And falls on the other.   (I. vii. 25)

The speech, already so rich in its development of living metaphor, now introduces a new, final comparison: that of the rider who puts an excess of energy into his effort to vault into the saddle, only to find himself, having overshot the mark, falling into vacancy. After the preceding swell of the apocalyptic vision of pity, at once produced by and accentuating a sense of moral emptiness, the speech turns brokenly to a consideration of the speaker's own state—his 'I' is lamely introduced in the middle of a line—while the verses which follow are deliberately interrupted at 'only' (the adverb in itself carries on a restrictive sense) and at 'o'erleaps itself', to fall away with lame inconclusiveness 'on the other'. Few speeches, even in this most tensely conceived of plays, achieve a closer, more intimate fusion between the psychological disintegration of an individual and the overriding supernatural conception which finds harmonious expression in the innocent and a broken, incoherent reflection in the hysterical fear of the guilty.[15]

By the time the murder of Duncan has taken place it is abundantly clear that Macbeth's crime is, as we have argued, a rift in the harmony and richness of the unity 'symbolized' in the royal rule and realized in the poetry associated with the dead king. Such a rift, once it has appeared, has to exhaust its destructive consequences before coherence can be restored; and in the central part of the play Macbeth's kingship, contrasted with that of Duncan as 'evil' with 'good', is shown as simply the working out of the negation upon which it was founded. The usurper, as he comes to realize that the crime he has committed to gain, in his wife's overweening words, 'solely sovereign sway and masterdom' (I. v. 71), has in fact failed to achieve this goal, progressively loses the illusion of freedom and plunges into a further series of unnatural actions. At the lowest point in his downward progress, he consults the Witches once more in a determination to know 'by the worst means the worst'; and the Witches respond (IV. i) both by offering further false 'certainties'—in the form of the various apparitions set before his eyes—and by confirming finally, through the vision of Banquo's succession, the sterility of his own line. With this revelation, and the last, useless killing of Macduff's wife and children which immediately follows (IV. ii), the central part of the action, exhausting the possibilities of evil and uniting Macbeth and the realm he has usurped in a common degradation, is logically complete. Its third and last stage will show a process of recovery in which the forces of 'good', of life and ordered harmony, drawing their strength originally from the holy ruler of England, flow back like a returning tide over Scotland to sweep away Macbeth's shadow of power and to restore, in the person of Duncan's rightful heir, Malcolm, the kingship of 'grace'. The complete effect, as will be seen, is that of a balanced construction, each successive stage of which, linked to the preceding action by threads of imagery and the logic of events, also prepares the ground for the final resolution.

From the moment of Duncan's murder until the final overthrow of Macbeth the action turns upon a contrast between two royalties: that of the dead king, founded upon natural allegiance and rich in generous bounty, and that of his murderer, which, initiated in a reversal of 'nature', can only have as its end unnatural chaos and inevitable death. The terms of the contrast are already established at the moment in which Duncan's dead body is discovered. Macduff, bursting in with the news of the 'discovery', stresses those aspects of it which imply the reversal of natural order and the commission of sacrilege:

> *Confusion* now hath made his masterpiece!
> Most *sacrilegious* murder hath broke ope
> *The Lord's anointed temple*, and stole thence
> *The life o' the building*.   (II. iii. 72)

On his own re-entry, a moment later, Macbeth in turn expresses, in the typically heightened and unnatural spirit which reflects his distraught condition, the positive values which he has deliberately chosen to attack. Royalty truly established and freely accepted is, indeed, 'the life o' the building', the foundation upon which all natural relationships in society depend; and Macbeth, in his effort to simulate a sorrow which he alone cannot feel, speaks more truly than he knows when he says:

> from this instant,
> There's nothing serious in mortality:
> All is but toys; renown and grace is dead;
> The wine of life is drawn, and the mere lees
> Is left this vault to brag of.   (II. iii. 99)

When the murderer thus surrounds the dead majesty of Duncan with images of life and 'grace', he both stresses the sacramental quality, so to call it, of the victim's office (even the implications of 'the wine of life' may hold a subsidiary meaning in this respect) and reveals how his own deed has left him nothing but the dregs and 'toys' which will from now on dominate his utterances to the end of the tragedy. The sense that the future is, for Macbeth, as obscure as the manifestations of darkness and chaos which now surround him leads finally to the complete reversal of the 'gracious' imagery of life and light which surrounded the figure of Duncan. 'Dark night *strangles* the travelling lamp,' the king's horses 'contend against obedience', and, most powerfully of all,

> darkness does the face of earth *entomb*,
> When *living* light should *kiss* it.   (II. iv. 9)

The point of balance between the happy past and the forebodings of the future is finally expressed in Macduff's remarks to Ross:

> *Ross:*   Will you to Scone?
> *Macduff:* No, cousin, I'll to Fife.
> *Ross:*   Well, I will thither.
> *Macduff:* Well, may you see things well done there:—adieu,
> Lest our old robes sit easier than our new.   (II. iv. 35)

Exchanges of this kind repeatedly mark what are in effect turning points in the spiritual not less than in the surface development of the action; their use, indeed, is a typical feature of this most carefully and deliberately constructed of plays.

During the central part of the tragedy, which opens with the shift from Inverness to Forres and closes with the murder of Lady Macduff (IV. ii), the contrast between the usurper's kingship and that of his victim is fully developed in a series of balanced images. Its outstanding dramatic expression is Macbeth's banquet (III. iv), which is set, in its spirit and final outcome, against Duncan's great feast at Inverness, when he distributed 'great largess' to his thanes and finally 'shut up in *measureless* content' (II. i. 16). The force of 'measureless', and its connection with the infinite generosity in which the spirit of Duncan's kingship is consistently expressed, should by now be amply clear. It is significant that Macbeth should be absent from this demonstration of free loyalty and corresponding royal bounty; the action upon which his imagination has already embarked is the flaw in 'the single state of man' which depends upon natural reverence for the throne. If we return to Macbeth's own banquet, which takes place just after he has advanced a step further on his empty progress only to learn that the escape of Fleance has once more meant the dropping of a link in the chain of rigidly determined acts in which he follows the illusion of freedom, we shall find the ghost of Banquo intervening to occupy the place destined for him as king at the head of his table. The apparition breaks in upon the show of loyalty and order which Macbeth seeks, by virtue of his

usurped dignity, to command; and the effect of its entry is such that the
whole scene is closed by Lady Macbeth's most significant words:

> You have displaced the mirth, broke the good meeting,
> With most admired disorder.   (III. iv. 109)

The use of the word 'disorder' is especially revealing. It is a precise
description of what Macbeth's crime has let loose upon Scotland, and
also—in the personal sphere—of the effects of evil as revealed more
intimately in his own person. The two disorders, individual and universal, stand in the closest connection; they develop side by side, until
both reach their culminating point, in terms of the external action, in
the murder of Macduff's family.

The state of intimate disorganization in which his crime has left
Macbeth is closely associated, from an early stage, with the loss of the
power to sleep. The darkness which he has invoked from the first
conception of his crime, far from bringing with it rest, natural renewal
after the exertions of the day, is associated for him with a wakefulness
which the dissociation of his various faculties—the divorce between
'eye' and 'hand' (I. iv. 52), consciousness and act—can only render more
horrible in its effects. The sleep in which Macbeth found Duncan when
he raised his hand against him is henceforth woven into the innermost
fabric of his conscience; his imagination, in which he sees himself as the
'murderer' of sleep itself, clutches incoherently at the healing properties
of rest in words which escape his wife's more literal understanding and
express the chaos which has taken possession of his mind:

> the innocent sleep,
> Sleep that knits up the ravell'd sleave of care,
> The death of each day's life, sore labour's bath,
> Balm of hurt minds, great nature's second course,
> Chief nourisher in life's feast.   (II. ii. 37)

By a process typical of this play, these words are at once a revelation of
breaking coherence and, through the positive force of the images with
which the speaker so disjointedly, hysterically fumbles, a contribution
to the spiritual content of the tragedy. Sleep should bring repose, the
renewing of the whole man in his rest; it is at once a sign of health,
moral and physical, and, for those to whom it is available, a means of
recovering health after exposure to the strain of daily living. Lady
Macbeth, confronted at a slightly later stage with her husband's uneasiness, says to him, 'You lack the season of all natures, sleep' (III. iv.

141); the 'season', the element that makes life sweet and acceptable, as to the natural taste. The full force of sleep as a Shakespearean symbol becomes increasingly clear in his last plays, in Pericles and in Leontes[16]; already in *Macbeth* it is related to seasoning and so, in a very vital way, to the natural functioning of the 'gentle senses'. Macbeth's words as he first contemplates the nature of his act constitute an inverted homage to the values he has wilfully destroyed. By his crime he has cut himself off from all that is natural, and so his sleep, under the palpable 'blanket of the dark' that henceforth envelops him, is shot through with

> the cursed thoughts that nature
> Gives way to in repose.   (II. i. 9)

This double nature of sleep, which nourishes the innocent at 'life's feast' and restores the faculties of 'hurt minds' at the same time that it releases, in the guilty, the subconscious images of terror present in their natures, is variously and richly related to the complex poetic structure of the tragedy.

To Macbeth, indeed, who has murdered not only a man and his kinsman, but, in the person of his king, order, unity itself, sleep can offer no refuge and no restoration. At best he can connect it, not with the renewal of vital energy, but with death, the only release from the continuation of a life the content and significance of which he has killed. In this spirit, when first alone with his wife after their crowning, he opposes his own insomnia nostalgically to the peace which his victim has found in death:

> better be with the dead,
> Whom we, to gain our peace, have sent to peace,
> Than on the torture of the mind to lie
> In restless ecstasy. Duncan is in his grave;
> After life's fitful fever he sleeps well.   (III. ii. 19)

To suggest, as Santayana once suggested,[17] that this phrase sums up Shakespeare's attitude towards life (in so far as one can be discovered) is remarkably misleading. Macbeth's state of mind can in no way be identified with the complete conception of this tragedy. Opposed to it there stands, as we have noted and shall see again in the concluding scenes, the norm and plenitude, the splendid ordering of experience achieved in the poetry of Duncan and finally confirmed in the 'symbolic' function of Malcolm. Macbeth's attitude towards death cannot be identified with that of Shakespeare in this play (something like it is perhaps the most unambiguous feeling in *Hamlet*), though the dramatist no doubt felt it keenly and persistently as an element in his experience. It is rather the product of Macbeth's original crime against loyalty and order, against the harmony and continuity which makes experience valuable. In murdering Duncan, his usurper murdered the coherence of his own life, so that henceforth we expect of him (as, in reality, he expects of himself) nothing but death.

The turning point of the entire action (if a turning point can properly be spoken of in a series of events so closely and continuously related to their point of departure) is finally reached in the two scenes in which Macbeth, after returning to consult the Witches, proceeds in full disillusionment to the murder of the family of Macduff. The new approach to the Witches involves a fully conscious acceptance of anarchy; he will know the future, he says, even though the result be universal chaos, even though

> the treasure
> Of nature's germins tumble all together,
> Even till destruction sicken.   (IV. i. 58)[18]

The reply he receives, ambiguous to the last in accordance with the nature of evil as it presents itself to its servants in this play, at once offers an illusory certainty and, in the succeeding apparitions offered to his eyes, foreshadows the future development of the action. Each of the apparitions, indeed, insinuates a double meaning, offers a fallacious confirmation to Macbeth's evil instincts at the same time that it symbolizes a stage in the birth, through tragedy and retribution, of a new positive order. The first appearance, that of the 'armed Head', while warning him of the struggle that awaits him, fixes the threat to his security upon the person of Macduff; it thus confirms him in his determination to eliminate the latter, who will thereby be given an added personal motive to seek his overthrow. The following apparition, that of the 'bloody Child', both strengthens Macbeth in his confidence by offering him immunity from all 'of woman born' and suggests the birth in travail of an innocence in which the usurper can have no part. This birth is confirmed, and given the seal of royalty, in the final apparition of 'a Child *crowned*, with a tree in his hand', offering, beyond the shadowy assurance associated with the wood at Birnam, a symbol of infant authority invested with the green of living hope and the fertility which, in this play, is the accompaniment of 'grace'. Seen in this way, the scene turns upon a contrast between the false certainties offered to Macbeth and the anticipated rebirth of innocence in ordered loyalty; the only unambiguous glimpse into the future conceded to the usurper is that which his insistence wrings from the Witches and which shows him the sterility of his line in contrast to the fruitful succession derived from the loyal Banquo. From this moment the murderer, now aware that his crime has been in vain, knows also that there is no retreat from its consequences, that what remains of his life is inexorably caught in the determined chain of circumstances which his own act has initiated.

The disillusionment produced in Macbeth by the revelation of the Witches henceforth dominates his whole being. The crown placed on his head has proved 'fruitless', the sceptre grasped by his usurping hands 'barren' (the continuation, implied in its opposite, of the imagery of fertility so closely connected with Duncan is most significant), and the supernatural fears of the early scenes have hardened into the conviction that he has indeed, and vainly, surrendered 'the eternal jewel' of his soul 'to the common enemy of man' (III. i. 69). The decision to murder Macduff and his family (IV. ii) marks his final enslavement to the determined course of events. To 'What's done is done' (III. ii. 12), the conviction urged on him by his wife when she first becomes conscious of the futility of their common crime, he has already replied with the statement of a philosophy of illusion: 'Things bad begun make strong themselves by ill' (III. ii. 55); and this conviction, or the need for clinging to it, henceforward dominates his actions. Macbeth follows a course which he originally chose, indeed, but now no longer controls. Crime leads to further crime, until—in a moment of despairing insight —he realizes that his real wish is to retrace his steps, to recover an original state of innocence, but that, being what he has now become, he cannot do so:

> I am in blood
> Stepped in so far, that, should I wade no more,
> Returning were as tedious as go o'er.   (III. iv. 136)

This, far from being the voice of the confident man of action, is that of the self-deluded criminal who has waked finally, but too late, to the hopeless weakness which all his actions imply.

The two scenes which thus mark the final disillusionment of Macbeth also convey the lowest point in the misery of Scotland, whose state is now so clearly contrasted with the happiness formerly enjoyed under

Duncan. Her sorrows, in Macduff's phrase, 'strike heaven in the face' (IV. iii. 6), the loyal remnants have fled, and Macduff himself, with a carelessness that he admits to be unpardonable, has left his family to die at the hands of their butcher. Yet, at the very moment when this particularly gratuitous crime is carried out, Shakespeare confirms through a single speech of Ross that a further decisive stage in the action has been reached. Ross is one of those minor personages to whom Shakespeare, more especially in his later plays, gives some of the functions of a chorus; he comments upon the events which take place before him, and his speeches are often statements of fact so made that their imagery unites them to the poetic construction of the play. Ross now addresses Lady Macduff in these words:

> cruel are the times, when we are traitors
> And do not know ourselves; when we hold rumour
> From what we fear, yet know not what we fear,
> But float upon a wild and violent sea
> *Each way and move.* I take my leave of you;
> Shall not be long but I'll be here again:
> *Things at the worst will cease, or else climb upward*
> *To what they were before.* (IV. ii. 18)

The conclusion clearly anticipates the course of events to follow: Macbeth's overthrow with the recovery of loyalty and the 'single state of man' in the triumph of Malcolm. This scene, in fact, in spite of the horrors enacted in it, marks a point of balance in the entire development (that is the effect so finely conveyed in the suspense of 'Each way and move'), with a first suggestion of the recovery. It is worth noting, too, how the opening lines drive home the impression of evil which Macbeth's own speeches have already stressed. The essence of evil, which communicates itself from the usurper to his whole realm, lies in uncertainty, in ignorance of one's impulses, of the true causes of one's own actions. This uncertainty has reached such a degree of anarchy that it must either 'cease', lead to the annihilation which Macbeth's whole career has presupposed as its end,[19] or else 'climb upward' and so return to the former condition under Duncan.

This speech, and the assassinations which follow, lead to a long scene (IV. iii), the effect of which is as puzzling as anything in the play. This is the episode in which Malcolm, after 'confessing' to a series of hideous faults which are not in fact even remotely connected with his character, reveals himself finally as a truly dedicated man and undertakes to place himself at the head of the movement which is to restore order and peace to his country. In terms of common realism, Malcolm's change of attitude is neither adequately motivated nor convincing, and we must surely regard it as a 'symbolic' experiment, the true meaning of which lies in its relation to the preceding and the following action. Read in this way, the episode is a dramatic projection of the balance of contraries recently affirmed by Ross. The catalogue of Malcolm's 'vices', in fact, is not meant to be intrinsically probable; it simply gathers up those really associated with Macbeth and is finally rounded off by an evocation of universal disorder that is connected with the usurper's previous utterances:

> Nay, had I power, I should
> Pour the sweet milk of concord into hell,
> Uproar the universal peace, confound
> All unity on earth. (IV. iii. 97)

'Vice', thus conceived, is more than personal in its implications, just as the virtue and purity which stand against it, and which Malcolm also finally associates with his own person, is related to the sanctity of the royal line; for, as Macduff puts it,

>   Thy royal father
> Was a most sainted king; the queen that bore thee,
> Oftener upon her knees than on her feet,
> Died every day she lived. (IV. iii. 108)

This association of sanctity with penance, this deliberate spiritualizing of the idea of death, corresponds perfectly to the state of the action. While Macbeth is spreading death through his usurped kingdom, the royalty round which the forces of recovery are beginning to gather finds in awareness of mortality a prelude to the restoration of 'grace' and the positive values of life. *Macbeth*, taking a stage further the presentation of the Shakespearean tragic hero, sets him against a universal moral background in what is essentially a fresh dramatic conception; the deliberate abandonment of realism in this scene corresponds to a new 'symbolic' purpose, related less to the simple portrayal of the events which constitute the tragedy than to the poetic unity which, underlying it, confers upon it its true meaning. This is not to say that the combination of vestiges of 'realism' with the new 'symbolic' purpose is here achieved with entire success.

The last act of *Macbeth*, the logical rounding off of a process conceived from its first moment as a unity, deals with the return of the kingship of 'grace'. The word, which we shall meet again in the last plays (notably in *The Winter's Tale*), is used by Shakespeare to express the harmony associated with the 'single state of man'. It is noteworthy that in the very scene between Malcolm and Macduff which we have just considered, the loyal elements scattered by Macbeth's tyranny anticipate the access of new strength to their cause from the action of yet another holy king—Edward the Confessor of England. The Lord who converses with Lennox just before Macbeth's return to the Witches first indicates the coming reaction when he speaks of the sanctity of 'the most pious Edward' and associates it openly with the restoration of natural harmony to a wounded society:

> by the help of these—with Him above
> To ratify the work—we may again
> Give to our tables meat, sleep to our nights;
> Free from our feasts and banquets bloody knives;
> Do faithful homage, and receive free honours.   (III. vi. 32)

The insistence upon threads of imagery already seen to be variously significant in the play—'meat' and 'sleep' as attributes of normal, healthy functioning, the disturbance of banquets by bloody visions of murder, the counterpoise of 'faithful homage' and 'free honours'—leads to the more explicit note of 'symbolism' which underlies Malcolm's account of the curing by Edward of the 'king's evil':

> 'Tis called the evil . . .
> How he solicits heaven,
> Himself best knows: but strangely-visited people,
> All swoln and ulcerous, pitiful to the eye,
> The mere despair of surgery, he cures,
> Hanging a golden stamp about their necks,
> Put on with holy prayers; and 'tis spoken,
> To the succeeding royalty he leaves
> The *healing benediction*. With this strange virtue
> He hath a heavenly gift of prophecy,
> And sundry blessings hang about his throne,
> That speak him *full of grace*.   (IV. iii. 146)

The force of this is so clear that it does not need to be enlarged upon; the explicit reference to the 'evil' and the final word 'grace' tell us who are the 'crew of wretched souls' of whom the Doctor has spoken, the nature of their infirmity and of the restoration that is approaching them. Scotland is to be healed and purified by the powers of harmony and reconciliation symbolized in 'grace' and 'benediction'; and the holy Edward will impart to Malcolm the spiritual strength needed for this task. By the end of the scene Malcolm can refer directly to the supernatural sanction which will bless his arms:

> Macbeth
> Is ripe for shaking, and the powers above
> Put on their instruments;   (IV. iii. 236)

and again, recalling directly the persistent darkness that has surrounded Macbeth's rule since he himself invoked its cover for his original crime: 'The night is long that never finds the day.'

As Malcolm returns with this army of deliverance, the divisions implicit in evil come to the surface in his foes. In contrast to Edward's healing power, the Doctor at Dunsinane cannot cure the disharmony beneath Lady Macbeth's sleepwalking. 'More needs she the divine than the physician' (V. i. 81); the words reveal the absence of the 'healing benediction' which Malcolm has triumphantly invoked. From the first, as we have seen, the sleep of the murderers has been wrapped in a darkness shot through with 'cursed thoughts', pregnant with subconscious images of retribution. As such, it fails to bring relief to either Macbeth or to his wife. As one sin against 'grace', conscience, and human obligation follows another, the chaotic intensity originally present in Macbeth's mind is replaced by a mere weary lack of feeling; even revulsion gives way to dead insensibility. Every student of the play has noted the nervous exhaustion which progressively overtakes Macbeth, until at the end we find that 'unfix my hair' which he had uttered in his first obscure reaction to the message of the Witches[20] echoed thus:

> I have almost forgot the taste of fears;
> The time has been, my senses would have cool'd
> To hear a night-shriek, and my fell of hair
> Would at a dismal treatise rouse and stir
> As life were in't: I have supp'd full with horrors.   (V. v. 9)

The fact of Macbeth's weariness is much less important than the manner of its expression. Note how the feeling associated with the 'fell of hair' is further connected with the cloyed palate and the satiated stomach, and so with a line of imagery variously related to feasting, royal munificence and the 'seasoning' proper to healthy living processes, throughout the play. Even the disorganized sensibility of the animal, once so keenly felt in the deepest stirrings of the speaker's consciousness, is now played out, exhausted. The murderer continues to the last to go through the motions of action, but his deeds are divorced from all desire or feeling, however inhuman. His end, when it comes, is no more than the logical conclusion of a process which aimed at the destruction of harmonious life to replace it by anarchy and death.

In the light of these considerations, we may understand better the final scenes of the tragedy, reading into them something more than a monotonous series of battle episodes leading to a foregone conclusion. To this end, we need to avoid above all the temptation to sentimentalize Macbeth in the hour of his downfall, regarding him primarily as a brave warrior making his last stand against hopeless odds. He is indeed that, in part and up to a point; but it is more important to see him above all as a man who has freely chosen his own particular and appropriate hell and who is now faced with the undisguised consequences of his choice. Life itself has now become for Macbeth a pale and senseless succession of incidents—

> To-morrow, and to-morrow, and to-morrow . . .
> a tale
> Told by an idiot, full of sound and fury,
> Signifying *nothing*— (V. v. 19)

a procession of events in front of which he is conscious only of a decline into meaningless old age and irreparable loss. As he puts it, more poignantly than ever before:

> I have lived long enough: my way of life
> Is fallen into the sear, the yellow leaf;
> And that which should accompany old age,
> As honour, love, obedience, troops of friends,
> I must not look to have; but, in their stead,
> Curses, not loud but deep, mouth-honour, breath,
> Which the poor heart would fain deny and dare not.
> (V. iii. 22)

Lest we be tempted to find this principally pathetic in its intention (though it is, of course, that, and to a high degree: otherwise there would be no tragedy in the spectacle of Macbeth's fall), we should consider that every item in this catalogue of loss—'honour, love, obedience, troops of friends'—has been forfeited by the speaker from the moment when he chose to strike his fatal blow against Duncan. *Honour:* can a general claim this who has betrayed the king whose armies he once, in happier times, led to victory? *Love:* how did Macbeth reply to the bounteous generosity which was the external sign of Duncan's trust, of his kingly love for him? *Obedience:* how, but by rebellion culminating in assassination, did he follow up the hollow declarations of allegiance originally made to his royal master? *Friends:* what claim to friendship can he advance, who conceived the murder of Banquo, once his comrade in victorious and patriotic arms? Of Macbeth, in short, it has to be said that, possessing the human privilege of choice (for this, as we have seen, is a play about free will and determinism), he chose to exercise it against nature: and when he awoke, but too late, to the essential vanity of his motives, he discovered the bitter truth that certain choices, once freely and consciously entered upon, become irrevocable, and end—following an inexorable law of human behaviour—by excluding the possibility of further freedom. Such, without recourse to any notion of the future life, which would be foreign to Shakespeare's purposes, is Macbeth's particular and appropriate form of damnation. *Macbeth* is, perhaps, of all Shakespeare's plays, the most Dantesque in spirit. His hero, unlike Dante's personages, finds his hell exclusively in this life; but the loss to which his choices lead him at the last is surely akin to that which Adamo da Brescia, usurer and coiner of false images, expressed with equal, and equally vain, regret, towards the bottom of hell, when he remembered the world that he had lost—'the streams that from the green hills of the Casentino flow down into the Arno'[21]—and who said of these things, with the sad pathos of eternity: 'Sempre mi stanno innanzi, e non indarno': '*Always* these things are before me, *and not in vain.*'

The final battle, seen in this light, merely confirms a process already foreshadowed, substantially complete. The seeds of chaos and death sown in the moral being of the usurper emerge to cover his fictitious rule. We hear almost at once that 'The tyrant's people on both sides do fight' (V. vii. 25), and the terrible Macbeth shrinks to something small and rather absurd as his fall becomes inevitable. In the words of Angus:

> now does he feel his title
> Hang loose about him, like a giant's robe
> Upon a dwarfish thief.   (V. ii. 20)

Before the advancing powers of healing good, evil has shrunk to insignificance. Macbeth is seen to be a puny figure dressed up in a usurped greatness, a dignity not his own, and we are ready for the final bravado flourish with which he dies after Macduff has stripped him of his false 'supernatural' hopes. Such is the end of the ambiguity stated by the Witches as the opening theme of the play: 'Fair is foul, and foul is fair' (I. i. 12). The consequences of this inversion of values have been far-reaching indeed, but—for the first time in a Shakespearean tragedy—not beyond repair. The answer to it is seen in the concluding announcement of the coronation of a king who refers to 'the grace of Grace' (V. viii. V. vii. 101, O.U.P. edition) as his sanction, and who is the rightful successor of Duncan; a king, in short, to whom the loyalty of free men is properly due, and from whom royal bounty may again be expected to flow.

3 King Lear

The tragedies of Shakespeare's maturity, from *Macbeth* onwards, are characterized by a consistent development of the dramatic 'symbolism' which that play first anticipates. This symbolism, which derives originally from an extension of the function of the poetic image in the dramatic scheme, leads naturally to a new conception of plot. The image, expanding by a growing number of contacts with the surrounding verse, becomes more intimately and more variously related to the exigencies of story and character, until the very possibility of a sharp distinction between the action and the poetry through which its meaning in emotional and spiritual terms is conveyed becomes inconceivable. The plot, thus regarded less in terms of common realism than as an extension of the poetry, becomes in effect an expanded metaphor,[22] the 'symbolic' reflection of an experience which the poet, following the promptings of his creative impulse, is concerned to mould into artistic form.

The story of *King Lear*, in some way the most complex and deliberately constructed of Shakespeare's great tragedies, is precisely of this kind. There is a very real sense in which the whole action of the tragedy might be described as a projection of the conflicting issues present in the mind of the central protagonist. As father, Lear produces in his daughters contrasting reactions that reflect different and contradictory facets of his own mind; as king, his wilful impulses liberate forces of anarchy which nothing less than utter exhaustion can ultimately contain. From the conflict whose dual aspect is thus concentrated in one mind the various subsidiary issues of the play radiate as partial reflections of a common image, at once contributing depth and variety to the central situation and deriving from it the subsistent unity which alone can give the complete story its full meaning. In none of Shakespeare's mature plays is the correspondence between action and motive, the external event and its inner meaning, so exactly and significantly established.

Both aspects of Lear's position, the personal and the social, contribute to the unity of a tragedy whose various stages correspond, in the external action, to a closely knit development. The first stage in this development, occupying roughly the first two acts, is concerned with the entry of uncontrolled passion as a disruptive force into Lear's mind and with the consequent overthrow of ordered balance in himself, in his family, and in the state of whose unity he has been hitherto the royal guardian. By the very act of parcelling his realm into three parts Lear in effect denies his unifying vocation and opens the way to the ruin and anarchy which follow inevitably from his gesture. In the second stage, which covers the central part of the play, personal disorder finds in the tempest to which the protagonists are exposed a symbol which at once reflects and transcends it; the elements at war, besides corresponding to the conflict in Lear's distraught person, act through the intense suffering which they impose upon him with the force of a self-revelation, and become the necessary prelude to a species of rebirth. That rebirth, however, although achieved in the personal order during the third and final stage, cannot affect Lear's external fortunes. His reconciliation with Cordelia is followed almost immediately by their final defeat and death against a background of almost unrelieved disaster; the personal and social themes, hitherto so closely united, now separate to produce the concluding catastrophe, and the tragedy, after touching unprecedented heights in its treatment of the personal theme, is rounded off in a mood of Stoic acceptance.

The first stage in an understanding of *King Lear* is a proper interpretation of the opening scene. When Cordelia, in answer to her father's implied request for flattery, follows up her uncompromising 'Nothing' with the equally direct assertion:

I love your majesty
According to my bond; nor more nor less, (I. i. 94)

she introduces the central conception of the whole play. The 'bond' to which she refers is, of course, far more than a legal obligation. Lear's fatherhood bears a 'symbolic' value similar to that of Duncan's kingship in *Macbeth*. The family, like the Scottish state, is a 'symbol' of ordered living. The authority of the father is balanced by the love of his children, and their devotion aspires normally to the grace of his benediction, just as Macbeth's loyalty in the early stages of his career is rewarded by Duncan's bounty.

The breaking up of this pattern of reciprocal loyalties in the opening scene is presented in terms of a conflict between 'nature' the true, permanent reality of things, and the vagaries of individual temperament. Only in Cordelia are these two elements, objective 'nature' and subjective impulse, truly united. For her, filial affection is a duty to be returned to the parent who has, in her own words, 'begot', 'bred', and 'loved' her, in the form of obedience, affection, and respect. Her insistence upon the 'bond', in other words, is based primarily upon a proper understanding of the constitution of things, and no rhetorical profession can strengthen it because it lies as a condition of health at the basis of human normality. Cordelia's behaviour during the whole episode, far from reflecting the stubbornness of which she has so often been accused, represents a norm, a plenitude, in relation to which the imperfect or distorted motives of the other members of the family are seen in their evident partiality.

Of this partial understanding, Lear's behaviour at this stage is a clear example. Old age has weakened his capacity for self-control, making him as soon as he is crossed the prey of an anger definitely rooted in the 'blood'. For, whereas Cordelia is, in a phrase later used of her, 'queen over her passion' (IV. iii. 15), Lear's external royalty is compatible with an intimate servitude which is the reverse of kingly. The splendid pagan imagery of the elemental fire of life and of the dark places of nature, the evocation of the orbs 'from whom we do exist and cease to be' (I. i. 114), represent the source of his anger against the 'reasonable' Cordelia, represent passion in revolt against control, driving the personality to destruction. The immediate and decisive effect of his curse is to reverse the position upon which Cordelia had taken her stand. In it Lear is moved to disclaim 'propinquity and property of blood' (I. i. 116), to break bonds which precede reason and order, but upon which depends the unity of the family and, in the long run, that of experience itself.

Lear's insistence, as father, upon the respect naturally due to his paternity leads, through the imperfect self-knowledge which vitiates it, to the division of his family into two parties both of which reflect contrasted aspects of the family nature simultaneously present in himself. Both Cordelia and her sisters are evidently Lear's children. The firmness with which Cordelia clings with unadorned simplicity to the position which she rightly regards as sanctioned by 'nature' is as clearly hereditary as the passionate devotion of her sisters to the selfish purpose they have proposed to themselves. It is, indeed, precisely in their contrary readings of 'nature'[23] that the difference between them lies. If Cordelia is able throughout to relate her behaviour to a balanced and objective conception of reality, Regan and Goneril, while—unlike their father—perfectly conscious of their own motives, are entirely unaware of the existence or relevance of any universal norm to which these motives may be related. In other words, while Cordelia's quiet insistence on the 'bond' may be said to represent the spirit of reasonable control which Lear's royal status should imply, in Goneril and Regan the passions which lurk in the darker recesses of his undifferentiated humanity are given independent life and logical consistency. Father and daughters, in short, are to be regarded as complementary aspects of a *single* development within the unity of the family. Lear's initial crime against his paternity is fittingly balanced by his elder daughters' disregard of all natural feeling, and this double reversal of the order of 'nature' demands, once set afoot, a complete working out in terms of tragic disunity.

One other aspect of this opening scene, though scarcely stressed in its development, needs to be remembered for a complete understanding of it. Lear is not only father but king, and the bond which binds him to his children is, in a certain sense, a reflection of the more comprehensive one that embraces him to his subjects. At this stage the political theme, still strictly secondary to the personal conflict, is mainly indicated through the person of Kent. To Cordelia's interpretation of the duties which bind her to her father, in fact, corresponds Kent's devotion to truth, regarded by him as the highest expression of his loyalty to his king. His allegiance is of the kind that holds its best service to consist in honest independence of judgment:

> Think'st thou that duty should have dread to speak,
> When power to flattery bows? To plainness honour's bound,
> When majesty stoops to folly;   (I. i. 149)

but that 'allegiance' itself, when directly invoked by his master, exacts obedience is, for him, a truth not open to question. Cordelia's devotion to the family 'bond' and Kent's acceptance of 'allegiance' are, in fact, twin aspects of the ordered sanity in which Lear's passion has opened a breach. The breaking of the more intimate relationship contains within itself the causes which, when projected against a vaster background, lead to the disruption of the social unity which provides the play with its 'universe'; but both proceed from the original breach opened by Lear's passion in the fabric of natural relationships, the evil consequences of which must work themselves out, as in *Macbeth*, through sorrow, disruption, and anarchy.

Having thus set forth in the opening scene the central tragic situation, Shakespeare proceeds to provide a comment upon it in the form of a parallel story. The story of Gloucester and his two sons, Edgar and Edmund, is clearly intended to bring out the deeper implications of Lear's own behaviour. Edmund, indeed, gives rational consistency to an attitude which proceeded in Lear from instinct and of the universal implications of which he was entirely unaware. Like Cordelia (and like no one else in this play), he shows from the outset a 'philosophy' of his own based on a consistent reading of 'nature'. Reacting against 'legitimacy', and therefore against the 'bond', in the name of 'nature', he gives a rational substance to the second of the two positions whose conflict is the theme of the tragedy. Cordelia's acceptance as supremely 'natural' of the bond that unites parent to child and is, in some sense, the reflection of universal order is set against Edmund's contrary reading of 'nature' in the light of his own origins. The law of 'nature' is replaced, from the point of view represented by Edmund's self-conscious sufficiency, his confidence in his own intelligence and drive, by the prejudice of 'legitimacy', itself a mere product of the 'plague of custom', of the 'curiosity of nations' (I. ii. 4), based upon nothing tangible or living in the order of things as interpreted by the dispassionate exercise of reason. Acting upon this interpretation of reality, Edmund first reverses the normal foundations of family life and then, with the unchecked craving for power that springs from his 'unprejudiced' nature, disrupts the accepted order of the state.

Behind Edmund's self-sufficiency, however, there lies a remarkable contradiction. Like Iago, his use of reason is a product of the passion which inspires him to revolt against sanctions which have, for him, no relationship to the sources of instinctive life. Edmund's 'philosophy', in fact, is itself the product of the breaking of the 'bond' which led originally to his begetting. A child of Gloucester's own disordered passion, traces of which survive to undo him in his senility, his destruction of the filial bonds imposed by 'nature' is a consequence of the 'natural' manner of his conception. The relation of Gloucester to his two sons constitutes a study, one of several in *Lear*, of the complexity implied in the term 'nature'. Edmund's 'natural' bastardizing destroys the still more natural relationship between the father and his trueborn son; in the same way passion, though 'natural' to the full development of man, may yet wreck the harmony of his experience and destroy his peace.

The situation thus set forth in these parallel opening episodes works out its consequences, in terms of disruption and disunity, during the first part of the play. Successively rejected by Goneril and Regan, the full effects of his previous disclaimers of 'propinquity and property of blood' emerge in Lear's passionate reaction against a 'reason', now itself deliberately self-seeking and self-determined, but nonetheless in a very real sense the child of his own error. It is the awareness of this error, indeed, and his obstinate refusal to admit it, that account between them for the explosion of violence which now takes possession of his whole being when confronted with Goneril. Appealing to 'nature', he prays that the natural fertility of his own daughter be suspended:

> Into her womb convey sterility;
> Dry up in her the organs of increase,
> And from her derogate body never spring
> A babe to honour her!   (I. iv. 302)

This curse, which proceeds from passion and calls upon 'nature', the source of instinct and spontaneous feeling, is nonetheless an attack on the natural fulfilment of passion: that is the heart of Lear's tragedy. The full extent of his departure from normal feeling is apparent a little later when we find him in his incoherent rage anticipating his reception by Regan. *She*, he is certain, will show herself 'kind and comfortable'; for that reason, on hearing of Goneril's behaviour:

> with her nails
> She'll flay thy wolfish visage.   (I. iv. 331)

This development of moral unreason in Lear is a clear sign of the tragic consequences wrought by passion in his nature. Its development is paralleled in the later history of his daughters, who are, as we have already seen, impelled to follow their father in a disregard of natural feeling which will lead them eventually to turn against one another over Edmund in the following of their individual desires. 'Appetite', upon which their apparently rational cruelty is grounded, makes them eventually rivals for the love of Gloucester's bastard son, and so prepares for their ruin. Once more, as in *Othello* and *Macbeth*, the evil elements in passion work themselves out to their natural conclusion, which is absolute disruption.

The encounter between Lear and Regan, which follows (II. iv), gradually works up to a climax with the appearance of Goneril and the complete agreement reached between the sisters. Towards the end of it, in the discussion after Goneril's arrival, Lear's palpable breaking down into the incoherence which precedes his madness is balanced by an equally evident growth in selfish ferocity on his daughters' part. Lear, on his side, touches with increasing frequency on images and ideas shortly to be revealed as essential to the play's deeper meaning; his utterances are a strange blend of dawning self-knowledge and wilful passion which finally breaks down into helplessness. In his last speech before leaving, he brings together into one utterance the conflicting emotions which are about, in their clash, to shatter his sanity:

> O, reason not the need: our basest beggars
> Are in the poorest thing superfluous:
> Allow not nature more than nature needs,
> Man's life is cheap as beasts: thou art a lady;
> If only to go warm were gorgeous,
> Why nature needs not what thou gorgeous wear'st,
> Which scarcely keeps thee warm. (II. iv. 267)

At this point we touch, almost for the first time, upon themes which the central part of the play, relating them to Lear's madness, will be concerned to develop. The conception of 'necessity', of the difference between 'true need' and that which passes for such in the accepted currency of society, has for some time been taking shape in the old man's distraught mind. Now, as his impotence comes finally home to him, it asserts itself as one of the principal themes to be exposed to the clarifying action of the coming tempest. The opening protest against the kind of 'reason' which his children have just turned upon him merges immediately, with a consideration of what is 'true need', into the social contrast which is one of the main features of the storm scenes. The true 'nature' of man, so Lear argues, requires 'superfluity', is distinguished by it from the beast, whose subjection to mere necessity is a sign of the cheapness of its life. The situation, however, contains a deep ambiguity, for the same superfluity which is a sign of his superior 'nature' can easily become, in man, attachment to the 'gorgeous', the merely superfluous, which leads in turn to the contrast between luxury, such as that shown by the sisters in their new pride of power, and the exposed misery of the beggar, who himself, nonetheless, is conscious of 'superfluous' necessities. The 'superfluity' which dignifies, humanizes the one leads, in short, to the arrogance and inhumanity of the other. The action of the tempest on Lear's consciousness, here indirectly anticipated in the references to 'warmth', will be needed before he learns to attach their true value to each of these two extremes. For the moment he passes on to a prayer for 'patience', itself caused by his grief and awareness of helplessness; but to this prayer is added a new desire to penetrate the obscure purposes of the 'gods' which will also be met in the storm. Thereafter the speech, under the renewed pressure of emotion, breaks down into a fragmentary intensity and finally into the first sinister awareness of coming madness. 'O fool, I shall go mad!' (II. iv. 289); it is no accident that this recognition, addressed to the Fool, who is, in a sense, the mirror of his own broken consciousness, is followed immediately by the first outburst of the gathering storm.

Under the shadow of the tempest the two opposed groups finally separate themselves out. 'Let us withdraw; 'twill be a storm,' urges Cornwall, and Regan and her sister are not slow to invoke the justifying voice of reason in support of their interest. 'The house is little'; ''Tis his own blame' (II. iv. 293); it is all impeccably logical, and—at the same time—completely inhuman. 'The king,' on the other hand, we are told by Gloucester, 'is in high rage.' His passions, prelude to lunacy, have gained the upper hand, and Cornwall rightly understands that, in this mood, he will be the instrument of his own destruction. ''Tis best to give him way; he leads himself' (II. iv. 301). In Regan's last comment this is developed further in words which, besides echoing the characteristically selfish moralizing of the speaker, contain a truth of the depth of which she is not herself aware:

> O, sir, to wilful men
> The injuries that they themselves procure
> Must be their schoolmasters.   (II. iv. 305)

That these words besides the speaker's obvious disclaimer of responsibility, have a connection with Lear's own growth in self-knowledge, his development in the tempest will show. Meanwhile, the doors are closed, and the worldly and the powerful come in, out of the 'wild night' and the approaching storm; the way is clear for a development of the central situation of the whole tragedy.

The third act of *King Lear*, which covers the storm and its counterpart in human behaviour, is a marvellous example of poetic elaboration for dramatic ends. At the centre of it, at once the main protagonist and symbol of the spiritual state of a humanity exposed to fundamental disorder, wrenched out of its 'fixed place' in the 'frame of nature', stands the figure of the aged king. The intimate dovetailing of personal conflict with external convulsions has often been noted, and is indeed an essential part of the conception. The storm which has broken out in Lear's mind, the result of his treatment at the hands of his children, is admirably fused with the description of the warring elements mainly entrusted to his lips; the external storm, while exercising upon his aged physique the intolerable strain under which it finally breaks, is itself a projection of his inner state, being fused with it as a single poetic reality. Thus related to the action of the elements, Lear clearly assumes a stature that is more than purely personal, becomes man, the microcosm of the universe, exposed to a suffering to which the frame of things itself contributes, but which finds its acutest symbol in the intimate disunion which the earlier action has introduced into the family bond.

The whole act is beautifully contrived around this central situation. If Lear has himself become 'unaccommodated man' (III. iv. 109), it is clearly felt that he is unable to bear alone the whole weight of the situation for which the tragic conception has destined him. He is, therefore, by a superb piece of dramatic tact, surrounded during his exposure to the elements by a number of characters who serve, as it were, as the external buttresses of a great architectural construction[24] to take from him some of the strain to which he would otherwise, as a dramatic conception, be subjected. It is the presence of these buttresses in *Lear* that are the best measure of the play's success, speaking in terms of artistic conception, when compared with a play which suggests a certain partial coincidence of mood, *Timon of Athens*.[25] Timon, seen in terms of the greater tragedy, is too isolated in his suffering, and his denunciation of the human environment is too extensive, too generalized, to carry complete conviction.[26] The situation of Lear is different.

Although he bears throughout the storm the main weight of suffering, and although his situation is, as I have suggested, a concentration of that of man in general, he is surrounded by beings who, in varying degrees, suffer with him, and who are further used, each in his appropriate way, to illuminate some aspect of his central situation. The Fool, Kent, and Edgar bear some fraction of Lear's tragic burden, show an insight into some part of its significance; and before the act ends, he is further joined by Gloucester, whose fortunes have been from the first evidently parallel to his own. The result is an intricate and progressive dovetailing of characters and situations which leads us, step by step, further and further into an understanding of the universal tragedy embodied in Lear's outraged fatherhood and shattered royalty.

Lear's first appearance in the storm shows him in the state of resentful denunciation which precedes the dawn of understanding. He calls upon the storm to execute upon 'nature', upon the whole universe, the curse of sterility he has already called down upon his daughters:

> Crack nature's moulds, all germins spill at once
> That make ingrateful man!   (III. ii. 8)

The root of his indignation, however, is still self-pity, still a sense of outrage at an 'unkindness', a lack of kinship, which he rightly feels to be contrary to nature, but whose relation to his own folly he does not yet grasp. The first step in bringing to light the deeper causes of his tragedy is taken through the Fool. In the relationship, during the tempest, between the King and his Fool, we have a clear case of those significant inversions of which this play is particularly fond. King and Fool, master and slave as they have so far been, now become, in the hour of Lear's helplessness, something very different; the bond between them grows ever closer and, in the inversion of Lear's mind, through which he sees himself, as it were, upside down, in reflection, we become aware of a deeper relation of contraries, that of the 'wise man' and the 'fool'. The essence of this relationship consists in a reversal of accepted values. The supposedly wise man of the opening scenes, the Lear who was in a position to have his slave whipped and to exercise his own will without fear of contradiction, has become, as his own acts have shown, the fool, and his former creature can now offer the comments of a practical, popular wisdom upon his behaviour and prospects. Yet both, like separated fragments of a single mind, have something in common. The Fool represents for 'royal Lear' the voice of reality which, to his own ruin, he sought to ignore, but which was somewhere present beneath his own favourable estimate of himself; and Lear, in turn, retains for the Fool at least part of that compelling authority which draws from him, even in his master's diminished state, a loyalty which his own disillusioned rationalism can hardly justify:

> The knave turns fool that runs away;
> The fool no knave, perdy. (II. iv. 85)

And both, in their divided unity, are bound together by common exposure to an external force that seems to pity 'neither wise man nor fool' (III. ii).

The Fool, moreover, soon penetrates beyond these obvious dramatic contrasts. In so doing, he enters directly into what we may call the subconscious ground of the play, bringing out motives which throw light upon Lear's behaviour but of which Lear himself, in his assumption of royal simplicity, has so far been quite unaware. The contrast between the 'wise man' and the 'fool' is seen in terms of a deeper conflict between controlling reason and a passion whose ultimate impulse is, as always, sexual. The Fool's own attitude to this contrast, and to the reversal of the state of 'nature' which is, in this play, connected with it, is characteristically ambiguous. Already in earlier scenes[27] his reason told him that the contrast between 'head' and 'heart' has an aspect which may be called social, can be interpreted as one between thrift, an economic foresight which is essentially self-regarding, and thriftless improvidence; the poor man who follows the promptings of natural instict, symbolized in the 'cod-piece', before he has made due provision against an evil day, is apt to find his whole being, 'head' and 'heart' alike, involved in a catastrophe which his rational faculties had no part in willing:

> The cod-piece that will house
> Before the head has any,
> The head and he shall louse;
> So beggars marry many. (III. ii. 27)

This saying reflects an ethic to which the whole of society, as pictured in *King Lear*, gives tacit assent. A more careful reading of this, one of the most significant of all his comments, will show, however, that the Fool himself does not regard his own statement as all the truth. At least part of his nature refuses to accept thrift as a supreme virtue; and so, in the second part of his rhyme, he shifts his ground deliberately, substituting

the contrast between 'head' and 'cod-piece' by another, not less close
to human nature, between 'heart' and 'toe', between proper feeling
and its unworthy caricature in unchecked indulgence. 'Head', 'heart',
and 'cod-piece', in fact, represent a triangular relationship which replaces the more superficial one between control and indiscipline, thrift
and improvidence, as a true reflection of the human situation.

The evident contradictions in human behaviour, personal and social,
can only be understood, in fact, by relating them to a reading of man's
nature which will carry us eventually beyond the Fool's vision of
reality, including it, but without being bound by its limitations. Of
this vision, indeed, his own words, reaching out beyond his normal
disillusioned realism, occasionally give a dim, broken indication. One
of these indications occurs precisely at this point, when the Fool, on the
entry of Kent, develops his point even more profoundly in the phrase
'here's grace and a cod-piece; that's a wise man and a fool' (III. ii. 40).
Wisdom and folly, rather than implying a contrast between reason and
passion, or still less between saving and spending, involves a deeper one,
which in turn illuminates the others, between 'grace', the state of
harmony in accordance with a 'natural' sanction, and the rebellious
'cod-piece'. The word 'grace', full of significance in Shakespeare's
later plays, here acquires something of its full meaning as expression of
a supernaturally sanctioned harmony; this harmony has been broken up
in Lear by the operation of a force based ultimately on the 'cod-piece',
on uncontrolled instinct operating outside the balanced order of
'nature' and leading, among other things, to improvident poverty. The
personal conflict is thus, by a further extension of significance, not only
related to its social consequences but given a universal spiritual content.

The next contribution to the expanding pattern of meaning is made
through Kent. With that solicitude for human frailty which is in him a
natural extension of loyalty, he emphasizes the incapacity of man's
'nature' to endure the action of the elements. Lear, in his reply, at once
stresses the existence of a fundamental unity between the external and
the inner commotion, the tempest in his mind and that which rages
without, and shows signs of a breaking coherence:

> the tempest in my mind
> Doth from my senses take all feeling else
> Save what beats there.   (III. iv. 12)

'Filial ingratitude' is conceived by him in terms of a bestial struggle
between the different parts of a single body:

> Is it not as this mouth should tear this hand
> For lifting food to it?   (III. iv. 15)

and from now on the imagery of beasts in conflict, of the human organism torn remorselessly apart as though by fang and claw, or by the pitiless action of the rack, will play an increasing part in the play. The 'concealing continents' (III. ii. 58) of man's nature, already invoked by Lear, are now being riven open, and the state of animal anarchy so revealed is no more than a physical projection of the 'guilts' which they normally cover. Under the strain imposed upon him by this spectacle Lear's own mental coherence visibly breaks down. Threats of undetermined future actions which he is obviously in no position to carry out ('I will punish home') alternate with assertions of his capacity to endure; these in turn are related to fresh expressions of self-pity ('In such a night as this! . . . Your kind old father'), and beneath these fragments of a once unified intelligence, present as a threat visibly approaching, lies the shadow of coming madness: 'O that way madness lies . . . No more of that!' (III. iv. 21).

Not all that is coming to the surface in Lear under the elemental pressure to which he is being exposed is negative. The distinctively human solicitude which is Kent's contribution to the total structure of the episode begins now to communicate itself to the aged King. After inviting the Fool to take shelter, he says: 'I'll pray, and then I'll sleep' (III. iv. 27). The content of his prayer is, in fact, new, represents the extension of his understanding to new areas of life. Its starting point is a new concern for the state of 'houseless poverty' inspired in him by contemplation of the Fool. Contemplating the pitiful state of those whose 'heads' are 'houseless' (once more, he is taking up concepts originally broached, in his characteristically enigmatic form, by the Fool) and whose 'sides' are 'unfed', he is brought to a fresh awareness of his own lack of understanding:

> O, I have ta'en
> Too little care of this!   (III. iv. 32)

and, as a reaction against it, to introduce more specifically than ever before a concern for justice. The elemental equity already invoked in previous scenes now gives way to a more clearly moral criterion, one which may even be described as concretely social. The contemplation of misery is a 'physic' for such 'pomp' as Lear himself has so far taken for granted; it leads, in terms of what we may call social morality, to a

desire to redress the balance of the superfluous well-being ('the super-
flux') of the privileged and thus—with tremendous daring—to show
the heavens more just.

It is at this point that the scope of the action is still further enlarged by
the entry of Edgar, in whom the state of 'houseless poverty' becomes a
visible reality. With his own nakedness confronted by that of Edgar, and
both subjected to the remorseless pressure of the elements, Lear's rapidly
awakening concern for 'justice' shows signs of shading into something
deeper, more universal. *King Lear* is a great tragedy precisely because
it is a play about human 'nature' before being a play about the abuses
of government or social inequality. It is this 'nature', indeed, that is
now being revealed, stripped and exposed to the prevailing 'cold' for
our consideration. The state of 'sophistication', through and beyond
which Lear now sees, is more than the mere pride of position or the
abuse of wealth. Both these things are, indeed, normal attributes of
human nature, part of the conventional superstructure with which man
seeks to hide even from himself his true character, as normal in their
own way as the garments which he owes to the brute creation and with
which he protects his otherwise 'uncovered body' from the 'extremity
of the skies' (III. iv. 105). To this state of false pretension the action of the
storm has come as a corrective. It has brought those exposed to it back
once more to the familiar but always forgotten truth that 'unaccommodated' man is no more but such a poor, bare 'forked animal' as Edgar.
This pitiable object is, by his own confession, a 'serving-man', at once
a courtier 'proud in heart and mind' (III. iv. 84) and a slave to his own
passions, who has now learned by bitter experience that it is a *'poor
heart'* which betrays itself to the transitory satisfactions of the flesh only
to find itself enveloped at the last—in accordance with Edgar's own
repeated catch—in the prevailing cold.

The confronting of Lear with Edgar, though an important stage in
the development of the main themes, is not an end in itself. It is the
prelude to a still more important meeting in which the two parallel
family histories with which *King Lear* is concerned are brought together and the two fathers whose behaviour has set them in motion
finally confronted. The Fool intervenes at this point with one of his
most significant observations. The occasion is in part Lear's frenzied
divesting of the 'lendings' which still differentiate him from elemental
humanity and in part the arrival on the scene of Gloucester, newly
moved to compassion. Gloucester, whose own past behaviour in the

begetting of Edmund is—like Lear's own—in the process of returning to him upon the whirlwind, has his own contribution to make to the general theme of passion. This is the meaning of the Fool's enigmatic greeting. Taking up the contrast, already developed by Edgar, between the brief fire of lust and the 'cold' which surrounds it, he is moved to see in the entry of Gloucester with a 'torch' a reflection of the fire of life blazing up briefly and ineffectively in the surrounding desolation: 'Now a little fire in a wild field were like an old lecher's heart, a small spark, all the rest on's body cold' (III. iv. 114). The 'old lecher' is clearly Gloucester himself and the 'little fire' the smouldering remains of the vitality which had formerly produced its 'unnatural' fruit in his illegitimate child. As a prelude to his meeting with Lear, the Fool's greeting emphasizes both the common, 'blood'-inspired source of their respective tragedies and the equally common helplessness with which they face it. Thus related in past behaviour, they are from now on envisaged as sharers in a common tragic destiny.

Gloucester's approaching sufferings, indeed, make him at this stage a fit commentator upon Lear's fortunes. Lear's recent outburst—

'Twas this flesh begot
Those pelican daughters— (III. iv. 73)

is fitly balanced by Gloucester's own situation with regard to his children; and, though he does not yet realize that the past sin of his own flesh is turning against him, he can already relate the disorders in man's behaviour to a corruption, a flaw in the fleshly fabric of human nature:

Our flesh and blood is grown so vile, my lord,
That it doth hate what gets it, (III. iv. 149)

and refer, in terms highly characteristic of this scene, to the son 'now outlaw'd from my blood'. In such utterances the 'embossed carbuncle' in the 'corrupted blood' to which Lear formerly referred in his denunciation of Goneril (II. iv. 227) is visibly working its way to the surface. At the same time, however, in Gloucester as in Lear, another development is simultaneously taking place. His new realization of what human nature may imply in terms of depth of degradation brings with it, at this very point, the beginnings of a saving reaction, a return to the natural concept of 'duty' which, in his own words, 'cannot suffer' to obey commands themselves unnatural. Edgar, in turn, touched more closely than ever by the appearance of his own father and aware of the full meaning of the tragedy which Gloucester is still unable to relate to his own situation, can only repeat his sense of the cold that surrounds human helplessness: 'Poor Tom's a-cold.' Once more the external, physical situation, conveyed through the words of one of those subjected to the tragic process, corresponds to the spiritual state of which it is the unadorned reflection. It is Edgar's persistence in grasping the naked truth that prompts Lear to hail him, at this very moment, as 'philosopher' and to inquire of him 'the cause of thunder' (III. iv. 159); the cause, that is, if any there be, of the pitiless intervention of nature to which all the actors in this episode are equally exposed. The elemental disorder which produces the thunder has its own psychological counterpart in the dissolution of sanity, and the scene ends with Kent referring once more to the oncoming of Lear's madness—'His wits begin to unsettle'—and Gloucester's parallel admission of the state to which the 'outlawing' of Edgar has brought him: 'I am almost mad myself . . . The grief hath crazed my wits' (III. iv. 170).

These points once established, Lear, after being sheltered by Gloucester from the action of the elements, passes on to a consideration, in the most ample terms, of the nature of 'justice' (III. vi). The execution of justice, indeed, is an essential part of the royal function, and Lear's torn mind when it recalls this fact is going back over the same range of responsibilities as he had once exercised to his own undoing. Now, with a complete reversal of the conventional values of society, the poor and the outcast, themselves seen as victims of an inadequate conception of justice, are raised to the position of executing ministers. The naked Edgar becomes 'thou robed man of justice', and the Fool, himself the living symbol of subjection to irresponsible power, his 'yoke-fellow of equity'; while those who have risen by their ruthlessness to the exercise of authority, who are 'gorgeously' clad, as indeed is the conventional judge in his robes, are now seen, stripped of their pretensions and with their subsistent animality exposed, as so many 'she-foxes'. The problem now presented, however, is not merely one of social categories. Behind the reversal of accepted standards of justice there lies a sense of the intractable, irreducible element of evil in human impulse with which justice itself has to deal. 'Let them anatomize Regan; see what breeds about her heart. Is there any cause in nature that makes these hard hearts?' (III. vi. 80). It is this question, rather than the extent of the personal disaster which has made it possible for him to pose it, that indicates the true extent of Lear's tragedy. A question less about the

nature of justice or its application to any particular situation than about
human nature itself, it lies at the heart both of Lear's madness and his
possible redemption. It creates a state of spiritual tension so deep that
the only possible transition from it is one into repose, sleep; and so it is
at this point that Kent calls upon his exhausted master to 'lie and rest
awhile' and that the Fool, having accompanied him to the lowest point
in his downward progress, now leaves him.

In the last episode of this central part of the tragedy (III. vii) the full
effects of the cruelty unleashed in human nature by passion are revealed
in terms of physical suffering. Gloucester, as a result of his concession to
natural human feeling in sheltering Lear, is apprehended on the charge
of treason, and Regan, Goneril, and Cornwall move round him with
an intensity which is clearly inspired by 'blood' and which reaches its
culminating point in the blinding of their helpless victim. The spectacle
of the suffering thus inflicted is almost intolerable, and only in relation
to the vast conception of the whole tragedy, in which it forms a
turning point, can its inclusion be justified. For it is no accident that the
moment in which Gloucester loses his sight, the victim of a gratuitous
act of evil, is also that in which the birth of his spiritual understanding
is confirmed. It is immediately after his blinding that he accepts his own
responsibility for the position in which he finds himself, in the light of
the knowledge, newly dawned, that the true son of his own blood,
whom he had believed to be a traitor, was in fact himself betrayed:

> O my follies! Then Edgar was abused.
> Kind gods, forgive me that, and prosper him!   (III. vii. 91)

When, at the same time, Cornwall's servant is moved to draw his
sword in protest against his master's savagery, and to lay down his life
in the name of common humanity and natural compassion, we must
feel ourselves to be at a turning-point of the entire action. These new
developments are, indeed, the exteriorization of a central paradox
implied in Shakespeare's use of the image of sight. Those who 'see',
who pride themselves on their clear-sighted appraisal of the world and
its ways, find themselves betrayed by their sight, are, in fact, in a very
real and tragic sense, blind; while those who have lost their eyes, or
whom their self-styled 'betters' may have regarded as incapable of
'vision', may, in the very moment of losing them, receive a flash of
moral illumination, in fact, 'see'. The achievement by Gloucester of
this kind of 'sight' at the moment of his blinding can only be compared

with the growth into moral insight, into understanding of the true human situation, that accompanies Lear's collapse into madness.[28]

At this stage in the development of his tragedy, Shakespeare was faced by an artistic problem of tremendous difficulty: the problem, that is, of balancing the disruption so thoroughly traced in the first part of the play by a harmony corresponding to that achieved in *Macbeth* in the second. The blinding of Gloucester represents the lowest depth reached in terms of physical action as a result of man's subjection to the bestial elements in his nature. The end of the storm is followed by a kind of lull in the emotional development of the tragedy, in which misery seems to pass into a Stoic resignation to the worst. As Edgar puts it:

> The lamentable change is from the best;
> The worst returns to laughter.   (IV. i. 5)

The mood is the only possible transition from the horrors we have just witnessed, and during it we become aware of two new developments. In the first place, the passion which has up to now impelled Goneril to ingratitude and cruelty now begins to ruin her own prosperity. She reveals her love for Edmund and her contempt for her husband ('My fool usurps my body'—the physical intensity is noteworthy), while Albany, appalled by her bestiality, turns upon her in language that itself suggests the beast:

> Were't my fitness
> To let these hands *obey my blood*,
> They are apt enough to *dislocate* and *tear*
> Thy flesh and bones.   (IV. ii. 63)

It is the development of *Macbeth* repeated, but now with an even higher degree of animal intensity; evil, having destroyed the foundations of order upon natural dependence, proceeds to destroy itself.

The second development at this stage is the reappearance of Cordelia, who introduces a type of poetry which, although it scarcely springs from anything yet noted in the play, at once assumes an essential part in it. Cordelia is first introduced in the description of a Gentleman, whose words initiate a harmonizing and healing element to balance the cruelty which has so far prevailed in the tragic action:

> patience and sorrow strove
> Who should express her goodliest. You have seen
> Sunshine and rain at once; her smiles and tears

> Were like a better way; those happy smilets
> That play'd on her ripe lip seem'd not to know
> What guests were in her eyes; which parted thence
> As pearls from diamonds dropp'd.   (IV. iii. 18)

One is struck at once by the tremendous range of imagery at the poet's disposal. Cordelia's sorrow is expressed in a whole series of comparisons few of which have a plain factual connection with the scene and emotions described; 'sunshine and rain', 'ripe lip', 'guests', 'pearls', and 'diamonds' are all connected with one another and with Cordelia less because of any visual image than because of the sense of value, of richness and fertility, which they impart. For the passage is moved by a presiding logic of its own. The struggle between the queen and her passions is now seen to be a strife between two emotions—'patience' and 'sorrow'—equally natural and worthy, each contributing to a 'goodly' expression of her nature. Her behaviour, in fact, is so normal, so spontaneous a manifestation of her virtues that it reflects the balance of nature in 'sunshine' and 'rain', each contributing to the single harmonious effect which presents itself as a 'better way', an indication of redemption; and this in turn causes us to feel no surprise when 'happy smilets' make their appearance, immediately below, as indicative of Cordelia's mood. 'Sunshine and rain', in turn, lead directly to the suggestion in 'ripe' of the maturing crops, and 'guests'—as in the first act of *Macbeth*—hints at the bounty which expresses itself in hospitality. Ripeness, again, indicates the riches implied in 'pearls from diamonds dropp'd'; these are 'rarities', and sorrow itself is in such a case less a tragic manifestation than a rarity enriching human nature, part of a harmony capable of being summed up in the terms of generous fulfilment already suggested in the phrase 'an *ample* tear trill'd down' and of being, in the most spiritual sense, 'beloved'. Last of all, by a final step profoundly characteristic of Shakespeare's late verse, Cordelia's tears become 'holy water' dropping from her 'heavenly eyes', and the poetical transformation of natural emotion into its spiritual distillation is complete.

To the norm of harmonious completeness thus established, the broken and partial experience of Lear looks as to its fulfilment. With his wanderings over, his condition is such that it is ready to receive the 'balm' of 'broken sinews'. The poetic expression of his suffering, indeed, is realized in Kent's account of his master's condition after his arrival at Dover:

A sovereign shame so elbows him: his own unkindness
That stripp'd her from his benediction, turn'd her
To foreign casualties, gave her dear rights
To his dog-hearted daughters: these things sting
His mind so venomously that burning shame
Detains him from Cordelia. (IV. iii. 44)

The changed quality of Lear's suffering is reflected in a new type of poetry, the natural response of his chastened humanity to the possibilities of transfiguration symbolized in Cordelia. The storm, with its sense of division, of the human body physically torn apart on the rack or defenceless under the teeth of beasts of prey, is superseded by the memory of a pain which is still intense but which may be—within those limits that life imposes—the prelude to restoration. Not only is his shame 'sovereign', at once the reaction of a king and his most rich and valuable emotion; not only is Lear's past 'unkindness' (in the sense of neglect of kinship) opposed to the harmony implied in the 'benediction' of which in the past he ruthlessly 'stripp'd' his daughter and to the possibility of which he is now painfully feeling his way back; but 'sting', 'venomously', and 'burning shame' suggest the cauterizing of a wound, as though his grief possessed a possible healing quality, were a necessary prelude to restoration. Read in conjunction with the overflowing fullness of Cordelia's emotion, the speech indicates that Shakespeare intends to balance the anarchy and cruelty of the first part of the play by a reconciliation of father and daughter in a natural and harmonious sublimation of their normal relationship.

Before the final meeting between Cordelia and the regenerated Lear, however, the play turns back once more to take up, and in a sense to summarize, its presentation of human suffering (IV. vi). The external purpose, so to call it, of the scene is to bring together Lear and Gloucester. The latter, brought to the limits of his endurance on the verge of Dover cliff (the fact that his lofty perch is imaginary, that its 'dizzy' heights exist only in Edgar's imagination, emphasizes the symbolic quality of the situation), turns away from his attempted suicide with a declaration that he has learned his lesson:

henceforth I'll bear
Affliction till it do cry out itself
'Enough, enough' and die. (IV. vi. 76)

This, no doubt, is still less a positive attitude than the preliminary foundation upon which such an attitude may be built. Gloucester's words contain as yet nothing to connect him with the positive experience which will emerge from the entirely different spirit of the reconciliation scene; but the thoughts which will henceforth occupy him, 'free' because liberated from the baser temptations of despair and 'patient' because acceptance, even in obscurity, is the necessary prelude to understanding, have their own place in the development of the play.

The entry of Lear, which immediately follows, serves to give final expression to the anguish with which the whole tragedy has been so heavily charged. At its culminating point the reaction of the aged King to the unnatural behaviour of his daughters universalizes itself, to take shape finally in an assertion of the dual nature of woman:

> Down from the waist they are centaurs,
> Though women all above:
> But to the girdle do the gods inherit,
> Beneath is all the fiends'.   (IV. vi. 127)

The light thus thrown on the dark and hidden nature of man's impulses, for which so much in the earlier action has prepared us, also illuminates Lear's own situation. It leads finally to his desire to 'sweeten' his imagination when confronted with behaviour which, like his own hand, 'smells of mortality' (IV. vi. 137). In his madness he is penetrating far more deeply than in his apparent sanity to the roots in universal human frailty of his own situation. His apparent obsession represents in fact, the elimination of a mental poison, the purgation of unclean impulses from the spirit which cannot, while they are still present, receive the saving visitation of sleep. Exposing instincts which normally remain hidden under the 'simperings' of affected 'virtue' and the pretentious garb of current social behaviour, he reveals, beyond his own infirmity and that of the society over which he formerly ruled, the true state of man by which Gloucester has been brought to blindness and himself to the condition in which we see him. If the contemplation of this state brings the speaker to the verge of moral disintegration, that is a necessary part of the complete pattern of the tragedy which must precede any conceivable restoration of harmony. The pressure of emotion at this point, besides twisting its expression into incoherent forms, is such that even the sightless Gloucester feels himself to be in the presence of a 'ruin'd piece of nature' (the universal implications of Lear's state could hardly be more explicitly stated) and anticipates that,

under the pressure of such concentrated emotion, the 'great world'
itself, of which Lear is so consistently the microcosm, will wear itself
out to 'nought'.

With Gloucester and Lear once more united in the contemplation of
the tragic experience which has brought them together, and with both,
as King and courtier, subdued to an acceptance of their dimly conceived
destinies, the way is at last open for a restoration of natural harmonies.
The scene in which this takes place is, from the point of view of
Shakespeare's capacity to unite the dramatic and poetic elements with
which he is working, the most advanced in the play. It is full of the
'symbolism' which from now on plays an increasing part in the poet's
work, a 'symbolism' which is not imposed upon the dramatic development but which springs from and completes it. Given the extraordinary
freedom, the breadth of reference which everywhere characterizes the
verse of this play, it is only a step further to introduce effects that are not
strictly part of the development of the drama, but which the unprecedented control of the poet succeeds in welding organically into the total
effect. 'Sleep' we have already found to form part of a 'symbolic'
effect of this kind; and Shakespeare now adds music, with its associations of harmony, and 'fresh garments', suggesting the purification
accomplished in Lear by the immersion of past sorrows into repose.
The Doctor calls upon music at the moment of Lear's awakening, and
Cordelia prays for his 'restoration' in language which relates the musical
symbol of harmony to the revival of unity and health in the torn and
divided personality:

> O, you kind gods,
> Cure this great *breach* in his abused nature;
> The *untuned* and jarring senses, O, wind up
> Of this child-changed father! (IV. vii. 14)[29]

By such means Lear's suffering is transformed, made into a condition of
his revival. When his awakening takes place, it comes little by little,
covering the bitter memories of the past by an incoming tide of fresh
emotions. We can feel this most clearly of all in his first exclamation of
wonder:

> Thou art a soul in bliss; but I am bound
> Upon a wheel of fire, that mine own tears
> Do scald like molten lead. (IV. vii. 46)

This at once looks back to past experience, to the 'burning shame' which, earlier in the act, had 'stung' him and kept him from Cordelia,[30] and indicates a fresh spiritual development. Lear's difficulty in believing that he really sees his daughter before him indicates both the depth and the remoteness of what he has passed through; the suggested idea of resurrection ('You do me wrong to take me out of the grave') contributes to the same effect. So, in a different way, does the sense of compassion which prompts him, in the moment of his awakening, to say:

> I should e'en die with pity,
> To see another thus,   (IV. vii. 53)

and which is an echo, like the combination of shattered pathos and fresh understanding which prompts his 'I am a foolish, fond old man,' of the humanity he has learned in his exposure to the tempest. Lear, in other words, still suffers on the 'wheel of fire' to which the consequences of his own passion and folly originally bound him, but his grief no longer springs from division, from the 'embossed carbuncle' in his own 'corrupted blood' which produced Regan and Goneril; it has become such that it can, for the first time and briefly, precariously, contemplate 'a soul in bliss'.

For the length of this scene, then, Shakespeare has succeeded in balancing the suffering of the first part of his play with an adequate harmony fulfilled in terms of external symbolism through Cordelia's prayer for 'benediction' and Lear's corresponding confession of guilt:

> I know you do not love me; for your sisters
> Have, as I do remember, done me wrong:
> You have some cause, they have not.   (IV. vii. 73)

This is the central moment of reconciliation, full of significance for an understanding not only of *King Lear*, but of the whole pattern of Shakespeare's later work. The restoration of the original relationship of child to father is the resolution of the ruin caused by 'blood' in the unity of the family. Two features of this development are especially worthy of note. In the first place, Lear, while still remembering his past experiences, looks back to them, as it were, across a great gap of intervening time, sees them as belonging to another world; in the second, his new state is explicitly described in terms of a spiritual rebirth. 'Thou art a soul in bliss,' 'You are a spirit, I know': such phrases, added to the sense of a break in temporal continuity—

> it is danger
> To make him e'en go o'er the time he has lost—   (IV. vii. 79)

have a double effect. They at once stress the spiritual meaning of Lear's new state by placing it outside the temporal process and show that it is not of this world, that in this world, indeed, it may even be cruelly interrupted. The achievement of a state which is that of 'souls in bliss' does not necessarily involve the end of exposure to suffering. If the spiritual life of Lear and his daughter is situated, from now onwards, on a level which is not that of the political action, the passions which move that action still have to work themselves out, and even annihilate the main protagonists, in the last part of the tragedy.

In the sphere of political action and worldly success, indeed, the course of events moves to a conclusion which seems to make no concession to the glimpses of newly found intuition thus hardly won. If these have validity (and this is a question which the play seems to leave deliberately open), it is on another and apparently unrelated level. The final battle seems to leave Edmund in full and undisputed control of events. To his order that the aged king and his daughter should be removed to prison, Cordelia can only reply with her determination to 'outfrown false fortune's frown' (V. iii. 6) and with the profound moral integrity implied in her quiet 'Shall we not see these daughters and these sisters?' If her attitude denotes a characteristic mastery, it is on a moral rather than on a practical level. Lear's response, equally typical of his new, 'resurrected' state, is more pathetic, in a sense even more sentimental in kind. Life for him has been entirely concentrated, since his recovery, upon the reconciliation with his daughter; and prison itself, while he is with her, is the whole of his universe. In this spirit he takes up once more the theme of paternal blessing and filial forgiveness which lies at the heart of the central symbolic situation:

> When thou dost ask me blessing, I'll kneel down
> And ask of thee forgiveness, (V. iii. 10)

and looks back, as though across the infinite distance imposed by the experience through which he has lately passed, at the 'gilded butterflies' and 'court news' which had once, in what seems a barely conceivable remoteness, meant so much to his headstrong nature. As Lear speaks at this point he is at once broken by his sufferings and beyond being affected by them. The speech moves from the gentle irony which enables the old man to contemplate the coming imprisonment of himself and his daughter in a spirit of tranquil acquiescence to the assertion, at once intensely moving and charged with a disturbing defiance, that

He that parts us shall bring a brand from heaven,
And fire us hence like foxes. (V. iii. 22)

The whole episode creates, as it were, an island of peace, precariously isolated in a world of iron. Lear has attained, at the expense of his own broken nature, a vision of spiritual acceptance; but across it, present if no longer uniquely so, lies the shadow of the way of the world.

The reconciliation thus realized in this moment of intense feeling, indeed, is not maintained. Reunited with Cordelia under the eyes of their captors, Lear has spoken to his daughter, with a kind of ironic nostalgia, of taking upon themselves

the mystery of things,
As if we were God's spies; (V. iii. 16)

but in fact, of course, neither Lear nor any other man has valid reason to pretend to so much. We have been engaged in an exploration of the human condition as it is under its tragic aspect, not working out a comforting moral doctrine of redemption through suffering; and so, such insights as have been gained in the course of the action fail to maintain themselves in the face of external pressure. The world is still hostile, almost intolerably cruel, in its treatment of the exhausted protagonists. The armies of Cordelia are defeated by Edmund, now undisputed master of the political action; and, though it is true that he finally dies in meeting the challenge of the disguised Edgar, his death does not take place until Cordelia has been hanged by his order. The whole of the final episode is set under the sign of dissolution, which is indeed the only possible outcome of sufferings so intolerably heavy and so protractedly borne. To conclude it, Lear enters for the last time 'with Cordelia dead in his arms' and in a world dominated by a double sense of darkness and emotional petrifaction, which finds its presistent echo in the words of the victims ('O! you are men of stones'; 'Fall and cease'; 'All's cheerless, dark, and deadly'), the curtain falls. Lear, finally reconciled to his daughter in adversity, himself dies with her body in his arms, gaining in death the only relief conceivable in temporal terms from the 'rack of this tough world', the course of which has proved so consistently indifferent to the spiritual intuitions which suffering itself has brought so painfully to birth. Kent, loyal to the end, anticipates in his own last words the 'journey' in which he is shortly to follow his master. and Edgar is left by Albany with the mission of sustaining 'the gored state' in a spirit in which exhaustion and sincerity, purged of all excessive pretensions by the contemplation of the sufferings just witnessed, join hands in a gesture of mutual sustainment.

4 Timon of Athens

It is tempting in some ways to think of *Timon of Athens* as a kind of appendix to *King Lear*. As such, it can hardly fail to suffer in the comparison. The direct, unvaried line of its action, concentrated on the hero's fall from greatness, must seem to lack the wealth of contrast which marks the earlier tragedy: the accumulated invective in which Timon expresses his disillusionment, his final rejection of life, must strike us, from the standpoint of the greater play, as excessive, one-sided, and monotonous. It is perhaps more useful, however, to see *Timon of Athens* as a play essentially different in kind from *Lear*. The comparative simplicity of its structure recalls certain features of the morality play, and its hero's excesses, both of generosity and disillusionment, are at least as much ironic as tragic in the impression they make upon us. Seen in this way, we can respond to a Shakespeare not engaged in repeating himself, but in contriving a new kind of dramatic action, an experiment which, though not entirely successful, is nonetheless the work of a great poet writing at the height of his unique powers.

The court in which Timon, as the action opens, exercises his 'magic of bounty' (I. i. 6) is clearly a reflection of the world, the ways of which are amply familiar to those who live in and by it. 'How goes the world?' asks the poet, and receives from his fellow-artist in counterfeit an answer—'It wears, sir, as it grows'—which is a commonplace of disillusioned experience. In this world both artists, creatures dedicated to the pursuit of self-advancement through flattery, are thoroughly at home. Their attitude to their respective arts is characteristically ambivalent, combines genuine appreciation of skill and civilized polish with the limiting implications of artifice cultivated as an end in itself or as a means to material advancement. The Poet praises the Painter for bringing out in his picture Timon's superhuman virtues—his 'grace', his 'big imagination', his 'mental power'—all real and impressive human qualities by the exploitation of which, however, both artists live and which are accordingly limited by a persistent impression of artificiality; for the picture is, as the Poet also sees, 'a pretty *mocking* of the life', an '*artificial* strife' which 'lives' indeed 'in these touches', but lives after a fashion suspiciously 'livelier than life' (I. i. 39).

In this way we are prepared for a realistic estimate of Timon's eminence, the situation in which his nature, recognized to be 'good and spacious', exercises a fascination as universal as it is finally suspect. 'You see,' explains the Poet,

> how all conditions, how all minds,
> As well of *glib and slippery creatures* as
> Of grave and austere quality, tender down
> Their services to Lord Timon; his *large fortune*,
> Upon his *good and gracious nature* hanging,
> Subdues and properties to his love and tendance
> All sorts of hearts.   (I. i. 53)

At this point Timon's court is seen to be nothing less than a reflection of the 'world', of society itself: a world dominated, as the Poet's parable goes on to stress, by the shifting vagaries of fortune, so that those who so readily follow Timon in his moment of exaltation, who are so suspiciously ready to

> Rain sacrificial whisperings in his ear,
> Make *sacred* even his stirrup, and *through him*
> *Drink the free air*,   (I. i. 82)

will follow the 'shift and change' of his mood and finally abandon him in his fall. Once more this reflects not merely a particular situation, but, as the Painter's comment makes clear, a universal law of life: ''Tis common.'

The presentation of Timon himself in these initial scenes is marked by a similar ambivalence. It is at once his virtue and his fault to be unaware of the precarious nature of his situation. His attitude towards those around him is marked by a true generosity, which expresses itself in images of conviviality and feasting—'We must needs dine together,' he tells the Painter—and in the encouragement of young love against the Old Athenian's depreciation of 'levity' in youth. In so far as these things are an expression of human solidarity we must respond to Timon's readiness to give away in bounty the 'jewel' which he values for its beauty, to affirm in friendship a genuine positive of life:

> I am not of that feather to shake off
> My friend when he must need me;   (I. i. 101)

but we must also see these things against the play's persistent equation
of art with artifice—'The painting is almost the natural man'—and the
hero's own tendency to equate 'bounty' with the sharing of 'pleasure'.
The contrasted attitude of Apemantus, in whom 'plain dealing' is a
reflection of inverted pride and in whom a realistic estimate of flattery
expresses itself through the hatred of society itself—

> That there should be small love 'mongst these sweet knaves,
> And all this courtesy! The strain of man's bred out
> Into baboon and monkey— (I. i. 259)

is there to balance excess with excess, the generosity that degenerates
into self-indulgence with a moralizing that ultimately implies the
negation of sociability itself. This is a world in which the sense of life
is turned persistently to suspect ends, in which Alcibiades can give a
peculiar twist to the imagery of banqueting—'I *feed* most hungerly on
your sight'—in which the attendant Lords '*taste* Lord Timon's bounty'
and hold that each of his apparently inexhaustible gifts will

> *breed* the giver a return exceeding
> All use of quittance. (I. i. 291)

It is, of course, 'gold' that so 'breeds' in an unnatural parody of life,
and the product will soon be shown to be, like the society which hangs
upon it, finally sterile. It is a sufficient comment on Timon's celebrated
'nobility'—

> The *noblest* mind he carries
> That e'er governed man— (I. i. 292)

that its celebration is persistently set in the mouths of those who are
clearly revealed as flatterers and timeservers.

Timon's ambiguous relation to an equivocal society finds its fitting
projection in the banquet which reflects his generosity. Timon, in offering it, stresses the unilateral quality of his gesture—

> there's none
> Can truly say he gives, if he receives— (I. ii. 10)[31]

and adds the more dubious conviction of the profligate when he affirms
that 'faults that are rich are fair'. Apemantus, who is universally regarded as 'unfit for society', is present to turn the prevailing imagery of
banqueting and participation to opposite ends. In this he is no doubt
moved by a misanthropy that is negative, life-destroying; but there is

sinister meaning in his implacable vision of Timon's associates as
'eating' him and in his insistent use of imagery that carries religious
implications of sacrifice and betrayal:

> It grieves me to see so many dip their meat in one man's blood . . .
> the fellow that sits next him now, parts bread with him . . . is the
> readiest man to kill him.   (I. ii. 42)

We shall not, of course, underrate the sardonic element in these
comments, or accept this bitter moralizing at its own estimate of
superior, detached insight. Apemantus' realism clearly rests on an excess
of selfishness that stands at the opposite extreme from Timon's 'generosity' and represents an attitude equally tainted; his conclusion 'I pray
for no man but myself' (I. ii. 65) is as limited, finally as self-stultifying,
as the facile open-handedness it justly condemns. When Apemantus
announces, in a mood akin to self-congratulation, that he will never
'trust man on his oath or bond', it is in the last resort nothing less than
humanity, in himself and others, that he is rejecting; and much the
same can be said, in a different way, of Alcibiades when he grotesquely
introduces into these convivialities a note of cannibalism in expressing
the soldier's pleasure in his blood-letting vocation:

> *Timon:*   You had rather be at a breakfast of enemies than a dinner of friends.
> *Alcibiades:* So they were bleeding-new, my lord, there's no meat like 'em.
>   (I. ii. 80)

In such a situation, the most unexceptionable sentiments become tinged
with irony. When Timon is moved to declare that he has often wished
himself 'poor' so as thereby to 'come nearer' his friends, the statement
has to be weighted against his evident inability to see these 'friends' as
they really are. When he utters his conviction that generosity lies at
the basis of all sociable living—'We are born to do benefits; and what
better or properer can we call our own than the riches of our friends?'
(I. ii. 107)—he is at once uttering a true law of life, a concept upon
which the very possibility of society is ultimately founded, and reflecting with unconscious irony upon his own future. For, beneath all
its surface of lavish splendour, the spirit of Timon's banquet is suspect.
The masque of Cupid, offered by the host as the culmination of his
feast, stresses a connection finally dubious between the 'bounty' so
abundantly revealed and the 'five senses'—

th'ear,
Taste, touch, and smell, pleased from thy table rise—   (I. ii. 133)

whilst there is a note of complacency, of easy self-satisfaction, in Timon's
own dismissal of what he calls his 'idle banquet'.

It is at this point, indeed, that ominous forebodings begin to make
themselves felt. The satiated Lords rise from the table with 'much
adoring' of their host, who speaks with glib facility of 'pleasures' and
'fair fashion', confusing the lavish surface of social entertainment with
true generosity. Apemantus foresees the future when he says that 'Men
shut their doors against a setting sun,' and Timon's faithful steward
Flavius condemns more explicitly his master's lack of foresight: ''Tis
pity bounty had not eyes behind.' His expressions of foreboding, and
the first open reference to Timon's 'debts', are momentarily drowned
in the finally self-gratifying gesture of Timon himself:

> Methinks I could deal kingdoms to my friends,
> And ne'er be weary.   (I. ii. 229)

When he turns to Apemantus to reprove him for railing against
'society', our reaction must be conditioned by these intimations of
ruin. Timon is at once making a valid criticism of the negative, inhuman 'virtue' which he feels to be the opposite of his own, and
brushing aside a true warning in a spirit of final irresponsibility.

The following scenes, which show these premonitions turning into
reality, have about them much of the 'morality' quality so marked in
this play. Timon's creditors are barely distinguished in terms of
character. They are rather presented as abstract representatives of greed
and selfishness, and as such contribute to the main patterns of imagery
which convey the sense of the action. The First Senator, describing
Timon's state in terms of fever, speaks of 'raging waste' and equates
his generosity with the breeding of gold:

> steal but a beggar's dog
> And give it Timon, why, the dog coins gold.   (II. i. 5)

The critical intention is apparent in the sardonic phrase, and clearly
answers to a truth; but the critic's own emphasis is throughout on
selfishness, on '*my* needs', '*my* turn': as he concludes,

> I love and honour him,
> But must not break my back to heal his finger.   (II. i. 23)

As the creditors, like so many vultures, gather round their declining patron, the faithful Flavius expresses in realistic terms the excess and indulgence which have constituted the reverse side of his master's generosity:

> When all our offices have been oppress'd
> With riotous feeders, when our vaults have wept
> With drunken spilth of wine, when every room
> Hath blazed with lights and bray'd with minstrelsy.   (II. ii. 168)

In the light of this it is important to avoid all identification with Timon,[32] to realize that his 'generosity' and the greed which feeds upon it are opposite excesses, made for one another and sharing a common disregard for proper human measure. Timon, thus reproached for prodigality, justifies himself with a certain complacency— 'Unwisely, not ignobly have I given' (II. ii. 184)—and clings to what is by now clearly his illusion of human solidarity. At bottom it is reality, both in himself and in those around him, that he is unwilling to contemplate.

It is not long, however, before reality forces itself upon him. As 'policy', barefaced self-interest, asserts itself with increasing urgency among his creditors, his remaining friends stress the malady that has affected sociability itself, the turning of 'nutriment' into 'poison' and 'disease', and return once more to the persistent sense of intimate betrayal:

> Who can call him
> His friend that dips in the same dish?   (III. ii. 73)

When Timon himself appears, it is to show that his surface 'nobility' has broken down into the hysteria that expresses itself in the injunction to 'Cut my heart in sums', 'Tell out my blood', 'Tear me' (III. iv); we are evidently faced now with the downfall of an excessive, finally a self-admiring confidence. The breakdown in Timon is seen in turn in relation to a larger flaw in society. Against the passionate and one-sided pursuit of martial honour by Alcibiades is set the frosty assertion of 'justice' on the part of impotent old age in authority, the conviction— as coldly stated by a senator—that 'Nothing emboldens sin so much as mercy' (III. v. 3). In this conviction, the senators are ready to exercise brutally against Alcibiades and his protégé such authority as they have— 'the law shall *bruise* him' (III. v. 4)—only to be faced by a warrior who is ready to commit his power to the contrary position—'pity is the virtue of the law'—and to assert, but in one-sided passion, the '*noble*

fury' and 'fair spirit' of the friend he is determined to save. The conflict
between passionate action and frigid control, over-confident youth and
impotent old age in authority, is a genuine one, but it is characteristic
of the society of this play that it should be pushed to destructive excess
on either side. On the one hand, we have the intransigent execution of a
law conceived in abstraction from human reality—'We are for law; he
dies'—by those who are incapable of sharing the generous, if uncontrolled impulses of passionate youth; on the other, the revolt of
passion itself, which, whilst purporting to reflect a generous reaction—

> Banish your dotage; banish usury,
> That makes the senate ugly— (III. v. 101)

leads the speaker to turn upon his own countrymen and to let loose
upon society the ruinous excesses of civil strife.

Timon's 'banquet', which follows at this point (III. vi), is placed
deliberately at the centre of the entire action. It contains a sardonic
parody of all the 'sociable' feasting which, in happier days, accompanied his largesse; and it culminates in a rejection of mankind which
is at once justified by his betrayal and provides a confirmation of his
excess, of the extent of his human failure. From now on, lust and
'appetite' are obsessively joined in Timon's mind; seeing his former
friends reduced to the status of beasts—'Uncover, *dogs*, and lap' (III. vi.
96)—he thanks the 'gods' for their revelation of human iniquity, and
sees humanity itself deprived of its distinctive attributes. It is significant
that, as the obsession with 'disease' replaces his former too easy generosity, Timon falls into a phrasing which echoes the misanthropy of
Apemantus:

> Of man and beast the infinite malady
> Crust you quite o'er. (III. vi. 109)

'Man and all humanity' have become, for Timon, the object of a repudiation as excessive and one-sided as his former generosity had been.
The astonished Lords are not far from the truth when they see his
behaviour as a collapse into insanity and point to the contradiction
which has led him to swing from one extreme to its opposite: 'One day
he gives us diamonds, next day stones' (III. vi. 131).

By the end of this crucial scene Timon's distinctively human, sociable
career is ended. The second half of the play brings him to the fate which
this unnatural detachment from his fellow men makes inevitable, and
at the same time shows the public conflict worked out, beyond civil

war, to a kind of restoration under Alcibiades. The great outbursts of misanthropy which mark these later scenes, and which have led to the comparison with *Lear*, need to be seen in their true ambivalence. As exposures of a corrupted and inhuman world they are true; but they are also the inevitable reverse of Timon's finally complacent prodigality. One excess leads to its opposite, and it is no accident that the main content of Timon's first long speech after the 'banquet' he has just staged is an attack upon 'degree', order, finally on the possibility of social existence itself. Timon, indeed, echoes the negative side of Lear's explosions of revulsion against humanity, but—we must add—can show less cause for it, less capacity to learn from an experience to which, finally, his own folly and lack of understanding have exposed him.

In view of this, we shall not underestimate the degree of negation, of sheer perverse destructiveness, which make themselves felt in Timon's tirades. To raise 'slaves and fools' to a position of ministering authority amounts to a parody of Lear's corresponding investment of the Fool and Edgar[33] with the attributes of justice; the connection of ideas exists, but the final result is, in Timon, ironic in its effect, whereas in Lear compassion and understanding are present beneath the crazed inversion. Shakespeare, once more, is not repeating himself. To incite 'the son of sixteen' to renounce 'piety and fear' and to turn 'degrees, observances, customs and laws' to their 'confounding contraries', so that mere 'confusion' may prevail; all this is *not*, in Shakespearean terms, to play the part of a moralist, however justly severe, but rather to indulge the hatred that represents the reverse side of Timon's 'generosity', that has always been present *as a possibility* in him and that has only been clothed in the garb of a facile sociability. Like Lear at certain moments, but more obsessively and one-sidedly, Timon in his madness indulges instincts which are finally anti-social, destructive of humanity itself; but, unlike Lear, no real degree of recovery is open to him, and only annihilation, the final exhaustion of any kind of human emotion, awaits him at the last. Only to a diseased imagination, interpreting an equally diseased society, can 'the unkindest beast' appear 'more kinder than mankind' (IV. i. 36); instead of seeking to read into Shakespeare's conception of Timon some kind of 'personal' crisis of despair, we shall do well to follow the stages by which a finely balanced imagination works itself out in terms of irony and contrast.

This, however, does not mean that we should refuse all pity to Timon. The faithful Flavius follows his master, as Kent followed Lear making a valid assertion of loyalty when all but loyalty has been lost; and Flavius accordingly, in a world which is made up of 'wolves'—and this here because it *is* so made up, not, as elsewhere in this play, because Timon *needs* to feel it to be such—is capable of seeing the hero's situation with a measure of true compassion:

> his poor self,
> A dedicated beggar to the air,
> With his disease of all-shunned poverty,
> Walks, like contempt, alone. (IV. ii. 12)

The servants too, who—again as in *King Lear*[34]—are more morally sensitive than their supposed betters, see Timon's end, and their own with it, in a common annihilation:

> we must all part
> Into this sea of air; (IV. ii. 21)

and because their feeling for the human situation is a true one, Flavius can salute them as 'fellows', describe them as 'rich in sorrow, parting poor', and so assert that very fellow feeling which Timon, whom his world has rejected, is so spectacularly engaged in renouncing. This is the answer, in terms of normal human experience, to Timon's own preceding prayer, in which he begs that

> as Timon grows, his hate may grow
> To the whole race of mankind, high and low. (IV. i. 39)

To fail to give due weight to this contrast is to destroy the true balance of Shakespeare's conception.

The scene which now follows (IV. iii), the longest in the play, amounts to a dissection, an exposure of Timon's attitudes in relation to a world which he has too readily accepted and which has now rejected him. As it opens, he is engaged in projecting his obsessions in an ever vaster scale upon the entire universe. 'Infection', 'rotten humidity', poison in his imagination the process of 'breeding', of life itself. This is a product of madness and an exposure of fundamental unbalance, though it is also true, and relevant, that Timon follows the mad Lear in his penetration of merely external social distinctions—

> Raise me this beggar and deny't that lord— (IV. iii. 9)

and in his perception of the universality of 'flattery'. 'The learned pate ducks to the golden fool': we must feel that there is truth here, though also and side by side with it excess in the generalization that 'all is oblique,' that

> There's nothing level in our cursed natures
> But direct villainy, (IV. iii. 19)

and in the conclusion that sociable living itself—'*All* feasts, societies, and throngs of men'—is to be 'abhorred', that the only solid conclusion about life is that contained in the perverse and finally ridiculous prayer: 'Destruction fang mankind.' This may be, and indeed is, the working out of a state of disease, the mirror of perverse possibilities that certainly exist in life; but it cannot be, and is not intended to be, a conclusive judgment on life itself. When he rejects 'gold' for 'roots' Timon is finally caricaturing himself, joining his shadow Apemantus in a common excess.

At this point, appropriately, the world intrudes upon Timon as Alcibiades approaches in the company of his whores. The conjunction implies a comment on 'blood', youthful passion and violent self-assertion, and Timon reacts to it by declaring himself 'misanthropos', a hater of mankind. In this he is again excessive, though he sees truly the vanity of what is offered him:

> Follow thy drum;
> With man's blood paint the ground, gules, gules: ·
> Religious canons, civil laws are cruel;
> What then should war be? (IV. iii. 58)

and relates the state of war to the individual's consuming passion for 'this fell whore of thine'. This is true and valid, if embittered, comment; but in Timon's following catalogue of diseases, and in his obsessive determination to cut himself off from his fellows, it is again a kind of inverted pride that prevails to grotesque and impossible ends. As a comment on the vanity of civil war, his conclusion,

> Make large confusion; and, thy fury spent,
> Confounded be thyself! (IV. iii. 128)

is fair enough; but it is also the product of a crazed and resentful mind, which is in turn exposed to a culminating irony when those whom he has rejected press him for the 'gold' they still hope to obtain from him. In this Alcibiades, exposing another aspect of his 'heroic' pretensions, leads the way—

> Hast thou gold yet? I'll take the gold thou givest me,
> Not all thy counsel— (IV. iii. 130)

to be joined, in sardonic echo of the warrior hero's greed, by the shrill
importunities of his accompanying prostitutes: 'Give us some gold,
good Timon: hast thou more?' (IV. iii. 133)

As Timon, in his increasingly crazed reaction, stresses his obsession
with prostitution—'Be strong in whore'—and with the idea of disease
that so persistently accompanies it, his vision of 'gold' as the ultimate
source of death finds an echo approaching the farcical in the demands of
those who hear him: 'More counsel with more money, bounteous
Timon!' The crowning irony is reached when Apemantus at last joins
the others and accuses Timon of imitating him:

> men report
> Thou dost affect my manners, and dost use them: (IV. iii. 199)

two extreme, and equally unacceptable attitudes, which meet here in
their common rejection of society; Apemantus, not without a certain
bitter truth, finds Timon's nature 'infected', ascribes his misanthropy,
not to any genuine moral attitude, but to the mere shock of his 'change
of fortune', the exposure of his former lavishness, upon an ill-prepared
mind. He advises Timon, with further appropriate irony, to assume the
behaviour of the 'flatterers' who so gratified him in former days, and
concludes with an uncomfortable truth—

> Thou gavest thine ears like tapsters that bid welcome
> To knaves and all approachers—

and draws the bitter conclusion:

> 'tis most just
> That thou turn rascal; hadst thou wealth again,
> Rascals should have't.   (IV. iii. 216)

The culmination of irony is reached when Apemantus, rubbing the
salt further into Timon's wound, stands on his dignity to reject him:
'Do not assume my likeness.'

Here, however, Apemantus in turn overreaches himself. His 'virtue'
has consistently lacked any sign of the generosity which Timon, in
however inadequate a form, presented to the world. He too deserves
the retort he receives: 'Were I like thee, I'ld throw myself away'
(IV. iii. 220). The two, both outcasts, though for contrasted reasons,

from the world, vie with one another in a finally absurd rejection. Apemantus accuses Timon of self-destruction—

> Thou hast cast away thyself, being like thyself,
> A madman so long, now a fool—

and bids him follow Lear in calling the 'naked creatures,'

> whose bare unhoused trunks,
> To the conflicting elements exposed,
> Answer mere nature,   (IV. iii. 221)

to 'flatter' him. When Timon in turn dismisses Apemantus as a 'fool', the latter replies: 'I love thee better now than e'er I did'; but when his victim retorts 'I hate thee worse,' and denounces him as a 'flatterer' of misery, he is driven to admit the perverse pleasure that 'vexing' gives him. Once more the truth is evenly divided; to Apemantus' insinuation that Timon would willingly be a 'courtier again', he can justly reply:

> Hadst thou like us from our first swath, proceeded
> The sweet degrees that this brief world affords
> To such as may the passive drudges of it
> Freely command, thou wouldst have plunged thyself
> In general riot, melted down thy youth
> In different beds of lust, and never learn'd
> The icy precepts of respect, but follow'd
> The sugar'd game before thee.   (IV. iii. 253)

This is at once a further true exposure of envious 'virtue' and something more. In the tone of Timon's references to the 'brief world' which was once at his disposal and which is now lost, to the 'sugar'd game', and in the following statement that he, in happier times, 'had the world as my *confectionary*', the implicit criticism of his former attitudes is apparent. Again, when he goes on to ask

> Why shouldst thou hate men?
> They never flatter'd thee,   (IV. iii. 270)

and adds petulantly 'What hast thou given?' he touches the truth, in so far as generosity, the willingness to give, is a necessary attribute of life on whose denial Apemantus' supposed 'virtue' rests; but there is an equal validity in the counter-accusation of pride which he himself invites:

> *Apemantus:*   Art thou proud yet?
> *Timon:*   Ay, that I am not thee.

Apemantus: I, that I was
              No prodigal.
    Timon: I, that I am one now.   (IV. iii. 277)

Each has his measure of truth, and each, converging on the wilderness
from his own point of departure, is now left with nothing but the dry
'roots', the empty husk of life, to sustain him. There is truth, again, in
the statement that Timon has never known 'the middle of humanity'.
That is why he is where he now finds himself, translated from one
'extremity' to its contrary; but, equally, when Apemantus declares his
wish 'to remain a beast with the beasts' Timon can justifiably call this a
'beastly ambition' and make his appropriate comment:

> What beast couldst thou be that were not subject to a beast? and what a
> beast art thou already, that seest not thy loss in transformation?   (IV. iii. 348)

The confrontation ends, appropriately, in an exchange of incoherent
insults—'Beast!' 'Slave!' 'Toad!'—delivered from positions mutually
exclusive and in which the futility of excess on either side is brought to
its farcical conclusion.

Even at this stage, however, Timon remains distinguished from
Apemantus by the ability to turn his life-weariness into distinctive
poetry. As he approaches his end, the craving for annihilation expresses
itself in ways which rouse an emotional response:

> Then, Timon, presently prepare thy grave;
> Lie where the light foam of the sea may beat
> Thy grave-stone daily;   (IV. iii. 380)

though even here he turns, immediately afterwards and with his own
kind of moralizing complacency, to the destructive properties of 'gold'
which have so long obsessed him. When Apemantus takes his leave, to
be replaced by the bandits, Timon sees in the newcomers a further
manifestation of the predatory instinct which, by now, he *needs* to see
universally present in mankind: 'You must eat men.' Typically, he
extends this vision to the entire universe—'each thing's a thief'—and
ends on the familiar evocation of anarchy:

> Love not yourselves; away,
> Rob one another.   (IV. iii. 450)

To this the thieves, with their eyes on Timon's gold, reply with a
caricature of reform. One declares himself almost 'charmed' from his
calling by Timon's eloquence; but the other, with whom the last word

rests, comments more sceptically in delaying his 'reformation' until such time as the state of 'peace' is established.

Flavius, also returning, has the clarity of vision to see Timon as he is, 'despised and ruinous', 'full of decay and failing'. His reaction to the spectacle, however, is one of 'honest grief', true compassion and fellow-feeling: an attitude which goes naturally with loyalty and which, alone in this play, can feel the tragic implications of the ruin of his master's 'nobility'. Timon's response is something less than adequate. When Flavius presents himself to his 'dearest master' as his 'honest poor servant', Timon clings to the misanthropy in which he has hitherto found a kind of compensation and refuses to recognize him or to admit the possibility of true disinterest. 'I never had honest men about me, I': the repetition of 'I', in a way which can be paralleled elsewhere in Shakespeare,[35] is not without meaning at this point. In spite of this, however, Flavius' tears end by appealing to Timon as a disclaimer of 'flinty mankind', though he adds that more normally in the world which they have been brought to contemplate in its reality sorrow turns to the irony of laughter: 'Strange times, that weep with laughing, not with weeping' (IV. iii. 495). This 'redemption' of human sorrow and fellow-feeling brings with it a sense of his own past folly which even now Timon is unwilling to face. Asserting his compassion in the name of 'duty and zeal', Flavius wrings from his former master the unwilling recognition of the existence of 'a singly honest man', covered, however, to the last by a continued admonition to hate:

> Go, live rich and happy;
> But thus conditioned; thou shalt build from men;
> Hate all, curse all, show charity to none.   (IV. iii. 534)

On this unqualified assertion of inhumanity and ruin the scene ends.

As the final stage of the play opens, the Poet and the Painter return to recall its opening. The rumour that Timon still has gold has reached them, and inspires them to a certain worldly optimism. This leads in turn to the courtier's habitual recourse to the flattery which comes as second nature to him; for 'promising is the very air o' the time' and ''tis not amiss we tender our loves to him in this supposed distress of his' (V. i. 15). Thus moved by the expectation of renewed gain, they greet Timon with echoes of the rhetoric that, in former times, constituted life to him: only to find that bitter experience has led him to see through these fictions to a new sense of the 'naked' truth, and that the

word 'honest', applied to these time-servers of his former eminence,
now rings with supreme irony in his ears. Beneath the obsessive tone
of his reference to 'honesty' Timon has come to see the artist who once
ministered to his vanity as a fraud—'Thou counterfeit'st most lively'—
and the poet as falsely 'natural':

> Why, thy verse swells with stuff so fine and smooth
> That thou art even natural in thine art, (V. i. 89)

and concludes the exchange with a bitter invitation to each to kill the
'villain' who is in reality none other than himself.[36] It is significant that
Flavius, in commenting on this, stresses the continued presence of an
element of self-absorption in Timon's reactions:

> *he is set so only to himself*
> That nothing but himself which looks like man
> Is friendly with him. (V. i. 122)

We shall not be following the true intention of the play unless we see
that Timon's attitudes, however explicable in terms of the way in which
the world has treated him, involve finally a rejection of man's true
nature in the name of personal disillusionment and, with it, a negation
of life itself.

Timon's attitude to his fellow-citizens points in the same direction.
To the Senators who plead for Athens, and who formerly deserted him
in his need, he reacts as an exaggerated and unilateral Coriolanus,[37]
having only 'blisters' and the 'plague' to offer. There is finally more
truth than he may realize in his observation that he himself is worthy
'of none but such as you, and you of Timon' (V. i. 140). The same
point is made when the approach of Alcibiades is announced, threatening the city with the consequences of its sin and inhumanity, imposing
the unnatural savagery of one who

> like a boar too savage, doth root up
> His country's peace; (V. i. 170)

it is significant that in answer to the plea for aid, uttered now in the
name of the familiar pieties, Timon can only confirm his indifference:
'I care not!' The logical end of such an attitude, by which Timon confirms his separation from society and all the natural positives, is an
acceptance of annihilation, and to this he now tends with the deepest
emotion left to him:

> my long sickness
> Of health and living now begins to mend,
> And nothing brings me all things. (V. i. 191)

From the moment of his initial disillusionment Timon has tended to see life in terms of disease, 'sickness'; the end of this perversion of life is now seen to be the illusion that seeks in 'nothing', the mere rununciation of continued living, the only end to which it can aspire.

This in turn is followed, again most logically, by a last invitation to suicide:

> Timon hath made his everlasting mansion
> Upon the beached verge of the salt flood; (V. i. 220)

even the 'sour words' in which he once expressed his misanthropy are played out as he stands, looking out to vacancy, from the farthest limits of his disillusionment. The resources of language itself, as a means to human communication, are exhausted—'let language end'— as 'plague and infection' are called in to redress universal human faults, and absolute death is seen as the end of all: 'Graves only be men's works, and death their gain' (V. i. 227). The death-wish, the natural reverse of Timon's former excess in self-centred generosity, has now taken total possession of his being.

As Timon speaks thus for the last time 'hope' is 'dead' in those who hear him, and Alcibiades is left to sound the trumpets of retribution against 'this coward and lascivious town' (V. iv. 1). His speech heralding the reversal of what has gone before is expressed with the sinewy strength of the best verse of *Coriolanus*:

> now the time is flush,
> When crouching marrow in the bearer strong
> Cries of itself 'No more': now breathless wrong
> Shall sit and pant in your great chairs of ease,
> And pursy insolence shall break his wind
> With fear and horrid flight. (V. iv. 8)

This is at once a reversal of Timon's negatives and an intimation of doom towards the society which brought him to them. The Senators, however, for all their manifold faults, can still offer through their spokesman a human regret which lies beyond Timon's latter comprehension. 'We were not all unkind' (in the sense of lacking in *kindred*, human fellow-feeling): 'All have not offended' (V. iv. 35). Even against the running tides of negation and excess, the natural instinct of sociability reasserts itself to win a measure of final recognition. The once predatory Alcibiades can at the last accept the spirit of the First Senator's plea, urging him to become the instrument of a justice based on the drawing of necessary distinctions:

> For those that were, it is not square to take
> On those that are, revenges; crimes, like lands,
> Are not inherited.   (V. iv. 36)

There could be no more direct comment on Timon's universalizing of a hatred based finally on flaws in his own nature; and it is followed, again logically, by an affirmation of the relevance of 'your public laws', as Alcibiades closes the action on a gesture of justice against which Timon's epitaph—the recalling of one who, 'alive', 'all living men did hate'—stands out as a manifestation of 'nobility' flawed, undone by its own self-engendered excesses. In the world that now opens before Athens, 'war' is to 'breed' peace, the 'olive' fittingly to accompany the 'sword'. The last word lies with a gesture of reconciliation in favour of the processes of life renewed.

III

THE ROMAN TRAGEDIES

SHAKESPEARE's major plays on Roman history span between them the supremely creative years of his dramatic career. The earliest of the three, *Julius Caesar*, was separated by no great distance in time from the two parts of *Henry IV* and *Henry V* and is concentrated, like these plays, upon the interplay of personal motives and public necessity; whilst the other two—*Antony and Cleopatra* and *Coriolanus*—belong to the dramatist's last years and combine an acute understanding of historical processes with the illuminating presence of a distinctive tragic vision. Thus variously situated in time, the plays, by bringing together into a mutually enriching unity two of the principal themes of Shakespeare's mature work—those expressed respectively in the historical chronicles and in the series of great tragedies which followed them—constitute one of the undoubted peaks of his achievement.

The historical matter of all three plays is principally derived from Plutarch's *Lives of the Noble Greeks and Romans*, as translated into English from the French of Amyot by Thomas North.[1] The fact is important for an understanding of the plays themselves; for, whereas it is, generally speaking, true that Shakespeare's acknowledged masterpieces—*Hamlet*, *Macbeth*, *King Lear*—owe little more than the barest outline of their plots to the comparatively artless narratives from which they derive, in the Roman tragedies we are conscious of dealing with what might almost be called a collaboration. It is well known that long passages from North's highly workmanlike translation were almost directly versified by Shakespeare; but a comparison of the relevant passages[2] shows that the dramatist, in following his original closely, was in fact developing his own conception, being fully himself. The style of these plays, far from reflecting a pedestrian process of versification, shows a unique combination of narrative lucidity, achieved through the easy, almost conversational use of spoken rhythms and vernacular phrases, with poetic intensities that flow effortlessly from

this foundation whenever the state of the action so requires. By the
side of these works, even some of the effects of the great tragedies
seem to have been reached with effort, to represent a sensibility
strained to the utmost in the intensity of its reaction to emotional
stresses; whilst the verse of the final comedies seems at times to achieve
its symbolic effects through conventions of greater and more artificial
complexity.

1 Julius Caesar

The action of *Julius Caesar* turns, in the tense simplicity of its narrative,
upon an event of unique historical importance. Round this event with
its varied and often contrasted significances for the Elizabethan mind,[3]
Shakespeare has developed a pattern of political passions which answers
to a closely knit dramatic plan. The early scenes show Caesar and his
enemies converging upon the striking of a blow which has in its
inevitability, in the universal concern it focuses upon itself, the quality
of a tragic sacrifice. The deed itself and the action which follows from
it lead, in the central episodes, to the conflict of public and personal
motives involved in the clash of Brutus and Antony over the dictator's
dead body. Finally, in the concluding stages, the consequences of the
murder are revealed through their effect upon each of the contending
parties. The conspirators, brought to see their motives in the unflattering light of reality, collapse into mutual recrimination and
confessed futility; whilst, against a background of practical assertion
and ruthless calculation of the odds, a new Roman order replaces that
which has been destroyed.

In one sense, and in one sense only, the entire action is centred upon
the murdered dictator. He disappears, it is true, at the end of the first
half of the play, and his appearances before his elimination have been
strangely brief and enigmatic; but the fact remains that, alive, the
action turns upon him, and when he is dead his spirit remains, as
Brutus unwillingly confesses,[4] persistently and implacably alive. The
emphasis, however, in the presentation of the character lies elsewhere,
in a notable sense of discrepancy between the figure which the dictator,
obliged by the force of circumstance, presents to the world and the
reality of what he in fact is. From the first, his use of the impersonal,

royal style implies an effort to live self-consciously up to the require-
ments which his isolated and uneasy eminence imposes. 'Always,'
in his own phrase (I. ii. 211), 'I am Caesar,' and in that 'always' there
is a sense of danger, of living poised over a void, an imminent disaster,
which, as we approach him more closely, his behaviour repeatedly
confirms. It is true that many of the initial intimations of weakness
in Caesar—Cassius' ascription to him of physical feebleness, Casca's
belittling report of his 'swooning' in the market place (I. ii. 249)—
come from his enemies, and are to be understood as the product of
envy: but true also that these same incidents contribute to the impression of one whom his circumstances oblige to play out a role, a course
moreover in which he is largely supported by a vanity which will at
last contribute to his disaster.

The scene (II. ii) in which Caesar is persuaded, against his intimate
will, to go to the Capitol is in this respect revealing. As Calpurnia,
shaken by premonitions which the elements confirm, presses him to
stay at home he clings obstinately to the determination which his
situation has imposed upon him. 'Caesar shall go forth': the dangers
that threaten him are always *behind* him, out of sight, waiting to assert
themselves against a man whose position obliges him to outface them:

> when they shall see
> The face of Caesar, they are vanished. (II. ii. 11)

Upon this illusion of constancy the dictator's position, and with it the
fortunes of the Roman world, depend.

Faced, indeed, by portents 'beyond all use', threats to human
conceptions of order and purpose, Caesar responds with what is at
once the striking of an attitude and a touch of sincerity:

> What can be avoided
> Whose end is purposed by the mighty gods? (II. ii. 26)

In the light of this implicit fatalism the renewed affirmation which
follows—'Caesar shall go forth'—must seem strangely obstinate. It is
followed by a further insistence upon the pose which we have come
to associate with his dignity, a stressing of self-consciousness which
ends by insinuating the presence of the weakness it seeks to deny:

> Of all the wonders that I yet have heard,
> It seems to me most strange that men should fear;
> Seeing that death, a necessary end,
> Will come when it will come. (II. ii. 34)

The lines answer to that sense of fatality, of subjection to the temporal process, which is present as a factor limiting human choices in all Shakespeare's plays of this period. Against this pervasive influence, Caesar is engaged in building up an impression of consistency which began no doubt as a real reflection of greatness, but which his situation, and the destiny which covers all human actions, now imposes upon him.

Caesar is revealed, in fact, less as brave and consistent at this moment than as talking himself into consistency. Beneath this determination, however, weakness once more asserts itself. Calpurnia persuades him to a course which his own instincts have already insinuated; he acquiesces ('Mark Antony shall say I am not well'), even while clinging to the excuse that it is the frailty of others that has imposed this change of plan: 'for thy humour I will stay at home.' The arrival of Decius Brutus to escort him to the Senate brings to the surface the contradictions by which he is torn. Decius is to tell the senators that he 'will not come to-day'; since it is false that he cannot, and that he 'dare not', falser, only the bare affirmation of his will can meet the case:

> The cause is in my will: I will not come;
> That is enough to satisfy the senate. (II. ii. 71)

The retort reveals the arbitrary nature of the consistency which circumstance imposes upon Caesar. It also covers an inner uncertainty; the pose has taken possession of the man, and will from now on lead him to his fate.

After Caesar's account of Calpurnia's dream and Decius' ingenious exercise in interpretation—both expressed in the heightened, almost hysterical language which surrounds conspiracy throughout—Decius drives home his point by a highly effective combination of flattery with an appeal to the dictator's unavowed love of power. The Senate have decided to confer a crown upon 'mighty Caesar', and if he does not attend the session, 'their minds may change'. More dangerously still, Decius emphasizes the mockery which may follow if the truth were known:

> It were a mock
> Apt to be rendered, for some one to say
> 'Break up the senate till another time,
> When Caesar's wife shall meet with better dreams.' (II. ii. 96)

The appeal to vanity supports that to ambition, and indifference to

Calpurnia—reflected in an attitude towards her that surely stands in significant contrast to Brutus' tender treatment of Portia (II. i)—is present in both. Above all—and here Decius is careful to cover his daring with a profession of love—it will be whispered that the master of Rome is 'afraid': a hint than which none is better calculated to play upon the strange complex of conflicting emotions at the dictator's heart.

With this last speech, Decius achieves his aim. The victim brushes aside all misgivings—'How foolish do your fears seem now, Calpurnia' —jokes with his enemies, and greets Antony with a manly jest. Throughout we feel a recovery of confidence, a readiness to accept willingly what has now become his fate. The emphasis on 'friendship', on taking wine together, underlines the monstrous treachery afoot; only Brutus, standing aside from the main stream, 'yearns' to think that appearances are 'false', that 'every like is not the same'. From this moment, Caesar's history marches together with that of his enemies to converge at the base of Pompey's effigy.

Caesar, however, though he dominates the action by virtue of his public position, is in no sense the principal moving force of the tragedy. This is provided, in the early scenes, by Brutus, who, in seeking the clarification of his own motives, gives the action its dynamic quality. His initial reflections are already charged with implications of character:

> Vexed I am
> Of late with passions of some difference,
> Conceptions only proper to myself,
> Which give some soil perhaps to my behaviours. (I. ii. 39)

The expression, notably reminiscent of certain utterances of Hamlet, stresses the nature, essentially inward-looking and exploratory, of his dilemma. To this Stoic theorist, tied to the contemplation of his own virtue, the 'passions' present themselves as disturbing elements, shadowing the unity and self-control which he craves as the key to action. It is of the nature of his conflict to be without communication, 'proper' to himself alone; and this inwardness, the product of his character and of his assumptions about life, affects him, when uneasily stirred to action, as a blot upon the harmonious personality at which he aims, a 'soil' upon the fair outward presentation of himself which he so persistently craves.

It is the function of Cassius, by playing upon this desire for communi-

cation, to mould him to ends not finally his own. The peculiar relationship between the pair, and the method of its dramatic presentation, are
both indicated in the query which opens his attack and in Brutus' reply:

> *Cassius:* Tell me, good Brutus, can you see your face?
> *Brutus:* No, Cassius: for the eye sees not itself
> But by reflection, by some other things.   (I. ii. 51)[5]

Under the guise of providing, in the shape of 'thoughts of great value,
worthy cogitations', a 'mirror' to reflect his friend's '*hidden* worthiness',
Cassius will bring him to see not a reality, an objective vision of his
strength and weakness, but the 'shadow' of the imperfectly understood
desires which will finally bring him, not to the affirmation of his ideals,
but to personal and public ruin.

Beneath these assertions of friendship and plain dealing, Cassius'
approach to Brutus is fraught with calculation. Those of 'the best
respect in Rome' look to him for redress; as they groan beneath 'this
age's yoke', their desire is that '*noble* Brutus'—the adjective initiates
a line of flattery which, precisely because it contains truth, will be
particularly insidious—understood his own wishes and motives, 'had
his eyes'. Brutus' first reaction is honest and true to character:

> Into what dangers would you lead me, Cassius,
> That you would have me seek into myself
> *For that which is not in me?*   (I. ii. 63)

It is some time before he will speak so truly again. Meanwhile, it is
Cassius' mission to undermine this candid self-estimate, replacing it by
a false confidence which carries no inner conviction. Taking up the
image of the mirror, he turns to his own ends the need for guidance
which makes his friend so pliable to his purposes:

> since you know you cannot see yourself
> So well as by reflection, I your glass
> Will modestly discover to yourself
> That of yourself which you yet know not of.   (I. ii. 67)

This is a dangerous proceeding, made the more so by the tendency,
which the following exchanges reveal, for the two friends to vie with
one another in setting up idealized images of themselves to minister
to what is finally, beneath their poses of Roman virtue and public
spirit, an intimate self-satisfaction. When Cassius denies that he is 'a
common laugher', 'fawning' on men with the intention of later

'scandalling' them, he is no doubt comparing himself, not altogether unjustly, with such as Antony and pointing to some true consequences of Caesar's exorbitant power; but, beneath the implied contrast, envy, the desire to debase what he has been unable to achieve, vitiates the judgment.

For Brutus, similarly, devotion to the public good expresses itself through assumption of that 'honour' which was, more especially at this time, so variously in Shakespeare's mind:

> What is it that you would impart to me?
> If it be aught toward the general good,
> Set honour in one eye and death i' the other,
> And I will look on both indifferently. (I. ii. 84)

Though expressed with a more 'philosophic' detachment, the spirit behind these words is akin to that which prompted Hotspur to his generous but useless sacrifice;[6] and it reveals much the same tendency to replace the balance of judgment by simpler but more illusory certainties. As Brutus concludes, not without a touch of self-esteem,

> let the gods so speed me as I love
> The name of honour more than I fear death. (I. ii. 88)

It will be, perhaps, one of the lessons of Brutus' tragedy that the 'names' of things, however noble and consoling in abstraction, are no substitute for a balanced consideration of their reality. 'Honour' is the way of becoming a trap set for those who, like Brutus, fail to temper idealism with a proper measure of self-awareness.

The soliloquy in which Brutus finally arrives at his decision, and thereby makes the murder of Caesar possible, is so riddled with implicit contradictions that some students of the play[7] have judged it incomprehensible. It is, however, thoroughly in character. Brutus, not himself an evil man, is about to perform an act which will release evil impulses whose true nature he persistently fails to grasp; the discrepancy between what he is and what he does is reflected in his recognizable effort to persuade himself, against convictions intimately present in his nature, that the resolve he is about to take is necessary and just. Had he been consistently the doctrinaire republican Cassius would have him be, the admitted fact that Caesar 'would be crown'd' would have been, for him if not for Shakespeare and most of his contemporaries, a sufficient reason for his elimination. Brutus, however, as the play presents him, is no such thing, but rather a man who seeks in decisive

action the confirmation of his own virtue, whose purposes are imposed
upon him by those who play upon inconsistencies, weak spots in his
own nature; and it is part of his tragedy that he cannot forget, much
as he now desires to do so, that his intended victim is a human being
and his friend. This situation bears fruit in his recognition, which a
convinced republican would have found irrelevant, that he has as yet
no valid *personal* reason for the deed he contemplates. 'To speak truth
of Caesar', he admits,

> I have not known when his affections sway'd
> More than his reason.   (II. i. 20)

'I know no personal cause to spurn at him': the admission is, for a
man who sincerely values friendship, personal relationships, serious
enough; but since another side of Brutus' nature craves abstract
consistency, the wedding of high principle to effective action, he turns
this recognition into an argument for clearing himself of dubious
personal motives and seeks to place the burden of justification squarely
upon an appeal to the 'general' good.

The argument, inevitably, is pressed home with less than complete
conviction. 'How that *might* change his nature, there's the question,'
Brutus urges upon himself, in a strangely tentative attitude, only to
recognize later that

> the quarrel
> Will bear no colour for the thing he is;   (II. i. 28)

but, since a contrary necessity urges him to conceal these doubts, calls
upon him to assert a certainty which he is far from feeling, emphasis
must be laid on a *possible*, an unproven danger:

> Fashion it thus; that what he is, augmented,
> Would run to these and these extremities.   (II. i. 30)

The vagueness, the readiness to 'fashion it thus' in accordance with
preconceptions in which observed reality has little part to play, is
highly symptomatic. Brutus, precisely because the vacillation which has
characterized his reactions since the beginning covers deep inner uncertainty, speaks to himself evasively in terms of specious 'philosophical'
commonplace—

> The abuse of greatness is when it disjoins
> Remorse from power . . .
>   lowliness is young ambition's ladder—   (II. i. 18)

and takes refuge in an imposed ruthlessness:

> think him as a serpent's egg
> Which, hatched, would as his kind grow mischievous,
> And kill him in the shell.   (II. i. 32)

The tendency to cover lack of intimate consistency with a show of impersonal brutality belongs to Brutus' peculiar brand of theoretical idealism. It is part of the presentation of human contradiction, whose exposure is so close to the spirit of this play. Brutus seeks at this moment to resolve an intimate, tragic disharmony through an act of decision foreign to his nature; the confusion revealed in his own motives, and in his attitude to the world of external realities, is one that will follow him through the contradictions of his career to the final resolution of suicide.

Confronted with the conspirators he has agreed to lead, Brutus further reveals his true nature. In presenting him to them Cassius stresses his need to live up to the conception of himself which his ancestors and his 'philosophy' have laid upon him. He suggests that, unlike these ancestors, Brutus is weak, indecisive; public opinion demands of him that 'opinion' of himself which every true Roman wishes to share. Brutus, in reply, urges his new associates to confirm their dedication and seeks confidence in a rhetorical declaration of his own:

> do not stain
> The even virtue of our enterprize,
> Nor the insuppressive mettle of our spirits,
> To think that or our cause or our performance
> Did need an oath: when every drop of blood
> That every Roman bears, and nobly bears,
> Is guilty of a several bastardy
> If he do break the smallest particle
> Of any promise that hath pass'd from him.   (II. i. 132)

The best comment on this earnest but slightly self-conscious harangue is provided by the return, which at once follows, to practical considerations. Cassius and his friends wish to enrol the support of Cicero, whose reputation will 'purchase us'—the verb is appropriately chosen —'a good opinion',

> And buy men's voices to commend our deeds.

Since, however, it is Brutus' adhesion that all desire, it is enough for him to reject Cicero as incapable of 'following' for all to agree that he should not be approached.

The basic weakness of the plot is more closely touched upon when Cassius urges that Mark Antony should die. Brutus' rejection of this advice is of very considerable interest as a further revelation of the kind of man he is. It combines an effort to be practical, revealed in the opening concession to expediency ('Our course will seem too bloody'), with failure to be so. It is finally the pose, the elevation of himself into a figure of magnanimous principle, that engages his emotions. The expression is not without a touch of the grotesque. 'Let us be sacrificers, but not butchers, Caius,' he urges, and follows up the plea with an unreal distinction between 'the spirit of men' and their material 'blood' which must so regrettably be shed:

> We all stand up against the spirit of Caesar,
> And in the spirit of men there is no blood!
> O, that we then could come by Caesar's spirit,
> And not dismember Caesar! (II. i. 167)

The distinction no doubt answers in part to the desire to make credible Brutus' nobility in the face of the nature of the deed on which he has set himself. The difficulty, however, is turned into an asset, a revelation of character. Brutus the idealist is seen as one more example of that typical Shakespearean creation, the man who, willing an end, is ready to deceive himself concerning the means necessary to gain it. 'Caesar must bleed for't,' he recognizes, but covers the admission with futile and self-conscious posing:

> gentle friends,
> Let's kill him boldly, but not wrathfully:
> Let's carve him as a dish fit for the gods,
> Not hew him as a carcass fit for hounds:
> And let our hearts, as subtle masters do,
> Stir up their servants to an act of rage,
> And after seem to chide 'em. (II. i. 171)

The speech points to the presence of a variety of motives in the process of decorating brutality with strained emotional expression. Addressing his future accomplices as 'gentle friends', Brutus, in admitting the fact of bloody death, embroiders it with the far-fetched and finally absurd evocation of 'a dish fit for the gods'. The odd mixture of unpracticality and a certain unconscious cynicism is brought home forcibly in the description of the conspirators' hearts as '*subtle* masters' who, in rousing their 'servant' feelings to a simulation, an 'act of rage', *seem* after, for the purpose of obtaining public approval, 'to chide them'. 'We shall be call'd purgers, not murderers': the reality, as so often occurs with men of Brutus' type, is disguised by a change of name, and this becomes the justification of a decision politically unwise, if humanly comprehensible, which will finally bring the conspiracy to ruin.

Such are the main elements which, converging, unite in the blow which strikes down Caesar in the central action of the play. The victim's last utterance, claiming the constancy of the 'northern star', is the most theatrical of all his assertions of fixity. Just as his fall is about to stress his common humanity, he accentuates unnaturally the distance that separates him from other men:

> men are flesh and blood, and apprehensive;
> Yet in the number I do know but one
> That unassailable holds on his rank,
> Unshaked of motion;   (III. i. 67)

but already his own unsuspecting words—

> and that I am he
> Let me a little show it, even in this—   (III. i. 70)

amount to a plea, an appeal to the world to support him in this self-estimate. It finds its answer in the repeated stabs of Brutus and his associates, and in his fall at the foot of the effigy of Pompey, whom he himself formerly overthrew.

The fall is followed by a tense moment of silence, set against the gathering climax which has so splendidly preceded it. Immediately after this, the emotions so far concentrated upon Caesar's overpowering presence break out with the rising hysteria of libertarian sentiment. 'Liberty! freedom! tyranny is dead!' cries Cinna; and even Brutus, after calling on those around him to maintain their calm, turns to a more emotional line of appeal:

> Stoop, Romans, stoop,
> And let us bathe our hands in Caesar's blood
> Up to the elbows, and besmear our swords;
> Then walk we forth, even to the market-place,
> And, waving our red weapons o'er our heads,
> Let's all cry, 'Peace, freedom, and liberty!'   (III. i. 105)

Here, if anywhere, and in the self-congratulatory exchanges that follow, a final comment on the true nature of conspiracy is unerringly made. The gap between profession and reality, the aspiration to freedom and the deed to which it has led, is remorselessly asserted in the insistence upon spilled blood: blood not, as in *Macbeth*, horrifyingly sticking to the assassin's hands, but lavish, free-flowing, answering to the strained emotions with which the murderers have sought to disguise, even from themselves, the true nature of their crime.

In this charged emotional climate, Mark Antony—first through a messenger and then in his own person—cautiously feels his way to the centre of the stage. By the end of his exchange with Brutus, which culminates in a grotesque parody—'Let each man render me his bloody hand'—of the reconciliation which Caesar's assassin has so impossibly proposed, he knows that his position is stronger than he can have dared to hope. Left alone with his thoughts, his last speech in this scene is a further revelation of character. Couched in the facile rhetoric which comes so readily to him, it apostrophizes the dead Caesar as 'thou bleeding piece of earth' and goes on to speak of 'costly blood' and to characterize his wounds as 'dumb mouths' and 'ruby lips'. In a world so fluent in feeling, where emotion swells in accordance with the forms of rhetoric, intensely rather than deeply, like the blood which issues from the wounds it contemplates, Antony's oratory is perfectly at home. It issues, however, in a vision of chaos. 'All pity' shall be 'chok'd' with 'custom of fell deeds',

> And Caesar's spirit ranging for revenge,
> With Ate by his side come hot from hell,
> Shall in these confines with a monarch's voice
> Cry 'Havoc!' and let slip the dogs of war;
> That this foul deed shall smell above the earth
> With carrion men, groaning for burial.   (III. i. 270)

This conclusion to the first open revelation of his pent-up feelings carries with it an estimate of Antony's limitations as a moral being. His rhetoric pays itself with its own expression, represents emotional irresponsibility in one who can also calculate and use his rhetorical gifts for ends deliberately and cunningly conceived. The vision of chaos, far from appalling Antony, finally attracts him, answers to a necessity of his nature; and that is why his type of emotion, not less than Brutus' frigid assertions of principle, is to be seen less in its own right than as a fragment, a partial aspect of the unity which Caesar's death has destroyed in Rome. The end of this process is 'carrion', self-destruction, death: that Antony, carried on the flow of words which reflects his emotional nature, can dwell with complacency on these dreadful realities is, by implication, an exposure of his most intimate motives.

The famous oration scene (III. ii) is too familiar to call for analysis in detail. It shows a Brutus caught in the consequences of his own act, deprived—now that the mood of exaltation which accompanied him to it has passed—of the impulse to go further. Against him is set an Antony who, in the act of affirming himself as the adventurer and theatrical orator he is, is also the instrument by which the *truth* about murder emerges to the light of day. This clash of aims and temperament takes place before a background provided by a new element in the action: the Roman populace. The crowd has not hitherto played a decisive part in events, though its fickleness has been indicated more than once in the early scenes.[8] It now makes the voice of its appetites heard in a more direct fashion, thereby showing from still another point of view the nature of the forces which Brutus and Cassius have so irresponsibly released from their normal restraints. At the end of the scene, as the mob moves off to burn and plunder, Antony's final comment is a revealing disclaimer of responsibility. 'Now let it work': the orator, resting on his laurels, looks with satisfaction on his achievement, dwells with a certain pleasure on the chaos he has let loose:

> Mischief, thou art afoot,
> Take thou what course thou wilt.   (III. ii. 265)

The final effect is a revelation of irresponsibility accompanied by sinister pleasure:

> Fortune is merry,
> And in this mood will give us anything.   (III. ii. 271)

That, later on, she will assume other moods, ultimately less congenial to the speaker, remains to be seen. Meanwhile, the grim little episode (III. iii) of the destruction of Cinna the poet for a chance coincidence of name comes effectively to announce the brutality which will from now on so frequently preside over the course of events.

The unleashing of the Roman mob brings to an end the more dynamic part of the action. The last scenes of the tragedy exhibit the consequences of Caesar's murder in a spirit of notable detachment.

They show a Rome divided by covert rivalries which can only end in the elimination of all but one of its contending factions and, after that elimination, in the restoration of unity under Octavius. Apart from this resolution, the personal tragedy of Brutus is rounded off in the self-inflicted death which is its logical conclusion.

It is important to note that this dispassionate evaluation falls impartially on both parties. As the fourth act opens, Antony and a notably frigid and non-committal Octavius are seen in the company of Lepidus, contemplating the death of their relations and former friends without illusion and without feeling. The initial words of Antony, who has so recently exhibited himself in the forum as a man of sensibility, are 'These many then shall die;' Octavius, typically passing from the general statement to its particular application, adds (turning to Lepidus) 'Your brother too must die,' and obtains his companion's assent:

> Upon condition Publius shall not live,
> Who is your sister's son, Mark Antony. (IV. i. 4)

The callousness of the exchange, the readiness to write off human lives by marks on paper, is rounded off by Antony's complacent rejoinder: 'He shall not live; look, with a spot I damn him.' The final suggestion that the will, which Antony has so recently used to stir up mob emotion in the name of generosity, should be studied to determine 'How to cut off some charge in legacies' adds a revealing touch of parsimony to the display of cynicism in action.

The world which is to replace that formerly dominated by Caesar is indeed mean, petty, and dangerous. The triumvirs are already engaged in the first stages of a ruthless struggle for power. As soon as Lepidus has been dispatched for the will, Antony refers disparagingly to him ('a slight unmeritable man'; 'meet to be sent on errands') and proposes his elimination. Octavius, whose moment is still to come, bides his time ('he is a tried and valiant soldier') and is answered by Antony with a further display of cynicism. 'So is my horse, Octavius;' with Lepidus thus removed from consideration, the two leaders return to discussion of the 'great things' in which their own future is involved. The last words of the scene, spoken by Octavius, stress the insecurity that now surrounds the entire political future:

> some that smile have in their hearts, I fear,
> Millions of mischiefs. (IV. i. 50)

Such is the world which has survived Caesar, and in which his avengers are fated to move.

On the other side the circumstances of Caesar's enemies, as they are shown in the process of coming to terms with their real as distinct from their rhetorical selves, answer to a conception which is, in its accepted pessimism, finally similar. In them, division and self-doubt replace the cynical manoeuvres of their foes. Cassius, no longer the ardent friend of the early scenes, whom the prospect of action united (perhaps, in the last analysis, spuriously) to a colleague whom interest also demanded as his associate, now salutes that associate with distant correctness, no longer shows

> such free and friendly conference,
> As he hath used of old.   (IV. ii. 17)

Brutus' reaction is heavy with the sense of fatality. Lucilius has described 'a hot friend cooling', and the process by which love begins 'to sicken and decay' has its symptoms in 'an enforced ceremony'. The wish of Brutus to maintain 'plain and simple faith' is at once moving and strangely inadequate. It springs from his most deeply held theoretical conception of life, in the absence of which his integrity, his belief in himself and in the purity of his motives, must founder; but it runs against the nature of things as determined by the course of action in which he has compromised his honesty. Against the background of advancing armies we feel already the 'sinking at the trial' which, proceeding from adverse external realities, mirrors inner dejection.

The motives behind this discussion are, from the first, of some complexity. Cassius, rushing typically into the void which opens before him, complains that he has been 'wrong'd'; but it is clear from his explanation that the wrong—an accusation of connivance in accepting bribes—has been inflicted in a dubious context. Brutus, indeed, having made his point in a tone of moral superiority—'You wrong'd yourself to write in such a case'—cannot refrain from rubbing salt into the wound. By accusing Cassius of 'an itching palm', he rouses the impetuous self-respect of his friend to violent protest:

> You know that you are Brutus that speaks this,
> Or, by the gods, this speech were else your last;   (IV. iii. 13)

and there is a touch of insensitivity in the responding reference to 'chastisement' which leaves Cassius speechless in its implication of

lofty superiority. The two characters, so precariously united against
Caesar, are seen to be perfectly designed to exasperate one another to
the limits of endurance.

As the gap between them widens, Brutus is led to recall the integrity
which inspired their actions: 'Did not great Caesar bleed for justice'
sake?' This thought, contrasted with the sad reality of the present,
leads him to back his reproof with a further gesture towards the
idealism of the past:

> What, shall one of us
> That struck the foremost man of all this world
> But for supporting robbers, shall we now
> Contaminate our fingers with base bribes,
> And sell the mighty space of our large honours
> For so much trash as may be grasped thus?   (IV. iii. 21)

The gesture is ample, noble, and yet it covers weakness. As always,
Brutus is taking refuge in a satisfactory picture of himself as one who
has dared, for 'honour' alone, to lead and inspire a conspiracy that
overthrew 'the foremost man of all this world'; but where disinterest
ends and egoism, the need to live up to an ennobling vision of his own
motives begins, we might be hard put to decide.

Whatever the truth about Brutus' purity (and no simple judgment
would be appropriate) his attitude could not be more precisely calculated to rub the raw edges of Cassius' sense of inferiority. As Brutus
ceases, he describes what he has heard as a 'baiting' of himself and utters
the ominous warning: 'I'll not endure it.' His touchy self-respect has
been offended, and now responds by appealing to his superior experience:

> I am a soldier, I,
> Older in practice, abler than yourself
> To make conditions.   (IV. iii. 30)

The repetition of 'I' indicates the nature of the wound inflicted upon
Cassius' own type of egoism. That of Brutus, though more complex,
is not less strong. It impels him, where tact would have passed over the
burning issue, to exasperate his companion further by contemptuous
denial. 'You are not, Cassius.' 'I am.' 'I say you are not': the result is
to create an ugly wrangle in which the last shreds of self-respect seem
likely to be swallowed up. At the culminating moment, Cassius'
threatening 'tempt me no further' is matched by the infuriating
superiority of 'Away, slight man!' and by the final insult:

> Hear me, for I will speak.
> Must I give way and room to your rash choler?   (IV. iii. 38)

At this moment, the realities of character which underlie the previous affirmations of constancy and devotion to principle are revealed for what they are. The rest of the scene is devoted to working them out fully, and to an attempt to cover them up in the interests of a cause already lost.

At first, however, it is not a matter of covering up, but of adding further irritation to Cassius' open wound. In this Brutus, by a trait which links curiously with his self-conscious idealism, but which is not on reflection incompatible with it, is a master. 'Must I endure all this?' Cassius cries, as though demanding clemency, and receives the bitter exasperation of the insult—'All this! ay more! Fret till your proud heart break'—and the contemptuous dismissal that follows:

> Go show your slaves how choleric you are,
> And make your bondmen tremble!   (IV. iii. 43)

The rest of the speech, so true to the frigid egoism of the man 'armed strong in honesty', rises to a final, almost sadistic determination to inflict humiliation:

> By the gods,
> You shall digest the venom of your spleen,
> Though it do split you; for from this day forth,
> I'll use you for my mirth, yea, for my laughter,
> When you are waspish.   (IV. iii. 46)

The lines are rich in inflection, in the varied revelation of character. There is pleasure in inflicting humiliation, moral callousness, and contempt, together with a bitter pleasure in true characterization in the final description of Cassius as 'waspish'. The fact is that the element of egoism present from the first beneath Brutus' noble façade is coming to the surface under the stress of his growing awareness of standing intolerably in a false situation. The effect of this outburst, though palliated, can never be undone; and Cassius' broken reply, 'Is it come to this?' clearly involves a glance back to the idealistic unity of purpose in which Caesar's murder was carried out and which is now being revealed in so unflattering a light.

The healing of this breach and the return to at least the appearance of unity are accomplished with no small tact. The conspirators, seeing the abyss opening at their feet, draw back in horror. Both, we may feel, are moved beneath the surface of their reproaches by a sense that it is their own past, their capacity for continued belief in their moral dignity, which they are in reality placing in jeopardy; and when Cassius breaks into further reproach, self-exhibition is subtly combined with a true sense of personal betrayal. 'Cassius is a-weary of the world': here it may seem that a conscious appeal to emotion prevails, but the following phrases surely strike a valid note in their criticism of Brutus' frigid moralizing:

> Hated by one he loves; braved by his brother!
> Check'd like a bondman; all his faults observed,
> Set in a note-book, learn'd, and conn'd by rote,
> To cast into my teeth. (IV. iii. 95)

Brutus, no doubt realizing that he has gone too far, meets this outburst, which culminates in Cassius' offer of his dagger, with a genuine attempt to reduce the tension. He is, however, characteristically clumsy in his effort to adjust his words to a new mood. His phrase 'Be angry when you will, it shall have scope' sounds stiffly, rather like the humouring of a self-willed child; men such as Brutus do not easily descend from the pedestal on which their lives are based. Beneath the clumsiness, however, there is now revealed a deep unhappiness, the immediate cause of which is still being held back from us:

> O Cassius, you are yoked with a lamb,
> That carries anger as the flint bears fire,
> Who, much enforced, shows a hasty spark,
> And straight is cold again. (IV. iii. 109)

The reference to feeling hardly struck as from a flinty surface, an innate coldness, reveals tellingly the diffidence, the emotional clumsiness, which is part of the character; and the sincerity of the revelation opens the way to a rueful, disillusioned reconciliation. The impression left by the whole exchange is one of the cooling embers of a passion doomed to extinction, but surviving, at least for the moment, the death of the original flame.

The immediate reason for Brutus' state, however, and for much that has gone before, has so far been held back by an admirable stroke of dramatic tact. It is now revealed. After calling for a bowl of wine, symbol—as it were—of harmony between friends, he meets Cassius' wondering comment 'I did not think you could have been so angry' and the reproof of 'Of your philosophy you make no use' with his simple revelation: 'No man bears sorrow better: Portia is dead.' The disclosure, followed by an admirably brief and tense exchange of phrases—

> —Portia is dead.
> —Ha, Portia!
> —She is dead—   (IV. iii. 146)

gives a centre of stillness to the bitter exchanges that have gone before. From this heart of silence, Cassius' emotion speaks in a new, transformed tone: 'How 'scaped I killing when I cross'd you so?' and backs it with the almost choric quality of his following exclamation: 'O insupportable and touching loss!'

The revelation is rounded off with the recovery by Brutus of his Stoic mask: 'Speak no more of her!' If the 'philosopher' in him dictates this assertion of emotional control, the husband's affection warns him not to give voice to a feeling which, once expressed, might shatter all containing limits. The hidden cause of emotional stress having been thus revealed, the bowl of wine is brought in, and in it Brutus pledges himself to 'bury all unkindness', receiving in return the fullness of Cassius' answering pledge:

> My heart is thirsty for that noble pledge.
> Fill, Lucius, till the wine o'erswell the cup;
> I cannot drink too much of Brutus' love.   (IV. iii. 159)

The reconciliation takes place under the shadow of tragedy. It cannot be a restoration of the original relationship, now irretrievably flawed by past choices; but, in spite of this, the human content is there, beyond all the purposes of political realism, and it rounds off suitably the issues so dramatically represented in what is, in some respects, the most interesting scene of the play.

The last stages of the tragedy represent the winding-up of the action in accordance with its underlying constants. The defeated Romans fall on their swords in a show of Stoic resolution, because no other choice is left open to them, and the victors turn away from the field 'to part the glory of this happy day'. As we follow these episodes to their conclusion, we cannot help feeling that something of the shadow of the Greek heroes in *Troilus and Cressida*, written possibly at a time not very far distant, already lies over them. Cassius commits suicide in an error caused by his own short-sightedness (as Titinius says:

'Alas, thou hast misconstrued everything!'), and the cold, practical
Octavius is shown on the other side as reacting against the tutelage
of Antony, who has made his victory possible and whom he will soon
be ready to discard. With all his flaws, which have been so uncompro-
misingly revealed in the course of the play, Brutus is the only character
who emerges with some measure of genuine personal stature. His last
farewell rises, in contrast with so much that surrounds it, to the dignity
of tragic assertion. 'Countrymen,' he says, addressing through his
remaining followers Rome and posterity:

> My heart doth joy that yet in all my life
> I found no man but he was true to me.
> I shall have glory by this losing day,
> More than Octavius and Mark Antony
> By this vile conquest shall attain unto. (V. v. 34)

Once more it is important to avoid any simple reaction to the mood
so expressed. The speech is truly noble, but is also an effort made by
the speaker, in the absence of more solid ground for satisfaction, to
encourage himself on the threshold of the annihilation which he has,
after all, brought upon himself, and perhaps even obscurely come to
desire.

The mood is, in any case, neither false nor triumphant, implies
rather an acceptance of the end Brutus has come to see as inevitable,
involved in the entire logic of his own past, and which he now
approaches with a certain nostalgic craving for the dark:

> Night hangs upon mine eyes; my bones would rest,
> That have but labour'd to attain this hour. (V. v. 41)

In this mood of self-awareness, and snatching some crumb of comfort
from the fact that Strato, the instrument of his release, is 'a fellow of a
good report', he dies in a mood akin to expiation:

> Caesar, now be still;
> I kill'd not thee with half so good a will. (V. v. 50)

In this admission, the whole contradictory nature of the enterprise to
which Brutus so perversely forced himself in the name of humanity is
gathered up in the prelude to a last act of self-annihilating resolve.

When Octavius enters to wind up the action with Antony, Strato
is able to turn on Messala, now a bondman to the conqueror, with an
assertion of the freedom that Brutus has found in death:

> Brutus only overcame himself,
> And no man else hath honour by his death.   (V. v. 56)

For all his devotion, however, he is ready to follow Messala by joining
the conqueror; the world of rhetorical aspiration and that of practical
reality rarely run parallel. The contrast between personal integrity
and the way of a world from which, we have good reason to believe,
it will be increasingly exiled, is implicit in Antony's epitaph, in which
he justifiably glorifies Brutus' personal qualities—

> This was the noblest Roman of them all—   (V. v. 68)

without concealing the 'envy' which surrounded this nobility and
used its inherent flaws for ends of its own. Octavius, having made
the victor's appropriate gesture of generosity, now that generosity can
no longer endanger his triumph, turns away with his companion to
enjoy the 'glory' they have won. The results to which this sharing
of the fruits of victory will lead are to be the theme for another play.

2 Antony and Cleopatra

It should be noted that in *Antony and Cleopatra* Act III the three scenes (viii, ix,
and x) set on the Plain near Actium are in the Oxford University Press edition
referred to collectively as Scene viii; thus there are eleven, not thirteen, scenes in
Act III. Similarly in Act IV the three scenes (x, xi, and xii) set on Ground
Between the Two Camps are referred to collectively as Scene x; there are
thirteen, not fifteen, scenes in Act IV.—Publisher's Note.

The critic of *Antony and Cleopatra* has, in offering an account of this
great tragedy—for the fact of its greatness is plainly evident in purely
poetic terms—to resolve a problem of approach, of the interpretation
of the author's true intention. This problem has in the past produced
a variety of strangely contrary solutions. Sooner or later, the critic
finds himself faced by two interpretations of Shakespeare's intention
in this play, each of them strongly defended and each of them arguing
from elements demonstrably present in the text, whose only dis-
advantage is that they appear to be mutually exclusive. Is *Antony and
Cleopatra*, to put the matter in other terms, a tragedy of lyrical inspiration, justifying love by presenting it as triumphant over death, or is it
rather a remorseless exposure of human frailties, a presentation of

spiritual possibilities dissipated through a senseless surrender to passion? Both interpretations, as we have said, can be defended; but to give each its due, to see them less as contradictory than as complementary aspects of a unified artistic creation, is as difficult as it proves, in the long run, to be necessary for a proper understanding of the play.[9]

The fact that these two readings can, in spite of their appearance of contradiction, *both* be derived from a dispassionate examination of the tragedy can be explained in the light of the past development of Shakespeare's art, as we have sought to follow it in the preceding pages, for both correspond to aspects of that development which we have already had occasion to consider. From one point of view, indeed, this tragedy is the supreme expression in Shakespeare of love as *value*, as triumphant over time through and in despite of death; from another, it exposes, again through a consideration of human relationships in love, the weakness which makes possible the downfall of the tragic hero, a weakness, moreover, which is given a *social* reference by being consistently related to the presentation of a society in the advanced stages of decay. Now all these factors, positive and negative alike, have been given expression in Shakespeare's earlier plays, and the novelty of *Antony and Cleopatra*—which is at once the last and greatest of his chronicle plays[10] and (with the exception of *Coriolanus*) his final exercise in tragedy—lies not in the fact of their presence but in the manner and complexity of their interrelation. The desire to see love as a manifestation of spiritual values derives, as we have seen,[11] from as far back at least as the sonnets, and in so far as *Antony and Cleopatra* succeeds in presenting it as such, the tragedy can be described as a positive counterpoise, given full depth and maturity, to *Troilus and Cressida*. The exposure of tragic weakness in the hero, first dramatically presented in *Othello*,[12] gathers strength through the great plays which follow and is finally related to an explicit political study, similar in kind though vastly developed in conception to that originally expressed in the later works on English history, in the Roman theme of *Coriolanus*. It is the supreme achievement, rather than the problem, of *Antony and Cleopatra* to show that these two lines of development, far from excluding one another, are in fact mutually illuminating.

The presence of these various elements, positive and negative so to call them, is admirably indicated in the short opening scene of the play, which serves, in a manner highly characteristic of the mature Shakespeare, as a kind of overture to the main action, a first brief exposition

of the themes which will be developed in the course of the tragedy by
relationship and contrast. The opening speech of Philo leaves us in no
doubt as to the adverse estimate which we are bound, on a dispassionate,
realistic view, to form of Antony's relationship to Cleopatra. His love is
described as a manifestation of 'dotage', which has, moreover, reached
the point at which it can no longer be tolerated, at which it 'overflows
the measure'; his former martial virtues, through which he maintained
his position of responsibility as a 'triple pillar of the world'—the phrase
is one which will be repeatedly echoed in the course of the political
action—have been shamefully abandoned, have become, in the scathing
comment of the common soldier,

> the bellows and the fan
> To cool a gipsy's lust.   (I. i. 9)

Nothing in the action to come, no poetic exaltation of the passion that
animates the main protagonists, can make this first estimate irrelevant;
it is part of the truth, and no later development can properly contradict
it.

The entry of Antony and Cleopatra, immediately after this indignant
comment, at once confirms it and introduces further themes for consideration. The first exchanges of the lovers are couched in an antiphonal
form that will become familiar in the passionate personal passages of this
play: emotion responds to emotion in a mutual heightening, a progressive accumulation of intensities. The effect at this point is a cunning
combination of lyricism with artifice, passionate dedication with the
conscious stimulation of feeling. To Cleopatra's request that Antony
should tell her 'how much' is his love for her, he replies, 'There's
beggary in the love that can be reckon'd'; and to her further statement,
made as it were to dare him, to provoke further and more far-reaching
expressions of devotion, that she will 'set a bourn how far to be beloved',
he responds with a lyrical declaration that suggests infinity, transcendence in emotion: 'Then must thou needs find out new heaven, new
earth.' Once more this sense of superhuman value apprehended
through love is one that the play will be concerned to repeat and
develop. Its final relationship will be to the experience of death imposed, as a consequence of their public failure, upon both characters at
the end of the tragedy; but meanwhile its emotional force must not
blind us to its irrelevance in terms of common realism. The fact that the
lovers who can thus address one another are in fact persons subdued to

the course of events in the world is stressed by the entry of a messenger from Rome and by the manner, remarkably discordant with the spirit of what we have just heard, of his reception. Antony's gesture in thrusting aside the newcomer in order to turn again to the mistress who has enslaved him is rather petulant, self-indulgent, than noble or generous; and Cleopatra, with the intention of playing upon his dependency, is not slow to chide him with the imagined anger of his wife or with that inferiority to the 'scarce-bearded Caesar' which already rankles in his uneasy conscience. The scene, in fact, by relating the political action to emotion poetically expressed, calls in the characteristic Shakespearean way for a balance in judgment which will have to be maintained throughout the play. On the one hand, Antony's readiness to turn away from outside events is given a certain weight by his first opulent gesture of triumphant love; on the other, that gesture is itself finally subjected to criticism, seen in its double nature as splendid and yet mean, a product of personal degradation. To bear *both* judgments in mind, refusing to neglect one in order to exalt the other, is to respond truly to the intention of the play.

This intention emerges further from Antony's full declaration of the emotion which moves him:

> Let Rome in Tiber melt, and the wide arch
> Of the ranged empire fall! Here is my space.
> Kingdoms are clay: our dungy earth alike
> Feeds beast as man: the nobleness of life
> Is to do thus; when such a mutual pair
> And such a twain can do't, in which I bind,
> On pain of punishment, the world to weet
> We stand up peerless.   (I. i. 33)

The expression, considered with care, introduces a number of elements which the later action will develop. The vast spaciousness of the political background, the sense that a world order, a universal structure of society, rests as upon its keystone on the individuals whose tragedy is to be presented is conveyed by reference to the 'wide arch' of the 'ranged empire'; and the very fact that Antony is ready to turn aside from issues so endowed with universality gives weight and a presumption of value to his emotion. By contrast with his assertion of devotion, the material nature of the outside world is stressed. Kingdoms become 'clay' and, in a phrase as daring as it is relevant, the earth itself is 'dungy', at once contemptible and yet, when brought to life by the transforming presence of passion, potentially fertile. Against this background, both vast and petty, equally related to 'beast' and 'man', the presence of intense personal emotion serves to emphasize 'the *noble-ness* of life', a nobility which has often concerned Shakespeare in his earlier tragedies[13] and which is here presented, for exaltation and criti-cism, in the story of his pair of lovers.

To what extent these will be able to maintain their worth, to justify the arrogant exaltation of themselves as 'a mutual pair', fit each for the other and ready to assert their 'peerless' quality before the world, time will show. Already there is a clear element of shame and indulgence, which the splendour of his rhetoric cannot conceal, in Antony's readiness to contemplate—publicly and with satisfaction—the crum-bling into ruin of the arch of empire; and his display of emotion is not left at its own estimate. Having been largely produced in reaction to Cleopatra's calculated ironies, it is followed immediately by the realism of her comment:

> Excellent falsehood!
> Why did he marry Fulvia, and not love her!
> I'll seem the fool I am not; Antony
> Will be himself.   (I. i. 40)

Antony's own following words confirm this estimate. From the high-flown expression of 'nobility', of transcendent emotion, we pass at a stroke to the cloying sensuality which is equally a part of his character. He exhorts her 'for the love of love and her *soft* hours' to set aside the reality of the outer world, which he dismisses in terms of 'conference *harsh*':

> There's not a minute of our lives should stretch
> Without some *pleasure* now. What *sport* to-night?   (I. i. 46)

The desire to fill every moment of life with its utmost content of sensa-tion belongs, perhaps, to a certain vital element in Antony's apprehen-sion of passion; but this vitality is qualified by the nature of the content which he foresees. *Sport* and *pleasure*: these turn out, when we pass from the universally lyrical to concrete reality, to be the true ends of Antony's devotion. The *sport* is, characteristically, obtained by neglect-ing the discharge of the speaker's political duties in the hearing of the Roman ambassadors; the seizing of the *pleasure* of the moment, and the desire to endow it with a spurious eternity by thrusting aside all other responsibilities, represent in fact the real content of Antony's generalized expressions of emotional nobility. The working out of the contrast so presented until, through a fusion of poetic and dramatic resources as comprehensive and complete as anywhere in Shakespeare, its diverse elements are shown to belong to a single range of emotion, is the true theme of *Antony and Cleopatra*.

Only a detailed analysis of the play can show Shakespeare achieving this aim by what is, in effect, a series of perfectly definable steps. The first of these concerns his use of the political action of the play, which is admirably adapted to a purpose that is no longer, as it had been in *Julius Caesar* and even, though to a lesser extent, in *Coriolanus*,[14] primarily political. The story of Antony and Cleopatra, as we have already seen in considering Antony's first speech, is set against an imperial background of far-reaching universality; and this vastness of range is itself an important factor in the play. The story of the lovers is influenced by events significant for the entire civilized world, and the poetry of the play deliberately and repeatedly stresses a sense of vast issues and tremendous dominions. Antony himself, as we have seen, is not only an infatuated lover but a 'triple pillar of the world'. Even the attendant who bears off the drunken Lepidus after the feast at which the triumvirs meet (II. vii) carries upon his shoulders 'the third part of the world'; and Octavia tells Antony that a quarrel between himself and Caesar would be

> As if the world should cleave, and that slain men
> Should solder up the rift. (III. iv. 31)

This emphasis on the world background of the tragedy can be related to Antony's own behaviour in either of two ways, each of which was anticipated in the opening scene and will assume its relevant place in the total effect. On the one hand, as Philo from the first asserted, the thrusting aside of responsibilities so great is at once an act of folly and a grave repudiation of duty; on the other, if Antony, although at times aware of this aspect of his conduct, is nonetheless repeatedly moved to confirm it, then we may think that the measure of his passion must be correspondingly universal, endowed with value in its own sight. The first estimate will be consistently confirmed by the comments of those who surround Antony and by the development of his tragedy; the second will find expression mainly in the lyricism of his own utterances and in the corresponding intensity of Cleopatra, but will loom increasingly large as the confirmation of his own failure in action is brought home by the course of events.

Our attitude towards this failure, indeed, is most subtly affected by the way in which Shakespeare has chosen to portray the political action of the play. For the world of the triumvirs, vast as it is and correspondingly opulent, is steeped in meanness and treachery. The presentation of it is full of touches which recall the realism of *Henry IV*; there is a good deal of the less admirable side of Prince Hal's character (though little, we must add, of Henry V's sense of the tragic burden of the royal vocation) in Caesar's controlled, ungenerous dedication to the pursuit of a power in itself necessarily and responsibly exercised; and Antony's own political folly, the reverse of Caesar's impressive command of the public situation, is not exempt from a note of hard calculation which his incapacity to calculate successfully does not make any more attractive. The expression of the play, indeed, lays continual stress upon the intrigue which, in Rome, takes the place of Egyptian corruption. Antony's account of the state of the Roman world near the beginning of the action is no more than typical:

> Our Italy
> Shines o'er with civil swords: Sextus Pompeius
> Makes his approaches to the port of Rome:
> Equality of two domestic powers
> Breeds scrupulous faction: the hated, grown to strength,
> Are newly grown to love: the condemn'd Pompey,
> Rich in his father's honour, creeps apace
> Into the hearts of such as have not thrived
> Upon the present state, whose numbers threaten;
> And quietness, grown sick of rest, would purge
> By any desperate change. (I. iii. 44)

It would be hard to find a better example of the way in which what can easily be read as no more than a straightforward piece of exposition is in fact charged with a linguistic vitality that relates it variously to the deeper issues of the play. Rome is in a dangerous state of 'equality', poised between two powers which, uncertain of the future and unable to trust one another in the present, 'breed' (the verb, with its sense of organic growth, has a quality of its own) a 'scrupulous', calculating 'faction'. Pompey, in turn, the common enemy of Caesar and Antony, is 'rich' only in his father's reputation; thus speciously endowed, he 'creeps' by a process of stealthy treachery into the hearts of those who have not made their fortunes, 'thrived' in the 'present state' of deceptive peace. These as a result grow (through the 'breeding' process already defined, we might say) into a threatening condition, and the result of the whole development is summed up in one of those images of dislocated organic function by which Shakespeare, from *Henry IV* at least onwards, has habitually chosen to express the implications of civil strife. The discontented elements in Rome are 'sick': 'sick' in themselves, because domestic war is the symptom of political disorder, and 'sick' too of the false state of 'rest', or stagnation, by which other interests in turn prosper. The end of this sickness here, as ever, is a 'purge', but one scarcely less uncertain, 'desperate' in its possible consequences, than that the desire for which had inspired Northumberland and his fellow conspirators to action in the Second Part of *Henry IV*.[15]

There are two scenes in the first, the predominantly 'political' part of the play, which particularly illuminate Shakespeare's presentation of the Roman world. The first is the episode (II. ii) in which Antony and Octavius, brought together for an attempted settlement of their differences, first eye one another in mutual distrust like two hard-faced gamesters, each jealous of what he is pleased to regard as his reputation and each equally distrustful of the trick which he feels his fellow 'pillar of the world' may have up his sleeve, and are finally persuaded by the calculating go-between Agrippa to build a sham agreement on the sacrifice by Caesar of his own helpless sister Octavia. The successive stages of this shameful proceeding are indeed beautifully indicated. To Caesar's frigid greeting, 'Welcome to Rome', Antony replies with an equally distant 'Thank you', and to his further laconic invitation 'Sit,' with the corresponding show of wary courtesy: 'Sit, sir.' These preliminaries over, the true discussion is opened by Antony with a phrase that shows, in its deliberate churlishness, his determination to be the first to take offence:

> I learn, you take things ill which are not so,
> Or being, concern you not. (II. ii. 33)

If, after a considerable amount of further recrimination, in which Caesar's thin-lipped, efficient disdain and Antony's libertine carelessness display themselves to the worst possible advantage, the trend of the discussion changes, it is because of one of those sudden, theatrical changes of mood for which Antony's behaviour is notable throughout. Caesar's accusation of perjury prompts a facile gesture to 'honour'—

The honour is sacred which he talks on now—

and this in turn leads to a show of self-excuse which reflects yet another
facet of Antony's shifting personality. His oath to come to Caesar's aid
has been, in his view, 'neglected' rather than denied; negligence,
indeed, has always been an outstanding feature of his character, and the
excuse is, not for the first time, that of the weak man who ascribes his
own failing to the machinations of others:

> when *poison'd* hours had bound me up
> From mine own knowledge. (II. ii. 94)

The 'poison', indeed, has worked more deeply than Antony knows.
His infatuation for Cleopatra, which he is now turning with singular
meanness into an excuse for his own indignity, is at least as much the
product as the cause of his self-betrayal.

Having thus shifted the fault, to his own satisfaction, upon Fulvia,
upon Cleopatra, upon anyone but himself, Antony's 'honour' is
satisfied and he is ready to come to terms. Around him are the helpless
tool Lepidus, always disposed to find 'nobility' in the words of the
shabby cut-throats who surround him, and Agrippa, ready as a courtier
should always be to whisper his supremely cynical suggestions into his
master's ear:

> Thou hast a sister by the mother's side,
> Admired Octavia: great Mark Antony
> Is now a widower. (II. ii. 124)

Thus seconded, and with the ground so prepared, the most dishonourable
project cannot but prevail. It is, indeed, insinuated before it is openly
proposed, and the jibe implied by Agrippa when he describes Antony
as a 'widower' is sufficient to produce in him, after Caesar's ironic
reference to Cleopatra, the parody of 'honour' contained in his 'I am
not married, Caesar': a false dignity which fittingly crowns a false
situation and leads to a transaction as cynical as it is clearly destined to
be impermanent. The degradation implied in Antony's relationship to
the political action which surrounds him will find no expression more
complete than this most specious and sordid of reconciliations.

Even more subtle, more beautifully constructed, is the great drunken
scene (II. vii) which celebrates this agreement, with its contrast between
the witless conviviality of the triumvirs and the 'quick-sands' of sober
treachery represented by Menas and turned aside by Pompey less

through honesty than through weakness. The opening remark of the servant—'Some o' their plants are ill-rooted already; the least wind i' the world will blow them down' (II. vii. 1)—refers as much to the farce of reconciliation now being enacted as to the business the speaker has in hand, and the further comment on the position of Lepidus—

> To be called into a huge sphere, and not to be seen to move in't, are the holes where eyes should be, which pitifully disaster the cheeks—   (II. vii. 16)

adds its own contribution to the note of hollowness, at once grotesque and sinister, which the whole episode is intended to convey. The following conversation between Lepidus and Antony, taking us further at each moment from common reality, leads up to its culminating phrase in Antony's

> These quick-sands, Lepidus,
> Keep off them, for you sink,   (II. vii. 66)

and thence to the return of sober calculation in Menas' blunt offer to Pompey which so effectively follows it: 'Wilt thou be lord of all the world?' The offer, of course, is rejected by Pompey, though with something less than conviction; but the moral tone of the episode has been established and the following descent into dissipation proceeds, as Lepidus, 'the third part of the world', is carried away, in the spirit of Menas' revealing observation to Enobarbus:

> The third part then is drunk: would it were all,
> That it might go on wheels.   (II. vii. 99)

The construction of the whole scene, which turns upon a superb counterpointing of the related motives of drunken folly and treachery, is far beyond the type of political realism formerly exhibited in *Henry IV*, but the inspiration is still demonstrably related to that of the earlier play.

Shakespeare's mature experience, therefore, moves him to present his characters in a world in which imperial pretensions, themselves laden with falsity, are associated through their poetical expression with the presence of over-ripeness and luxury in individual experience. 'Rest', as we have seen in Antony's account of the social significance, so to call it, of Pompey's rebellion, is the state of stagnation produced by opulence which inevitably leads to the purge of civil war. When the messenger, in the following scene (I. iv), brings Caesar news that 'flush youth revolt,' he is relating imperial disorder further to bodily surfeit and its consequences; his words underline those of Octavius which immediately precede them:

> This *common* body,
> Like to a vagabond flag upon the stream,
> Goes to and back, lackeying the varying tide,
> To *rot* itself with motion. (I. iv. 44)

Such a speech has its own function in the play, pointing to a tightening in poetic terms of the bond which unites the political, the 'Roman' action, to the 'Egyptian' fortunes of the tragic protagonists. The passion of Antony and Cleopatra, whatever may be said further of it, shares the weakness, the corruption of the world in which it grows to expression. One scarcely needs, in establishing this point, to feel the Elizabethan association of 'common' with sexual promiscuity; the link which binds the use of 'rot' to the images of decay associated more than once with Cleopatra[16] is enough to show how Shakespeare, through the continuous stressing of imagery invoking disorder and physical corruption, connects the universal situation of his play with the particular tragedy of mature love with which it is immediately concerned.

The realism thus shown, and poetically integrated into the spirit of the play, in the public affairs of the Roman world, is balanced, where more intimate relations are concerned, by a corresponding effect in the expression of the love of Antony and Cleopatra with its consistently Egyptian setting; indeed, the connection which underlies these contrasted realities, presented dramatically in terms of character and poetically by continuity in the use of imagery, is one of the principal keys to the total effect. Antony's advancing years are repeatedly stressed, and Caesar's exposures of his vices are too full of individuality in phrasing, too closely related to the characteristic over-ripeness of the play, for them to be taken at less than their full value:

> he fishes, drinks and wastes
> The lamps of night in revel. (I. iv. 4)

Nor are we allowed to overlook the disintegration which falls upon Antony in adversity. The qualities of self-deception, and the weakness which has led him repeatedly to place responsibility for his own actions in the hands of others, bear fruit in the hour of defeat in reactions which are almost invariably illogical and at times tinged with hysterical cruelty. In such a mood he finds consolation for his state in ordering the messenger of Octavius to be whipped until 'he whine aloud for mercy' (III. xi. 101). The futile viciousness revealed by this action is an essential part of Antony's nature. His relations with Cleopatra, whatever else they may be, are ruthlessly presented in terms of a weakness which the experience of disaster amply confirms. Every meeting between them, from the opening which we have already considered, is the exposure of an ageing libertine and a decaying queen; though it is the peculiar triumph of this tragedy that the most important meetings, being that, are also a great deal more. Shakespeare did not write a great play by ignoring Antony's failings or the presence of a corresponding corruption in Cleopatra; rather, while giving full weight to the weaknesses, he assimilates them into a poetic mood in which other elements, positive and triumphant in their associations, contribute to the total effect. Antony's love asserts itself at the play's supreme poetic moments in spite of his continual awareness that Cleopatra is 'a whore of Egypt', and the discarded mistress of Julius Caesar, in spite of the fact that his is the infatuation of an ageing soldier for a woman who has already served the pleasure of many men. It is the play's achievement to leave room for *both* estimates of the personal tragedy, the realistic as well as the lyrical; and if each has to be continually balanced against its opposite, so that the total impression can never, even at the last, rest upon one to the exclusion of the other, full understanding of what is intended depends upon an appreciation of the poetic quality so marvellously, richly present throughout the play. The gap between what is clearly, from one point of view, a sordid infatuation, and the triumphant feeling which undoubtedly, though never exclusively, prevails in the final scenes is bridged by a wonderful modification of connected imagery. Rottenness becomes the ground for fertility, opulence becomes royalty, infatuation turns into transcendent passion, all by means of an *organic* process which ignores none of its own earlier stages, which, while never denying the validity of the realistic estimates of the situation which accompany it to the last, integrates these in the more ample unity of its creative purpose.

This poetic effect, in turn, can be seen as firmly anchored, still in the case of Antony, on the reading of character. In the moment of his supreme degradation, just after he has vented his vain resentment on Caesar's emissary and accused Cleopatra of betraying him, he is capable of a clear-eyed statement of the hardening of the moral vision which accompanies the persistent surrender to the compulsions of appetite:

> when we in our viciousness grow hard—
> O misery on't!—the wise gods seal our eyes;
> In our own filth drop our clear judgements: make us
> Adore our errors; laugh at's while we strut
> To our confusion.   (III. xi. 111)

Antony, seeking to console himself, to place elsewhere the responsibility for his disaster, is driven in his own despite to a very clear comment on his condition. He is, indeed, one who has grown 'hard' in his 'viciousness', lost sensibility by his submission to 'appetite'; and the result has been to close his eyes, as though by a dispensation of fate, cruel but just, appropriate to the nature of his choices, to moral realities. The 'judgement' which should have been his distinctive quality as a man, a purposeful reasoning being, has been dropped into 'filth' of his own creation; the consequence of his 'errors' has been to reduce him to an absurd figure 'strutting'[17] in a caricature of self-approbation to his final confusion. The stroke which brings this moment of intimate revelation out of hysteria and attempted self-deception is one of the most revealing in the play.

In Antony, however, realism of this kind is still compatible with a sense of personal tragedy. At a later stage in his downfall, as his last moments of illusory triumph in battle fade away at Actium, he is capable of uttering, beyond the sentimental heroic gestures which are also part of his nature, a remorseless exposure of tragic weakness, of a personality dissolving in the contemplation of its own contradictions:

> All come to this? The hearts
> That spaniell'd me at heels, to whom I gave
> Their wishes, do discandy, melt their sweets
> On blossoming Caesar; and this pine is bark'd
> That overtopped them all. Betrayed I am.
> O, this false soul of Egypt! this grave charm,
> Whose eye beck'd forth my wars and call'd them home,
> Whose bosom was my crownet, my chief end,
> Like a right gipsy hath at fast and loose
> Beguiled me to the very heart of loss.   (IV. x. 33)

The sense of dissolution makes itself felt first through the contemplation of those who have abandoned Antony's failing fortunes; those who formerly followed him with dog-like servility in return for his generosity now 'discandy', 'melt their sweets', with cloying insistence, on the growing fortunes of 'blossoming Caesar'. By contrast the 'pine' that was Antony, who formerly 'overtopped them all' (and here we look forward to Cleopatra's image of 'the soldier's pole'[18]), is 'bark'd', stripped of its trappings of nobility and honour. This leads Antony to express his sense that he has been betrayed, that the 'grave charm', the superstitious amulet that Cleopatra has been to him, has become his 'false soul': 'soul' in recalling her former inspiration, and 'false' on account of the ruin to which his infatuation has led him. Even at this moment, Antony confesses to her magnetism and his own subjugation. It has been his tragedy to place his manhood in the hands of one who at once inspired his wars and irrationally, illogically 'call'd them home'. Upon her, abandoning all sense of his male responsibilities, he rested, her bosom his 'crownet', her love his impossibly exclusive end; and the result has been a betrayal, the 'beguiling' of his manhood into what he now sees—in a phrase that wonderfully combines haunting emotion with the sense of intimate failure—to be 'the heart of loss'.

It is because his moral being is flawed by this double vision that Antony falls; but it is also on account of it that he rises, at his best moments, to genuine tragic stature. The starting-point of this poetic 'redemption' (if we may so call it without unduly simplifying the complete effect) is the very rottenness we have observed in the world around him. The over-ripeness of that world is variously related to the personal tragic theme; if it is a fitting background to the story of mature passion, which indeed springs from and reflects it, it also lends point to Antony's assertion of the supremacy of his personal feeling. Antony undoubtedly gambled away his dignity as 'a triple pillar of the world', but the corruption and treachery of that world in part redeems his folly and justifies the contempt which at certain moments he expresses for it. To assert, however, that Shakespeare was content to make this contrast after the manner of the seeker after moral axioms (*All for love, or The World Well Lost*: axioms based indeed on a strangely indulgent morality) is vastly to underestimate his achievement. The play, as we have said, relates the rottenness of their world *poetically* to the individual fortunes of the protagonists; the love imagery springs from the over-ripeness, sharing its decay and yet exacting from it something not entirely limited to it. The presence of this further element, incommensurate with the realistic presentation of the tragedy but not contradictory to it, is most clearly grasped not in Antony (who may be said to receive it through participation), but in the more vital and complex poetry given, at her moments of supreme emotion, to Cleopatra.

Cleopatra's relationship to Antony is one in which complexity and falsehood, stressed from the first, are interwoven with other elements. As Antony, when he announces initially his decision to leave her to return to Rome and his public duties, interposes his efforts to justify himself—'Cleopatra', 'Most sweet queen'—her emotion responds to his own and soars finally into what is, while it lasts, an intuition of permanent value:

> Nay, pray you, seek no colour for your going,
> But bid farewell, and go: when you sued staying,
> Then was the time for words; no going then;
> Eternity was in our lips and eyes,
> Bliss in our brows bent, none our parts so poor
> But was a race of heaven. (I. iii. 32)

The supreme statement of mutual dedication is made to rest, for its force and poignancy, upon a foundation of accepted parting. Like Antony, Cleopatra needs to have her emotions stimulated, brought to a pitch by what is in the last analysis a contemplation of their lack of solid foundation. 'Bid farewell, and go,' she says, and we know that she means the opposite; and yet the power of what follows forbids us to see in her gesture merely a stratagem, obliges us to regard it as a trick indeed, but as a trick based finally on a measure of truth. In the world of time parting is the order of the day: but there has been for these lovers a time when 'eternity' at least *seemed* at their command, 'was in our lips and eyes', and when the 'bliss' reflected in their mutual gaze had a transforming quality, appeared to raise ordinary human attraction to an intuition of superhuman perfection:

> none our parts so poor
> But was a race of heaven. (I. iii. 36)

Belief in Antony's integrity, so dubious to the dispassionate eye of common sense, is made to rest on the validity of an experience which can only be held in a moment of emotional intensity and in reaction against what Cleopatra knows, even as she speaks, to be reality. While it lasts, and so far alone, the 'parts' of the lovers, the attributes of their physical presence, are transformed, rendered heavenly to the eyes of the imagination; and to maintain that vision is the aim, impossible but now necessary (because for it all else has been sacrificed), of life. Antony has chosen this life with Cleopatra, and by the constancy of his devotion to it he can fairly, if not exclusively, be judged. This constancy may be, is indeed, incommensurate with his other, public responsibilities; but the choice has been made and cannot now, without an acute sense of loss, be renounced.

This does not mean, of course, that Cleopatra is exempted from the realistic judgment which falls, at one time or another, on all the characters in this play. We have seen already that Shakespeare insists on her ripe maturity, on her dubious past, on the corruption undoubtedly represented by her person. This, however, is not all. Cleopatra, like Antony, is to be judged not only through her own words but through the reaction of those who surround her. Even Enobarbus' famous account of her meeting with Mark Antony at Cydnus (II. ii) is at least as much an exposure as a glorification. The beauty unquestionably conveyed by his description is, like so much else in this play, deliberately over-ripe, artificially opulent in its effect. The poop of Cleopatra's barge was 'beaten gold', the oars 'silver', and she herself lay in a pavilion 'cloth-of-gold of tissue'; surrounded by 'pretty dimpled boys, like smiling Cupids', her own person was an elaboration, wrought less by nature than by conscious artifice, on what is already conceived as a work of art:

> O'er-picturing that Venus where we see
> The fancy outwork nature. (II. ii. 208)[19]

On this vessel, indeed, nature has no place, and genuine feeling correspondingly little; its sails are 'purple' (the colour itself is, in a boat, unnatural) and so 'perfumed' that the very winds, sharing in the prevailing tone, are 'love-sick' with them. The smiling boy-Cupids and the 'gentlewomen, like the Nereides', belong, as do their rhythmic motions, to a world of elaborate decoration from which Cleopatra herself was not freed until she became involved in the popular acclaim—

> The city cast
> Her people out upon her—

and until we hear of her a little later, again through Enobarbus, as able to

> Hop forty paces through the public street;
> And having lost her breath, she spoke and panted,
> That she did make defect perfection,
> And, breathless, power breathe forth. (II. ii. 237)

The presence of these two contrasted elements in the description corresponds to the essential diversity of the character. Cleopatra, though the creature of the world which surrounds her, can at times emerge from it, impose upon her surroundings a vitality which is not the less astonishing for retaining to the last its connection with the environment it transcends. This combination of 'nature' with artifice, vitality with corruption, in a single, infinitely complex creation, is at once the essence of her personality and the key to the conflicting estimates which her relations to Antony inspire in the course of the tragedy.

The manner in which much of Cleopatra's poetry derives from the idea of Egypt, of the overflowing fertility of the Nile, is especially significant in this respect, for in Egypt, and more particularly in its sacred river, the ideas of corruption and natural growth are most closely interwoven. Her love is, in the words of Antony's promise, 'the *fire* that *quickens* Nilus' slime' (I. iii. 68), a living fertility, expressed in terms of fire, that grows by a continuous process of nature out of the corruption of 'slime'. The play is full of this balance between decay and fruitfulness; in her declining fortunes Cleopatra describes herself as 'the blown rose' (III. xi. 39), combining beauty and decline in a complex unity of sensation. So assured is Shakespeare's mastery that he can impart dignity even to Cleopatra's relations with Julius Caesar. In those days, she says, she was 'a morsel for a monarch' (I. v. 31), and the 'monarch' redeems, at least in part and while the emotional spell of her utterance is maintained, the indignity of 'morsel', of having been a 'cold' scrap upon 'dead Caesar's trencher' (III. xi. 117). But perhaps the most complex example of Cleopatra's conversion of slime into fertility is her speech to Antony immediately after the whipping and dismissal of Thyreus:

> as it determines, so
> Dissolve my life! The next Caesarion smite!
> Till by degrees the memory of my womb,
> Together with my brave Egyptians all,
> By the discandying of this pelleted storm
> Lie graveless, till the flies and gnats of Nile
> Have buried them for prey. (III. xi. 161)

The proper reading of this speech brings us very close to the spirit in which this tragedy is conceived. The astonishing poetic power involved is not open to question, nor is the fact that it contributes, within certain limits, to an assertion of constancy in the face of death: but the emphasis is at least equally on decay, and the emotional compensation offered to Antony is significantly couched in terms of dissolution. Dissolution, indeed, the 'melting' of a personality into its component elements of corruption, has been the essence of the entire episode, and here Cleopatra is engaged in turning it into her own kind, at once intense and equivocal, of poetry. 'Discandying' imparts a sense of melting sweetness to corruption, and 'dissolve', whilst presenting the end of the corrupt process itself, gives it an ease and inevitability which looks forward to the final aspic scene; and 'the memory of my womb' again suggests the full fertility associated with the speaker's desires, the reflection of a certain richness of life (real or fictitious?) which seems to blend with its foreseen conclusion, the decay so vividly implied in 'the flies and gnats of Nile'. Within these variations, at once hauntingly lyrical and ruthless, the speech contains the whole range of an emotion particularly relevant to this stage—combining disenchantment with a first, flushed anticipation of the conclusion—of the play's development.

These complexities, indeed, have one principal aim—to evolve a certain tragic greatness for Cleopatra's passion out of its very stressed imperfections, out of the impermanence of the flesh and the corrupt world with which it is organically connected. As the story proceeds, Antony is subjected to a similar development, making him, without evading or in any way minimizing his weaknesses, fit for an end in which *value* and therefore true tragedy have a part to play. From the first, certain moments of generosity and bravery, fragments which might, under different circumstances and without the accompanying weakness, have made him a complete man, are brought out in him by contrast with Caesar's calculating self-control and the treachery of the surrounding world. Even the folly and shame of his renunciation of practical affairs is to some degree compensated by the splendid assertion of his love; 'kingdoms are clay' for him, as we have seen, and the only value of the clay is to be at certain moments a ground in which the fertility of love may take root. In accordance with this intention the decline of Antony's fortunes is balanced by a series of devices which, while they do not free him from responsibility for his fate, set him apart from the increasingly disreputable issues which so persistently shadow the public conduct of the Roman world; that issues so great, so imperial in their scope can come, even if only for certain moments, to be felt as trivial is in itself a measure of the quality of his passion. The evolution of his fortunes balances a similar development in Cleopatra until, after their defeat, they are ready for the great meeting on the monument (IV. xiii), in which irony and criticism are against all probability dissolved (the word is appropriate) into transcendent poetry.

It will be seen that the total effect of the tragedy is one of no small complexity. How far this is so is amply confirmed in the final scenes. Antony's death is a natural consequence of political folly and personal infatuation. We are not allowed to forget that its immediate cause is a miscarriage of Cleopatra's ingenuity, which leads her to announce falsely her own death and so drives him to despair; to the last Antony is involved in subterfuges and deceptions which spring logically from the nature of his passion. But just as 'slime' was converted into the memory of fertility, just as the folly of renouncing the 'ranged empire' was to some degree balanced by the rottenness of that empire, so does death, which is the consequence of Antony's prodigality, bring with it a certain liberation from triviality and an opening of the way to the poetic assertion of a truly tragic emotion. We can feel this liberation in the very movement of the blank verse, in which 'labour' and its opposite are marvellously fused in what is simultaneously weakness, a renunciation of all effort in the light of admitted failure, and an intuition of peace:

> now all labour
> Mars what it does; yea, very force entangles
> Itself with strength.   (IV. xii. 47)

A little further on, death is explicitly associated with love:

> I will be
> A *bridegroom* in my death, and run into't
> As to a *lover's* bed.   (IV. xii. 99)

In the face of death the contrary judgments which this tragedy invites are maintained and marvellously fused. Not for the first time in Shakespeare the tragic hero, as he approaches the moment of resolution, incorporates expressions that proceed from the weakness, the self-indulgence that is destroying him, into an effect that transcends them. Antony's suicide, indeed, becomes thus an integral part of the final lyrical assertion of emotional *value* and therefore, up to a point, of life. It looks forward to its counterpart in the poetry of Cleopatra's death, in which 'baser life' is finally transmuted into imagery of fire, air, and immortality.

The spirit of the great scene on Cleopatra's monument (IV. xiii) is thus prepared for by what has gone before. Its poetry is marked by the extraordinary range of imagery which characterizes the play, and which implies an equally extraordinary power of fusing it into a single and continuous effect. Shakespeare himself could not have written this at any previous point in his career:

> O, see, my women,
> The crown o' the earth doth melt. My lord!
> O, withered is the garland of the war,
> The soldier's pole is fall'n; young boys and girls
> Are level now with men; the odds is gone,
> And there is nothing left remarkable
> Beneath the visiting moon. (IV. xiii. 62)

One has only to attempt to separate a few of the images in this 'knot intrinsicate' of poetry to realize the extent of the poet's control. 'The crown o' the earth' carries on naturally enough the tone of transcendent royalty with which Cleopatra has emphasized Antony's greatness and the depth of her love and grief. The verb 'melt', so repeatedly used in this play and with such a varied range of associations, from deliquescence to spiritualization, is not *factually* related to 'crown'; it has been chosen because it removes the sense of harshness from Antony's death by suggesting a natural, gentle dissolution into purest air (there is to be a similar feeling about Cleopatra's own death—'As sweet as balm, as soft as air, as gentle') and so prepares for the sense of triumph associated with her grief. 'The soldier's pole' is probably the standard of war; but 'pole', taken together with 'crown' and the following 'boys and girls', bears a complex suggestion of May Day, when love and the renewed life of spring meet in triumph. If we set these joyful associations against the corresponding depths of desolation, we shall feel something of the tremendous emotional range covered by the episode. The final reference to the 'visiting moon' lends further point to this relation of joy to death and sorrow. The fact that after Antony's death there is left nothing 'remarkable' beneath the moon not only suggests the extent of Cleopatra's loss but also implies that their union, while it lasted, reduced all earthly things to a dull uniformity. The whole passage is built upon a breadth of imagery which does not yield in complexity to the greatest ambiguities of the sonnets which treat equally of love; but, unlike them, its variety is subdued to a harmony which regards both desolation and triumph as integral parts of a complete mood. The poetry which sublimates emotion in *Antony and Cleopatra*—and it is not suggested that the mood thus expressed is permanent or covers the whole meaning of the tragedy—no longer turns, like that of even the later tragedies, upon a cleavage between 'good' and 'evil' within the unity of experience. It depends rather, while it lasts, upon a perfect continuity between the 'flesh', with its associations of earth and death, and the justification of passion in terms of emotional value and intensity. This continuity is in no way vague or sentimental, but is splendidly realized in a harmonious scale of related imagery; this scale is most completely expressed in Cleopatra's final speeches.

Cleopatra's death is preceded by a successive loosening of the bonds which have so far tied her to the political action. The loosening is, characteristically, gradually achieved. Her last negotiations with Caesar are marked, deliberately, by calculation and even fear; she seeks to obtain from him what she can, and is even detected in a stratagem to set aside material provision for her future purposes. The true direction of the scene, however, is set from the first deathwards; and death itself is indicated, in the very first speech, in a manner as complex as it is intensely poetical:

> it is great
> To do that thing that ends all other deeds;
> Which shackles accidents and bolts up change;
> Which sleeps and never palates more the dug,
> The beggar's nurse and Caesar's. (V. ii. 4)

Once more we are in the presence of the astounding breadth of reference which is typical of the imagery of this play; and once more each element in it contributes, beyond itself, to the total effect of the tragedy. That the intention of suicide is, at this moment and in the mind of this speaker (the reservation is important, for other judgments are possible and relevant), nobly conceived is beyond doubt; it is 'great' precisely in that it ends Cleopatra's slavery to the world of contingencies, that—in the splendid emphasis of her own phrase—'It *shackles* accidents and *bolts up* change.' The prisoner of her fate, in other words, now aims to take her own fate captive. She does so, moreover, by an act which she conceives to be gentle as 'sleep', a sleep differentiated only by its eternity from that shown, in all times and conditions, by the baby at rest on its mother's breast. Only—it is essential to remember, lest the beauty of the image should induce in us a mood of surrender, of unqualified acceptance which is foreign to the total intention—the baby will, in due course, turn out to be the aspic, whose 'biting', in the words of the Clown, who combines realism with fascination, is 'immortal' (V. ii. 245), and the sleep, though associated with images of peace and fulfilment, will be that of death.

The next stage in Cleopatra's progress lies in her exaltation, through memory, of the Antony whom she has lost in life. Once more the breadth of reference is only paralleled by the poetic power which can fuse impressions so diverse into a single, unstrained effect:

> For his bounty,
> There was no winter in't; an autumn 'twas
> That grew the more by reaping: his delights
> Were dolphin-like; they show'd his back above
> The element they lived in: in his livery
> Walk'd crowns and crownets; realms and islands were
> As plates dropp'd from his pocket.   (V. ii. 86)

That such an apostrophe can be accepted as natural, unstrained, and that images so diversely and intensely conceived can be gathered together to produce one impression, is a sign that we are dealing with emotion of no common depth: that Dolabella explicitly denies that it corresponds to reality[20] warns us, at the same time, against making exclusive claims upon its relevance to the whole conception. Cleopatra is living in a world which is the projection of her own feelings. That world, while it lasts, is splendidly valid, vital in its projection; but only death, which is the end of vitality, can prevent an awakening from it. For that reason, if for no other, Cleopatra is resolved to die.

Her last great speech opens significantly with an assertion of 'immortal longings'. The reference to immortality is in full contrast to the impression of 'dungy earth', from which her love sprang and in virtue of which Antony's fall and her death were both inevitable. Yet the 'immortality' so evoked has a content of 'nobility' which memory supplies; it is simply the highest assertion of her love for the dead and infinitely exalted Antony, whom she can now call for the first time in the play, precisely because he is dead, 'Husband!' In the light of this association of love and immortality, death assumes a fresh poetic function. It becomes a dissolution, a purging of all the earthly elements upon which love had been based:

> I am fire and air; my other elements
> I give to baser life.   (V. ii. 291)

On the edge of death the sense of dissolution acquires a further significance; only the purest elements of feeling remain in Cleopatra—and those, by a paradox particularly meaningful at this moment, which are most fully, most intensely alive. From a great distance, as it seems, we are reminded of the other elements of 'baser life', the earth and fertile slime from which love sprang, with which its degradation was associated, and in virtue of which defeat and death were inevitable; but defeat and death themselves have now become subdued, at least in the speaker's exaltation, to the 'immortal longings' which they themselves brought into being, and the adverse fortunes of the world are dismissed as

> The luck of Caesar, which the gods give men
> To excuse their after wrath.   (V. ii. 288)

In spite of this note of transcendence, however, the firm foundation on the senses of the imagery by which the speech achieves its purpose is essential to the full effect. It conveys no abstract triumph imposed upon what has gone before. The elements of 'fire and air' represent a continual refining process from the comparative earthliness of the opening, and the effect of Cleopatra's longing is reinforced by the keenly sensed reference to 'the juice of Egypt's grape', suggesting all that is most alive and delicate in the activity of the senses.

This impression of continuity balanced by infinite remoteness is a principal key to the development of *Antony and Cleopatra*, in which self-indulgence and valid emotion are bound together in the death which is their common end. Shakespeare has so refined, so intensified his love poetry by a progressive distillation of sensible experience that it is able to assimilate the apparently incompatible fact of death, which is simultaneously release and the reflection, on the plane of common realism, of moral failure:

> The stroke of death is as a lover's pinch
> Which hurts and is desired.   (V. ii. 297)

'Hurts' and 'desired', which seem so contradictory, reinforce one another in a splendid balance of sensations; the pain implied in 'hurts' is so delicately, so intensely felt that it becomes fused with the keenness of the lover's desire. An emotion originally sensuous, unashamedly physical in kind, has become, besides that, something more, a taking up of the sensible into a world that shadows permanence: a gesture which originated in rhetoric and deception, and which retains its connection with these base realities, has become assumed into tragic validity. The death which is the supreme proof of failure, to which everything in this equivocal relationship has tended, becomes an untying of 'this knot intrinsicate' of body and soul, of infinite desires hitherto subject to adverse and earthly circumstance.

It remains only for the entry of Caesar's envoy, bringing back the external, the real world, to break against the final confidence of Charmian's defiant farewell:

> It is well done, and fitting for a princess
> Descended of so many royal kings. (V. ii. 328)

Caesar himself, when he arrives, can only utter one of those fitting epitaphs in which he specializes, and follow it by the profounder reflection:

> she looks like sleep,
> As she would catch another Antony
> In her strong toil of grace. (V. ii. 347)

In this last phrase, something very like the spirit which animates the entire presentation of Cleopatra finds its summary. For Antony, her fascination has been a 'toil', a snare which he had accepted for both of them once he had fallen victim to her enchantment, and which led to their common downfall; but it was also a toil of 'grace', in which beauty and, at the supreme moment of dedication in death, a certain fitness have made themselves apparent.

The whole development of the play has been tending to this point. The balancing of the generosity which Antony's folly sometimes implies against Caesar's successful meanness, the gradual ascent of the love imagery from earth and 'slime' to 'fire and air', are all part of one great process which now needs death to complete it. For death, which had seemed in the sonnets and early tragedies to be incontrovertible evidence of the subjection of love and human values to time, now becomes by virtue of Shakespeare's poetic achievement an instrument of release, the necessary condition of an experience which, although dependent upon temporal circumstance, is by virtue of its *value* and intensity incommensurate with it—that is, 'immortal'. This effect, moreover, is achieved at the same time that death is seen, from another point of view, as the natural end of a line of conduct in which folly and self-indulgence have consistently predominated. The emotions of Antony and Cleopatra, like their weaknesses, are built upon 'dungy earth', upon 'Nilus' slime', and so upon time which these elements by their nature imply; but, just as earth and slime are quickened into fire and air, while retaining their sensible qualities as constituent parts of the final experience, so time itself, in which this tragedy of waste and vanity was nurtured, becomes simultaneously a necessary element in the creation of 'immortality'.

3   Coriolanus

It would be hard to imagine a greater gulf than that which separates the world of *Coriolanus* from that of *Antony and Cleopatra*. The poetry of the latter play takes in with effortless ease the fortunes of a world in conflict; that of the former achieves its effects through intense concentration upon the familiar and the material.[21] Its prevailing imagery is rigid and unadorned, more appropriate to a village or a country town than to a capital of historical significance. The aristocratic ladies of Rome sit at home upon their 'stools'[22] and the people carry 'bats and clubs'[23] to their riots; the action abounds in references to simple pastimes, such as 'bowls',[24] or turns upon disputes over the immediate necessities of life, 'corn', 'coal', and 'bread'.[25] To a great extent the difference is imposed by history; whereas the events which provided the background to Antony's fall concerned an empire which spanned the known world, those which condition the tragedy of Coriolanus are concentrated within the limits of a city and its immediate surroundings and reflect the tension between its classes, the threat to its indispensable unity.

This tension, this threat, marks the struggle for power in a world at once restricted and pitiless. The sense of this struggle is conveyed almost immediately by the patrician Menenius when, in rebuking the citizenry for their rebellion against constituted authority, he embarks upon a fable which reveals more than he can himself realize of the true situation in Rome. The central image of the fable, derived from Plutarch, but considerably developed, is that of the functioning of the human body in its related parts:

> There was a time when all the body's members
> Rebell'd against the belly: thus accused it:
> That only like a gulf it did remain
> I' the midst of the body, idle and unactive,
> Still cupboarding the viand, never bearing

> Like labour with the rest; where the other instruments
> Did see and hear, devise, instruct, walk, feel,
> And, mutually participate, did minister
> Unto the appetite and affection common
> Of the whole body.   (I. i. 101)

The wording of the parable tends to the transformation of a political commonplace, a theoretical vindication of natural 'degree', into a criticism, not of this attitude or that, but of Roman society itself. The impression of a general obstruction of all vital activity communicates itself through the unhealthy stagnation of 'idle and unactive', the coarseness of 'cupboarding'. These effects are set against the very noticeable livening of the verse when Menenius turns to the 'other instruments', the senses and active faculties of the body which represent, however, not the class he is defending, but its enemies. These contrasted elements, thus concentrated, in a manner profoundly typical of the play, upon images of food and digestion, answer to the real state of the Roman polity. Stagnation and mutual distrust, mirroring the ruthlessness of contrary appetites for power, are the principal images by which we are introduced to the public issues of *Coriolanus*.

It does not follow that our sympathies are to lie, as Menenius intends, solely with the patricians. He criticizes justly the failure of the populace to recognize the part played by their superiors in the social organism; but there is a sense in which the figure he uses to illustrate his point turns the argument against his own thesis. The patricians are presented in the likeness of the 'belly'; and though this was indispensable to the proper functioning of the body it was also, in the view of its detractors, 'idle and unactive', self-satisfied and complacent in the security of its central position. In this connection we should not overlook that brilliant stroke,

> with a kind of smile,
> Which ne'er come from the lungs, but even thus,   (I. i. 113)

where the fine balance between the ironic and the self-contented implies so much more than the patrician speaker realizes. By making the belly speak 'tauntingly' against the 'mutinous' members, Menenius asserts the invincible self-satisfaction which has already made itself felt in the assumption of infallibility—

> Confess yourselves wondrous malicious,
> Or be accused of folly—   (I. i. 93)

with which he embarks upon his reproof. Thinking of the motives of

those who dare to challenge the authority of his own class in terms of
sterile 'malice', he fails to penetrate to the causes of a dislocation deeper
than any partial vision can adequately compass.

So much is confirmed by the force of the Citizen's rejoinder. His
vigorous defence of the superior organs—the 'kingly-crowned head',
'the vigilant eye', 'the tongue our trumpeter' (I. i. 121)—has little
indeed to do with the reality he is defending; but it cuts across the complacency of the patrician rebuke with a force that the patronizing
interruption—''Fore me, this fellow speaks!'—cannot diminish. The
total effect of the fable is to convey, through and beyond Menenius'
justification of privilege, the condition of the social organism from
which the hero's tragedy will spring. We are shown, indeed, a populace incapable of discerning its true good, confirming by its short-
sighted behaviour its need for the guidance which only a class recognized to be superior can give it; but we are shown also a patrician caste
unreasonably contemptuous of the rest of society, who have forfeited
much of their claim to superiority by their attitude towards those upon
whose existence and effort their own well-being, in the last analysis,
depends. Both the factions thus confronted in sterile obstinacy are set
in an iron framework which permits no real contact or community of
purpose, nothing but ruthless repression countered by outbursts of
animal discontent. So situated towards one another, they cannot fail to
come to blows. 'Rome and her rats are at the point of battle': Menenius
describes the situation in one, and relevant, way, but other possible
interpretations suggest that there can be no final victory in this struggle,
that the contending factions are involved in a common disaster which
their mutual obstinacy has brought upon the city.

Menenius' first speech in verse, preluding his fable, reflects his
assumption that the position by which his own class stands to benefit
belongs to the natural and unalterable nature of things. His habitual
kindliness, which allows him to show himself benignly human towards
those whom he assumes to be his inferiors, should not blind us to the
iron beneath his words. He takes it for granted that it is the duty of
himself and his like to exercise 'charitable care' over the people; but
his concept of 'charity', kindly and condescending so long as it is
unquestioned, is compatible with the denial of responsibility when
'charity' is not enough:

                         For your wants,
         Your suffering in this dearth, you may as well

> Strike at the heaven with your staves as lift them
> Against the Roman state, whose course will on
> The way it takes, cracking ten thousand curbs
> Of more strong link asunder than can ever
> Appear in your impediment. For the dearth,
> The gods, not the patricians make it, and
> Your knees to them, not arms, must help.   (I. i. 70)

The effect is more searching in its revelation of complacency than may at once appear. Rhythm and expression combine to embody the irresistible motion of an impersonal and overbearing force with which the speaker finally feels himself identified. The effect of the division in the earlier part of the speech between 'cracking' and 'asunder', both words which carry a strong sense of violent physical separation, is to convey an impression of ruthless dedication to an indifferent fatality. The emotional impetus so generated is then brought to a sudden curb after 'impediment': the long period comes to an emphatic pause in the middle of its implacable development and Menenius, turned from the bland counsellor into the mouthpiece of an unrelenting social destiny, throws upon the 'gods' the responsibility for a catastrophe which no thought of human solidarity is allowed to mitigate.

The speech, indeed, strikes for the first time a note which will be almost obsessively present in the following development. Its spirit emerges perhaps most clearly from the phrase 'strike at the heaven with your staves,' with which Menenius dismisses the protests of the citizens and the efficacy of their '*stiff* bats and clubs'. These phrases, and others of a like nature scattered through the play, answer to the peculiar sensation of hardness with which its conflicting attitudes are presented. The rough implements of the people and the iron weapons of their masters threaten one another in a closed and indifferent universe; the 'heavens' remain stonily impenetrable, so that the 'stiff' weapons can almost be heard to clang when raised, not so much against injustice as against the imposition of an impersonal fatality. This sense of hard hostility answers to an order in which patricians and people are out of contact, hostile and exclusive in positions which seem to have been imposed upon them by the nature of things. If Menenius is right to stress this fatality—

> You are transported by calamity
> Thither where more attends you—   (I. i. 79)

the fact remains that the prospect of 'calamity' rouses no real echo of sympathy in his mind. When he blandly asserts that his fellow patricians care for the people like 'fathers', he lays himself open to a retort which the facts of the situation in no small measure confirm:

> They ne'er cared for us yet: suffer us to famish, and their store-houses crammed with grain; . . . repeal daily any wholesome edict established against the rich, and provide more piercing statutes daily, to chain up and restrain the poor. (I. i. 83)

Envy and blind resentment no doubt play their part in the Citizen's accusation of patrician egoism; but the concluding answer to so much complacent paternalism is, as far as it goes, blunt and effective: 'If the war eat us not up, they will, and there's all the love they bear us.'

Into the cauldron of dissension thus ominously overflowing the most disconcerting and incongruous of all Shakespeare's heroes plunges with a characteristic outburst of uncontrolled and misdirected energy:

> What's the matter, you dissentious rogues,
> That, rubbing the poor itch of your opinion,
> Make yourselves scabs? (I. i. 170)

The long speech thus introduced is an unconscious self-revelation, alternating the slow and weighty amplitude proper to the speaker's martial dignity with descents into an explosive directness which tells its own tale of imperfect control. The most striking effect is one of intense contradiction—

> Your virtue is
> To make him worthy whose offence subdues him
> And curse that justice did it.
> . . . your affections are
> A sick man's appetite, who desires most that
> Which should increase his evil— (I. i. 180)[26]

a chafing of contrary sensations, as spontaneous in impulse as they are laboured, unnaturally hard in expression, which rises to the crowning denunciation:

> He that depends
> Upon your favours swims with fins of lead
> And hews down oaks with rushes. (I. i. 185)

The plain but ponderous images fall like sword-strokes, deadly, force-ful, metallic, upon the abuses which they repudiate; but the periods in which they are embedded break habitually in the middle of their

rhythmic structure, fail to cohere in a cumulative impression of life
The general sense is of a violent torrent of energy concentrated upon a
narrow range of ideas and prejudices, deriving finally from an irreparable lack of spontaneity in the intimate relationships which have made
the speaker what he is.

The full significance of this attitude will only emerge as the tragedy
progresses. In the meantime Coriolanus, convinced by breeding and
temperament that to defer to his natural inferiors is to 'flatter beneath
abhorring', asserts in its most extreme form the patrician claim to
unlimited authority:

> You cry against the noble senate, who,
> Under the gods, keep you in awe, which else
> Would feed on one another. (I. i. 192)

The claim is one which the facts in part justify, but which is in danger
of being turned into a brutal imposition. So much is clear when
Marcius winds up his tirade with a ruthless assertion of force which
amounts to a caricature of true valour:

> Would the nobility lay aside their ruth,
> And let me use my sword, I'ld make a quarry
> With thousands of these quarter'd slaves, as high
> As I could pick my lance. (I. i. 203)

Here, at least, the strength of emotion, hitherto half strangled by its
own indignation, issues in an image close to the speaker's heart; but,
though it is clear that the people against whom this anger is directed
are weak, worthless, and brutal in many of their reactions, this truth
cannot lend validity to what remains a barbarous perversion of traditional heroic values.

This initial confrontation does not lead immediately to disaster.
Rome's need of its warrior hero is stressed by news of the Volscian
rising, which he welcomes as offering the authorities an opportunity to
'vent' the 'musty superfluity' of the state into a foreign adventure.
But before Marcius is set in motion on the first, ascendant stage of his
career, we are offered a revealing glimpse of his family circle, and more
particularly of the mother whose demands upon him will determine the
course of his tragedy. The First Citizen has already linked these demands
to his martial prowess when he has said, in explanation of his service to
Rome, that 'he did it to please his mother and to be partly proud'
(I. i. 40). This pride proceeds from a strange mixture of solicitude and

ruthlessness, possession and renunciation in Volumnia's own nature. Remembering 'the only son of her womb' as 'a tender-bodied child', the repository of all her affection, whom 'for a day of King's entreaties' she would not 'sell an hour from her beholding', she can yet recall how she found herself 'considering how honour would become such a person' and how she directed his youth to a stern and fanatical conception of duty. Fearing that her son might 'picture-like hang by the wall', she willed that he should 'seek danger where he was likely to find fame'; and, as she dwells on this decision, her thoughts rise to a severe exaltation of the sacrifice which she imposed upon her affection and which she is now determined to assert as freely and responsibly taken. 'To a cruel war *I sent him*: from whence he returned, his brows bound with oak.' (I. iii. 15). Seen in this way, the hero's glory becomes the reflection of his mother's purpose, a compensation for the sacrifice which sent him forth, in despite of a mother's natural attachment, to affirm in dedication to 'honour' the exalted destiny she has chosen for him.

Before long, and in the course of the same scene, this concentration rises to a ruthlessly masculine participation in her son's achievements. Her ideal, to which he will amply correspond, ceases to be human, becomes the exaltation of an engine impersonally dedicated to destruction. Marcius will 'pluck Aufidius down by the hair', be shunned by his enemies as children 'fly from a bear'; as she imagines him defying the Volscians it is as if she were herself engaged in the bloody work, sharing in its ruthless fascination. The picture of her victorious son—

> his bloody brow
> With his mail'd hand then wiping, forth he goes
> Like to a harvest-man that's task'd to mow
> Or all, or lose his hire—   (I. iii. 38)

balancing against a touch of spontaneous poetry the grim aspect of the warrior bathed in blood, is not allowed to deflect her from the dedication which her nature so insistently demands. When Virgilia, with wifely concern, pleads 'no blood', her answer is ferociously concentrated on the idea which entirely possesses her. 'Away, you fool': the repudiation ends in a glorification of bloodshed more fantastic and inhuman than all that has gone before:

> the breasts of Hecuba,
> When she did suckle Hector, look'd not lovelier

> Than Hector's forehead when it spit forth blood
> At Grecian swords, contemning.   (I. iii. 44)

Even at this moment of supreme dedication to her martial ideal, the thought of maternity lingers on as an obsessive presence in the mother's mind. Sacrificed to the masculine cult of 'honour', its survival emphasizes the moralin completeness which will bring her son to ruin.

These narrow and perverse intensities are not allowed to pass without implicit comment. This is provided by Volumnia's picture of her grandson in the nursery:

> O' my word, the father's son; I'll swear, 'tis a very pretty boy. O' my troth, I looked upon him o' Wednesday half an hour together; has such a confirm'd countenance. I saw him run after a gilded butterfly; and when he caught it, he let it go again; and after it again; and over and over he comes, and up again; catched it again: or whether his fall enraged him, or how 'twas, he did so set his teeth, and tear it; O, I warrant, how he mammocked it!
> (I. iii. 62)

There could be no better comment on the deadly lack of feeling which has surrounded Marcius from birth and of which his child, in turn, partakes; the boy is, after all, 'the father's son'. To complete the effect we need only the crushing, if unconscious, irony implied in Valeria's observation, 'Indeed, la, 'tis a noble child.' The entire episode, with its glimpse of the father's narrow and inhuman concentration mirrored in the precocious savagery of his child, makes a revealing introduction to the episodes of war which follow.

All this, however, acutely and finely observed as it is, is only one side of the picture which this strangely inconsistent hero presents. On the other, and not less real, we are made to feel in this same exclusive family circle the reality of an affection so intense, so concentrated, that it binds the son irrevocably to his mother, making him indeed a hero and the saviour of his city, but finally, in its one-sided possessiveness, leading to his ruin. Subject from birth to the relentless pressure of his mother's affection, Coriolanus has grown into a man at once capable of the deepest feeling and unable to give it free expression, even at times ashamed of what he feels: the man who at one moment can salute his wife, on his return from the hazards of war, with a marvellous, shy tenderness—

> My gracious silence, hail!
> Would'st thou have laugh'd had I come coffin'd home,

That weep'st to see me triumph? Ah, my dear,
Such eyes the widows in Corioli wear,
And mothers that lack sons—   (II. i. 194)

and who, at another, thrusts aside his own heroic deeds, bashfully and
awkwardly, as scarcely worthy of mention or recall: in other words,
at once a hero, an inexorable fighting machine, and a childishly naïve
and undeveloped human being. The play is consistent in presenting
Coriolanus under both these aspects. As a warrior, neither material
rewards nor normal pity can make him other than a superb but inhuman engine of war placed at his country's service; as a son, his
intimate resolution is helpless before his mother's successive demands
upon him, and he is brought to isolation and disaster by following the
strain of natural sensibility which lies present in the deepest recesses of
his nature, but which he has never really been brought to consider or
to understand.

   This combination of nobility and weakness is fully revealed in its
true nature when Coriolanus returns to Rome to celebrate his victory
at Corioli. The victory has been won in the name of his city's aris-
tocracy, the ruling patrician class, to which he is so proudly conscious
of belonging, and in the pursuit of personal rivalry with Tullus
Aufidius. The common soldiery whom he regards with contempt as
the 'musty' raw material for slaughter have had no share in his exploits:
so much so that, when he rallies them on the field of battle, they watch
him go, as they think, to meet his fate behind the closing gates of the
enemy city to the accompaniment of an indifferent comment: 'To the
pot, I warrant him' (I. iv. 47). Now, as he receives the offer of supreme
authority in Rome, the virtues which have made him a hero are
balanced against his lack of flexibility and human understanding, both
wonderfully present in the great eulogy with which Cominius, his peer
and colleague, proposes him for the supreme office. The speech underlines by its weight and gravity a decisive turning-point in the action.
At this dangerous moment in the hero's career, when his triumph and
his ruin stand face to face, it stresses the energy, the splendour of
superabundant power, made manifest in his victorious campaign. This
impression of life is conveyed not only in the triumphant image which
mirrored his youthful rise to glory—'he waxed like a sea'—but in the
intensity which records in terms of vivid sensation his inexhaustible
response to the challenge of danger:

> the din of war 'gan pierce
> His ready sense; then straight his doubled spirit
> Re-quickened what in flesh was fatigate. (II. ii. 120)

This magnificent rousing of the spirit to the sounds of conflict carries us back to the nostalgia felt by Othello for 'the spirit-stirring drum, the ear-piercing fife'[27]; both passages convey, in their respective evocations of what is, for each of these heroes, life and fulfilment, a sense of the imagination reaching out to the confines of sensual intensity. The exaltation of the warrior as he advances towards his goal, the crowning of triumph with the 'garland' of victory, impresses itself through a fine keenness of sensation, this play's parallel to that which, at certain moments, transfigures the utterances of passion in *Antony and Cleopatra*.

Just, however, as *Antony and Cleopatra* does not finally invite to uncritical romantic surrender, so the celebration of the soldierly virtues in *Coriolanus* is balanced by a contrary impression. Side by side with its superb sense of vital energy, Cominius' speech asserts the presence of a dead heaviness, an almost grotesque insensibility. The expansive splendour of 'he waxed like a sea' is immediately qualified by the ponderous, dead impact of

> in the brunt of seventeen battles since,
> He *lurch'd* all swords of the garland;   (II. ii. 105)

even as the hero attained with manhood the complete martial assertion of his being, the power so revealed converted itself into a heavy indifference to life. From the comparison, at once splendid and sinister, of the warrior to a 'vessel under sail', bearing down upon the lives which he regards as 'weeds', we pass to the evocation of his sword as 'death's stamp', invested with the destructive weight of a battering-ram. As the eulogy draws to its close, its object is converted into a mechanical instrument of carnage, indifferent to the ruin he has caused:

> from face to foot
> He was a thing of blood, whose every motion
> Was timed with dying cries. (II. ii. 113)

The impression of inhumanity is further reinforced by the irresistible impact with which the hero 'with a sudden reinforcement' *struck*

Corioli 'like a planet'; the effect is to make Coriolanus no longer a mere soldier but an instrument of 'shunless destiny' launched against 'the *mortal* gates of the city'. In the word 'mortal' is contained not only a sense of the frailty of those who sought to bar his progress, but the protest of down-trodden life against the power which began as an affirmation of vital energy and is now revealed in ruthless dedication to destruction. Then, to balance the effect yet again, the machine quickens in response to new perils in the lines about 'the din of war' already quoted: a quickening followed immediately, however, by the renewed calousness of

> he did
> Run reeking o'er the lives of men, as if
> 'Twere a perpetual spoil;   (II. ii. 123)

and we are left, as Cominius bows to the acclamation which greets his close, with a final picture of Coriolanus pausing to 'pant' like a hot-blooded bull after his orgy of carnage.

On the tide of emotion which the speech rouses, Coriolanus is lifted to the culmination of his public glory. If he fails to remain there it is because his true enemy lies finally, not in those around him, but in himself. The prospect of addressing himself to the people produces in him a deep-seated, almost physical repugnance associated with the fear of finding himself 'naked', intimately exposed in his hidden weakness. In this reaction the tribunes see an opportunity which they hasten to press home. The people '*must* have their voices'; they will never 'bate one jot' of the 'ceremony' which they know to be their due. The growing rift is healed for the moment by Menenius and the hero is left to 'blush' boyishly and to express an unwillingness to 'brag' which, however creditable in itself, answers to motives deeper than he can readily understand. The entire situation is already variously and impossibly fragile. The demagogic demands of the tribunes are balanced by an unreasoning obstinacy in the warrior, who is being compelled, against every instinct of his stubborn nature, to exhibit his most intimate feelings to further ends which others have imposed upon him.

In this situation the final triumph of the hero's enemies is assured. Before they finally achieve their end, however, Coriolanus, feeling himself lost, at sea in a world too complicated for his understanding, turns, as he has always been accustomed to turn, to his mother, seeking

from her a confirmation of what he regards as his sacred integrity, his
belief in himself: only to find himself *there*, in the very place where all
his confidence has rested, inexplicably betrayed. For it is indeed
Volumnia who now strikes the decisive blow at his consistency by
calling him 'too absolute'—as if he could be so in his own esteem—
and by wrapping her counsel in what must strike him, being what he
is, as a deep moral ambiguity. In war, she urges, it is in accordance with
'honour' to seem 'the same you are not' and to shape 'policy' accordingly; why then should it be 'less or worse' to do precisely this in an
emergency of peace? From this opening, which he can only receive in
bewilderment ('Why force you this?'), she goes on to urge him to
dissimulation:

> now it lies you on to speak
> To the people; not by your own instruction,
> Nor by the matter which your heart prompts you,
> But with such words that are but rooted in
> Your tongue, though but bastards and syllables
> Of no allowance to your bosom's truth.   (III. ii. 52)

The wording of this advice is calculated to bring home to Coriolanus
the moral monstrosity, as it must seem to him, which it implies. To
tell such a man that he must speak, not from the 'heart', according to
the dictates of that 'honour' which is life to him, but according to the
promptings of expediency is to run counter to the self-respect, the
narrow but absorbing sense of fitness, for which he has been taught to
live. Most shocking of all is the assumption that dissembling is an
acceptable and even a necessary part of the warrior's occupation:

> Now, this no more dishonours you at all
> Than to take in a town with gentle words,
> Which else would put you to your fortune and
> The hazard of much blood.   (III. ii. 58)

The one-sidedness, the artificial simplicity, of the hero's attitude to his
martial profession could hardly be more devastatingly exposed. When
his mother tells him,

> I would dissemble with my nature, where
> My fortunes and my friends at stake required
> I should do so in honour,   (III. ii. 62)

the notions of 'honour' and 'dissembling', hitherto so clearly separated in his mind, are presented to him as intolerably mingled, have become pointers to disorientation and inner doubt.

The manner in which Volumnia goes on to depict the piece of play-acting she is urging upon her son can only add to his shame. His 'bonnet' is to be stretched out in supplication, his knee to be seen 'bussing the stones'; the 'waving' of his head must correct the impulse of the 'stout heart', which is to become

> humble as the ripest mulberry
> That will not hold the handling.   (III. ii. 79)

Worst of all, the hero is to prostitute his soldiership, declaring himself the servant of the people and exhibiting himself as tongue-tied and inapt of speech:

> being bred in broils,
> Hast not the soft way which, thou dost confess,
> Were fit for thee to use, as they to claim,
> In asking their good loves.   (III. ii. 81)

By the end of this harangue, Coriolanus is a hero shattered in his inner integrity, exposed to the play of forces which can have for him no intimate reality. It is supremely ironic that Volumnia, having achieved her purpose by tying up her son in doubt and self-mistrust, should claim at the last to have left him free: 'Do thy will.' In fact, his will is now for his friends and, above all, for her to dispose of. As he goes to meet the populace, with the words 'honour' and 'mildly' ringing inarticulate and clashing changes in his stunned thought, we know that they have prevailed. The consequences of their victory for Rome and for himself will emerge in the remaining course of the tragedy.

In the immediate event we are shown the hero, puzzled and without conviction, struggling to apply in the world the lesson he has so incomprehensibly been forced to learn. He tries to woo the people, to show them the wounds which his mother has so frequently exalted as a sign of honour—'He is wounded: I thank the gods for it' (II. i. 135)— and which are now so strangely to become a public spectacle. Inevitably this attempt to reverse his entire being cannot have lasting effects. Emotion wells up in him as he faces the mob who have been roused against him, and he ends by repudiating violently the role that has been forced upon him. As a result he is condemned first to death and then to banishment, uprooted from his family and his country and the values which have hitherto sustained him, left a man at sea, adrift, with only passionate devotion to an unnatural and impossible revenge to sustain him. Consistency, truth to his narrow but absorbing conception of himself and his honour is, perhaps, the virtue he has most highly prized in life. It has now become a virtue which, in Rome, he can no longer practise, having become in his own phrase, at once darkly tragic and finally self-dramatizing,

> a lonely dragon, that his fen
> Makes fear'd and talk'd of, more than seen;   (IV. i. 30)

and so it now becomes his fate, in the very act of unnaturally stressing this same consistency, to follow his avenging purpose into the camp of his former enemy.

Coriolanus' approach to Aufidius shows him aware of the equivocal situation which his presence in Antium implies. Having cut himself off from Rome, exiled himself to what he bitterly describes as 'the city of kites and crows', he recognizes that he has made himself acceptable to none:

> I have deserved no better entertainment,
> In being Coriolanus.   (IV. v. 10)

The sense of his untenable position leads him, as though in compensation, to an attitude of defiance. Stressing the 'hurt and mischief' which he has done to the Volscians, he proudly recalls

> The extreme dangers and the drops of blood
> Shed for my thankless country;   (IV. v. 74)

all this, he insists, gained for him in Rome the surname which must be most galling to those to whom he now offers his services. These glories, however, belong to the past. In the present, 'only that name remains'; dedicated to a purpose of negation and destruction, he ends by taking refuge from his sense of his own vanity in an empty caricature of purpose:

> I will fight
> Against my canker'd country with the spleen
> Of all the under fiends.   (IV. v. 96)

Whatever voice speaks here, it is not that of heroism or firm consistency. The true spirit of his resolution is contained in Coriolanus' admission that, if his offer is not accepted, he is 'longer to live most weary': moved by the sense of vanity which now dogs his career, he offers his throat to be cut by his rival even as, with a remnant of his native pride, he stresses yet again the harm he has done to the enemy into whose hands he is delivering himself.

If Coriolanus shows himself lost in a world of ill-considered perplexities, Aufidius' reply is notably and, in view of his normal attitudes, strangely romantic in tone:

> Let me twine
> Mine arms about that body, where against
> My grained ash an hundred times hath broke,
> And scarr'd the moon with splinters: here I clip
> The anvil of my sword, and do contest
> As hotly and as nobly with thy love
> As ever in ambitious strength I did
> Contend against thy valour. Know thou first,
> I loved the maid I married; never man
> Sigh'd truer breath; but that I see thee here,
> Thou noble thing! more dances my rapt heart
> Than when I first my wedded mistress saw
> Bestride my threshold.   (IV. v. 112)

It may seem curious that Aufidius, habitually moved by envy and emulation, should give fine expression to the ecstatic values of war just as Coriolanus is finally renouncing them. The inconsistency, however, is true to the tragic conception, in which contradiction plays an essential part. Aufidius, who welcomes his former enemy so generously, who feels bound to him in an emotional relationship which he expressly declares to be in some sense akin to love, will not on that account be less ready to take advantage of his weakness. Heroism and consuming jealousy live together in his nature: in much the same way Coriolanus himself is divided between heroic integrity and an intimate sense of failure.

The later stages of Aufidius' welcome notably modify the opening lyricism. The romantic values of war are replaced by the memory of tough physical rivalry—

> I had purpose
> Once more to hew thy target from thy brawn—   (IV. v. 125)

and by the recalling of a dream in which he has seen himself and his rival 'Unbuckling helms, fisting each other's throat', intimately engrossed by the clash of armed bodies in ruthless conflict. After this transition, the speech ends on a combination of offered friendship and careful calculation. Aufidius confers upon Coriolanus the leadership of his own 'revenges', not simply out of deference to his soldiership, but because he is 'best experienced' to know 'his country's strength and weakness' and so to bring about its ruin. Upon these conditions he declares himself ready to greet his one-time opponent as 'more a friend than e'er an enemy'; but there is an undertone in the rounding-off of his welcoming gesture—'Yet, Marcius, that was much'—which suggests that this strange coincidence, though acceptable while it serves the turn of the moment, must not be expected to last.

Having taken his grotesque resolution, Coriolanus advances upon Rome in a progress of which the absolute and unnatural ruthlessness is stressed. Cominius returns from him with his mind dominated by the pervasive image of consuming fire:

> I tell you, he does sit in gold, his eye
> Red as 'twould burn Rome; and his injury
> The gaoler to his pity.   (V. i. 64)[28]

Menenius, speaking before the news of Volumnia's successful mission has reached the city, describes most vividly the hard inflexibility which has so recently impressed him at their meeting:

> The tartness of his face sours ripe grapes: when he walks, he moves like an engine, and the ground shrinks before his treading: he is able to pierce a corslet with his eye; talks like a knell, and his hum is a battery. He sits in his state, as a thing made for Alexander ... He wants nothing of a god but eternity and a heaven to throne in.   (V. iv. 19)

The emphasis rests, as so often before, on bitter and implacable determination. When Menenius sums up his impression by saying that, except for 'eternity', Coriolanus lacks none of the attributes of divinity, the tribune Sicinius—speaking for once profoundly—adds by way of comment, 'Yes, mercy, if you report him truly,' only to find confirmation in the patrician's rejoinder: 'there is no more mercy in him than there is milk in a male tiger' (V. iv. 31). We are reminded once again of the element of arrogant presumption that has been stressed in Coriolanus from the first, and to which the other tribune, Brutus, referred at an earlier stage when he said:

> You speak of the people,
> As if you were a god to punish, not
> A man of their infirmity.   (III. i. 79)

But the element of weakness which was then only implicit in his attitudes is now on the point of coming to the surface to destroy him. Coriolanus needs to stress his inhuman dedication precisely because the emphasis covers an emptiness, a lack of true belief in himself. He seems in the eyes of his former friends to be consistent, fully dedicated to his avenging purpose; but at the crucial moment, and when the Romans have lost all hope, the submerged side of his strangely divided nature asserts itself to bring about his ruin.

The final confrontation between the hero and his family (V. iii) is beyond doubt one of Shakespeare's most moving and eloquent creations. Coriolanus, bracing himself instinctively to meet the challenge which it implies, calls on his Volscian allies to witness what he intends to be a demonstration of his firmness; but when Volumnia actually stands before him, with his wife and child, a notable admission of natural feeling escapes his lips—

> I melt, and am not
> Of stronger earth than others—   (V. iii. 28)

before he takes refuge in further emphatic denials of instinct and family alike. The expression of these is, indeed, revealing. Coriolanus seeks, by sheer emphasis of assertion, to return to the simplicity of purpose which his being craves. Let the Volscians, whom he has so often defeated in his country's service, 'plough Rome' and 'harrow Italy'. To 'obey instinct' by accepting the validity of the intimate emotion he has just allowed himself to reveal is—so he seeks to persuade himself—to confess himself a 'gosling', incapable of asserting integrity of will in his new situation. Self-depreciation here is a cover for doubt and inner contradiction. To smother the powerful voice of 'instinct' Coriolanus needs to postulate the impossible, to assert that a man may be 'author of himself' and 'know no other kin'. The effect is to make him a renegade, not only to his city and to the family which has bred him, but—in a sense deeper than he can fully understand—to his own being.

When he ceases to speak, enough has been said to show where the hero's resolution will be vulnerable. The first indication of what is to come is a recognition of the clumsiness with which, like a 'dull actor' who has forgotten his lines, he moves towards the exposure of his 'full disgrace'. The admission leads naturally to a more personal expression of the emotions which, do what he will to smother them, remain so close to his heart. 'Best of my flesh', he salutes his wife, and goes on to

beg forgiveness for the 'tyranny' which his attitude towards her
implies; but, once feeling has thus forced its way to the surface, he
makes yet again to cover it, pleads to be allowed to maintain the fiction
he has chosen to present to the world:

> do not say,
> For that, 'Forgive our Romans.'   (V. iii. 43)

The plea, however, is already advanced in the name of a lost cause, and
the emotion he seeks to repudiate finds issue in a further lyrical outburst
which gains enormously by contrast with Virgilia's reticence and his
own assertions of iron sufficiency:

> O, a kiss
> Long as my exile, sweet as my revenge!
> Now, by the jealous queen of heaven, that kiss
> I carried from thee, dear, and my true lip
> Hath virgin'd it e'er since.   (V. iii. 44)

Beneath the depth of feeling, the sense of a return, through emotions
so long and so perversely excluded, to the natural foundations of the
speaker's being, there lies a further revelation of character. The emphasis on virgin purity answers to an essential simplicity of nature: the
simplicity which underlies, on its more positive side, the code of
martial 'honour' for which he has lived and which he cannot, without
involving himself in ruin, sever from its intimate inspiration. Because
the simplicity is true, Coriolanus' downfall must affect us as truly tragic;
because his own perverse choices have led him to deny it, a pitiless
element of irony shadows his end.

Once so much has been admitted, the gesture of natural submission
at once imposes itself:

> sink, my knee, i' the earth;
> Of thy deep duty more impression show
> Than that of common sons.   (V. iii. 50)

There could be no better comment on the determination, so recently
asserted, to show himself 'author' of his own decisions, autonomous,
released from the ties of nature. As the hero's knee bends, a frame of
tense and self-imposed rigidity bows to the reality it has sought to
evade, even while it seeks, in a vestige of obstinate pride, to assert its
devotion in terms more absolute than those afforded to the rest of men.
The emphasis cannot conceal the reality of the transformation which is
taking place under our eyes. Nature, so long and so vainly denied, has

begun to reassert herself. The way is open for Volumnia to press her
plea and to compass, through her very success, the downfall which her
son's choices have from the first implied.

It is highly significant that Coriolanus should have gone so far in
admission before his mother has really had occasion to marshal the full
force of her arguments. In her marvellously eloquent reply she pleads,
in fact, for all the pieties that she has instilled into him, which have
made him what he is, and which he has so unnaturally been brought to
deny. Her plea gains its end because, as we have already been shown,
there is nothing true, nothing but inner emptiness, beneath the resolution
that the exile has sought to oppose to it. As she ceases, he is left 'silent',
holding her by the hand and contemplating the sorry spectacle of his
shattered integrity. When at last he speaks, the effect is overwhelming
in its recognition of personal disaster. 'O mother, mother,' he exclaims,
'What have you done?' (V. iii. 183). The question comes from one
bewildered, conscious not of a true resolution to his conflicting loyalties,
but of obscurely threatening deities who look down upon an 'unnatural
scene' and 'laugh' at what they see. The sardonic note which has
throughout lent the scene a distinctive quality finds issue at this point
in a vision of life, as it presents itself to the hero, finally desolate and
meaningless:

> O my mother, mother! O!
> You have won a happy victory to Rome;
> But, for your son, believe it, O, believe it,
> Most dangerously you have with him prevail'd,
> If not most mortal to him.   (V. iii. 185)

At this moment, if anywhere, we are face to face with the tragic
contradiction on which the entire action has rested. Coriolanus' submission, made under the eyes of a withdrawn and notably non-
committal Aufidius, represents an affirmation of natural feeling, but
one made in vacancy, which answers to the pathetic crumbling of an
impossible purpose with nothing real or consistent to take its place.
He has spared Rome, but cannot in the nature of things return to it.
The patriot is left without a country to serve, the son, having chosen a
course which is now seen as in turn enslaving him, is debarred from
accompanying his mother. Uprooted, with a strange, almost adolescent
gesture of clumsiness, he turns away for the last time from the women
and the child before him: turns away to what he knows already to be
his ruin.

The ruin, indeed, is not long in coming. In the city he has left forever,
a new mood of 'merriment', of relief from tension, makes itself felt in
a poetic transformation which bursts the iron bonds that have habitually
restrained imagination in the public scenes of the play. The messenger
is as certain of the truth of his tidings of peace as he is that 'the sun is
fire,' and he follows up his assertion with a most graphic picture of the
returning tide—

> Ne'er through an arch so hurried the blown tide—   (V. iv. 51)

as the 'recomforted' swarm in jubilation through the city gates. 'All
together', as the stage direction has it,

> The trumpets, sackbuts, psalteries and fifes,
> Tabors and cymbals and the shouting Romans
> Make the sun dance.   (V. iv. 53)

The restoration of peace, however, though it restores Roman society to
sane unity and produces these manifestations of life and joy, is powerless
to ward off the hero's own fate. Aufidius, who no longer has any use for
his former enemy, finds it easy to accuse him of betraying his new
masters. Returning to Corioli, which he had once conquered in the
name of Rome, Coriolanus is taken unawares, surrounded and stabbed
ignominiously to death. His reaction, somewhat like that of Othello
before him,[29] is a last pathetic glance back to the days of his glory: the
days when he had been a triumphant warrior in the service of Rome,
and before division had become the substance of his soul:

> If you have writ your annals true, 'tis there,
> That like an eagle in a dove-cot, I
> Flutter'd your Volscians in Corioli;
> Alone I did it.   (V. v. 114)

'Alone': perhaps here, in the turning into a heroic virtue of what is in
fact a weakness, the isolation from his fellow-men which birth and
prejudice have combined to impose upon him, lies in great part the key
to Coriolanus' tragedy. Both the angry scolding and the attempt to
reaffirm a lost dignity represent some aspects of the truth about this
strangely divided, inopportune hero; and since these aspects do not
harmonize, since he cannot now hope to recover the shattered simplicity which he abjured when he turned his back on his city and his
family, the tide of vengeance flows over him with the repeated clamour
of 'Kill!' and Aufidius, in a last gesture of gratuitous brutality,
'stands on his body' in triumph.

IV
THE FINAL ROMANCES

THE two great Roman tragedies of Shakespeare's last years do not represent the last stage in his dramatic development. They were followed by a series of plays—*Pericles, Cymbeline, The Winter's Tale,* and *The Tempest*—which are clearly related in theme and represent an effort to give, through the extension of conventions familiar in the earlier comedies, artistic form to a new 'symbolic' purpose. Of these romances *Pericles* and *Cymbeline* seem to be, each in its very different way, frankly experimental; the first appears to contain passages not from Shakespeare's pen, and the latter suggests an effort to adapt current forms of romantic comedy to express the intensely individual vision which is clearly present in the whole series. *The Winter's Tale* and *The Tempest* are, on the other hand, finished masterpieces that can stand comparison with the best of Shakespeare's writing.

That the whole series forms a close artistic unity is clearly revealed in the pattern discernible in the respective plots of the plays. At the heart of each lies the conception of an organic relationship between breakdown and reconciliation, between the divisions created in the most intimate human bonds by the action of time and passion and the final healing of these divisions. Near the opening of each play—even in *Cymbeline,* where the central theme is partially obscured—a father loses his offspring through the effect of his own passion-driven folly; the main action is devoted to the sufferings and remorse which follow from their mutual estrangement, and at the end of each play, the lost child (normally a daughter whose name has evident symbolic associations: Marina, Perdita, Miranda) is restored to her father's blessing and becomes the instrument of a reconciliation which in turn throws a light of its own upon some of the principal themes—more particularly those of the individual's relation to society, and of the relationship between untutored 'nature' and civilized 'nurture'—with which Shakespeare's earlier work is consistently engaged. In these final romances the harmonizing theme first attempted in *King Lear*[1] and there broken, after the brief restoration of the aged king to Cordelia, by the prevailing tragic development produces a conception of drama largely removed from common realism and scarcely paralleled in English literature.

1   Pericles, Prince of Tyre

Pericles is, by the common consent of criticism, a problematic play. A late arrival to the accepted canon,[2] it is clearly in some sense a stratified construction, in which passages in Shakespeare's latest manner are superimposed upon others relatively crude and undeveloped. Whatever explanation these inequalities may bear, however, it seems likely that the play represents an early approach to the conception of drama which later produced *The Winter's Tale* and *The Tempest*. Conceived as an experiment in poetic symbolism, it shows the basic conceptions of the last comedies, still in the process of formation, striving to impose artistic unity upon an imperfect theme; and it is this fact, rather than the uncertain authorship of disputed passages, that constitutes the primary interest of the play.[3]

If this be a true account, we can regard Pericles, when the play opens, as embarked upon a pilgrimage in search of true happiness. His appeal before Antiochus (I. i) is to the 'gods that made me man and sway in love', who have inflamed in his breast the desire 'to taste the fruit of yon celestial tree', and his reaction to the King's ambiguous warning is an affirmation of deepened moral understanding:

> Antiochus, I thank thee, who hath taught
> My frail mortality to know itself.   (I. i. 41)

Driven by the discovery of hidden evil to abandon his first dream of felicity, Pericles is exposed to a succession of experiences which, crudely expressed as they often are, can be interpreted as representing various stages in moral growth. The anger of the tyrant obliges him to leave his kingdom, exposing him first to penury and then to a storm which, as in so many of Shakespeare's later plays,[4] reflects the hero's subjection to tragedy. In the storm, and through the action of three Fishermen, he recovers the armour bequeathed to him by his father, an incident (II. i) itself capable of bearing a symbolic interpretation;

and, once more clothed in it as his defence, he wins in tournament the hand of Thaisa, daughter of Simonides of Pentapolis. With the consummation of their marriage the first part of a play so far remarkably uneven, not to say imperfect, is complete.

The rest of the story brings us, beyond all reasonable doubt, into contact with Shakespeare's first attempt to develop the theme of symbolic reconciliation in the manner of his final romances. With Pericles exposed to a storm at sea which he ascribes to the will of the 'gods' (III. i), and with the death in childbirth of his wife, the true sense of the action at last begins to emerge. Thaisa, dying through exposure to the elements, bequeaths her husband a living continuation of herself ('this piece of your dead queen'), and Pericles hails the event in words in which stress and calm, tragedy and following peace, are blended:

> Now, mild may be thy life!
> For a more blustrous birth had never babe:
> Quiet and gentle thy conditions! for
> Thou art the rudeliest welcome to this world
> That ever was prince's child. Happy what follows!
> Thou hast as chiding a nativity
> As fire, air, water, earth and heaven can make,
> To herald thee from the womb.   (III. i. 27)

The balance of contrasted images here is at once unmistakably Shakespearean, a product of the same imagination as that which conceived Cordelia's regal grief,[5] and an indication of the point reached at this stage in the symbolic pattern. Pericles prays that the 'mildness' of his daughter's life may compensate for the unprecedented 'blustrous' condition of her birth, the future hope of a 'quiet and gentle' environment for the 'rudeliest welcome' to the world which she has undergone at the moment of her begetting. Behind the more superficial aspects of this prayer for peace lies the characteristic Shakespearean intuition of subsistent continuity, the sense that birth and death, tempest and following calm, are in reality related aspects of a single process to which the elements themselves are, in their universal presence, witnesses. Thus imaginatively supported and given poetic substance, the episode, which at once looks back to the sufferings of Pericles in his pilgrimage (of which it is the consummation) and anticipates the birth of a new and deeper understanding, becomes the pivot of the whole action.

Before the compensating development of the future can receive its

dramatic expression, however, the death so recently announced needs
to be introduced more fully into the symbolic pattern. The dialogue
with the sailors by which this is achieved is set against a background of
tempest evoked in prose that clearly anticipates the similar scene in
The Winter's Tale[6]; whilst Pericles, responding to external pressure
with a corresponding growth in moral insight, combines the patience
expressed in

> Courage enough: I do not fear the flaw;
> It hath done to me the worst (III. i. 39)[7]

with tender concern for the well-being of this 'fresh, new sea-farer'.
Death and birth, the old and the new, are seen to be more closely
connected than ever in a single process. When, as a final tribute to the
storm, the sailors insist that the 'ship be cleared of the dead', the
symbolic action is taken a step further; for the burial of his wife at sea
is not only a sacrifice on the part of the Prince, but is seen to imply the
elimination of death as prologue to its poetic transformation. The shift
of emphasis begins to make itself felt in Pericles' dispositions for the
funeral. Thaisa's death, though the result of the 'terrible child-bed' to
which she has been exposed, has found issue in a new life; and so even
her burial, conceived as the sacrifice of her corpse to the 'unfriendly
elements', becomes subject to a process of mutation reflected in the
motion and texture of the verse:

> nor have I time
> To give thee hallow'd to thy grave, but straight
> Must cast thee, scarcely coffin'd, in the ooze;
> Where, for a monument upon thy bones,
> And aye-remaining lamps, the belching whale
> And humming water must o'erwhelm thy corpse,
> Lying with simple shells. (III. i. 59)

This deliberately poetic recalling of the body's consignment to the sea,
destroyer and preserver, aims at giving the idea of death a transforming quality of remoteness, at making it, in the words of Ariel in
The Tempest,[8] 'suffer a sea-change' to which the supporting indication
of expanding moral understanding will give the necessary substance.
The imaginative quality conveyed in the use of 'ooze' to indicate the
sea,[9] in the transmuting musicality of '*humming* water' and '*aye-
remaining* lamps', is a fit introduction to the burial of Thaisa with her
'casket and jewels', whilst the mention of the 'satin coffer' and the rich

'spices' by which her body is preserved from the temporal action of the
elements and disposed for the coming resurrection contributes to the
creation of a subtle effect of harmony which will be taken up into the
final scenes of reconciliation.

The following scene (III. ii) transports the action to Cerimon's house
at Ephesus. Cerimon occupies in *Pericles* a position intermediate
between that of the physicians who ministered to spiritual infirmities
in *Macbeth* and *King Lear* and that of Prospero in *The Tempest*, whose
studies give him power over nature and an insight into the true
character of things. His studies are as much spiritually as medically
conceived. They concern the '*blest* infusions' that dwell in the properties
of nature and tend to the cure of deep-seated 'disturbances'; they
proceed, in fact, from a contemplative depth that recalls that of
Prospero and aims at restoring the broken moral harmony of human
nature.

To the figure thus conceived the coffin of Thaisa, recovered in accordance with the prevailing symbolic design from the sea, is brought in.
Her resurrection is, as in the parallel case of Lear,[10] a gradual process,
during which the returning tide of life is first hailed by the bystanders
in terms of the manifestations of renascent nature—

> see how she 'gins to blow
> Into life's flower again—   (III. ii. 95)

and at last confirmed in the reopening of her eyes to the light. Her
revival is greeted by Cerimon with fresh intimations of value and
beauty:

> She is alive; behold
> Her eyelids, cases to those heavenly jewels
> Which Pericles hath lost,
> Begin to part their fringes of bright gold;
> The diamonds of a most praised water
> Do appear, to make the world twice rich. Live,
> And make us weep to hear your fate, fair creature,
> Rare as you seem to be.   (III. ii. 98)

In this speech, a new, transhumanizing element (so to call it) enters the
verse, giving its full symbolic quality to what has now become a poetry
of resurrection. This is perhaps the first time in Shakespeare that the full
range of his mature poetry is lent to an effect so deliberately remote, so
charged with a quality that can truly be described as supernatural, and

yet so free from any suggestion of abstraction or strain. Thaisa, once 'lost' to Pericles in her death, is again *alive*, and the first sign of her restoration is a renewal of value by which her very physical attributes are transformed. Her eyelids have become 'cases' to the 'heavenly jewels' of her eyes, jewels which were formerly the most valued treasures of Pericles and which their loss has made doubly precious to him. The lashes on these lids have become transmuted into 'fringes of bright gold' and the eyes themselves 'diamonds of a most praised water', whose influence in their resurrected beauty is able to enrich, even more than in her first life, the world which had already celebrated their loveliness. The beauty of Thaisa, thus exalted above common realism, is of a 'rarity' that has now only to wait for the final reconciliation to Pericles to exercise its power as the key to a new life.

The time for this reconciliation, however, is still distant. The next scene (III. iii) shows Pericles resigned to his irreparable loss:

> We cannot but obey
> The powers above us.   (III. iii. 9)

The need for acceptance, conformity to ends still only dimly apprehended in the course of exposure to tragic experience, is an essential part of the conception on which each of Shakespeare's last plays is built. Such resignation, however, is not final. Already, in the stress of the very tempest that robbed him of Thaisa, his daughter Marina, herself symbolically named, has been born. Pericles now leaves her in the hands of Cleon, so that she may receive from him 'princely training' and 'be manner'd as she is born', stand out by her possession of the civilized virtues in a society whose courtly spirit has already been indicated (I. iv) and whose shortcomings will soon be revealed. The act concludes (III. iv) with Thaisa learning from Cerimon of her situation and balancing Pericles' vow to leave his hair uncut until his daughter's marriage by assuming a 'vestal livery' in the temple of Diana. With this pair of resolutions duly adopted, and waiting upon the future development of events, this central stage in the play, poised between past tragedy and future reconciliation, is brought to a close.

Most of the action of *Pericles* covered by the fourth act shows a partial decline in emotional tension and poetic mastery. The reasons for this are not easy to define. It could be argued that the greater part of the action at this point belongs to an earlier version of the play, perhaps only occasionally touched by Shakespeare to bring his material into a minimum of concordance with his general purpose. The argument, however, would need to be advanced with caution. The contrast between Marina's purity and the trials to which she is subjected in the brothel is excessively facile and sentimental, but its spirit, and some of its phrasing, can be paralleled in earlier plays. The first exchange between Pander and Boult (IV. ii) and the final discussion between the latter and Marina (IV. vi) recall, at times closely, the scenes in *Measure for Measure*[11] which present social dissolution as a background to the central conflict. Like the prostitutes of Vienna, the 'unwholesome wenches', 'pitifully sodden' (IV. ii. 21) of the Mytilene brothel are conceived as victims, subject to creatures conscious of the iniquity of their trade ('the sore terms we stand upon with the gods') but powerless to react against adverse circumstances[12]; the physical infirmities which accompany the exercise of their 'profession' are as much morally as bodily significant, symptoms of a process of social disintegration to which the universal force of 'appetite' subjects them and against which only the consistent purity of Marina stands out in flawless integrity. The weakness of these scenes, indeed, lies precisely in the excessive clarity of the contrast. Marina, unlike Isabella, does not answer to the realistic conception of drama which still prevails in the presentation of her background. Her motives are not analysed, and still less subjected to the possibility of conflict; they are inflexibly simple, self-consistent, and therefore, in terms of the dramatic objectivity with which Boult, Pander, and their like are presented, artistically incompatible. The fault lies in the attempt to adapt the realism of Shakespeare's earlier manner to symbolic purposes still in the process of elaboration; but the presence of this inconsistency does not alter the fact that the whole episode is conceived as a necessary stage in the development of the action to which it belongs.

In the concluding episodes, which bring the principal strands of the play together in a harmonious close, the main symbolic line is once more taken up in full poetic mastery. Pericles appears on board ship, curtained from the sight of onlookers and so cut off, in a sense, from a world he has decided in his sorrow to abandon. Marina, still unaware that she is in her father's presence, goes in to him to exercise her healing gifts. She begins by singing to Pericles, for 'music' is here, as always, the prelude to restoration. The effect upon him is not immediate; but when she invokes her subjection to a 'grief' equal to his own and refers to her noble but 'forgotten' parentage, Pericles is moved to break his silence with words which in their halting incoherence record the first tentative groping towards a restored life. Thus we are brought, step by step, to the presentation of the central symbolic situation, when Pericles finally brings himself to ask Marina

> What countrywoman?
> Here of these shores?

and meets with a reply in which fact and symbol are blended:

> No, nor of any shores:
> Yet I was mortally brought forth.   (V. i. 103)

From now on, Marina clearly fulfils a double function. She is at once 'mortal', the issue of Pericles' own flesh and blood, and the instrument of entry into a new, transfigured life; the conditions of her birth both link her to 'mortality', and so to the strain and suffering symbolized in her past subjection to the elements, and exalt her to the spiritual freedom of a fresh creation. Through her, past and present, death and life, temporal servitude and spiritual freedom are fused in a single organic process tending to the affirmation of a new state of being.

The gateway to this new state is, as Pericles now realizes, the 'grief' imposed upon him by his tragic past and accepted as the necessary condition of moral growth. As this truth comes home to him, he breaks into renewed speech and finally salutes her in terms that carry a step further the spirit of poetic symbolism in which all this part of the play is steeped:

> I am great with woe, and shall deliver weeping.
> My dearest wife was like this maid, and such a one
> My daughter might have been: my queen's square brows;
> Her stature to an inch; as wand-like straight;
> As silver-voic'd; her eyes as jewel-like,
> And cas'd as richly: in pace another Juno;
> Who starves the ears she feeds, and makes them hungry,
> The more she gives them speech.   (V. i. 107)

Pericles' opening words indicate that his past grief has been, spiritually speaking, fertile and introduce once more the birth-theme with which so much of the play is steeped. The physical birth in the tempest is, in fact, at last opening into its counterpart in the spiritual order. What is in process of being born, under the revival of poignant past memories, is now expressed as a new vision of humanity restored to a stature almost divine. In the healing figure of Marina are reborn the 'square brows' of Thaisa, her perfect carriage, her 'silver voice' and 'jewel-like' eyes (the epithets, with their indication of infinite riches, recall those formerly used to indicate the quality of Cordelia's royal grief[13]), and, above all, the 'pace' of Juno, the queen of the gods; and to round off the transforming splendour of the description, her utterance is such that it gives nourishment without surfeit (she 'starves the ears she feeds') and, as it nourishes her hearers, makes them 'hungry' for further speech. Almost all the recurrent themes of Shakespeare's symbolic imagery are here gathered together into a vision of life reborn, exalted in 'grace'.

To the spectacle thus miraculously presented to his eyes Pericles responds by an exercise of faith. He calls upon Marina to tell her story, promising to believe even what still seems impossible; for the truth of the words she speaks is guaranteed, for him, by the echo they call forth from the depth of his past experience, and, as he puts it,

> thou look'st
> Like one I lov'd indeed.   (V. i. 126)

As Marina replies, and the tide of memory flows back in a process which reminds us even more strongly than what has gone before of the gradual restoration to life of Hermione in *The Winter's Tale*,[14] his desires convert themselves step by step into reality. First she tells him that her name is Marina, then that her father was a king; and when he feels himself, as it were, mocked by this miraculous rehearsal of his abandoned hopes, she comes finally to the full revelation:

> *Pericles:*   Where were you born?
> And wherefore call'd Marina?
> *Marina:*   Call'd Marina,
> For I was born at sea.   (V. i. 156)

By this declaration of her origins, Marina finally assumes her full place in the symbolic pattern. Connected by her birth 'at sea' with the tempest that bore Pericles apart from Thaisa and confirmed their separation in her supposed death, Marina, having passed unscathed through the trials to which her separation from her father exposed her, now returns as the harbinger of harmony restored. With the response aroused in Pericles by the contemplation of her transfigured humanity, the necessary conditions for the final reconciliation are at last established.

In complete possession of a truth which gives meaning to his own past, and after receiving the confirmation of Lysimachus, Pericles at last gives expression to the rebirth in himself of natural emotion. The stages of his final awakening are conveyed with an exquisite tenderness. As Lear, when restored to Cordelia, called for a pin to put himself to the test in order to discover whether he was in fact alive,[15] so Pericles calls upon Helicanus to 'strike' him, give him a 'gash',

> Lest this great sea of joys rushing upon me
> O'erbear the shores of my mortality,
> And drown me with their sweetness. (V. i. 194)

At this point, and after Marina's recent declaration, the references to the 'sea' and to 'mortality' are more than ever relevant. Their emotional content has now been finally transformed; for the sea to which Pericles' wife and child were exposed, and which has so far served as a symbol of tragic suffering, has now become a 'sea of joys' which threatens to overthrow his weak 'mortality' and to cause a death conceived in terms of 'sweetness'. Against this background, Pericles calls Marina to himself in words which express the symbolic kernel of the whole play:

> O, come hither,
> Thou that beget'st him that did thee beget;
> Thou that wast born at sea, buried at Tarsus,
> And found at sea again. (V. i. 196)

What is here asserted, under the guise of the play's poetic symbolism, is nothing less than a concept of spiritual resurrection. Its instrument is Pericles' own child, formerly begotten as the fruit of a marriage that was itself the result of search in pilgrimage, and now, in the moral sphere, the instrument of his rebirth. Marina, recently described in terms that confer a certain status of divinity upon the human, has brought her father the intuition of a new and deeper life; and this she has been able to do as a result of her own experience, the pattern of which involved her birth in tempest, her 'death' and burial, her exposure to human malevolence, and finally her triumphant resurrection—once more at sea—as symbol of a reintegrated and regenerated humanity.

Having declared this truth, Pericles calls upon those around him to give thanks to the 'holy gods' whose provident action has shaped his story. He also recalls, through Marina, her mother and his 'lost' wife who, in his daughter's words,

did end
The minute I began. (V. i. 213)

In this mood of enlightened conformity, Pericles is ready to acknow-
ledge his child and to assume—in clear symbolic reference to his new
state—'fresh garments'; once more there is an obvious parallel with
the reawakening of Lear.[16] Like Lear again, his first gesture on being
restored to his position as father is to respond to Marina's kneeling to
him by embracing her and giving her his blessing; and finally, as a
background to restored harmony, his speech becomes penetrated by the
'music of the spheres' which fills his enraptured imagination. This
'heavenly music', in turn, brings Pericles the sleep which is the necessary
prelude to lasting restoration.

The last scene (V. iii) brings the chief protagonists together before
the altar of Diana at Ephesus; the final reconciliation of Pericles with
his wife takes place in the presence of the 'gods' to whom she has, in
the intervening years, dedicated herself. Pericles begins by recalling
the death of Thaisa 'in childbed' and the bringing forth of their 'maid-
child'; the self-dedication of Marina to Diana is also referred to, as are
the 'better stars' which have preserved her from adverse 'fortunes' and
restored her finally to her father's care. Hearing her own story thus
repeated, Thaisa faints, and Cerimon, taking up the prevailing symbolic
imagery, describes how he found her 'early in blustering morn' upon
the shore with 'rich jewels' in her coffin, and how, having restored her,
he placed her in the holy temple. Thaisa's recovery from her swoon is
also, and simultaneously, the awakening into a new condition. Like
Pericles before her, she gropes her way towards the truth, leaning for
enlightenment upon her obscure understanding of the symbolic situation by which birth and death, united in common exposure to adversity, are seen as related aspects of a single process issuing in a new
life:

did you not name a tempest,
A birth, and death? (V. iii. 33)[17]

With this, and the showing of the ring given her as symbol of union by
Pericles' father, her husband is convinced. In the light of the harmony
thus restored, his 'past miseries' are seen as 'sports', and his happiness
is such that only in terms of death can its absolute, *final* quality find
expression:

O, come, be *buried*,
A second time within these arms. (V. iii. 43)[18]

Marina, in turn, feels her heart leap 'to be gone into my mother's bosom', kneels, and is presented by Pericles to her mother with the pregnant simplicity of 'Flesh of thy flesh, Thaisa'. It is significant, indeed, of the play's intention that, even in this moment of achieved spiritual harmony, physical normality is given its full and essential part. The central balance of filial prayer and answering paternal benediction having thus been established, the healing function of Cerimon ('through whom the gods have shown their power') is given its proper spiritual context, and Helicanus for the last time affirms his loyalty. With the concluding betrothal of Marina to Cerimon, the pattern of reconciliation in *Pericles* is finally complete.

2 Cymbeline

The second play of this period, *Cymbeline*, though without the disconcerting crudities of the early scenes of *Pericles*, is in some ways a less immediately striking piece. More closely connected with the fashionable dramatic convention of the moment, which called for sentiment and a glorification of the simple life on lines popularized by John Fletcher, it nonetheless shows Shakespeare attempting—with partial success—to use these conventions for his own purposes. The theme of loss and reconciliation, though less clearly defined than in *Pericles*, is present in the new story. Cymbeline loses his children, Guiderius and Arviragus, whose place at court falls to Cloten through the machinations of his twice-married queen; they are exposed for long years to the simplicities, crude but noble, of the primitive life under the charge of the banished Belarius, and finally return to their father's embrace. Thus restored to civilized life, they bring with them the virtues of barbaric honesty which are henceforth to be integrated into the order of true courtliness.

This order is introduced into the play, and related in turn to the master-theme of loss and gain, through yet another story of division and exposure to trial, that of Imogen and Posthumus. In the treatment of this second action, which derives equally with the first from Cymbeline's primary error of judgment in his second marriage, Shakespeare's language comes to life in a way that distinguishes the play decisively from the sentimental conceptions of Fletcher. The clash

of loyalties occasioned by Imogen's forced betrothal to Cloten is given
a definite universality of context in the opening words of the play:

> our bloods
> No more obey the heavens than our courtiers
> Still seem as does the king.   (I. i. 1)

Against the background of concord which relates the observation of
courtly 'degree' to the operation of the 'heavens', the arbitrary act of
the monarch produces in his subjects an underlying sense of profound
disquiet. First indicated, perhaps, indirectly in 'seem', it is openly
expressed a little later in the First Gentleman's assertion that

> not a courtier,
> Although they wear their faces to the bent
> Of the king's looks, hath a heart that is not
> Glad at the thing they scowl at.   (I. i. 12)

The linguistic quality of this passage, with its suggestion in 'wear their
faces'[19] of the masking of true sentiment and the conflict of natural
feeling and duty implied in the contrast between 'glad' and 'scowl at',
indicates the prevailing state of moral dislocation. This uneasiness,
implying a disturbance of the bond which binds individual conduct to
the functioning of the cosmic order, has its part to play in the complete
conception. The return to normality through the integration of natural
simplicity and true courtly virtue, and the subordination of both to a
higher loyalty, is the true theme of *Cymbeline*.

  In accordance with this general plan, Imogen's repudiation of the
uncouth pretensions of Cloten, whose supposed courtliness can only be
acceptable to Cymbeline's passion-distorted vision, implies her choice
of a superior conception of humanity, at once natural and deeply
civilized. This conception inspires the opening description of Posthumus, whom the king formerly endowed with

> all the learnings that his time
> Could make him the receiver of; which he took,
> As we do air, fast as 'twas minister'd;
> And in's spring became a harvest; liv'd in court—
> Which rare it is to do—most prais'd, most lov'd;
> A sample to the youngest; to the more mature
> A glass that feated them; and to the graver
> A child that guided dotards.   (I. i. 43)

The virtues thus celebrated in Posthumus are those of true courtliness, fostered by a 'learning' imbibed as naturally as air and proceeding, in the normal course of youthful development, to its spontaneous 'harvest'. In a world in which true virtue is indeed rare, he has become an example to all ages and conditions, a mirror of the finer human qualities which Imogen, in loving him, has appreciated at their proper worth.

The 'rarity' of this example is emphasized first by contrast with the aristocratic pretensions of Cloten—a court parody of the truly 'natural' man, enslaved to the prompting of his own passions—and later by the success which attends the cynical intrigues of Iachimo. The arrival of Posthumus in Rome (I. iv) introduces the convention of Italianate court cynicism, which is allowed to play with critical detachment, or the appearance of it, upon the values incarnated in Posthumus' idealization of Imogen. Iachimo's attitude of negation should not obscure his part in expanding the moral content of the action. He sees Posthumus' virtues not as illuminating social existence, as the crown of human living, but as conditioned by it, tainted by its inescapable hollowness. His devotion to Imogen becomes from this new stand-point a proof of imperfection; for, to a critical eye, it seems to imply that 'he must be weighed rather by her value than his own', whilst the very 'approbation' of those that welcomed the match can be explained in terms of a desire to 'fortify' the weak judgment of Imogen, 'which else an easy battery might lay flat, for taking a beggar without less quality.' The intricate verbal pattern thus woven round the central situation has, beyond its obvious purpose as a reflection of sophisticated 'Italianate' cynicism, a strictly analytic content. To Iachimo, absolute 'value' of the kind postulated in love by Imogen and Posthumus is inconceivable. His intelligence, acute in its limitations, plays upon such 'value' and the virtue which is its moral expression, reducing both to a mixture of sentiment and interest; and if his attitude is rootedly negative, if such a phrase as 'how *creeps* acquaintance' clearly reflects a tendency towards systematic debasement, under-valuation, it is none-theless true that his position needs to be taken into account, first isolated in its expression and then assimilated, through the positive reaction it will eventually produce, into the final pattern.

To this clash of contrary attitudes to 'value', the symbol of the ring serves as a point of focus. Posthumus is ready to defend his belief in his mistress' virtue in terms of tangible worth, and Iachimo uses this readiness to insinuate that the two concepts of value, the moral and the material, are in fact identical, that the one is only to be conceived in terms of the other. In this he is helped, if not justified, by a strain of romantic rashness in Posthumus, which is indicated in his preparatory exchange with the Frenchman. What strikes the latter, in remarking upon an incident in Posthumus' earlier career, as a disparity between the 'mortal purpose' of a challenge and the 'trivial' nature of its cause, is at once acknowledged by him to have been the product of impulse in a 'young traveller' and confirmed by what he now considers to be his 'minded judgement'. The distinction both affirms a valid principle—for Posthumus' adoration of his mistress is clearly intended to be ratified by his mature evaluation—and indicates a possible danger; for, although it is undoubtedly true, as he asserts later, that there is a fundamental difference between 'what may be sold or given' and what is 'only the gift of the gods', the assumption that the two values are connected, that the one may properly be discussed in terms of the other, is perhaps a little too easily made. Certainly it gives Iachimo his opening. To Posthumus' sweeping assertion that his jewel and the object of his love stand alike unparalleled in his estimation—'I praised her as I rated her: so do I my stone' (I. iv. 88)—the answer inspired by his rooted relativity is, as far as it goes, indisputable: 'I have not seen the most precious diamond that is, nor you the lady.' The attempt, whether successful or not, to turn romantic commonplace to the ends of moral analysis is undoubtedly present. The romantic love of Posthumus, far from being a final and sufficient relationship, needs to be subjected to a destructive process which will eventually bring it to full maturity. 'She your jewel' and 'this your jewel', thus brought together in the subtleties of court conversation, represent a knot of contrasted interpretations of value which the play, in so far as it is consistent with its deeper purposes (which is only in part), will be concerned to unravel.

With the two conceptions of 'value'—the romantic and the critical, so to call them—thus contrasted, the rest of the first stage in the development of the play deals with the undermining of the former by the latter. To Iachimo, apparently dispassionate but in reality enslaved to his own sensuality,[20] pure virtue is inconceivable. In his attack upon Imogen, the overflow of physical imagery, product of

> the cloyed will,
> That satiate yet unsatisfied desire, that tub
> Both filled and running, (I. vi. 47)

is at once intense and deeply repellent; this is a speaker to whose cynical intelligence passion seems sterile, even disgusting, but to whom no limiting conception of value is conceivable as a check to the sense-less operations of desire. It is his resentment against the physical embodiment of such a conception in Imogen that causes him to intrigue against her chastity. She repels, easily enough, his direct assault, but is powerless to meet the guile by which he steals from her in sleep the 'proof' of his conquest: powerless, above all, to overcome a plot which owes its success, finally, to the gullible complacency of her lover.

From this point, it is natural to pass to the scene (II. ii) in which the 'temple' itself is finally subjected to direct siege by the furtive entry of Iachimo into Imogen's bed-chamber. The assault upon her honour is characteristically wrapped, for Iachimo, in a pervading sense of decoration. Her eyes are 'lights'

> canopied
> Under these windows, white and azure, laced
> With blue of heaven's own tinct;   (II. ii. 21)

the sleep in which she lies is 'ape of death' and her sense

> a monument
> Thus in a chapel lying!   (II. ii. 32)

The introduction of a literary parallel with the 'tale of Tereus', and the reference to the open book by Imogen's side, contribute to the same effect. They convey a sense of artificiality and opulence which correspond to a contrived quality of feeling. Iachimo's sensuality, which habitually dwells, for all its appearance of intensity, on the surface of things, is as much at home in this elaboration as Imogen's virtue is obscured, in a sense stifled by it; the liberation of her integrity by removal to another environment, as well as the awakening of her lover from the artificial dream which has led him to confuse the reality of love with its material symbol and to allow love itself to become involved in a cynical and irresponsible game of hazard, are essential features of the full development of the play.

At this point, and as a result of their common expulsion from the so-called civilized world, the story of the two lovers, transferred to Milford Haven, meets that of the lost sons of Cymbeline in a common exposure to 'nature'. They, in their discussion with Belarius (III. iii), balance a realization of the advantages of the simple life against their sense of its limitations. On the one hand,

> Haply this life is best,
> If quiet life be best;   (III. iii. 29)

on the other, Arviragus acknowledges his state to be 'beastly' and
feels its limitations as a prison:

>   our cage
> We make a quire, as doth the prison'd bird,
> And sing our bondage freely.   (III. iii. 42)

Simplicity has limitations of its own, freedom under conditions of
primitive life involves the 'bondage' of the higher, specifically civilized
faculties. These will only be awakened in Cymbeline's sons when they
are restored to free loyalty and to a proper relationship with the father
they have lost.

The scene (IV. ii) which brings Imogen and her brothers at last
together is clearly intended, in its length and elaboration, to be of
central importance. Through her exposure to tragic circumstance
Imogen is learning how far beneath the surface appearances of courtliness lie the true sources of a 'nobility' which 'nature' possesses indeed,
but which needs to be confirmed and deepened before being assumed
into a more ample, civilized order; and through this development,
she will attain to a true brotherly relationship as well as to the confirmation of her love for Posthumus. Meanwhile, it is precisely the
failure of the merely sociable to sustain her that is stressed in her
attitude:

>   society is no comfort
> To one not sociable.   (IV. ii. 12)

The whole episode rests on an atmosphere of moral commonplace to
which the development of the action and its poetic unfolding are
meant to contribute a distinctive life. 'Nature', following Belarius'
aside, 'hath meal and bran, contempt and grace,' and Imogen's
sojourn in his cave will lead to a more discerning separation of the one
from the other.

The entry of Cloten and the threats with which he approaches
Guiderius revive once more the theme of true nobility as the gift of
'nature', in opposition to its appearance, symbolized in the possession
of gorgeous clothes. 'Natural' nobility may not be the crown of
human virtue; but, when confronted with Cloten, it is seen to be in
a very true sense its foundation. Cloten demands to be recognized by

his possession of surface splendour—'know'st me not by my clothes'—
before seeking to intimidate his opponent by declaring himself 'son
to the queen'; Guiderius replies by stressing the need for correspondence between inner worth and the pretensions of origin:

> I am sorry for't; not seeming
> So worthy as thy birth.   (IV. ii. 93)

The fight which follows, leading to the elimination of Cloten, serves
as a decisive evaluation of his claim to nobility.

The final removal of Cloten is followed by the playing of the
'solemn music' which announces Imogen's 'death', and with it the
opening of one of the most deliberately worked passages in the play.
The phrasing is from the first pervasively sentimental. Personal
emotion is set in an elaborate decorative framework, sound and image
combining to give feeling a sense of remoteness on the basis of which
the desired effect of acceptance may be achieved. Such is the purpose
which underlies Belarius' grave apostrophe to sadness—

> O melancholy!
> Who ever yet could sound thy bottom? find
> The ooze, to show what coast thy sluggish crare
> Might easiliest harbour in?—   (IV. ii. 203)[21]

and such too the intention of Guiderius' following invocation:

> With female fairies will his tomb be haunted,
> And worms will not come to thee.   (IV. ii. 217)

The tone of such passages presents a critical puzzle highly characteristic
of *Cymbeline*. Their beauty cannot fail to strike us less as a new creation
than as an evasion of true tragic feeling; unlike the best of Shakespeare's
mature verse, their aim is primarily decorative, their relation to the
situation described tenuous and remote. Were it not for the presence
of similar passages in more successful plays of this period, such as
The Winter's Tale and *The Tempest*, we might pass these off as imita-
tions of the fashionable sentimentality of Fletcher. There is no reason,
indeed, to prevent us from supposing that an influence of this kind
exists; but, in view of the later successes, we shall probably do better
to regard these speeches as a first attempt to elaborate a type of poetry
which, if not convincing in isolation, will later be an essential element
in a fuller and more various effect. It is part of the technique of the
last plays to absorb direct emotion into a more complex poetic

harmony, and this seems to be Shakespeare's intention here in his handling of the romantic conventions; except that in this part of *Cymbeline* the prevailing tone seems to be still that of a sentimentality which is its own justification, rather than that of a harmony in which tougher and more realistic states of feeling can find their context in reconciliation.

The impression of an incomplete security of purpose is heightened in the two central passages of the burial episode: Arviragus' catalogue of flowers and the famous dirge over Fidele's 'body'. The delicacy of feeling of the first strikes an unmistakable note:

> With fairest flowers,
> While summer lasts, and I live here, Fidele,
> I'll sweeten thy sad grave: thou shalt not lack
> The flower that's like thy face, pale primrose, nor
> The azured harebell, like thy veins; no, nor
> The leaf of eglantine, whom not to slander,
> Out-sweeten'd not thy breath.   (IV. ii. 218)

The whole passage turns on a romantic balance of beauty and subsistent melancholy. The 'sweetening' effects of the 'fairest flowers' promised by the speaker are set against a sense of temporal impermanence—'While summer lasts'—and of the sadness associated with the grave; and, as counterparts to the emotional background thus created, the flowers—'*pale* primrose' and the 'azured harebell'—are evoked to produce a sense of personality dissolved, poetically transmuted in death. The beauty of the passage has obvious points of contact with Perdita's more perfect flower speech in *The Winter's Tale*.[22] It leaves us with a sense of evasion, even of dissatisfaction, to which Guiderius himself gives expression when he makes his realistic comment:

> Prithee, have done;
> And do not play in wench-like words with that
> Which is so serious.   (IV. ii. 230)

Throughout this part of *Cymbeline* there are signs of a certain effort to balance, in the utterances of the two brothers, contrasted attitudes to tragic experience. Arviragus proposes to express tragedy in song, transmuting feeling into harmonious dirges, whereas Guiderius says: 'I cannot sing: I'll weep, and word it with thee,' stressing the necessity for concordance between feeling and its expression:

> For notes of sorrow out of tune are worse
> Than priests and fanes that lie. (IV. ii. 241)

If the voice of 'nature' clearly speaks here, condemning the fictions of courtly life and modifying his brother's more decorative attitude, Belarius, recalling Cloten's end, reminds us that differences in rank have in the world their proper relevance:

> though mean and mighty, rotting
> Together, have one dust, yet reverence,
> That angel of the world, doth make distinction
> Of place 'tween high and low. (IV. ii. 246)

Guiderius' reaction, again characteristically blunt, speaks with the voice of 'nature':

> Thersites' body is as good as Ajax',
> When neither are alive; (IV. ii. 252)

but the following dirge envelops the whole in a quality of poetic remoteness, evoking indeed the elements of a tragic experience, but seeing them as it were from afar. The feeling behind the reference to the 'completed worldly task' and the following catalogue is evidently a residue of elements present in the tragedies; but the mellow sensation behind 'golden', which is repeated elsewhere in the play,[23] combines significantly with a feeling for youth and innocence which has already been present in the early part of the scene and lends a note of peaceful 'consummation' to the whole.

This, however, is not the last word. When Imogen wakes, after the departure of Belarius and his 'sons', her first words give a moral quality to the rites we have just witnessed:

> These flowers are like the pleasures of the world;
> This bloody man the care on't. (IV. ii. 295)

The speech thus introduced, however, leaves us yet again with a sense of imperfect concordance between action and expression. Imogen's statement that she has awakened from the dream of simple life in which she was a 'cave-keeper' aims at a universality of human reference which recalls, for a moment and imperfectly, the phrasing of *King Lear*:

> 'Twas but a bolt of nothing, shot at nothing,
> Which the brain makes of fumes: our very eyes
> Are sometimes like our judgements, blind. (IV. ii. 300)

The feeling, however, is not sustained. When Imogen passes from general moral statements to face her particular tragedy—the death, as she believes, of Posthumus—her words slip into an incoherence which is justified by the situation but adds little to its poetic development:

>   Damn'd Pisanio
> Hath with his forged letters—damned Pisanio—
> From this most bravest vessel of the world
> Struck the main-top. (IV. ii. 317)

This is rather a normal, ample gesture of Elizabethan verse drama than a contribution to the poetic integration of the main theme. It gives way to the entry of the Roman Lucio and the carrying of the plot a stage further by the incorporation of Imogen, disguised as Fidele, into the Roman army. The episode at Milford has played its part in the development of the general theme; what follows is the incorporation of the values there expressed into a wider range of action and, more particularly, the assimilation of 'natural' virtue through patriotic dedication and further exposure to death into a more ample field of harmony.

The last act of *Cymbeline*, whilst maintaining the inequalities so typical of the play as a whole, has some of its most interesting effects to offer. The main symbolic structure leading to the final reconciliation is clear enough, as is the aim of absorbing personal vicissitudes into a more universal inclusiveness. To this conception the 'death' of Imogen already belongs. It implies, as we have seen, a certain liberation, and to it now corresponds the captivity of Posthumus and the tone of his meditations in prison:

> Most welcome, bondage; for thou art a way,
> I think, to liberty. (V. iv. 3)

Both attitudes, in so far as they reflect a mood of tempered acceptance, are proper preludes to the battle in which Posthumus and the sons of Cymbeline find their natural place fighting against the foreign invader in the orbit of patriotism. Patriotism, however, is not the last word. The Britons, though they defeat the Roman invader, are finally absorbed into an order more than patriotic, and accept the payment of tribute, which is the sign of a unity that surpasses the national. The play ends, not on a note of victory, but on one of reconciliation, coupled with an ample gesture of thanksgiving. To the Soothsayer's declaration of the relevance of supernatural purpose—

The fingers of the powers above do tune
The harmony of this peace— (V. v. 467)

Cymbeline, restored to true self-knowledge and to his position as royal symbol of unity, replies with a gesture of forgiveness and a final offering of thanks:

Laud we the gods;
And let our crooked smokes climb to their nostrils
From our blest altars. (V. v. 478)

In no part of the play, perhaps, is the link which binds it to the development of the final Shakespearean conception so fully realized.

The sense of having reached a new and decisive stage in the action is brought home to us as a suitably chastened Posthumus, for some time past displaced by Imogen and the sons of Cymbeline, is reintroduced in his disguise. The description of the battle, as placed in his mouth, is, to the most cursory reading, intensely alive in its free, supple adaptation of the resources of speech to the blank verse construction. Against the suggestion of divine control, indicated in 'the heavens fought', the speaker builds up a fine impression of vast and powerful action. The first lines stress the magnitude of the British defeat, transforming it into a tide of adversity by which they are carried, their wings 'destitute', their army 'broken', 'all flying' towards the 'strait lane' which is to be the focal point of the whole episode. Against this helplessness, and balancing the British dejection with the corresponding confidence of victory, the Roman enemy is evoked in all his exaltation, 'full-hearted', 'lolling the tongue with slaughtering'. The sense of an irresistible tide is wonderfully conveyed, at the peak of the Roman success, by the carry-over of the blank verse rhythm in the description of the victims—

struck down
Some mortally, some slightly touched, some falling
Merely through fear; (V. iii. 9)

and this, in turn, culminates once more in the 'strait pass', where the critical moment is beautifully indicated in the complex final reference to

cowards living
To die with lengthened shame. (V. iii. 12)

By this culminating phrase, the action is carried to its decisive turning-point in the 'lane', and with it to the affirmation that life dishonourably saved is a form of death which calls for redemption by a reaction on the moral as well as the military level.

The reaction, indeed, is given substance in the second part of Posthumus' description. After the short question interposed by the Lord, his account proceeds to a decisive reversal of the original ebbing rhythm. It opens with a more detailed description of the crucial 'lane', of the 'ancient soldier', and of the two 'striplings' who stood in its defence. In their reported words to the routed British troops, the verse for the first time ceases to ebb, reflects in its change of movement a repeated emphasis on the idea implied in the thrice-repeated call to 'stand':

> To darkness fleet souls that fly backwards. Stand;
> Or we are Romans, and will give you that
> Like beasts which you shun beastly, and may save
> But to look back in frown: stand, stand!   (V. iii. 25)

The pattern of words and rhythms at this point responds admirably to the purpose in hand. The first line flows naturally to its culmination in 'backwards', and then balances it in the single, isolated syllable of command. The threat of the very death which the soldiers are seeking 'beastly' to escape, but which will come upon them 'like beasts', emphasizes the balance of physical situation and decisive moral choice; and, in the light of this, the earlier 'backwards' is balanced by a 'back' that implies the opposite of flight and leads finally to the firmness of 'stand, stand.' The accumulation of phrases, in other words, whilst recalling that of the early part of the speech, is now built up round the idea of resistance and leads finally to the reversal implied in 'Part shame, *part spirit renewed*'.

From this moment, the rhythm of recovery makes itself felt irresistibly to the end of the description:

> Then began
> A stop i' the chaser, a retire; anon
> A rout, confusion thick: forthwith they fly
> Chickens, the way which they stoop'd eagles; slaves,
> The strides they victors made: and now our cowards,
> Like fragments in hard voyages, became
> The life o' the need: having found the back-door open
> Of the unguarded hearts, heavens, how they wound!
> Some slain before, some dying, some their friends
> O'erborne i' the former wave: ten chased by one

> Are now each one the slaughter-man of twenty;
> Those that would die or ere resist are grown
> The mortal bugs o' the field.   (V. iii. 39)

At this point, and henceforth, the reversal of the previous ebb is decisive. The verse grows from the opening check implied in 'stop', in which the reversal of the retreat is finally concentrated, through the 'retire' of the pursuer to the accumulated effect of 'rout' and 'confusion thick'. Confusion itself, indeed, is here given controlled expression, subordinated to the development of a coherent artistic purpose. The beautifully telescoped syntax of the reference to

> Chickens, the way which they stoop'd eagles; slaves,
> The strides they victors made,

at once adds breathless immediacy to the change of fortunes and relates it to the new rhythmic development of the whole; intensity and the breathlessness of the moment are combined in a single comprehensive effect. To this splendid rhythmic control answers an equal vigour and immediacy of speech, conveyed in phrases such as 'fragments in hard voyages' and 'the life o' the need,' as well as in the grotesque power of

> having found the back-door open
> Of the unguarded hearts.

With language and verse movement thus fused in a single, forward-flowing impression, the way is open for a full expression of the rhythm of recovery, and the speech attains complete freedom of movement in the cumulative power of the final lines. 'A narrow lane, an old man, and two boys'. The central situation, further invested by the Lord's wondering comment with a symbolic overtone of its own, has become the point of departure for a process by which rout has been turned into recovery, confusion into restored harmony.

Posthumus, however, before he can take his place in this movement, must pass through the shadow of death and imprisonment. In the scene which follows (V. iv), he declares himself more 'fettered' by the accusations of his own conscience than by the external fact of his imprisonment. The 'penitent instrument' of his reflections is coupled with a sense of the 'mercy' of the 'gods' and of his own mortal dependence:

> For Imogen's dear life take mine; and though
> 'Tis not so dear, yet 'tis a life; you coin'd it:

> 'Tween man and man, they weigh not every stamp;
> Though light, take pieces for the figure's sake:
> You rather mine, being yours; and so, great powers,
> If you will take this audit, take this life,
> And cancel these cold bonds.   (V. iv. 22)

What is being stated here is something very like an adaptation to the circumstances of the Christian view of atonement. Springing from the deep sense of mortality which Shakespeare shares with other writers of the age, the argument proceeds, after admitting the inequality between the 'value' of Imogen, murdered as an indirect consequence of the speaker's own behaviour, and his repentance, to stress their common dependence on the 'gods' in restoration of the balance. His life, though less 'dear' than Imogen's, has been equally 'coined' by the 'gods', and in their common dependence at least there is an implication of equality. ''Tween man and man, they weigh not every stamp'; in their common need for mercy, at least, men are equal, and the processes of divine forgiveness can properly ignore the discriminations and evaluations of relative guilt which are a necessary part of the 'cold bonds' of human justice.

The peculiar vision which appears to Posthumus in his following dream, though it falls naturally into place at this point as a supernatural intervention, is one of the puzzles of the play. The verse, taken as a whole, is poor enough to make the theory of interpolation plausible, and yet there is no denying that the episode, like so much in the early part of *Pericles* and like the masque in *The Tempest*, is firmly integrated into the structure of the play. Whatever may be thought of its expression, there can be little doubt, in particular, that the words of Sicilius immediately after Jupiter's withdrawal are impregnated with a sense of supernatural 'grace' that is entirely in line with the spirit of these final romances:

> He came in thunder; his celestial breath
> Was sulphurous to smell: the holy eagle
> Stoop'd, as to foot us: his ascension is
> More sweet than our blest fields: his royal bird
> Prunes the immortal wing and cloys his beak,
> As when his god is pleased.   (V. iv. 114)

The feeling conveyed in 'celestial breath', 'holy eagle', and 'sweet ascension', in 'blest fields' and 'immortal wing' is, cumulatively speaking, unmistakable. It belongs to the imagination that put into the mouth of Banquo the description of Macbeth's castle at Inverness[24] or evoked, in *The Winter's Tale*, the holiness of the 'sacrifice' to the oracle in Delphos in terms of 'sweet air', 'delicate climate', fertility, and the 'celestial' quality—'ceremonious, solemn, and unearthly'—of the offering.[25] Royalty, holiness, and immortality are fused in an impression of transforming 'grace' which will, in due course, be taken up in the splendid, sun-drenched vision which rounds off the concluding scene.

The full implications of this complex scene are still, however, to be completed. Posthumus in prison is in a state of trial, balancing appearance and substance against the sense of imminent death; and, accordingly, it is proper that the revelation enigmatically offered comes to him not as enlightenment but as puzzlement and obscurity, a further instance of the apparently inconsequent fabric that goes to make up the dream of living:

> 'Tis still a dream; or else such stuff as madmen
> Tongue, and brain not: either both, or nothing:
> Or senseless speaking, or a speaking such
> As sense cannot untie. Be what it is,
> The action of my life is like it.   (V. iv. 146)

Just as Prospero's famous vision of the dream fabric of our experienced world[26] proceeds from his 'beating brain', is set against the brutality of Caliban's design upon him in a way that forces actuality upon us, so here the vivid energy of phrasing corresponds to the felt pressure of reality. Of that pressure, Posthumus' imprisonment and impending death are the external impression. The moment has come for self-examination, for the unravelling of complex and contradictory themes; the final resolution indicated in Jupiter's words—

> Whom best I love I cross; to make my gift,
> The more delay'd, delighted—   (V. iv. 101)

is still bound up with fantasy and dream.

The final grave prose dialogue with the Gaoler rounds off this fine scene in a most fitting manner. The elements that go to make up the Gaoler's 'philosophic' attitude are, of course, Elizabethan commonplaces, used as such by many inferior writers; a phrase like 'he that sleeps fears not the tooth-ache' bears an air of self-conscious truism that can easily be paralleled among Shakespeare's lesser contemporaries.

What really matters, however, is the delicate and deeply individual balancing of contrary attitudes, the setting of death conceived as liberation—an emotion itself deeply, genuinely felt—against an equal sense of the uncertainty which the contemplation of mortality inspires: 'look you, sir, you know not which way you shall go.' The Gaoler hesitates between the conceptions of death as release, as implying freedom from the burden of life, and as obscurity, entry into the unknowable; and to this Posthumus opposes a feeling akin to religious conviction, which naturally accompanies the distinctively moral outlook which characterizes his utterances throughout this part of the play: 'there are none want eyes to direct them the way I am going, but such as wink and will not use them.' The tone of the dialogue, however, remains one of balance, of poised alternatives. Posthumus' mood of religious acceptance is set against the Gaoler's scepticism, expressed above all in his clear statement of the alternatives that face the prisoner:

> you must either be directed by some that take upon them to know, or take upon yourself that which I am sure you do not know, or jump the after-enquiry on your own peril. (V. iv. 184)

The alternatives as here stated are an acceptance of spiritual authority, itself given a certain sense of pretension in 'some that *take upon them* to know', an admission of the helplessness of individual judgment ('take upon yourself that which *I am sure you do not know*'), or a plunge into the unknowable that recalls, in its expression, Macbeth's frustrated impulse to 'jump the life to come'.[27] All these are, in the Gaoler's eyes, equally confessions of impotence, for the only certainty is, in his own terms, 'how you shall speed in your journey's end, I think you'll never return to tell one.' In this balance of opposing attitudes, none accepted as final but each serving to add immediacy to its fellow, the genuine Shakespearean note makes itself unmistakably felt.

The final scene uses the familiar mechanism of romantic reconciliation for symbolic ends of its own, working through successive stages to a final inclusive effect. The first stage is to bring Belarius and his charges before Cymbeline, who is still unaware of his true relationship to them, so that they may receive the knighthood conferred by his royal 'grace'; the second disposes of the queen and her machinations through her suicide, in which, having been 'cruel to the world', she concludes 'most cruel to herself'. These, however, are no more than preliminaries. The entry of the Roman prisoners opens the way for

Cymbeline to demand of Iachimo, with Imogen's prompting, an account of the diamond he wears upon his finger. The confession leads to the self-revelation of Posthumus and to his admission of a guilt that amounts, in his own eyes, to sacrilege:

> it is I
> That all the abhorred things o' the earth amend
> By being worse than they. I am Posthumus
> That kill'd thy daughter. (V. v. 216)

Finally, in his hysterical remorse, he strikes 'Fidele', and her fall is the occasion for Pisanio to declare the true identity of the victim. It is at this point that the spirit of the episode comes to life in Cymbeline's charged phrase:

> If this be so, the gods do mean to strike me
> To death with mortal joy. (V. v. 235)

The balance thus asserted between life and death, joy and mortality, is clearly akin to the mood of the final scenes of *Pericles*.[28] It raises the tone to one of spiritual integration, in which sorrow, neither forgotten nor set aside, is transmuted into an element of deeper joy. With the mystery of her 'death' finally revealed, the way is open for Posthumus and Imogen to be reconciled, in lines pregnant with symbolic meaning and unmistakably belonging to the spirit of Shakespeare's last romances. 'I was dead,' says Imogen, and her words, beyond the mere recalling of a past event, bear a distinctive quality of marvel that itself implies the integration of the action on the symbolical level. In the light of her following question—

> Why did you throw your wedded lady from you?— (V. v. 262)

Posthumus' intense, broken exclamation, 'My queen, my life, my wife,' combining the personal and familiar with the vivifying and the regally transcendent, is given its proper counterpart, and the embrace of the lovers surrounded by intimations of a harmony more than merely personal:

> Hang there like fruit, my soul,
> Till the tree die! (V. v. 264)

The feeling, in fact, is so fine, so precious, that it can only be described in terms of 'soul', and by relating the spiritual suggestion to an evocation of the rich fertility of nature. Cymbeline, in turn, responds

with words that stress the closeness and value of the reconciliation
which has just flooded him with a rebirth of emotions long presumed
dead; again, like Pericles, he salutes his daughter as 'my flesh, my
child',[29] and the strength of his feeling is such that he senses himself
reduced to the state of a 'dullard' by his incapacity to express it.
Finally, the reconciliation assumes its proper external form. Imogen,
kneeling, requests the 'blessing' of her father, the tears of whose
mingled happiness and grief become, in his own mind, 'holy water',
a transformation of mortal sorrow into spiritual joy. In the light of
these discoveries, the queen and her machinations have become
'naught', the unwitting cause of the miracle taking place before his
eyes:

> long of her it was
> That we meet here so strangely. (V. v. 272)

The pattern of plot, thus filled out with a corresponding harmony of
poetic imagery, assumes its complete, balanced form.

The spirit of restored unity which dominates the conclusion needs,
however, to be further confirmed by Cymbeline's recognition of his
lost sons. Belarius prepares the way by invoking upon his charges,
even as he delivers them to their father, 'the benediction of the covering
heavens'; the notions of benediction and reconciliation are, as ever,
closely connected, and Cymbeline's answering expression of grief at
the very moment when the way is clear for him to return to felicity—
'Thou weep'st, and speak'st'—is also significant. The convenient
recalling of the mole on Guiderius' neck belongs, of course, to the
external commonplaces of romance; but it is followed by an intensifica-
tion of the idea of recovered paternity in Cymbeline's exclamation:

> O, what am I?
> A mother to the birth of three? Ne'er mother
> Rejoiced deliverance more. (V. v. 370)

The lines clearly contain the various elements that contribute to the
final emotional transformation of Cymbeline's grief. Birth, and a
certain rediscovery of the self, are indicated; so are the pangs of
'deliverance' by which sorrow finds relief in compensating joy. In
the light of this intensified feeling, the paternal blessing falls naturally
into place—'Blest pray you be'—and is in turn associated with the
restoration of natural order:

> That, after this strange starting from your orbs,
> You may reign in them now.   (V. v. 372)

The completing dialogue with Imogen:

> *Cymbeline:* Thou hast lost by this a kingdom.
> *Imogen:*   No, my lord;
>   I have got two worlds by it—   (V. v. 374)

with its characteristic sense of overtone, of a poetic content that
surpasses its occasion, combines with a stressing of the sanctity of
intimate family relationships—

> O, my gentle brothers . . .
>   you call'd me brother,
> When I was but your sister; I you brothers,
> When you were so indeed—   (V. v. 375)

to produce at least a verbal sense of latent significance springing through
to the surface; later plays will wed this sense more closely to a relevant
plot, but the poetic conditions for the full development are clearly
present, at least in potentiality. How far they can be taken will be seen
in *The Winter's Tale* and *The Tempest*.

The development of the action is now ready for completion.
Cymbeline, once more king over himself and the realm he has seen
victorious, points the way to a final act of religious affirmation, in
which the consummation of marriage between Imogen and Posthumus
will be one with the rendering of thanks for victory achieved:

> Let's quit this ground,
> And smoke the temple with our sacrifices.   (V. v. 398)

Once more, the ideas of sacrifice and worship anticipate a fuller
development in *The Winter's Tale*.[30] With Iachimo's confession of guilt
and the forgiving gesture of Posthumus the way is open for an act of
religious integration which will give its justification to the 'gracious
season' into which the action has at last entered. To confirm this
conclusion on the 'political' level, victorious Britain, through its
king, acknowledges its 'wonted tribute' to the universal empire of
Rome, reintegrates itself in bonds of peace and equality to a conception
vaster even than its own vindicated patriotism; and finally both states
are united in subjection to a spiritual vision, full of mellow, 'golden'
richness, which is itself expressed in Shakespeare's best manner:

> The fingers of the powers above do tune
> The harmony of this peace. (V. v. 467)

'Harmony', indeed, on a scale of ever-increasing spaciousness, is the keynote of this conclusion. 'The Roman eagle', lessening herself, is gathered into the 'beams of the sun', vanishes, is absorbed into a greater union; and the final reference, sustained by verse at once free, ample, and superbly concise, is to sacrifice and the praise of the 'gods'. In this final vision of consecration to a unifying purpose, the personal issues of the play, the love of Imogen for Posthumus maintained through trials and separation, and the integration of natural simplicity to the graces of civilized order, find in subjection to a universal unity, through the figure of Cymbeline as father and king, their proper culmination.

3 The Winter's Tale

The plot of *The Winter's Tale* is a perfect example of the symbolic technique perfected by Shakespeare in his last plays. It is a story of the division created in love and friendship by the passage of time and by the action of 'blood', and of the healing of these divisions through penitence and renewed personal devotion. The play's successive stages coincide with the development of the plot. This opens with a statement by Leontes' counsellor, Camillo, of the close friendship which has since childhood bound together Leontes and Polixenes, kings, respectively, of Sicily and Bohemia. Camillo's prose, however, not only prepares for the facts of the story but also proceeds to develop the obscurities which underlie them. Beneath the closeness of their intimacy, as yet un-realized but implicitly present, lie hidden seeds of division:

Sicilia cannot show himself over-kind to Bohemia. They were trained together in their childhoods; and there rooted betwixt them then such an affection, which cannot choose but branch now. Since their more mature dignities and royal necessities made separation of their society, their en-counters, though not personal, have been royally attorined with interchange of gifts, letters, loving embassies; that they have seemed to be together, though absent; shook hands, as over a vast; and embraced, as it were, from the ends of opposed winds. (I. i. 23)

As a mere exposition of fact, this would be elaborate to a fault. It is,

however, more than that, The force of the passage lies in the combination under one set of images of two processes apparently contradictory
—that of natural, unified development existing side by side with that of
spreading division. The word 'branch' can imply either the natural
unity of living growth from a central trunk or a spreading division
within that growth. If the affection that unites the kings is such that 'it
cannot choose but branch,' this may mean either that it must continue
to grow and bear fruit or that it must inevitably separate and break
down as it grows. In other words, this friendship, though rooted and
natural in its origins, bears within itself the possibility of future disunion. The concluding lines stress the same idea, and the reference to
'opposed winds' further anticipates not only the emotional storm in
which the present unity is shortly to be tested but also the actual
tempest in which Leontes' daughter Perdita is lost and found, and which
is to play a decisive part in the whole construction.

The opening scene, then, suggests how the plot will develop. There
will be a conflict between Leontes and Polixenes, a conflict caused by
Leontes' jealous conviction that Polixenes has usurped the affections of
his wife Hermione. The first movement will be the break-up, already
anticipated, of happy human relationships by the folly of Leontes; the
exact nature of this break-up needs careful study. Since Shakespeare, as
usual, develops at the same time both his plot and its implications, we
are soon given a further key passage:

> *Polixenes:*   We were, fair queen,
> Two lads that thought there was no more behind,
> But such a day to-morrow as to-day,
> And to be boy eternal.
> *Hermione:*   Was not my lord
> The verier wag o' the two?
> *Polixenes:* We were as twinn'd lambs that did frisk i' the sun,
> And bleat the one at the other: what we changed
> Was innocence for innocence; we knew not
> The doctrine of ill-doing, nor dreamed
> That any did. Had we pursued that life,
> And our weak spirits ne'er been higher rear'd
> With stronger blood, we should have answer'd heaven
> Boldly 'not guilty', the imposition clear'd
> Hereditary ours.   (I. ii. 62)

The importance of youth and springtime in this play is sufficiently obvious, and this passage first shows the reason for it. Shakespeare is using this description to point a contrast between spontaneous human emotion and the continual pressure of time—a friction clearly connected with the 'metaphysical' ambiguity we have already considered in certain of the sonnets.[31] Time, in brief, which brings friendships to maturity also destroys them, just as, in the earlier works, it destroyed the love which developed with it. But Polixenes' speech adds something which is new in *The Winter's Tale*—the connection of this friction with sin, 'the doctrine of ill-doing'. The action of time, as seen at this stage in the play, is a corrupting action; experience, as it enters into the life of innocence, destroys the foundations of spontaneous friendship. The youthful freshness which is set against this deterioration is coupled with an ominous ignorance of 'ill-doing'. Its beauty is nostalgic and pathetically defenceless ('Temptations have since then been born to 's', as Polixenes puts it), an easy prey to the inevitable action of the 'sneaping winds' whose imminence has already been suggested.

Polixenes' account, however, takes us even further than this. The cause of Leontes' quarrel with his friend is, significantly enough, jealousy, the conviction that he has betrayed him with Hermione, who is known to be with child. Polixenes' introduction of the idea of 'blood', coupled with the birth of this obsession in Leontes, gives the 'idyllic' content of the speech a fresh meaning by relating it to the problems raised by the nature of sexual passion. 'Blood', in fact, and the action of time are here fused into a single intuition; that is what is behind the contrast between 'stronger blood' and 'weak spirits'. The friendship between the two kings has rested so far on the youthful state of innocence; based on a sentimental ignoring of the reality of the temporal process, it has assumed with pathetic simplicity that it was possible to remain 'boy eternal'. The realities of human nature, however, make this impossible. Boyhood is necessarily a state of transition. The development of the sensual life, 'stronger' than the innocence which preceded it, is necessary to complete maturity of the spirit. Without it, the ideal of eternal youth and pastoral innocence is 'weak', though lovely. It is an ideal which at once depends upon its illusory timelessness and is vitiated by it; the continual action of time, here equated with the growth of a man into sexual maturity, gives the necessary fullness of the 'blood' to human experience, but also destroys it by exposure to the impersonal laws of mutability. The sensual life of man, while giving substance to his development, implies the subjection of his ideal innocence to the capacity for evil. Only through a conscious reaction to tragedy, and the consequent acceptance of deeper experience, can this idyllic state of childhood grow into an independent, conscious maturity.

For the moment, however, this harmonious development is no more than a remote possibility. Meanwhile, the capacity for sensual passion which time imposes upon man bears a double interpretation. It may be good, if it leads to its natural fulfilment in the creative unity of the family, or evil and destructive, in the form of egoism and its consequences, jealousies overcoming all restraint of reason. In Leontes it is the evil impulse which first comes to the surface, destroying his friendship with Polixenes and leading him to turn upon Hermione with an animal intensity of feeling. That his jealousy, so often dismissed as the product of a dreary obsession, is in fact the moving force in this, the first stage in the development of the play, should by now be clear. The power of the verse in which it finds expression is, indeed, a sufficient guarantee of this:

> Too hot, too hot!
> To mingle friendship far is mingling bloods.
> I have *tremor cordis* on me: my heart dances;
> But not for joy; not joy . . .
>
> But to be paddling palms and pinching fingers,
> As now they are . . .   (I. ii. 109)
>
> They're here with me already; whispering, rounding
> 'Sicilia is a so-forth': 'tis far gone
> When I shall gust it last.   (I. ii. 217)

Shakespeare's rhythms were never more impressive, never more delicately adjusted to the breaks in an overwrought consciousness, never more vivid in their ultra-sensual repulsion from the physical. This is apparent in the superbly palated 'gust', allying Leontes' loathing to the offending of a highly sensitive taste. *Troilus and Cressida* abounds in such imagery, though the adaptation to the dramatic ends proposed is there less completely realized. The delicately broken line—'I have *tremor cordis* on me; my heart dances'—could, again, only have come from Shakespeare at the height of his power. Leontes plays his part in the play at this stage as the 'embossed carbuncle'—to echo *King Lear*[32]— in the organism of human relationships, as one by-product, perversely and destructively dynamic, of that organism's growth through rising 'blood' to maturity.

It is significant that, having reached this stage, Leontes declares himself ready to invert reality itself in the following of his released instincts.
'Affection,' he affirms, makes 'possible things not so held,' truth is
confounded with dreams, and the unreal is 'coactive' with reality to the
'infection' of his peace of mind:

> Should all despair
> That have revolted wives, the tenth of mankind
> Would hang themselves. Physic for't there's none;
> It is a bawdy planet, that will strike
> Where 'tis predominant. (I. ii. 198)

With the universalizing of his own infirm obsession into a not very
impressive piece of Elizabethan commonplace, the infection of Leontes'
mind is substantially complete. In the following exchange with
Camillo his concern is not so much to discover the truth as to confirm
what he holds in his own mind to be certain. In his perversity, indeed,
and not unlike Othello before him, he craves for this confirmation as
an alternative to the sense of chaos which is one of the accompaniments
of unleashed passion; for, 'if this be nothing,'

> Why, then, the world and all that's in't is nothing;
> The covering sky is nothing; Bohemia nothing;
> My wife is nothing; nor nothing have these nothings,
> If this be nothing. (I. ii. 293)[33]

The whole of Leontes' behaviour has now become a frenzied building-
up of supposed certainties on 'nothing', on the baselessness of an
irrational emotion followed to the limits of self-centred impulse. The
consequences of this development, as they affect the world beyond
him, soon make themselves felt in the choice offered to Camillo. To
the loyal courtier it is clear that his master is of a 'diseased opinion' and,
as such, intensely dangerous; but the only effect of his protest is to
provoke the accusation of lying and the command, based on royal
authority, to poison Polixenes. Thus placed in a position where loyalties
clash, Camillo's final comment stresses at once the irrationality of his
master's behaviour, 'in rebellion with himself' (I. ii. 355), and its
extension implied in the determination to have 'all that are his so too'.
As always, the introduction of passionate division in the mind of a
king is followed by a split in the fabric of society, whose unity is only
conceivable under a royal guarantee.

A full understanding of Leontes' position is furthered by referring

to the contrasts of feeling in Polixenes when he becomes aware of
Leontes' suspicions:

> O, then my best blood turn
> To an infected jelly, and my name
> Be yoked with his that did betray the Best!
> Turn then my freshest reputation to
> A savour that may strike the dullest nostril
> Where I arrive, and my approach be shunn'd,
> Nay, hated too, worse than the great'st infection
> That e'er was heard or read.   (I. ii. 417)

The sensitive quality of these lines, based on a delicate balancing of
opposed impressions, is notable. On the one hand, there is an insistence
upon 'infection' allied to the odour of decay; on the other, freshness is
associated with the idea of boundless value twice stressed, and given a
specifically religious sanction in the use of 'best'. This peculiar quality
of 'freshness', with its persistent symbolic overtones, is as familiar in
the great tragedies as the notion of contagious infirmity set against it.
Lear, awakening from his madness, was dressed in 'fresh garments',[34]
and in *Macbeth* infection plays an important part in the account given
of the 'healing benediction' of the English king,[35] in the Doctor's work
at Dunsinane, and in the diseased disorder of the murderer's mind. The
contrast, in fact, implies that Shakespeare is once more using his
unrivalled control of sensual imagery to set forth, through Leontes'
jealousy and its effects, a contrast between the good and evil elements
of experience, between the fullness of maturity crowned by 'grace'
and the vicious and disintegrating savagery of uncontrolled 'blood'.

The mention of 'grace' reminds us that the behaviour of Leontes
throughout this scene, and indeed in the whole play, is only fully comprehensible in a context provided by the concept of family unity. Of
that concept, in its full moral significance, Hermione is the gracious
symbol. 'Grace' is a word to note in Shakespeare's later plays. We have
already found it in *Macbeth*[36] applied to Malcolm's restoration of just
kingship and to the sanctity and healing powers of Edward the Confessor. Cleopatra's triumphant beauty on her throne was described as
her 'strong toil of grace',[37] and the last plays are full of the word. Its
implications, which shift and develop in the intricate pattern of the
plays, are hard to define. In *The Winter's Tale* Shakespeare seems to
reinforce the Christian associations already acquired in *Macbeth* with a
deeply personal intuition of natural fertility, fulfilled in the intimate

unity of the family. The play, indeed, contains a profound and highly
individual effort to bring the impasse suggested by his exploration of
the part played by 'blood' in human experience—a part at once
destructive and potentially maturing—into relation with feelings which
imply the understanding of a positive spiritual conception. Only so can
we read the poetry of Hermione. From her earliest appearance she is deliberately surrounded with religious associations and intimations of
value. Polixenes addresses her at the outset as 'most *sacred* lady' (I. ii. 76),
and backs the apostrophe with a further reference to 'your *precious*
self'. Value and spiritual perfection are, indeed, closely associated with
her in the eyes of those who surround her, and it is not long before her
own words bring the idea of 'grace' still more intimately before us:

> My last good deed was to entreat his stay:
> What was my first? it has an elder sister,
> Or I mistake you: O, would her name were Grace!   (I. ii. 97)

And when Leontes has replied, she comments, ''Tis Grace indeed.'
In her trials too, the same note is stressed—

> this action I now go on
> Is for my better grace—   (II. i. 120)

in which the idea of purification behind Lear's sufferings is repeated
with a much more explicit sense of religious values.

This, however, is only a part of Hermione's significance; the rest of
it lies in her relationship to Leontes and in her child. Leontes' jealousy,
as its true nature finds confirmation in his mounting brutality, is much
more than criminal shortsightedness. It is a sensual repudiation by the
uncontrolled 'blood' of a right sexual relationship, of natural fertility
consecrated, given its proper spiritual context in the bond of marriage.
In his insults Leontes stresses brutally the fact that his wife is with child:

> let her sport herself
> With that she's big with; for 'tis Polixenes
> Has made thee swell thus.   (II. i. 59)

His words echo, in the form of perverted brutality, the conversation
between Hermione's ladies at the beginning of the scene, words which
give a rich and natural quality to her state:

> — The queen your mother rounds apace; we shall
> Present our services to a fine new prince
> One of these days . . .

> She is spread of late
> Into a goodly bulk: good time encounter her!   (II. i. 16)

The 'rounding' of the queen is here envisaged as part of a natural, beneficent process, 'goodly' and destined, in 'good time', to find its proper fulfilment in maternity. The unsoftened harshness of Leontes' use of 'big' and 'swell', with their implication of the grotesque and the deformed, appear in the light of this contrast as a deliberate inversion of nature which will produce its own fruit in the disruption of normal human relationships.

That disruption, indeed, follows logically from the nature of Leontes' sin, now bearing fruit in action. His is more than a personal offence; it is against 'nature', and so against the 'grace' for which Hermione in her simple integrity stands. The perverted keenness of his senses, at once sharpened and debased by the action of 'blood', have become a spiritual 'infection'. It is the essence of Leontes' tragedy that, having raised an irrational and indeed unnatural impulse to the status of certain knowledge, he makes it the foundation of his whole being. Regarding his suspicion, with unconscious irony, as 'just censure' and a 'true opinion', he follows Othello in craving for lesser knowledge and in regarding himself as less 'blest' than 'accursed' by what he believes he knows. His knowledge, indeed, as it emerges through the powerful expression of his disillusionment, is 'infected'. It leads to abhorrence, to a sense of nausea which characterizes the whole of his utterance in the early stages of the play:

> There may be in the cup
> A spider steep'd, and one may drink, depart,
> And yet partake no venom; for his knowledge
> Is not infected; but if one present
> The abhorr'd ingredient to his eye, make known
> How he hath drunk, he cracks his gorge, his sides,
> With violent hefts. I have drunk, and seen the spider. (II. i. 38)

Like Othello again, he rests the entire foundation of his being upon the assertion as truth of his error, in words which clearly convey the universal implications of his disorder:

> if I mistake
> In those foundations which I build upon,
> The centre is not big enough to bear
> A school-boy's top.   (II. i. 99)

The whole of Leontes' subsequent progress, from this moment to that
in which he finally awakens to his folly, is contained in this image.
Upon the central point of his illusory certainty his mind revolves in an
ever-increasing rhythm of lunacy to the final collapse. Before that
collapse is complete, he has dragged the whole of his world with him
into ruin. Because of the 'infection' in his spirit Hermione suffers, the
natural human relationship which binds him to Polixenes is rudely
broken, the young prince Mamillius dies out of the course of nature,
and the winter of the gods' displeasure rests upon them all. The first
stage of the play's development is complete with the withdrawal and
supposed death of Hermione. The rest of it is to show how 'grace' can
spring from the jarrings and maladjustments of 'blood', the summer of
right human relationship out of the winter of disorder and penance.

The turning point of *The Winter's Tale* is not so much the long,
central gap of sixteen years as the scene (III. iii) in which Antigonus
leaves Hermione's child, banished by order of Leontes, on the desert
shore of Bohemia, where it is found and cherished by shepherds. Before
this, at the very point where the consequences of Leontes' passionate
impulses are becoming apparent, the action shifts for a moment to an
entirely different plane, indicates in passing the positive spiritual forces
which are already, at this apparently unpropitious moment, in charge
of the action. Such is the meaning of the short dialogue between
Cleomenes and Dion (III. i) on their return to Sicily with the gods'
vindication of Hermione's innocence. Placed at this particular moment,
before the full tragedy has been unfolded, the peculiar 'freshness' which
invests Cleomenes' account of Delphos is doubly significant:

> The climate's delicate, the air most sweet,
> Fertile the isle, the temple much surpassing
> The common praise it bears. (III. i. 1)

We are immediately reminded of Banquo's description of Macbeth's
castle,[38] similarly placed to point a contrast with the growing darkness
of the surrounding action. There too the air was 'delicate', and the
impression of holiness associated with the King's arrival was reflected in
images of fertility and the nimble sweetness of the senses. This is
poetry, indeed, in which exquisite sensual refinement appears as the
tangible manifestation of a hallowed state. Associated in Dion's reply
with the 'celestial habits' and 'reverence' of the priests and the spiritual
quality, 'ceremonious, solemn, and unearthly', of the sacrifice, it

becomes the prelude to a return journey which is 'rare, pleasant, speedy', filled to the brim with a pervading impression of the supernatural (an impression, however, which is itself conveyed through the continuous, intense operation of the senses), and leads to a taking up of the key word of the play in the final prayer, '*gracious* be the issue'.

This scene, however, for all its beauty, is no more than a prelude to the introduction into the action of Perdita. The first 'movement' of the play is closed by the series of calamities which concluded Hermione's trial, ending in Leontes' broken confession of guilt:

> Apollo's angry; and the heavens themselves
> Do strike at my injustice, (III. ii. 147)

and the gesture of acceptance which follows it:

> Come and lead me
> To these sorrows. (III. ii. 243)

The next scene (III. iii) which, short as it is, may be said to constitute the second 'movement' of the play, links the past and future action in the person of Perdita, looking back to the folly of Leontes at the same time that it anticipates the final resolution. The singularly beautiful prose in which the storm and shipwreck are evoked strikes a new note, which can, however, be paralleled in other plays of this period, notably in *Pericles* and *The Tempest*. The disturbed skies and the angry sea carry on the impression of the divine displeasure ('The heavens with what we have in hand are angry,' as the Mariner puts it), and create a background for the central remark of the whole scene: 'thou mettest with things dying, I with things newborn.' This scarcely needs the parallel from *Pericles*—

> did you not name a tempest,
> A birth and death?— (V. iii. 33)

to give it point. The implication of the two phrases is indeed the same. Out of storm and tempest, themselves connected in the symbolic scheme with the results of human folly, is born a new life, destined to grow in the course of time into the harmony of 'grace' and to lead to final reconciliation. From this moment, Hermione's child is connected with the general theme of 'grace' and fertility born out of passion and jealousy. The child is the product of that 'mingling of bloods' which, misinterpreted in the light of his obsession, so repelled Leontes and jarred upon his peace; but it is also the outcome of that natural human fertility which is the soil of 'grace' itself, so that it looks not only back to the decisions of the past but forward to the reconciliation of the future.

In this way we are led up, in what we may agree to call the third 'movement', to the great pastoral scene (IV. iv. IV. iii in O.U.P. edition) which is by no means a simple, almost naïve contrast to the preceding bitterness, but an artistically logical development of the situation. The closely woven strands of feeling that run through the apparent simplicity of this episode have already been foreshadowed in Polixenes' account of his youthful friendship with Leontes; they are now further developed in the dialogue upon the flowers between himself and Perdita. The pastoral convention has never been put to more individual use than in Perdita's speech:

> Sir, the year growing ancient,
> Not yet on summer's death, nor on the birth
> Of trembling winter, the fairest flowers o' the season
> Are our carnations and streak'd gillyvors,
> Which some call nature's bastards: of that kind
> Our rustic garden's barren; and I care not
> To get slips of them.   (IV. iv. IV. iii 79 O.U.P. edition)

A reader aware of the possibilities of Shakespearean language will not pass by the beautiful linking of summer and winter, birth and death, into continuity. 'Death' is joined to 'summer' and 'birth' and 'trembling' are given to 'winter' so as to suggest that the passage of the seasons is only part of one inseparable process; and, since we know that the relations of birth and death are central to the play, we now realize that the various developments of *The Winter's Tale* are, like the cycle of the seasons, a necessary and connected whole. The contrast of the two seasons, moreover, has a further meaning. Summer is linked with the flowering of youth into the love of Florizel and Perdita, Bohemia's son and Sicilia's banished daughter, while 'winter' reminds us that the age of their parents will before the end of this same scene once more affect their children's relationship. It is, indeed, a winter of lust and egotism, which implies the vain barrenness of jealous, impotent age[39] in contrast to the fair summer of youth. The coming brutality of Polixenes in separating the lovers, and especially in his ferocious attack on Perdita's beauty ('I'll have thy beauty scratched with briars'), is an exact complement to Leontes' earlier sin; it proceeds from the same impotence of ageing blood, the same failure to see in the youth before it a normal, natural fulfilment by succession. By the time Camillo has brought them together, *both* his masters will have had cause to regret the importunities of passion. At present, however, the play has only reached a stage midway between the winter of disordered passion and the full summer of 'grace'. Perdita's speech goes on to make this clear. Between the two terminal seasons, so to call them, of winter and summer, unregenerate 'nature' and the fullness of 'grace', there are flowers which have a certain beauty of their own, but a beauty imperfect and, as it were, alloyed, like that of human passion unconsummated by 'grace'. These flowers are '*carn*ations', in which the *carn*-stem has a clear connection with the flesh, and 'streak'd gillyvors', 'bastards' between crude nature and the realm of 'grace'.

It is important to catch these associations; but more striking still is Perdita's attitude towards these flowers in the dialogue which follows. Polixenes greatly extends the scope of the discussion when he points out that the 'streak'd' process is, after all, engrained in nature; in the same way the action of 'blood', though capable of producing the disruption of harmony and natural relationship, is essential to a full growth into maturity:

> over that art
> Which you say adds to nature, is an art
> That nature makes. You see, sweet maid, we marry
> A gentler scion to the wildest stock,
> And make conceive a bark of baser kind
> By bud of nobler race; this is an art
> Which does mend nature, change it rather, but
> The art itself is nature.   (IV. iii. 90)

To Perdita's conception of 'art' as an addition to 'nature', and therefore, from the standpoint of her absolute simplicity, as a deformation of it, Polixenes opposes another of 'art' as completing 'nature', based on it indeed but as its crown and perfection. The conception is clearly capable of expression in social terms, and Polixenes, in what follows, proceeds to make this relation explicit by discussing the process of grafting in terms of marriage—the union, in this case, of 'the wildest stock' (in other words, 'nature', or, in human terms, 'blood', unregenerate humanity) to a 'gentler scion', the product of civilized urbanity, of 'nature' in its complete, fulfilled sense, which is 'grace'. The 'bark of *baser* kind'—the adjective is now clearly indicative of the lack of the civilized graces—is made to 'conceive' by 'a bud of *nobler* race': the idea of birth following on marriage thus acquires a new and wider meaning, becomes a completion, itself natural, of 'nature', an assumption by normal humanity of the crowning qualities, social and spiritual, of 'grace'.

To Polixenes' attempt, on the strength of this argument, to dissuade her from excluding these flowers, Perdita, however, turns away with an extreme repulsion which is most significant:

> I'll not put
> The dibble in earth to set one slip of them;
> No more than were I painted I would wish
> This youth to say 'twere well, and only therefore
> Desire to breed by me.   (IV. iii. 99)

The introduction of the familiar Elizabethan horror of being 'painted', together with the force of 'breed', shatters pretty thoroughly any suggestion that this scene is exclusively concerned with a state of idyllic make-believe. Clearly the innocent poetry so far given to Florizel and Perdita is no sufficient resolution of the great disunities developed in the early part of the play, and the brief moment of pastoral felicity is, in fact, broken by the open intervention of Polixenes. Only when the action has been decisively raised from the pastoral level will a final integration become conceivable.

The impression so far conveyed is, indeed, confirmed by the presence of a certain pathetic weakness, a kind of wilting from life, in the great list of flowers presented to Florizel which immediately follows. The emphasis on 'virgin branches' and 'maidenheads' is full of meaning in the light of the intense reaction against unregenerate passion which preceded it; still more so is the contrast with 'hot lavender'—the epithet is full of associations with 'blood'—and the other flowers given to men of middle age. Above all, there is the feeling behind the lines:

> pale primroses,
> That die unmarried, ere they can behold
> Bright Phoebus in his strength, a malady
> Most incident to maids.   (IV. iii. 122)

The beauty of these lines is devoid of strength, even clings pathetically to its own lack of vigour. The final reconciliation will be far less precarious. The spring-like beauty of this episode will have to be intensified and reinforced by the deep penitence of Leontes. Only thus can the idyllic pastoral be given sufficient substance to balance the harshness of the early scenes; and only so can a feeling for innocent beauty be raised to the level of Shakespeare's unique sensation of the fertility and maturity of 'grace'.

Meanwhile the vitality which, in spite of what we have said about certain elements in her flower speech, underlies Perdita's love for Florizel is indicated by the reference to the royal flowers—'bold oxlips' and 'the crown imperial'—with which she rounds off her apostrophe, and by the intense feeling for life which emerges from her final turning to her lover:

> *Perdita:*   O, these I lack,
>   To make you garlands of; and my sweet friend,
>   To strew him o'er and o'er.
> *Florizel:*   What, like a corse?
> *Perdita:* No, like a bank for love to lie and play on;
>   Not like a corse; or if, not to be buried,
>   But quick and in mine arms.   (IV. iii. 127)

The previous references to 'maladies' and unconsummated fading find their natural climax in Florizel's pathetically romantic evocation of the idea of death; but equally natural, equally a part of the beautifully balanced effect, is the spontaneous warmth and confidence of Perdita's reply. The consummation of their mutual love is *not* to lie in death, but in a reaction towards life. Florizel is not to be 'buried' by the flowers which she will bestow on him, but these are to be a sign of the vitality which is to deliver him 'quick' into her arms. The powerful strength of Perdita's youthful emotion has already, at this moment, laid the foundations for the final consummation, and the reference, which follows, to 'Whitsun pastorals' is far more than a piece of decorative folklore. It introduces, deliberately and at this most fitting moment, the theme of the Holy Spirit to stress the note of 'grace' (for Whitsun is, in the Christian cycle which conditions, however indirectly, the deeper purposes of *The Winter's Tale*, the feast of the descent of the Holy Spirit, harbinger of grace) as a crown to that of spring and love with which this part of the play is concerned.

These utterances of Perdita are balanced, immediately below, by the quality of Florizel's reply, which can be said to gather up in a most immediate form some of the basic sensations of the play:

>   What you do
>   Still betters what is done. When you speak, sweet,

> I'd have you do it ever: when you sing,
> I'd have you buy and sell so, so give alms,
> Pray so; and for the ordering your affairs,
> To sing them too; when you do dance, I wish you
> A wave o' the sea, that you might ever do
> Nothing but that; move still, still so,
> And own no other function; each your doing,
> So singular in each particular,
> Crowns what you are doing in the present deed
> That all your acts are queens.   (IV. iii. 135)

The most striking quality of this passage is the sensation it conveys of balance, of a continual relationship between motion and stillness. The verse is carefully constructed to reproduce this sensation, this balance, in terms of the rise and fall of the speaking voice. Consider the effect of the double 'so' in the fourth line, the first bringing the movement of the speech to its height and the second deliberately leading from that height while a third 'so' in the next line binds the central idea to those which follow; a little further on there is another 'so', again associated with two balanced phrases, bringing out still further the relationship of motion to stillness, the unity of experience to the incessant flow of its material. The same effect is obtained by the choice of echoing sounds in 'singular' and 'particular'. Still more important is the final association of 'present deed' with 'all your acts'; every action of Perdita's involves all her perfections and is a complete expression of her natural queenliness. And this, in turn, connects her with the central image of the whole speech—that of the wave which is always in motion and yet is ever the same. This image, like the speech of which it forms a part, is much more than a beautiful piece of decorative poetry. It is rather the particular expression of the theme vital to the play, and indeed to all Shakespeare's mature plays—the relation between the values of human life, which postulate timelessness, and the impersonal 'devouring' action of time which wears these values ceaselessly away. The wave image conveys perfectly the necessary relation between the mutability of life and the infinite value of human experience which it conditions but which is finally incommensurate with it. When this intuition and that of Perdita in the expression of her love have been gathered up into the wider framework of penitence and reconciliation, the full scope of *The Winter's Tale* will be finally clear.

The expression of this integration is the work of the last act. This opens with a return to Leontes, who is introduced, through the words of Cleomenes, at the moment when the 'saint-like sorrow' which has prevailed in him since the revelation of Hermione's innocence is ready to be crowned by reconciliation to the divine powers he has offended. The years since his last appearance have been passed in a sorrow that now appears to Cleomenes as a prelude to sanctity. His faults have been 'redeem'd', and the time has come when he can be called upon, without undue levity, to 'forget' his past, to accept by reassuming his royal functions the forgiveness which the 'heavens' are now ready to grant him.

Leontes, however, cannot immediately accept the invitation of his courtiers. For him, if not for those around him, the consequences of his sin are still alive, and their memory makes it impossible for him to act as a free man:

> Whilst I remember
> Her and her virtues, I cannot forget
> My blemishes in them; and so still think of
> The wrong I did myself; which was so much,
> That heirless it hath made my kingdom, and
> Destroy'd the sweet'st companion that e'er man
> Bred his hopes out of. (V. i. 7)

The rhythmic construction of this speech, with its break at the crucial words 'the wrong I did myself', stresses the enunciation of its most important points. In the first part, the weight of memory in Leontes leads him to recall the perfections of Hermione and to weigh them against the magnitude of his faults. These have been so great ('so much': the poignancy of the simple expression is stressed by its place at the end of a rhythmic unit) that they have left his kingdom 'heirless' and 'destroy'd' (once again the break after the inconclusive 'and' of the preceding line adds power to a word itself loaded with tragic meaning) the 'sweet'st' companion

> that e'er man
> Bred his hopes out of.

The sharp bitterness of 'destroy'd' is balanced by the intense pathos of 'sweet'st' and leads up to the final evocation, in 'bred', of fertility as the tangible expression of the deepest 'hopes' of paternity. The speech, in fact, is calculated to bring out the two emotions which now prevail in Leontes; they give new depth to the preliminary utterance of Cleomenes, which they extend without, however, contradicting. The first of these is his 'saint-like sorrow', a repentance for past sins kept alive in him by the unfailing memory of Hermione, and the second is his desire for an heir to be the fulfilment, as king and father alike, of which his sin has deprived him. It is here, however, that the past more especially lives on in the present as a limiting, restraining influence. A new son for Leontes can only be born from Hermione, whom he believes to be dead and can only therefore be the daughter whom, in his past folly, he condemned to die.

The other side of the picture, however, though Leontes cannot yet accept it, is nonetheless relevant. For his other courtly adviser, Dion, he is king as well as husband, and his duty to the state justifies a line of conduct which, as an individual, he might not be required to follow. The speech, indeed, has a meaning far beyond its value in developing the argument:

> What were more holy
> Than to rejoice the former queen is well?
> What holier than, for royalty's repair,
> For present comfort and for future good,
> To bless the bed of majesty again
> With a sweet fellow to't?   (V. i. 29)

The desire for an heir is thus taken out of the purely personal sphere, acquires a fresh universality in relation to the traditional conception of royalty in its social function. Dion's words, moreover, stress the note of sanctity ('holy', 'holier'), and add to it the emphasis on human fertility which preceded it, thus extending decisively the scope of an emotion which, on the purely personal plane, could hardly compensate the preceding tragedy. We now begin to see how the pattern of the play is to be completed. Penitence and devotion, kept alive in Leontes by his memory and by Paulina's stressing of his responsibility for his loss, can be raised to the level of sanctity, and the functions of 'blood', no longer the cause of jealousies and divisions which have exhausted their tragic consequences with the passage of time, can now become a source of life to the unified and gracious personality.

The necessary prelude to reconciliation, meanwhile, is a further projection of the past into the present, a poignant deepening of Leontes' love for Hermione. This is apparent when he says of her:

> I might have look'd upon my queen's full eyes;
> Have taken treasure from her lips,   (V. i. 53)

and when Paulina takes up and emphasizes the sensation of spiritual
wealth in her reply:

> And left them
> More rich for what they yielded,

the lover's gift of himself in emotional fullness becomes, typically, a
cause of deeper enrichment. Again, when Leontes abjures all other loves
as he remembers the eyes of his former queen—

> Stars, stars,
> And all eyes else dead coals!—

the intensity of his emotion suggests how the sense of the constant
pressure of time is in the process of being overcome. The answer, of
course, is not that of the philosopher but of the artist. It consists in
opposing to the action of time, sensibly apprehended, the value of
Leontes' experience, intensifying it as a sensation of boundless wealth,
until time itself is felt to be only a necessary element in the creation of
this rich intuition. Time, as at certain moments in *Antony and Cleopatra*,
has become irrelevant; in *The Winter's Tale* it has simply served to
shape the fullness of 'grace'. Only, whereas in *Antony* the achievement
of transcendent, vital justification is purely personal, balanced against
aspects of corruption and egoism which threaten it continuously with
collapse, here we are moving in a world less limited, more symbolic
and universal in its implications. The restored fulfilment of Leontes'
love is to take place against a background more ample than anything in
that love itself. The past, far from being forgotten, will need to live
again in the present as a formative influence, individual feeling will
find its proper context in the social obligations of the King, and both
will be subject together to a common dedication to the ends of 'grace'.
There could be no better indication of the essential novelty of Shakespeare's purpose in these, the last plays of his full maturity.

The transformation towards which the whole action has been
pointing is completed, given visible dramatic expression, in the final
scene (V. iii). In it the Shakespearean experience, different in kind and
quality from anything else in English poetry, reaches a complete
integration. The fetters of the plot are dissolved; or rather the plot
itself, conceived as an extension of the poetic development, is at last
finally assimilated to the interplay of imagery. The words of the reconciled parties at the foot of Hermione's 'statue' are as significant in their

sequence as in their sense; they proceed by an antiphonal building-up towards the final inclusive harmony. This sequence is given continuity, dramatic projection, by the process of Leontes' slow awakening to the fact that Hermione herself is before him, and by the almost imperceptible stages of her coming to life, which itself corresponds to the definitive birth of the new 'grace' out of the long winter of his penance. In this final scene, plot at last assumes its full status as the crown of an intricate development of poetic resources. Technique becomes the free and adequate instrument of experience, and the development of imagery through which we have tried to trace the various stages of the Shakespearean pattern is logically complete.

Compared with this general impression, irresistibly conveyed by the very movement of the action towards its conclusion, the analysis of detail becomes of secondary importance. Leontes' first reaction to the 'dead likeness' of his queen, presented to him by Paulina as a work of art which excels art, is one of 'silence' and 'wonder'. His first words, recalling his past treatment of Hermione, are a request that she should 'chide' him; his second utterance contrasts his sense of sin explicitly with the perfection he remembers, and associates his memory of that perfection with a new birth:

> for she was as tender
> As infancy and grace. (V. iii. 26)

It is, indeed, a rebirth whose successive stages we are now witnessing, a rebirth the impression of which is strengthened in Leontes by his acute sense of the passage of time; for the Hermione he sees is 'wrinkled' as the wife of his memories never was, and Paulina has to explain that this is due to the artist's skill in taking into account the years which have passed since her 'death'. The relation of the time-theme to those of rebirth and reconciliation is thus retained to the last as necessary to the complete effect.

The revelation of the restored image, as he believes it to be, of his 'dead' wife inspires Leontes initially to a mood of profound disquiet. The sight is now as 'piercing' to his soul, as full of memories of the follies he has committed, as her life, by himself destroyed, might have been to his 'good comfort'. In Perdita, on the other hand, the vision produces the first move towards reconciliation. She kneels and, like all the children of these plays in like situation, implores her parent's 'blessing'. Her prayer, moreover, is addressed to her 'that ended when

I but began', binding together—as in *Pericles*—mother and daughter in the single process of re-created life which the play aims at conveying. It is, in fact, the triumph of this continuity, a triumph as natural and inevitable as life itself, that we are witnessing. When Leontes is 'transported' by the contrary emotions which assail him, when, in spite of the grief which the sight of the 'statue' has roused in him, he begs that the deceptive life-likeness, as he still considers it, may not be taken from him—

> Make me to think so twenty years together—

and echoes the idea so emphatically in his exclamation, 'No, not these twenty years', he is once more suggesting that time can stand still as he contemplates the image of his love. This can only be justified by the power of the poetic process, which shows that this conception of love is one of life and value, incommensurate with time, which has now become only a condition of it. It is not an accident that Hermione's slow reawakening—slow both to ease the intolerable burden to Leontes' own senses and to reflect the successive stages of his full restoration to reality—is from now on surrounded by symbols explicitly religious. The 'statue' is said to be placed in a 'chapel', and the war between Leontes' contradictory feelings is envisaged as one in which good and evil spirits are at odds for possession of his soul. Above all, and most explicitly, Paulina stresses that as a prelude to Hermione's 'descending'.

> It is required
> You do awake your faith;   (V. iii. 94)

and her final call removes any doubt as to the true scope of the 'resurrection' we are about to witness:

> 'Tis time; descend; be stone no more; approach;
> Strike all that look upon with marvel. Come,
> I'll fill your grave up; stir, nay, come away,
> *Bequeath to death your numbness, for from him*
> *Dear life redeems you.*   (V. iii. 99)

The first line, broken into short phrases, intense, insistent, is as much the evocation to a descending spirit as a call to Hermione to leave her pedestal. Her restoration to Leontes is to be hailed as a 'marvel' of more than physical content, as the miracle of life spiritually reborn. The sense of temporal impermanence overcome is indeed present in the reference to the filling up of the grave, the returning of former 'numbness' to death, and, above all, in the assertion of the redemption by 'dear life' from the bonds of mortality.

With Leontes and Hermione finally embraced, it only remains for the play to be rounded off by the gesture, typical of these comedies, by which the family unity is finally restored and in which the father bestows his blessing. First Paulina restores Perdita to her mother, laying emphasis on the symbolic meaning carried by her name:

> kneel
> And pray your mother's blessing. Turn, good lady;
> Our Perdita is found;   (V. iii. 119)

and secondly, Hermione, in terms equally familiar, makes it her first act in her restored state to beseech the gods to 'look down' and pour their 'graces' upon her daughter's head. With the marrying of Paulina to Camillo, ratified by 'us, a pair of kings', Leontes and Polixenes newly rejoined in amity, the pattern of reconciliation is finally complete. It would be hard to find, even in Shakespeare, a more profound purpose more consistently carried out to its proper artistic conclusion.

4 The Tempest

Whether *The Tempest*, which we may assume to have been written almost immediately after *The Winter's Tale*, is or is not a more satisfactory play is a question about which opinion may reasonably differ. What seems certain is that it represents a further and logical development in the 'symbolic' technique evolved in the series of Shakespeare's last comedies. We might define this development by saying that, whereas *The Winter's Tale* is still concerned with the evolution of experience towards its completely adequate symbolic representation, *The Tempest* assumes that this consummation has already been achieved, so that the various characters and situations exist from the first entirely in terms of their 'symbolic' function. The sense of motion and development which is so prominent in the earlier comedy is no longer a primary feature of *The Tempest*. Its absence, although we may agree that it makes the play poorer in a certain human content, was the inevitable consequence of a great artist's inability to repeat himself; for *The*

Tempest is, whether we prefer it or not, the logical conclusion of the integrating process that produced *The Winter's Tale*, and consequently of Shakespeare's art.

The main outline of the 'symbolic' pattern of the play follows familiar lines. We should never forget, in this respect, that it is called *The Tempest*, and that it opens in a storm at sea. As in *The Winter's Tale*, the storm and the calm which follows it are related respectively to the tragedy caused by human passion and the reconciliation which, after an acceptance of the suffering implicit in that tragedy, follows upon repentance in its aftermath. At the centre of the action, formerly victim of the storm roused by unleashed human egoism, but now as much its master as he is in control of the physical tempest he has raised to bring his enemies to the stage upon which their destinies are to be decided, stands the enigmatic figure of Prospero. At once the victim and the master of circumstances—and it is perhaps this double aspect of his nature which has proved, for many, the stumbling block in the way of a full acceptance of the play—Prospero emerges increasingly as the plot takes shape as the instrument of judgment. Through his actions, and those of Ariel, the different motives which prevail in his former enemies are brought to the surface, evaluated, and finally judged. In the process of judgment, the meeting of Prospero's daughter with the son of Alonso provides a symbolic ground for reconciliation in the familiar Shakespearean manner. Only after the final restoration of harmony has taken place on the island does Prospero, with his associates, return to resume his place in the human society from which envy and ambition had originally driven him.

With Prospero's opening exposition to Miranda (I. ii) the symbolic design of the play begins to take shape. His aim is to bring her, by recalling her forgotten past, to an understanding of her present position, not only as an exile on the island, but as a human being on the threshold of her moral maturity. Although this understanding comes, in the nature of things, gradually, the tone and phrasing of Prospero's first speech are significant:

> There's no harm done . . .
> > No harm.
> I have done nothing but in care of thee,
> Of thee, my dear one, thee my daughter, who
> Art ignorant of what thou art, naught knowing
> Of whence I am; nor that I am more better

Than Prospero, master of a full poor cell,
And thy no greater father. (I. ii. 15)

Prospero's confidence contrasts with the compassionate fear which is Miranda's instinctive emotion. This fear, natural, human as it is, springs from her ignorance. It is a product of the same inexperience which has just led her to imagine 'some noble creature' upon Alonso's ship and to live throughout with visions of a 'brave new world' and of the ennobled humanity that is to live in it. Prospero does not disapprove of these visions, or of the 'virtue of compassion' which he has deliberately roused to expression in his daughter. Eventually he will endorse her feelings, give them their proper place in his own comprehensive view of spiritual reality; but, before this can be done, they need to be reconciled to a fuller experience of the possibilities of human nature. It is the story of Florizel and Perdita over again. As their full happiness involved, as a preliminary condition, the breaking-up of the rustic paradise in which they first met, so must Miranda leave behind her the 'ignorance' of her own nature, come to know 'what she is' in a way that can never be achieved in the isolation of her life on the island.

In the telling of the story which follows, Miranda is, as it were, awakened gradually into maturity. More properly speaking, as he penetrates the veil which shrouds for her 'the dark backward and abysm of time' (I. ii. 50), Prospero makes her aware, in terms of her own past, of the knot of mingled motives which constitute the behaviour of men in society. In the course of this exposition her state is closely and variously related to the main conception; for the successive stages by which her mature judgment emerges from the dream in which it has so far been enveloped correspond to the development which, by bringing together Prospero and his former enemies, is to restore both to a full participation in civilized life. Dream and reality, sentimental idealization and mature judgment, are in fact integrated by participation in the successive stages of a single action.

Remembering previous plays, we are not surprised to find as we follow the story of Prospero's expulsion from Milan that evil in *The Tempest* has two aspects—personal and social—which stand in the closest connection with one another. Throughout the tragedies the first consequence of evil is anarchy, and its starting-point the overthrow of 'degree' by the dominating force of passion. 'Degree', in turn, is associated in ever-increasing measure with the human institutions, the family and the body politic, in which personal 'value' receives, as it were, an external projection, a sanction in the objective order of reality. In the story of Prospero's banishment evil strikes both at the roots of social stability—for, as head of the state, he was the guarantee of that 'degree' by which alone societies can prosper—and at the unity of the family to overthrow the natural order of things. In casting Prospero with his daughter on the open sea, Antonio transgressed both against the Duke of Milan and his own brother.

His first crime in the social-political order—so to call it—is deliberately related to the character of his victim. Like the Duke in *Measure for Measure*, Prospero lived 'retired', withdrawn from the world and devoted to contemplation and the 'liberal' arts:

> I, thus neglecting worldly ends, all dedicated
> To closeness and the bettering of my mind
> With that which, but by being so retired,
> O'erprized all popular rate; (I. ii. 89)

and, like him again, he delegated his whole power to another. In so doing, both opened the way for evil to enter their respective dominions. Prospero is quite explicit about this when he tells Miranda that his own 'closeness', his 'neglect' of the ends of government,

> in my false brother
> Awak'd an evil nature: and my trust,
> Like a good parent, did beget of him
> A falsehood in its contrary, as great
> As my trust was, which had indeed no limit,
> A confidence sans bound. (I. ii. 92)

Prospero, of course, is more secure than the earlier Duke in his mastery. His apprenticeship to experience has already been served before *The Tempest* opens, whereas the Duke, conceived before the process of deepening insight shadowed in the great tragedies had taken place, is still involved in his own search for clarification.[40] But the position of both is, at bottom, similar. Both begin by consecrating themselves to an ideal of purely personal perfection, and both in so doing neglect not only social duties but also an instrument, when properly considered, for the attainment of that perfection itself. In the case of Prospero, however, the corruption which brings him suffering and loss springs from his own family.

At this point the political is replaced by the presentation of the family theme. Prospero's brother becomes

> The ivy which has hid my princely trunk,
> And suck'd my verdure out on't. (I. ii. 86)

Perhaps only the very intimacy of the ties which bind a man to his brother enables Antonio to assume a part so completely contrary to Prospero's own; the man of the world is, as it were, the enemy of the contemplative precisely because of the unity of blood that joins them. To Antonio's crime against the state is added at all events a crime against the bond of unity in the family which Prospero feels even more deeply:

> I prithee, mark me, that a brother should
> Be so perfidious. (I. ii. 67)

The two crimes are, in fact, one, a descent into anarchy prompted by personal selfishness which is, in the Shakespearean outlook of the great plays, the supreme cause of tragedy. But Prospero's past retirement has unwittingly helped to bring these crimes about; and so only now, after exposure to the tempestuous seas and years of confinement on 'a most desolate isle'—desolate, in spite of all the graces with which his wisdom has endowed it, because deprived of human society—is he in a position to assume with authority his vocation of judgment.

Beyond judgment, however, Prospero has yet another purpose—reconciliation. It is here that the process of Miranda's 'education' links up with the more general 'symbolic' theme. The instrument of reconciliation, as in *The Winter's Tale*, is to be the love spontaneously born in the children of the very fathers whose friendship envy and hatred have destroyed; and so Miranda, now instructed into the secret of her own past, is led to see Ferdinand. Moved still by innocence, she greets him at once as something supernatural, the representative of a humanity exalted, in her view, to something above the normal condition of man:

> I might call him
> *A thing divine*, for nothing natural
> I ever saw so *noble*. (I. ii. 415)

The idea of *nobility* exalted to something like a state of divinity is essential to Shakespeare's purpose. It is, indeed, the conclusion towards which Prospero himself is moving; but the moment for asserting it

has not yet come, and so he interrupts his daughter's ecstasy, breaks off
the developing love, to which Ferdinand has immediately responded,
with what seems unnecessary brutality. For the fact is that Miranda's
idealization, her divinization of Ferdinand, based though it is upon
sound instincts, is premature. She greets Ferdinand as a god simply
because she has seen nothing like him before; and yet, as Prospero is
quick to remind her, she has seen no other man than himself and
Caliban. The behaviour of the men who have been cast ashore on the
island by Prospero's providential storm—many of them presumably
not much less 'god-like' than Ferdinand to an inexperienced gaze—
will show how dangerous are her simple assumptions. Their behaviour
calls for consideration in the main body of the play. Only after Prospero's former enemies have done their worst and been, in turn, dominated by the superior power and insight of the man upon whose wrong-
ing their temporal good fortune has so far depended will he be able to
unite his daughter convincingly to Ferdinand in terms that are little
short of god-like. But the divinity—such as it is—will then be founded
upon a true experience of human nature and will express a spiritual
reality, not merely a sentimental intuition; and this experience will
have been obtained in the process of passing judgment on all the
characters in the play.

It is to pass judgment, as a prelude to reconciliation, that Prospero
has caused all those concerned in his former banishment to be cast
ashore on the island. From their first appearance there (II. i) he subjects
them to what is, in effect, an analysis of their respective guilts. Of all
the newcomers, Alonso, the King of Naples, comes best out of the
test.[41] Having lost, as he thinks, his son and feeling that his journey to
Tunis has been the cause of the disaster in which he and his companions
have been involved, he refuses to be comforted. It is, indeed, the very
inconsolable quality of his sorrow that shows him to be capable of
repentance; and Shakespeare no doubt intends to emphasize this when
he makes him capable of receiving the visitation of sleep. Alonso, in
short, is morally sensitive, and so his response to Ariel's music is a
positive one:

> I wish mine eyes
> Would, with themselves, shut up my thoughts. I find
> They are inclined to do so. (II. i. 199)

So Alonso sleeps, and his sleep is a sign that he will, when the time

comes and his understanding has been completed, find his place in the
final pattern of reconciliation.

The next stage in the analysis concerns Antonio and Sebastian. Their
first appearance marks them out, in the repartee to which they subject
Gonzalo's efforts to cheer Alonso, as cynics of the familiar Shakespearean type, their intelligence applied exclusively to purposes of
destruction and self-assertion. Taken in itself, their cynicism does not
seem of great moment, but we are soon shown that it is the prelude to
greater crimes. As soon as Alonso succumbs to sleep Prospero's
'nimble'-spirited enemy feels himself once more moved by the desire
for power:

> methinks I see it in thy face,
> What thou should'st be: the occasion speaks thee, and
> My strong imagination sees a crown
> Dropping upon thy head.   (II. i. 214)

This strikes a note familiar in earlier plays. Lady Macbeth, after crowning her husband in her thoughts, played in the murder of Duncan very
much the part played by Antonio in the plot to dispose of Alonso. His
motive power, like that of Iago and Edmund, is a peculiarly self-
sufficient conception of fortune:

> Noble Sebastian,
> Thou lettest thy fortune sleep—die, rather, wink'st
> Whiles thou art waking.   (II. i. 223)

The new twist thus given to the prevailing sleep image is deeply characteristic of the speaker. To act is to be awake, to seize the chance for
self-assertion which fortune has offered; to hesitate, on the other hand,
is to 'wink', to sleep beneath the appearance of watchfulness. This is
the 'philosophy' which, carried to its logical conclusion, formerly led
Antonio to play the chief part in his brother's banishment and which
now, energetically communicated to Sebastian, leads his weaker
associate to contemplate a similar betrayal of Alonso.

The nature of Antonio's domination over Sebastian is most clearly
revealed in his reply to the latter's tentative expression of doubt. 'But
for your conscience?' The very word, as indicating any reality, is
meaningless to him:

> Ay, sir, where lies that? if it were a kibe,
> 'Twould put me to my slipper: but I feel not

> This deity in my bosom: twenty consciences,
> That stand 'twixt me and Milan, candied be they,
> And melt ere they molest. (II. i. 284)

The opening image, with its comparison of conscience to a purely physical inconvenience, is pure Iago. So is the sneering reference to 'deity', a word which can mean nothing to Antonio but a sentimental illusion intervening between a man and the furthering of those selfish ends in the attainment of which alone he feels his manhood. The sense of sentimental unreality is driven home by the references, common in Shakespeare and everywhere expressive of loathing, to 'candied' and 'melt'[42]; the stomach of the practical man of action is turned by these finicky attempts to restrict his progress. The speech continues in the same strain:

> Here lies your brother,
> No better than the earth he lies upon,
> If he were that which now he's like (that's dead)
> Whom I, with this obedient steel, three inches of it,
> Can lay to bed for ever; whiles you, doing thus,
> To the perpetual wink for aye might put
> This ancient morsel, this Sir Prudence, who
> Should not upbraid our course. For all the rest,
> They'll take suggestion as a cat laps milk;
> They'll tell the clock to any business that
> We say befits the hour. (II. i. 288)

No one can deny Antonio's brilliance as a speaker. His words reflect an intense destructive energy, to which the intelligence is bound in faithful service. Behind them lies a deep-seated pessimism, the conviction that a dead man is 'no better than the earth he lies upon' and that only three inches of 'obedient' steel lie between his victim and extinction. If this be so, if there be no moral sanction governing our acts and if conscience be a mere 'kibe', an inconvenient 'deity' which a moment's reasoning can put securely to sleep, then the murder of a man who stands between him and power is the most natural thing in the world: so natural that he can discuss that man's death in terms of putting him 'to bed for ever'. As for Gonzalo and those who, like him, still feel conscience as a living thing, they are brushed aside in the contemptuous 'ancient morsel', 'Sir Prudence', and in the brilliant, scornful comparison implicit in 'They'll take suggestion as a cat laps milk.' The whole thing, given the will, the determination to act, is simplicity itself.

Sebastian has nothing to oppose to this conviction of anarchy. He yields at once, and as he yields Shakespeare is careful to remind us of Antonio's other crime:

> Thy case, dear friend,
> Shall be my precedent; as thou gott'st Milan,
> I'll come by Naples. Draw thy sword; one stroke
> Shall free thee from the tribute which thou payest,
> And I the king shall love thee.   (II. i. 298)

The last words show how fully Sebastian has succumbed to the spirit of Antonio. 'One stroke', one simple action, is sufficient to cut through all the obstacles which antiquated ties of conscience and custom put in the way of the plotters; and in a world in which only the blow really counts, the decisive stroke backed by the will resolved to achieve its ends, everything is simple. The blow when struck, moreover, is to free Antonio from 'tribute', from the material pledge of that natural allegiance on which all order finally depends. It is all simple, so simple that it leads fatally to destruction: a destruction logically implied in the act itself even before it is condemned by Prospero and judged by the standards of the moral law which upholds him and which he in turn, within his limited sphere, upholds.

In the same scene Shakespeare takes his analysis of the situation on the island a step further by relating it to a personal interpretation of the doctrine of man's original innocence.[43] In landing upon the island Alonso and his followers are placed in the possession of virgin soil. Here, according to Gonzalo, is their opportunity to organize a community untainted by competition or the shadow of ambition, an Arcadian anarchy founded upon the free following of instinct. His remarks, with the accompanying comments of Antonio and Sebastian are full of interest:

> Gonzalo: Had I plantation of this isle, my lord—
> Antonio: He'd sow it with nettle-seed.
> Sebastian: Or docks or mallows.
> Gonzalo: And were the king on't, what would I do?
> Sebastian: 'Scape being drunk for want of wine.
> Gonzalo: I' the commonwealth I would by contraries
>   Execute all things; for no kind of traffic
>   Would I admit; no name of magistrate,
>   Letters should not be known; riches, poverty,
>   And use of service, none . . .

No occupation, all men idle, all;
And women too, but innocent and pure;
No sovereignty:—
Sebastian: Yet he would be king on't.
Antonio: The latter end of his commonwealth forgets the beginning.
          (II. i. 150)

The dispassionate, academic catalogue reflects the unreality of the whole
dream. The sources of human misery are to be excluded, according to
Gonzalo, from the commonwealth; but with them, as soon appears,
every distinctive quality of human life. The state of innocence is also
necessarily the state of inexperience:

> All things in common nature should produce
> *Without sweat or endeavour*; treason, felony,
> Sword, pike, knife, gun, or need of any engine
> Would I not have; but nature should bring forth
> Of its own kind, all foison, all abundance,
> To feed my innocent people. (II. i. 166)

All this is to come about, according to Gonzalo's dream, 'without
sweat or endeavour'; but also, we must add, without the salutary
experience of effort from which is born, often slowly and painfully,
the capacity to distinguish between good and evil which is the foundation of the moral life. The inadequacy of Gonzalo's simplicity, already
implied in the flat, abstract tone of his speech, is confirmed once more
by the comments of Antonio and Sebastian:

> Sebastian: No marrying 'mong his subjects?
> Antonio: None, man, all idle; whores and knaves. (II. i. 172)

Gonzalo's commonwealth is founded upon an amorality which leaves
place for 'nettle-seed', 'docks', and 'mallows' to take possession of the
ground. The fact that men like Antonio and Sebastian exist proves that
some kind of cultivation of the human terrain is necessary.[44] The state
of nature is one which man must in the course of things outgrow; the
crucial problem is whether this development will be towards good, in
the aceptance of some adequate moral standard (sanctioned, in this play,
by the Destiny which upholds Prospero) or towards the anarchy of
unlimited personal desires.

At this point, with the problem of the state of nature before us, it
is time to consider Caliban. For Caliban, half man and half beast,
represents the real state of nature far more truly than any of Gonzalo's

courtly theorizings, and in his relations with Prospero the connection
between 'nature' and the moral, civilized state is far more profoundly
considered. Finding him already on the island, Prospero tried from the
first to incorporate him into the new civilized order of moral realities;
and Caliban himself at once admits this and turns the admission into a
formidable indictment of the whole civilizing process which began by
flattering him and finally became his tyrant:

> When thou camest first,
> Thou strok'st me, and made much of me; would'st give me
> Water with berries in't; and teach me how
> To name the bigger light, and how the less,
> That burn by day and night; and then I lov'd thee,
> And show'd thee all the qualities o' the isle,
> The fresh springs, brine-pits, barren place and fertile:
> Cursed be I that did so! All the charms
> Of Sycorax, toads, beetles, bats, light on you!
> For I am all the subjects that you have,
> Which first was mine own king.   (I. ii. 332)

From this we may learn more than one thing fundamental to the play.
In the first place, the poetry we admire in Caliban was given to him,
at least in part, by Prospero; the instinctive appreciation was, if we like,
his own, but the gift of expression, essentially a social, a civilizing gift,
came to him from Prospero. The burden of Caliban's grievance is that
Prospero has deprived him of his freedom, subjected his physical individuality to the pre-eminence of spiritual rule; and he goes on to
accuse his master of keeping him in prison who had originally been
master of the island. Prospero's answer once more shows the problem
in all its complexity:

> I have used thee,
> Filth as thou art, with human care, and lodg'd thee
> In mine own cell, till thou didst seek to violate
> The honour of my child.   (I. ii. 345)

The intensity of Prospero's reaction ('*Filth* as thou art') is a clear indication of the gravity of the issues involved, and of the tension which so
persistently underlies the moralizing harmonies of this play. Caliban,
who is necessary to Prospero, whose animal instincts are a true part of

human nature (for Prospero, who thus declares his contempt for him, is dependent on him for his services), is yet recalcitrant to all restraint or discipline. Regarding himself as rightful owner of the island, he echoes, in his own way, Antonio by the assertion of his right to enjoy all that appeals to his passions as desirable; so that when Prospero gave him liberty and the use of his own cell, he used this liberty to attack his master's dearest possession in the person of his daughter.

The deficiencies of Caliban's natural anarchism, thus indicated by Prospero, are further brought out by his meeting with Stephano and Trinculo. The arrival on the island of men from the outer world of 'civilization' is fatal to the natural creature, who escapes from the bondage of Prospero only to fall into that, infinitely more degrading, of the basest camp-followers of a supposedly civilized society. Caliban is, of course, in many ways greatly superior to Stephano and Trinculo. The poetry which marks the simplicity of his response to nature is enough to ensure that; but, divorced as he is from spiritual judgment and seeking only the anarchic freedom of his desires, he falls into a slavery which the superiority of his expression, being so incongruous, so divorced from the reality of his behaviour in the play, only serves to make more grotesque. Seduced by the 'celestial' liquor which Stephano gives him, he offers to serve him as a god:

> I prithee, be my god.
>
> That's a brave god and bears celestial liquor;
> I'll kneel to him.
>
> I'll kiss thy foot: I'll swear myself thy subject. (II. ii. 161, 126, 165)

His aim in doing so is to free himself from service—I'll bear him no more sticks, but follow thee' (II. ii. 176)—but in following the freedom thus offered him by his fallacious instincts, he goes out drunk, crying 'Freedom hay-day,' indeed, but reduced in reality to a slavery far more degrading than any to which he had been subjected before.

At this point the development of the situation on the island is substantially complete. Two plots—one against Alonso and another against Prospero himself—have been fully launched, and the original seclusion of Prospero's domain has been most effectively shattered by the entry of human passion and sin. Yet Prospero, in spite of all, maintains the threads in his hands and it is precisely at this moment that he chooses to indicate, through the instrument of his purposes, the moral resolution at which he aims. Ariel's great speech addressed to Alonso and his

companions just before he deprives them of the enchanted banquet
that has just been set before them is, in fact, nothing less than the turning-
point of the whole play:

> You are three men of sin, whom Destiny,
> That hath to instrument this lower world,
> And what is in't, the never-surfeited sea
> Hath caused to belch up you; and, on this island
> Where man doth not inhabit, you 'mongst men
> Being most unfit to live ... But remember
> (For that's my business to you) that you three
> From Milan did supplant good Prospero,
> Expos'd unto the sea (which hath requit it)
> Him and his innocent child: for which foul deed,
> The powers delaying, not forgetting, have
> Incens'd the seas and shores, yea, all the creatures,
> Against your peace. Thee of thy son, Alonso,
> They have bereft; and do pronounce by me
> Lingering perdition (worse than any death
> Can be at once) shall step by step attend
> You and your ways, whose wraths to guard you from,
> Which here, in this most desolate isle, else falls
> Upon your heads, is nothing but heart's sorrow
> And a clear life ensuing.   (III. iii. 53)

Here at last is an explicit statement of what *The Tempest* is about. The
speech is introduced with a degree of pageantry and circumstance that
makes it stand out with great dramatic force from the general action.
Ariel—generally the 'gentle Ariel' of Prospero's preference—is brought
onto the stage in the form of a harpy to the accompaniment of thunder
and lightning. He causes the banquet to vanish, and then, left face to
face with those he has come to judge, he speaks. His words have a
weighted simplicity that underlines their unique seriousness. The effect
is obtained by means so direct that they barely call for analysis.
Partly by the persistent use of heavy vocalic stresses, partly by the
emphatic use of pauses in the middle and at the end of lines, partly by
the significant insertion of parenthetic pauses into long unfolding
sentences, the speech attains a measured magnificence unsurpassed in
its kind anywhere in Shakespeare. Unsurpassed because, perhaps for the
first time in his work, the voice of Destiny delivers itself in judgment.
'I and my followers,' says Ariel, 'are ministers of Fate.' As such he
speaks, and, by so speaking, brings out the full meaning of the play.

The most important feature of the speech, indeed, is its affirmation of Destiny. This affirmation is, in its unequivocal expression, unique in Shakespeare's work. Much of the symbolism of the later plays—the use, for example, of the associations of 'grace' in relation to fertility—has religious implications; but nowhere, not even in *The Winter's Tale*, with its still rather misty references to 'the gods', is Destiny so *personally* conceived or conceded such power in the working out of human affairs. Destiny, says Ariel, 'hath to instrument the lower world.' 'Delaying, not forgetting', it watches over the whole story and brings the characters concerned in it, with absolute foreknowledge, to the conclusions willed by absolute justice. All this, however it may have been foreshadowed in earlier works, is substantially new, but at the same time inevitable. For all Shakespeare's symbolism, with the harmonizing purpose which underlies it, moves towards the presentation of the problems, moral and artistic, involved in this final acceptance of the reality of Destiny. Without that acceptance the intuition of 'grace' is only an insubstantial dream, a tenuous harmony woven out of elements that have no more permanence than that of a personal mood; with it, possibly, the author lays himself open to the charge of going beyond his experience, of introducing an element of discontinuity into what had been so far the harmonious pattern of his work. Needless to say, it was not part of the artist's purpose to substantiate this objective conception of Destiny by argument; but it was his aim, inevitable and necessary given the general direction of his previous writing, to place it in the centre of his play, to allow the symbolic web of experiences to form around it and to see if it would, in the last analysis, fit. For this reason we are justified in seeing Shakespeare's last great romance not simply as one more exercise in his final manner, but, beyond this and most remarkably of all, as a new kind of play.

The keynote of the whole action, as Ariel now emphasizes it, is indeed *judgment*. Only when the good and evil in human nature have been understood and separated will the final reconciliation take place. For this end—and really for this end alone—the various actors in the forgotten story of Naples and Milan have been brought together through the providential action of the storm upon this 'most desolate isle', 'where man doth not inhabit'. 'Desolate' surely because the work of purgation about to be accomplished needs to be accompanied by abstinence and a certain asceticism; and desolate too because it is not a place upon which men are to live their full, civilized lives—after the

final reconciliation it is left by all, including those whose nature debars
them from playing a part in the 'brave new world' of beings at once
spiritualized and social to which they are being offered entry—but on
which they are to achieve moral understanding and learn to accept the
judgment passed on them. Unless their sojourn on the island has shown
them the need for 'heart's sorrow' and a 'clear life' to follow, their
doom is certain. For it is in the nature of unbridled passion, as Shakespeare had presented it in the great series of tragedies from *Othello* to
Timon of Athens, to lead its victims to self-destruction; and *The Tempest*,
with its insistence upon ideas of penance and amendment that can only
follow from acceptance of a personal, spiritual conception of Destiny,
is conceived as nothing less than a counterpoise to this process of tragic
ruin.

The work of drawing to their appointed conclusion, after Ariel's
intervention, the symbolic threads of *The Tempest* has several stages.
The first is to consummate the union of Miranda and Ferdinand; for
upon the union of the children, in *The Tempest* as in *The Winter's Tale*,
the reconciliation of the parents, and of all the characters, depends.
Their love, indeed, as it unfolds under the eyes of Prospero, brings
both the lovers to a new and intenser life. Miranda becomes 'precious
creature', 'perfect', 'peerless'; whilst she, in turn, says all of Ferdinand
when she says

> I would not wish
> Any companion in the world but you;
> Nor can imagination form a shape,
> Besides yourself, to like of. (III. i. 54)

Moved by such love for one another, both are ready for Prospero's
blessing upon their union. He gives it, still invisible, in lines pregnant
with fertility and 'grace' which are most splendidly interwoven with
those of the lovers:

Ferdinand: I,
> Beyond all limit of what else i' the world,
> Do love, prize, honour you.
Miranda: I am a fool
> To weep at what I am glad of.
Prospero: Fair encounter
> Of two most rare affections! Heavens rain grace
> On that which breeds between them.
Ferdinand: Wherefore weep you?

Miranda: At mine unworthiness, that dare not offer
What I desire to give; and much less take
What I shall die to want. But this is trifling,
And all the more it seeks to hide itself,
The bigger bulk it shows. (III. i. 71)

Once again the parallels with other Shakespearean utterances are numerous and significant. All the symbolic imagery of the last plays is here: the 'grace' which blesses union and expresses itself in fertility and a grief which is itself life-giving. Miranda's love opens to expression like the child growing in the mother's womb. Her grief becomes something rich and infinitely precious, itself of redeeming quality; and her father, who has given Ferdinand 'a third' of his own life, lays by his gift the foundations of reconciliation in the eyes of Destiny:

here, afore heaven,
I ratify this my rich gift. (IV. i. 7)

The rather perfunctory masque, which follows this decisive gesture, is by comparison with what has gone before a little disappointing. The best of it, and the most germane to the general purpose, is the song shared between them by the spirits representing Juno and Ceres, where the note of fruitfulness is least artificially expressed, and where the season of birth and that of autumnal fulfilment is bound together in a manner that reminds us of a similar union in *The Winter's Tale*[45]:

Spring come to you at the farthest
In the very end of harvest. (IV. i. 114)

As a whole, however, it is hard to deny that this interlude, like its not altogether dissimilar predecessor in *Cymbeline*,[46] belongs more to the structural unity of the play than to its intimate poetic sensibility. As such, we may pass over it to the other issues which await Prospero.

For, in spite of these notes of reconciliation and redeeming love, the presence of passion still makes itself uneasily felt. Prospero, indeed, never forgets the sombre background of these idyllic exchanges. His preoccupation with it has been present from the first in a notable irritability which contrasts, at times strongly, with his prevailing serenity; and now even as he is bringing Ferdinand and Miranda finally together, it comes out in a warning which strikes us at first as almost cryptically out of place. A wintry tone, compatible with his age if not with the pervading beneficence of his purpose, appears to take possession of his words in a mood closely related to the sense of weariness and

disillusionment which the contemplation of human behaviour, on the
island and off it, seems to awaken in him:

> Look thou be true; do not give dalliance
> Too much the rein: the strongest oaths are straw
> To the fire i' the blood; be more abstemious ...   (IV. i. 51)

The fact is that Prospero has good reason to remember the evil effects
of passion. The forces of evil are still at work around him. He has
brought them there himself for the final and decisive conflict. As we
already know from Ariel's speech, he is called upon to judge as well as
to reconcile; and as soon as the marriage 'ceremony' is over his other
cares press back on his mind:

> I had forgot that foul conspiracy
> Of the beast Caliban and his confederates
> Against my life.   (IV. i. 139)

The thought, as Ferdinand observes, moves Prospero deeply, and in
the shadow of it he makes his famous reflections on the insubstantiality
of human affairs. The spirit in which these are spoken is manifest in the
concluding lines:

> Sir, I am vexed;
> Bear with my weakness, my old brain is troubled;
> Be not disturbed with my infirmity;
> If you be pleas'd, retire into my cell,
> And there repose; a turn or two I'll walk,
> To still my beating mind.   (IV. i. 158)

It is a mood very akin to pessimism that the thought of Caliban's plot
arouses in Prospero. We feel him steeling himself to meet it, to overcome evil in accordance with the moral conception of which he is the
instrument. The note of age, and that of a certain impotence which,
albeit momentarily, it inspires in Prospero, is the equivalent in this play
of the disillusioned resentment of Polixenes in the pastoral scene of
The Winter's Tale.[47] Both are characteristic of the last plays and to
ignore them is to convey something less than the total impression which
they should properly make.

There is, indeed, a deep sense of tension and impending conflict in
Prospero's following greeting to Ariel: 'We must prepare to meet with
Caliban.' With Caliban, be it noted, rather than with his fellow-
conspirators. They, when the time comes, will be easily led from their

purposes by the prospect of trumpery spoils. Caliban is more formid-
able, because his evil is rooted in an animal nature which it seems that
no amount of civilized attention can change. He is an original in-
habitant of the isle as Prospero found it; and his is the irreducible
element of bestiality in unredeemed human nature:

> A devil, a born devil, on whose nature
> Nurture can never stick; on whom my pains,
> Humanely taken, all, all lost, quite lost;
> And as with age his body uglier grows,
> So his mind cankers.   (IV. i. 188)

The lines are pregnant with the rotting, cankering effect of evil on
man's being, driven home by the contrast between 'nature' and
'nurture', between inherent savagery and the civilizing sense implied
in 'humanely'. All Prospero's efforts to regenerate Caliban have failed,
and when he actually comes in, driven by Ariel with his fellow-
conspirators, he alone shows himself obdurate in his purposes. While
his companions are carried away by the hope of easy loot, he remains
firm in his murderous intention: 'Let it alone, thou fool, it is but trash'
(IV. i. 226). Stephano and Trinculo have corrupted him indeed in so
far as they have added to his original nature a ridiculous deification of
the vices of civilization symbolized in the figure of the bottle-bearing
god; but the evil was in him before their arrival, since he was—after
all—the heir of Sycorax, against whom Prospero had struggled to
purify the island. The purpose of Caliban is to achieve liberty, to
destroy civilized restraints and live a life of anarchic, passion-directed
freedom; the existence of this purpose is not affected, though the possibility of attaining it is, by his willingness to become, in the very hour of
his apparent liberation from Prospero, the servant of Stephano:

> Do that good mischief which may make this island
> Thine own for ever, and I, thy Caliban,
> For aye thy foot-licker.   (IV. i. 218)

Yet this amounts to an admission that the liberty desired by Caliban is
unattainable, that his freedom from Prospero's direction can only be
brought at the price of slavery to something infinitely lower and more
degrading; and, in fact, with the help of Ariel, they are all three—
Caliban, Stephano, and Trinculo—easily defeated.

With their defeat the way is clear for a building-up of the final
resolution. To Ariel's picture of the penitent state in which he has left

Alonso and his companions Prospero responds, as the last scene (V. i)
opens, by a declaration of his intention to forgive:

> Though with their high wrongs I am struck to the quick,
> Yet with my nobler reason 'gainst my fury
> Do I take part; the rarer action is
> In virtue than in vengeance; they being penitent,
> The sole drift of my purpose doth extend
> Not a frown further.   (V. i. 25)

The wording of the speech is worth pausing over. The victory of
compassion over retribution is now a victory of the 'nobler reason'
over passionate fury. Reason and nobility have been closely associated
through all Shakespeare's tragic period. For Hamlet it was the use of
reason that distinguished man from the beast, made him, however
precariously, 'the paragon of animals'[48]; and it is just because reason
did not lead him to realize this ideal in action that he was plunged into
tragedy. Now, in *The Tempest*, the nobility of reason is finally asserted
in an act of compassion which transcends the exercise of reasonable
justice itself. In Ariel's great speech, as we have seen, the reality of
retribution is stated. Now, once it has been affirmed, it gives way to the
higher, still more 'reasonable' (because 'nobler') virtue of compassion;
and the bond between them, the thing that makes the transition possible,
is simply the reasoned admission of guilt on the part of those whom
Destiny has punished. To their reason, which has at last ennobled itself
by acceptance, only a similar nobility in forgiveness can fitly respond.
When it does so, in the words of Prospero, the pattern of the play is
to all intents and purposes ready for completion. The illusion which he
has been concerned to build up on the island, the state of dream-like
suspension from self-awareness in which each offending or meritorious
instinct has been released as though in sleep, is now ready to be broken,
the sway of magic to give way to the return of conscious reality.

The moment of resolution, indeed, heralded by the return of Ariel,
is at hand. Alonso and his companions are brought in, spellbound, and
Prospero's first action is to restore them to their full reason. The
instrument of restoration is music, to the notes of which they wake,
recover their being, or—more accurately—are transformed into a new
life:

> The charm dissolves apace,
> And as the morning steals upon the night,
> Melting the darkness, so their rising senses

> Begin to chase the ignorant fumes that mantle
> Their clearer reason . . .
>   Their understanding
> Begins to swell, and the approaching tide
> Will shortly fill the reasonable shores
> Which now lie foul and muddy. (V. i. 64)

Once more the symbolic purpose is clear enough. The restoration to normality of Alonso and his followers is at the same time a triumph of the dawning reason over the night of passion-inspired sensuality. The 'approaching tide' of life, purified and re-created, fills the 'reasonable shore' and heralds the arrival of a new, more gracious humanity.

The final reconciliation, which follows Prospero's rebuke to Antonio and Sebastian, is completely typical of Shakespeare's latest manner. Upon its poetic quality depends the success of the symbolic purpose. For, realistically considered, the whole action of these last scenes— Alonso's repentance, Prospero's 'loss' of his daughter to counter-balance the supposed loss of Ferdinand at sea—is thin and inadequate. But the details of the plot here have no more importance than that which attaches to them as the necessary thread of incident upon which is based the choreography of a great ballet; and indeed the whole of the last scene of the play is really conceived as a formal ballet in which words replace visual images as the main artistic medium. The crucial passage opens with a recognition by Ferdinand of the part played throughout by the sea as the minister of Destiny:

> Though the seas threaten, they are merciful;
> I have curs'd them without cause. (V. i. 178)

The tragedy and suffering caused by human sinfulness have turned, in other words, into the instruments of reconciliation, the gateway to a richer and fuller life. The entry into this life is symbolized, as usual, by the mutual act of blessing and forgiveness by which fathers and children are reconciled. Ferdinand kneels for blessing and is joined to Miranda. In their words the intuition of a reconciled, redeemed state is at last given clear poetic expression:

> *Alonso:*   Now all the blessings
>   Of a glad father compass thee about!
> *Miranda:*   O, wonder!
>   How many goodly creatures are there here!
>   How beauteous mankind is! O, brave new world,
>   That has such people in't! (V. i. 179)

The vision of a new humanity, already glimpsed by Miranda in her innocent compassion when she first saw Ferdinand, and now deepened by the trials to which Prospero has put her, here reaches its full expression; and in the lines which follow immediately after, Ferdinand recognizes both that this bride has been given him by 'immortal Providence' and that he has received from Prospero nothing less than a 'second life'. In that second life his fellows—those who have shown a proper disposition—naturally participate. As the children are finally joined the two fathers are also brought together, Alonso craving pardon and Prospero granting forgiveness, both with the blessing of the divine grace:

> *Alonso:*   O, how oddly will it sound that I
> Must ask my child forgiveness!
> *Prospero:*   There, sir, stop,
> Let us not burthen our remembrances with
> A heaviness that's gone.
> *Gonzalo:*   I have inly wept,
> Or should have spoke ere this. Look down, you gods,
> And on this couple drop a blessed crown!
> For it is you that have chalked forth the way
> Which brought us hither.   (V. i. 197)

In the light of earlier plays this is not difficult to interpret. Alonso, like Lear, like Leontes, has come through penitence to realize his errors and to ask his child forgiveness; and Prospero replies that the time has come to cast off the burden of past memories and to look forward to a harmony that long and often bitter experience has gained. Apart from them both, the faithful Gonzalo is given for a moment a dignity that he has not so far reached in the play, a dignity that makes him at this stage—rather even than Prospero—the mouthpiece of Destiny. In his words the gods are invoked to 'crown' the newborn vision of humanity with a symbol of royalty: the 'gods' who have unwound the whole plot and brought it at last to its harmonious conclusion. The crown that they bestow is, in effect, a sign of the 'second', the redeemed and 'reasonable' life which has been given the protagonists of the play through their experiences on the island. As Gonzalo puts it:

> In one voyage
> Did Claribel her husband find at Tunis,
> And Ferdinand, her brother, found a wife
> *Where he himself was lost;* Prospero his dukedom

In a poor isle: *and all of us ourselves,*
Where no man was his own.   (V. i. 208)

In the light of these lines the whole action—the loss no less than the finding, the separations no less than the reunions—is clearly seen to be a closely woven texture of symbolic elements. Recognized as such, it grows vastly into a significance that rounds off our understanding of the whole play. For it is at this point, if anywhere, that the pattern of *The Tempest*—and with it the whole pattern initiated in the historical plays and carried through the tragedies to these last symbolic comedies —is substantially complete.

NOTES

Introduction

1. First published in 1904.
2. The stock example is provided by Charles Lamb's famous observations on the stage impression produced by *King Lear*.
3. Granville Barker's *Prefaces to Shakespeare* were published in five series from 1927 to 1947.
4. See Volume I, Chapter VII.
5. *Shakespeare's Imagery and What It Tells us* (Cambridge, 1935).
6. Published in 1932.
7. *A Midsummer Night's Dream*, I. ii:

> The raging rocks
> And shivering shocks
> Shall break the locks
>   Of prison-gates;
> And Phibbus' car
> Shall shine from far,
> And make and mar
>   The foolish Fates.

Professor Wilson Knight comments on this as follows: 'The sombre plays were plays of tempest and earthquake, and yet their shattering violence itself cleaves that confining pain, breaks it as a shell, bursting the "prison-gates" of mortality to disclose a newer life in *Antony and Cleopatra* and *Pericles*. In *Antony and Cleopatra* "Phibus' car" rises, dispelling the murk of *Macbeth* and the mists of *Lear*, and does indeed mysteriously "make and mar" the fates, which are, in that vision, by themselves "foolish".'

8. The title of my original essay was '*An* Approach to Shakespeare', not—as a choleric critic once stated—'*The* Approach to Shakespeare'.
9. These phrases are taken from the original 1938 edition of my essay. They were only slightly amended in the reprint and expansion of 1957.
10. This quotation represents the thought of the 1938 essay as slightly amended, for greater clarity, in 1957.
11. Once again the argument developed in this passage, though valid in its general aim, now strikes me as less than complete. In particular it seems to suggest a serious undervaluation of the originality and power of Shakespeare's early work: an undervaluation which I hope that the account of these plays in the pages that follow will serve to correct.

12. I am referring here, of course, to the Globe playhouse. The theatre at Blackfriars, for which the last romances were written, was different in kind, and the difference is no doubt reflected in the plays themselves: but the difference does not affect the general line of the argument here put forward.

I The Problem Plays

1. These plays have been discussed in the first part of this study. See Volume I, Chapter VII, pp. 200–60.

2. See Volume I, Chapter IV.

3. Sonnet XCIV. See Volume I, p. 108.

4. See pp. 65–83 below.

5. The relation of this to *Hamlet*, and in particular to the soliloquy 'How all occasions do inform against me' (IV. iv. 32) is worth consideration. See also pp. 59–61 below.

6. Compare *Hamlet*:

> blest are those
> Whose blood and judgement are so well commingled
> That they are not a pipe for fortune's finger
> To sound what stop she please. (III. ii. 73)

7. This point of view was restated some years ago by Bertram Joseph in his study *Conscience and the King* (London, 1953).

8. Professor Wilson Knight, in his important studies of the play in *The Wheel of Fire* (London, 1930), is occasionally led by his desire to stress the elements of perversity and corruption in the hero to underestimate the sinister implications of Claudius' rule.

9. 'Sullied' is actually accepted as a true reading of the text by Dover Wilson and other editors of the play, but it seems scarcely necessary to go so far. It is the presence of both *senses*, rather than the choice of one, that concerns us here.

10. Hamlet will use this comparison again. See his speech to his mother (III. iv 53), quoted on p. 56 below.

11. Notably T. S. Eliot, who partly followed J. M. Robertson's *Problem of Hamlet* in his well-known essay on the play (*Selected Essays*, London, 1932, pp. 140–6).

12. The phrase belongs to a later stage in the play (V. ii. 62), but it could be used of all the lesser characters whose manipulation by Claudius has, up to the play-scene and beyond it, blunted the full force of the central conflict.

13. The comparison with Hyperion has been used by Hamlet before, and to much the same effect:

> So excellent a king, that was to this,
> Hyperion to a satyr. (I. ii. 139)

14. By Marcellus in the opening scene: 'The nights are *wholesome*, then no planets strike' (I. i. 162).
15. The reading here followed is a scholarly emendation for 'a good kissing carrion' which many, perhaps most, editors have preferred. The emendation seems to me to give added force to Hamlet's words and to answer well to the deeper implications of his thought; but its value, under these circumstances, can in the nature of things be no more than conjectural.
16. See Volume I, Chapter VII passim, and especially pp. 222–6.
17. Compare the use of the same adjective to express Hamlet's distaste in the phrase 'things rank and *gross* in nature' from his first soliloquy (I. ii. 136).
18. Since the above account of Hamlet was originally published, I have been glad to find not a few of its ideas confirmed, from a different standpoint, in a most suggestive study of the play by Francis Fergusson (*The Idea of a Theater*, New York, 1953, pp. 109–53).
19. *Measure for Measure*, I. iii. 20. The textual reading of this line has been questioned on the ground of obscurity, and 'wills' or 'steeds' are possible alternative to 'weeds'; but the more unexpected word is not necessarily foreign to Shakespeare's intention.
20. 'Success', of course, could carry for an Elizabethan mind a sense different from that with which we are to-day familiar. 'Certain word of my success' is likely to mean primarily something like 'firm news of the way things go'; but there is surely in Isabella's words at least a touch of impulsive confidence which is true to her character and which the suggestion of a subsidiary and more modern sense in 'success' may be held to confirm.
21. R. W. Chambers in his essay on the play published in *Man's Unconquerable Mind* (London, 1939) argues strongly for an opposite conclusion; but his plea for an absolutely and simply virtuous Isabella, eloquent as it is and partially justified as a protest against more cynical interpretations, reads with a strange naïveté in relation to what the play actually seems to offer.
22. The points of resemblance between Vincentio and Prospero were perhaps first noted by G. Wilson Knight in his fine essay on '*Measure for Measure* and the Gospels' in *The Wheel of Fire* (London, 1930). Many later writers have followed him.
23. See p. 66 above.
24. See our discussion of *As You Like It* in Volume I, pp. 282–302.
25. See *Hamlet*, I. ii. 29.

26. It is interesting to note that the Countess' advice to Bertram reminds us, at certain moments, of Polonius' parting injunctions to Laertes (*Hamlet*, I. iii).

27. Rosalind and Viola are the most notable examples of this resourcefulness and just confidence in Shakespeare's comic heroines.

28. See the discussion, Volume I, of comedies as far apart as *The Two Gentlemen of Verona* (pp. 89–95) and *Twelfth Night* (pp. 302–21).

29. For Touchstone see, especially, pp. 294–5 in Volume I.

30. Compare Falstaff's likening of himself, in his 'withered' state, to 'an old apple-john' (*Henry IV—Part I*, III. iii. 4).

31. Notably V. ii, with its emphasis on 'admiration' and 'wonder', its talk of 'a world ransomed, or one destroyed'.

32. See *The Merchant of Venice*, III. ii. and p. 190 in Volume I.

33. Parolles' plea in the moment of his exposure—'Let me live'—could be seen as an echo, transposed into a more cynical key, of Falstaff's more exuberant 'Give me life' (*Henry IV—Part I*, V. iii. 62) when confronted with the lifeless remains of Sir Walter Blunt.

34. For the implications of this word in Shakespeare's early comedies see Chapter III of Volume I, and the discussion of *A Midsummer Night's Dream* in Chapter V.

35. Lucio uses the word of himself in *Measure for Measure*, IV. iii. 193, but it could appropriately be used also of Parolles in his relation to Bertram.

II The Mature Tragedies

1. *Troilus and Cressida*, II. ii. 53. See p. 36 above.

2. See the relevant sections of Chapter IV below.

3. This point of view, which later students of the play have sometimes echoed, was first vigorously advanced by Thomas Rymer in *The Tragedies of the Last Age*, as long ago as 1678.

4. See Chapter IV in Volume I.

5. Sonnet XCIV.

6. There is an excellent discussion of this aspect of Othello's behaviour in the final scene in R. B. Heilman's *Magic in the Web* (Lexington, 1956).

7. It is useful to recall at this point the frequency with which the rose is associated in the sonnets with the 'canker' of faithlessness:

> How sweet and lovely dost thou make the shame
> Which, like a canker in the fragrant rose,
> Doth spot the beauty of thy budding name.   (Sonnet XCV)

'Fragrant' here, incidentally, can be associated in its effect with 'balmy breath' in the speech under consideration. There are other parallels earlier in the play: Othello, in accusing Desdemona, has addressed her as 'rose-lipp'd cherubin' and subsequently as a 'weed' so lovely 'that the sense aches at thee' (IV. ii. 66).

8. In his essay on 'Shakespeare and the Stoicism of Seneca' (*Selected Essays*, London, 1932 pp. 130–1).

9. A somewhat similar part is played in *King Lear*, III. vii, by the servant who protests against the gratuitous savagery of Gloucester's blinding and who wounds Cornwall to the accompaniment of Regan's contemptuous exclamation: 'A peasant stand up thus!'

10. The play may have been written immediately after, rather than before, *King Lear*, but the argument here advanced is not seriously affected by either alternative.

11. On this, as on other points connected with the play, it is still worth consulting Professor L. C. Knight's essay 'How Many Children Had Lady Macbeth?' originally published in 1933 and reprinted in *Explorations* (London, 1946).

12. For example:

> The service and the loyalty I owe,
> In doing it, pays itself. Your highness' part
> Is to receive our duties: and our duties
> Are to your throne and state, children and servants;
> Which do but what they should, by doing everything
> Safe toward your love and honour. (I. iv. 22)

13. It has been noted that the 'martlet' can also represent, in the language of Elizabethan low life, the gulled and gullible dupe, the victim of deception. To the extent to which Duncan is unfitted, in a world in which confusion and treachery abound, and in which—as he himself confesses—

> There's no art
> To find the mind's construction in the face, (I. iv. 11)

to deal with the malignity of human motives, this aspect of his trust is relevant and important. It cannot, however, invalidate the positive content of the description as a whole.

14. *Troilus and Cressida*, I. iii. See pp. 41–2 above.

15. F. R. Leavis has an interesting analysis of this speech in an essay published in *Scrutiny*, March 1941, pp. 316–19.

16. See Chapter IV below.

17. In an essay published in *Three Philosophical Poets* (Harvard, 1927).

18. It is perhaps worth noting the presence of similar phrasing in *King Lear*:

> Crack nature's moulds, all germins spill at once
> That make ungrateful man. (III. ii. 8)

19. He has accepted it himself, as we have seen, at the moment which preceded his last meeting with the Witches. See p. 139 above.

20. I. iii. See p. 126 above.

21.
> Li ruscelletti che de' verdi colli
> del Casentin discendon giuso in Arno,
> facendo i lor canali freddi e molli.
>
> (*Inferno* XXX, 64–66)

22. Professor Wilson Knight was the first student of Shakespeare to use the phrase 'an expanded metaphor' to describe the effect made by a given play. The phrase, like others which he originated, has since achieved considerable popularity.

23. An admirable discussion of the various uses of the word 'nature' in *King Lear*, and of their importance for an understanding of the play, is to be found in John F. Danby's book *Shakespeare's Doctrine of Nature: A Study of King Lear* (London, 1949).

24. I owe this comparison to H. Granville Barker's study of the tragedy (*Prefaces to Shakespeare*, Series I, 1927).

25. *Timon*, however, is more profitably approached as a play different in aim and spirit from *Lear*. See pp. 171–87 below.

26. It must be added that Timon's misanthropy differs from Lear's rejection of humanity in being much more a manifestation of *excess* and in being at least as much satirically as tragically conceived.

27. Notably I. iv.

28. Shakespeare's use of the imagery of sight in this play has been well studied by Robert B. Heilman in *This Great Stage: Image and Structure in King Lear* (Louisiana State University Press, 1948).

29. It is worth noting that, in her appeal to 'gods' expressly addressed as 'kind', Cordelia is echoing the words of Gloucester at an equally decisive moment in his development: '*Kind gods*, forgive me that, and prosper him' (III. vii. 92). This play's attitude to its dimly conceived 'gods' is a matter for endless debate, and no facile conclusion is acceptable; but upon our reaction to the challenge which the very use of the adjective in such contexts imposes our final understanding of the play will undoubtedly depend.

30. See p. 165 above.

31. On the necessity of 'giving' as a law of love, and therefore of life, see our discussion of Shakespeare's comedies in Volume I.

32. Professor Wilson Knight, in his long and often valuable study of the play in *The Wheel of Fire* (London, 1930), seems to me to err notably in this direction.

33. See *King Lear*, III. vi, and p. 161 above.

34. Most notably on the occasion of Gloucester's blinding. See *King Lear*, III. vii, and p. 162 above.

35. Compare 'And I am Brutus, Marcus Brutus, I' (*Julius Caesar*, V. iv. 7). It would be unsafe to assume here that Shakespeare is simply filling out his line to the necessary length.

36. It is interesting to see Shakespeare returning here to a device already used by the hero at the end of *Titus Andronicus*:

> Look round about the wicked streets of Rome,
> And when thou find'st a man that's like thyself,
> Good Murder, stab him; he's a murderer.
>
> (*Titus Andronicus*, V. ii. 98)

see p. 73 in Volume I of this study.

37. Compare, for one example among many, the tone of Caius Marcius' violent eruption into his tragedy, quoted on p. 236 below.

III The Roman Tragedies

1. North's translation was first published in 1579, and there were further editions during Shakespeare's lifetime in 1595, 1603, and 1612.

2. The material for such a comparison can be found conveniently assembled in Kenneth Muir's *Shakespeare's Sources*, Vol. I (London, 1956).

3. See, for an account of these significances, Professor T. J. B. Spencer's essay, 'Shakespeare and the Elizabethan Romans', published in *Shakespeare Survey* 10 (Cambridge, 1957).

4.
> O Julius Caesar, thou art mighty yet!
> Thy spirit walks abroad, and turns our swords
> In our own proper entrails.   (V. iii. 94)

5. Compare, for an elaboration of this idea, which is closely related to Shakespeare's dramatic method in presenting character in action, Achilles' speech in *Troilus and Cressida*:

> The beauty that is borne here in the face
> The bearer knows not, but commends itself
> To other's eyes: nor doth the eye itself,
> That most pure spirit of sense, behold itself,
> Not going from itself; but eye to eye opposed
> Salutes each other with each other's form:
> For speculation turns not to itself,
> Till it hath travell'd and is mirror'd there
> Where it may see itself.   (III. iii. 103)

6. Compare Hotspur's outburst to Worcester:

> Send danger from the east unto the west,
> So honour cross it from the north to south,
> And let them grapple.
>
> (*Henry IV—Part I*, I. iii. 195)

7. Coleridge gave classical expression to this point of view in his study of the play.

8. Most notably by Casca in I. iii.

9. An interesting study of *Antony and Cleopatra*, included in J. F. Danby's collection of essays *Poets on Fortune's Hill* (London, 1952), is worth consulting, but should be balanced by a reading of Wilson Knight's argument in *The Imperial Theme*. Neither seems to me to offer a completely satisfactory answer to the challenge represented by the play, which is possibly the supreme test of balanced Shakespearean criticism.

10. *Henry VIII* is, of course, later, but it is at least doubtful whether this was entirely Shakespeare's play.

11. See Chapter IV in Volume I.

12. See pp. 100–21 above.

13. Most notably, perhaps, in *Hamlet*. See p. 51 above.

14. Here, and elsewhere in discussing the Roman plays, I am aware that *Antony and Cleopatra* may well have been written *before Coriolanus*. Doubt on this point does not affect the substance of the argument.

15. See Chapter VII in Volume I, and especially pp. 235 and 237.

16. See, more particularly, Cleopatra's speech in III. xiii (III. xi. O.U.P. edition), quoted on p. 224 below.

17. Compare, for the spirit of this, Macbeth's famous

> Life's but a walking shadow, a poor player
> That *struts* and frets his hour upon the stage
> And then is heard no more. (*Macbeth*, V. v. 24)

18. See IV. xv. (IV. xiii. 65 O.U.P. edition) and p. 227 below.

19. The relation of 'nature' to artifice is one which increasingly interested Shakespeare in his later plays. Parallels to the spirit of this description can be found in *Cymbeline*, and notably in Iachimo's account of Imogen's bedchamber (*Cymbeline*, II. ii). See p. 267 below.

20.
> *Cleopatra:* Think you there was, or might be, such a man
> As this I dreamed of?
>
> *Dolabella:*   Gentle madam, no.
>
> (V. ii. 93)

21. This aspect of the poetry of *Coriolanus* has been well brought out by G. Wilson Knight in *The Imperial Theme* (Oxford, 1930).

22. Stage direction to I. iii.

23. I. i. 58.
24. V. ii. 20.
25. I. i. and passim.
26. Compare, for the conception,

> Our natures do pursue,
> Like rats that ravin down their proper bane,
> A thirsty evil; and when we drink we die.
> (*Measure for Measure*, I. ii. 137)

27. *Othello*, III. iii. 353.
28. The idea of 'burning' becomes almost obsessively related to Coriolanus' revenge as he approaches Rome in the closing scenes of the play. The point is well made by A. C. Bradley in his lecture on the play (*Oxford Lectures on Poetry*, London, 1909).
29. See pp. 120–1 above.

IV The Final Romances

1. See, more particularly, pp. 167–9 above.
2. The play was first printed with the rest of Shakespeare's work in the Third Folio, 1664.
3. It is of interest to note that a theory to account for the textual problems presented by the play, put forward by Philip Edwards ('An Approach to the Problems of *Pericles*', in *Shakespeare Survey* 5), would coincide with the argument here developed on non-textual grounds. Edwards holds that the 1609 Quarto is a debased text reconstructed by two reporters, 'the first responsible for the first two acts, the second for the last three'. From this he goes on to state that 'the problem that has to be solved is whether the different aptitudes of the two reporters are the *sole* cause of the difference in literary value between the two halves of the play, whether, in fact, the original play of *Pericles* was all of one standard, all by one author, and that the first reporter, in his crude attempts to rebuild a verse structure . . . has perverted language such as is found in the later acts.'
4. *King Lear* is the obvious example, but *The Winter's Tale* and *The Tempest* are also relevant. The most complete discussion of the whole subject is to be found in G. Wilson Knight's *Shakespearean Tempest* (London, 1932).
5. See p. 163–4 above.
6. *The Winter's Tale*, III. iii. See p. 291 below.
7. It is perhaps worth recalling Edgar's similar acceptance of 'the worst' as a turning point or prelude to moral reaction in *King Lear*, IV. i. 1. See p. 163 above.

8. *The Tempest*, I. ii. 398.

9. Compare Alonso's use of the word: 'Therefore my son i' the *ooze* is bedded' (*The Tempest*, III. iii. 100) for a somewhat similar effect.

10. *King Lear*, IV. vii. See pp. 167–9 above.

11. See pp. 67–8 above.

12. Note, for example, the implications of Boult's remark: 'What would you have me do? go to the wars, would you? where a man may serve seven years for the loss of a leg, and not have money enough i' the end to buy him a wooden one?' (*Pericles*, IV. vi. 185). We are also reminded of the end foreseen by Pistol in the final scenes of *Henry V*.

13. See, again, p. 163–4 above.

14. *The Winter's Tale*, V. iii. See pp. 299–301 below.

15. *King Lear*, IV. vii. 56.

16. See p. 167 above.

17. Compare *The Winter's Tale*: 'thou mettest with things dying, I with things newborn' (III. iii. 116).

18. Compare, for this juxtaposition of love and the grave, Perdita's words to Florizel:

> —   What, like a corse?
> — No, like a bank for love to lie and play on;
>   Not like a corse; or if, not to be buried,
>   But quick and in mine arms.
>
> (*The Winter's Tale*, IV. iv. IV. iii. 129 O.U.P. edition)

19. For another instance of Shakespeare's interest in the connection, liable to various degrees of ambiguity, between 'face' and feeling, appearance and reality, we might quote Sonnet XCIV: 'They are the lords and owners of their faces.'

20. In this attitude, Iachimo is in the line of the great Shakespearean 'villains': Angelo, Iago, Edmund, and Antonio.

21. It is just worth recalling other appearances of the word 'ooze', with a similar suggestion of nostalgic melancholy and remoteness, in *Pericles* and *The Tempest*. See pp. 255–6 below.

22. *The Winter's Tale*, IV. iv. (IV. iii. O.U.P. edition). See p. 294 below.

23. In the final scene. See p. 281–2 below.

24. *Macbeth*, I. vi. See pp. 124–5 above.

25. *The Winter's Tale*, III. i. See p. 290 below.

26. *The Tempest*, IV. i. 148.

27. *Macbeth*, I. vii. 7.

28. See pp. 258–63 above.

29. Compare *Pericles*, V. iii. 46: 'Look who kneels here! Flesh of thy flesh, Thaisa.'

30. See p. 290 below.

31. In Chapter IV of Volume I.
32. *King Lear*, II. iv. 227.
33. Compare, for Leontes' attitude at this point, Othello's outburst:

> Perdition catch my soul,
> But I do love thee! and when I love thee not,
> *Chaos is come again.*
>
> (*Othello*, III. iii. 90)

See p. 113 above.
34. *King Lear*, IV. vii. 22.
35. *Macbeth*, IV. iii. 156.
36. *Macbeth*, IV. iii. 159. See p. 142 above.
37. *Antony and Cleopatra*, V. ii. 349.
38. *Macbeth*, I. vi.
39. Leontes and Polixenes are not, perhaps, to be considered old on a strict count of years, but their attitudes at this stage in the play bear all the marks that so frequently accompany old age and experience, when divorced from true understanding, in Shakespeare's plays.
40. 'One that, *above all other strifes*, contended especially *to know himself*' (*Measure for Measure*, III. ii. 252). See p. 77 above.
41. Excluding, of course, Gonzalo, who cannot be said to develop in the course of the action.
42. For a similarly close association of these two verbs, see Antony's speech in *Antony and Cleopatra*, IV. xii. (IV. x. 35 O.U.P. edition), quoted on p. 220 above.
43. Here, of course, Shakespeare is returning to themes touched upon in his earlier comedies, and especially in *As You Like It*. See our discussion of the implications of the Forest of Arden, and of Duke Senior's retreat to it, in Volume I.
44. A similar point is made by Polixenes in *The Winter's Tale*, I. ii. See p. 283 above.
45.
> Sir, the year growing ancient,
> Not yet on summer's death, nor on the birth
> Of trembling winter ...
>
> (*The Winter's Tale*, IV. iv. IV. iii. 79 O.U.P. edition)

See p. 292 above.
46. *Cymbeline*, V. iv.
47. See p. 292 above.
48. *Hamlet*, II. ii. 327.